Essays of Master Xun

Yulie Lou

Essays of Master Xun

Based on *Xunzi Xin Zhu* by Yulie Lou

Yulie Lou
Peking University
Beijing, China

Translated by
Xiaopeng Liang
Qingdao University of Science
and Technology
Qingdao, China

Xiaomei Yang
Qingdao University of Science
and Technology
Qingdao, China

ISBN 978-981-97-6086-2   ISBN 978-981-97-6087-9 (eBook)
https://doi.org/10.1007/978-981-97-6087-9

Jointly published with Zhonghua Book Company
The print edition is not for sale in China (mainland). Customers from China (mainland) please order the print book from: Zhonghua Book Company.
ISBN of the Co-Publisher's edition: 978-7-101-12725-6

Translation from the Chinese language edition: "Xinzi with a Fresh Annotation—荀子新注" by Yulie Lou, © Zhonghua Book Company 2018. Published by Zhonghua Book Company. All Rights Reserved.

Sponsored by Chinese Fund for the Humanities and Social Sciences

© Zhonghua Book Company 2024

This work is subject to copyright. All rights are solely and exclusively licensed by the Publisher, whether the whole or part of the material is concerned, specifically the rights of translation, reprinting, reuse of illustrations, recitation, broadcasting, reproduction on microfilms or in any other physical way, and transmission or information storage and retrieval, electronic adaptation, computer software, or by similar or dissimilar methodology now known or hereafter developed.

The use of general descriptive names, registered names, trademarks, service marks, etc. in this publication does not imply, even in the absence of a specific statement, that such names are exempt from the relevant protective laws and regulations and therefore free for general use.

The publishers, the authors, and the editors are safe to assume that the advice and information in this book are believed to be true and accurate at the date of publication. Neither the publishers nor the authors or the editors give a warranty, express or implied, with respect to the material contained herein or for any errors or omissions that may have been made. The publishers remain neutral with regard to jurisdictional claims in published maps and institutional affiliations.

This Springer imprint is published by the registered company Springer Nature Singapore Pte Ltd.
The registered company address is: 152 Beach Road, #21-01/04 Gateway East, Singapore 189721, Singapore

If disposing of this product, please recycle the paper.

Preface to *Xunzi Xin Zhu*

A native of Zhao, a state in the mid- and late-Warring States Period in ancient China, Master Xun[1] was active in 298~238 BC. He had been to the states of Qi, Chu, and Qin. He taught in the Jixia Academy of Qi and served three times as a libationer (head of the Academy) there. Later, he went to Chu where he was once appointed magistrate of Lanling and spent the remaining years writing.

Master Xun is one of the great Chinese thinkers in history. The influence he effected was not restricted to ideology and academic research only. It was also reflected in the social and political system, ritual and moral principles, and law as well as the practical aspects of personal self-cultivation, education and learning.

It has been controversial over which school Master Xun's thought belongs to and over its theoretical significance and social influence. Sometimes the views are sharply different or even opposed, for men like him are rare in Chinese history. Some scholars decided that Master Xun represented the Confucian school since he was most respectful to Confucius and Zigong[2] for their learning. He called them great scholars and told men to learn from them. More importantly, Master Xun had an in-depth study on rites and strongly advocated the education of ritual principles, the establishment of a ritual system, and the government by ritual. Other scholars held that Master Xun ought to be regarded as a legalist, too, rather than a pure Confucian, since he asserted that man was evil by nature and emphasized that his transformation was made through conscious efforts. He advocated ritual and in the meanwhile stressed the importance of law. Two of his disciples, Fei Han and Si Li, were quite famous, both being considered legalists. The former was an important founder of the legalist theory; the latter was a powerful practitioner of legalism, who assisted the state of Qin in implementing the legal system and practicing the rule of law.

---

[1] Formerly known to the West as Xunzi, he was named Kuang Xun but generally known as Qing Xun, *qing* being a style name or a respectful form of address. His surname was sometimes Sun, either a different spelling or an effort of the later times in the Han to avoid as taboo the name of Xun Liu, Emperor Xuan of the dynasty.—Tr.

[2] Either Yong Ran, one of Confucius' disciples, who is best known for his moral integrity, or Bi Han, a scholar of *The Book of Changes*.—Tr.

Classification aside, Master Xun's theory exercised such a great social influence in the Qin and Han dynasties that shortly after his death the scholars learning from his teachings were regarded as models and examples for all. He was sympathized for not having lived in the right times. "He was virtuous as Yao and Yu, but his virtue was rarely recognized. His plans and strategies were viewed with suspicion rather than adopted. His wisdom was divine, and his conduct was upright and accorded with Dao. Both could be taken as the rules of conduct (Sidelights). By the time of the Tang Dynasty, there was doubt about Master Xun's Confucian identity and his theory. His thoughts drew skeptical comments when he was doubted to be a real Confucian in comparison with Mencius, a pure Confucianist, and refused to be included in the pantheon of ancient sages unless his ideas contradictory to Confucianism were removed from his essays.[3] The suspicion was pushed to an extreme in the Song Dynasty when Yi Cheng[4] responded Yu Han by remarking that Xun was thoroughly impure, which could be proved solely by his insistence on the evil nature of human beings. Master Xun was consequently judged to be against the sages and to have refused to promote their correct principles. He was accused of being shallow in learning in spite of his talent, of regarding ritual as being conscious efforts and human nature as evil, of neglecting the sagely and worthy, and of frequently deviating far apart from Zigong whom he respected.[5] As a result of Yi Cheng's influence in the academic world, Master Xun was denied an important place in society in its entirety although many men held a fair evaluation of his thought and even highly praised it. In modern times, the understanding of Master Xun's thought had undergone relatively great changes. For example, in his criticism and disapproval Sitong Tan saw the important role of Master Xun's thought in the 2000 years' history. He said, "It is frequently believed that the political system of the past 20 centuries was that of Qin characterized by usurpation and the learning in the same period of history was that of Master Xun characterized by hypocrisy."[6] Taiyan Zhang highly praised Master Xun by regarding him as a sage after Confucius,[7] saying, "Qing Xun stressed moral transformation by accumulated efforts and government of all under Heaven by promoting ritual and harmony in communities ... In this way, many worthy men would be found in an area as small as a hundred *li* across. In comparison with Confucius, his importance is absolutely identifiable to both old and young."[8]

Although Master Xun highly respected Confucius and Zigong, we should not necessarily regard his thought simply as a repetition or continuation of either. With the passage of over 200 years from Confucius to Master Xun, there were many changes and a lot of new schools emerged in the world of philosophy, including the branches of the old schools and the integration of those schools, of which some could be found in the Jixia Academy of Qi in the middle of the Warring States Period. By

---

[3] Yu Han, *Du Xun* ("Reading Xunzi").

[4] Aka Cheng Yi, founder of idealism and neo-Confucianism.

[5] *Er Cheng Yishu* ("Posthumous Works of the Two Chengs").

[6] *Ren Xue* ("Study of the Humanity").

[7] *Hou Shen* ("Sages of the Later Times").

[8] *Ding Kong* ("A Reevaluation of Confucius").

the time of Master Xun, such contention of the Hundred Schools of Thought was quite normal. With his divine wisdom, Master Xun commented on various theories that were still popular in the society then. He affirmed or praised some; he criticized others, pointing out their biases and denouncing the harm they brought to the society. It may not be an exaggeration to think that Master Xun had so widely absorbed the strengths of various schools in his theories that he epitomized the pre-Qin thoughts. Today when we look at him, we may be free from the sectarian biases of various schools in history. We only need to explore from his thought those things that embody the fundamental spirit of traditional Chinese culture and serve to promote the stable and harmonious development of the society. Basing on our experience, we believe the five aspects below are worthy of careful studies.

I. The Self-knowledge of Man as an Individual and as Mankind on the Whole

In traditional Chinese culture, it is believed that all was created by Heaven and Earth, including human beings, and man is the most intelligent and special. As is said in *The Book of History*, "Heaven and Earth are the parents of all creatures; of all creatures man is the most highly endowed."[9] Master Xun pointed out,

> Fire and water possess *qi* but are without life. Grasses and trees possess life but are without consciousness. Birds and beasts have consciousness but are without the sense of justice. Humans possess *qi*, life, consciousness and the sense of justice; therefore, they are the most honorable beings under Heaven (On Kingcraft).

"The sense of justice is the recognition of what is appropriate."[10] This sense of justice is characteristic of humans who are in possession of the power to tell right from wrong and to be aware of the order of importance and emergency. For this reason, Master Xun remarked, "What is it that makes a man man? It is his ability to make distinctions." (Criticism of Physiognomy) The way of man is characterized by his power of differentiation. That is why man is understood to be more intelligent than anything else in the universe. Therefore, man must follow the principle of justice; otherwise, he is inhuman. This is the first characteristic of human beings Master Xun persuaded men to understand.

The second characteristic of man Master Xun told men to remember is the ability to form communities. "They are no match for oxen in strength or with horses in speed, but they make the animals work for them. How so? Because humans can form communities while the other animals cannot." (On Kingcraft) The ability to form communities is a feature of human society, a highly conscious and organized group taking control of cattle and horses for its use. Master Xun held that "men cannot survive without forming communities" (On the Wealth of a State), and the reason

---

[9] Great Declaration I.

[10] *The Doctrine of the Mean.*

why people can be grouped is because they are capable of making distinctions on the basis of justice. He said, "social divisions based on morality and justice lead to harmony which promises unity. Unity means power means strength means triumph over all things" (On Kingcraft).

This reveals the all-dominating potential of communalism of man who participates in generating and nourishing all things ordinarily attributed to Heaven and Earth when Master Xun said,

> Heaven has its seasons, Earth its resources and man his governance. This involves the coordination of the three (On the Way of Heaven).

And when man "regards himself as a match to Heaven and Earth," he should not be regarded as boastful or self-important (On the Way of Heaven). The action of participation is the third characteristic Master Xun wanted men to be aware of. In the production and development of everything, Heaven has the control over time, Earth has its wealth to offer, and man applies his principles of government. Therefore, men must be careful about their way of participation for the purpose of a harmonious coexistence with all things between Heaven and Earth.

The fourth characteristic Master Xun wanted men to realize is the evil nature of man, which has been most intensely controversial in the history of ideology. While most people may agree on the first three qualities Master Xun pointed out for human self-knowledge, it is not so easy for them to reach a consensus on this fourth point. In history, there have been various views on the nature of man. Some held it to be good, some thought it evil, some made a mixture of both,[11] some came up with the theory of the three categories,[12] while others proposed the theory of neither good nor evil of human nature.[13] They defined human nature differently or explored this issue from different perspectives and are therefore reasonable to a certain extent. Opposing Mencius' theory of goodness of human nature, Master Xun held that "Man is evil in nature; whatever is good in man is the result of conscious effort." He demonstrated this opinion from the viewpoint of maintaining a harmonious human community and eliminating those factors in human nature that may result in mutual struggle and chaos. He believed that a man could recognize his identity as a man only through education, learning and self-cultivation before consciously observing the code of conduct, that is, being clear about his place in the society. Judged on the level of social reality rather than that of pure abstract theory, his understanding was not only reasonable but also practically significant. It involved the practice of the fundamental spirit of humanistic transformation in traditional Chinese culture. People need to recognize those factors in human nature that may cause disputes and chaos or evil. Through the conscious efforts of education, learning and self-cultivation the goodness might be aroused in human nature so that the goodness of the society could be developed and good custom formed.[14]

---

[11] This was initiated by Xiong Yang of the Western Han Dynasty.—Tr.

[12] A theory initiated by Zhongshu Dong of the Western Han Dynasty dividing human nature into the upper and the lower categories and that of ordinary men.—Tr.

[13] Put forward by Master Gao of the Warring States Period.—Tr.

[14] *The Book of Rites.*

II. The Relationship Between Heaven and Man

Heaven in traditional Chinese culture is a complicated concept with multiple meanings. It is the same case in Master Xun's discussions, although he used it synonymously with nature and chiefly paired it with Earth to signify the origin of all things. "Heaven evolves according to its own order," he said. "It does not exist for the sake of Yao or perish because of Jie." (On the Way of Heaven) He believed that Heaven has its role to play and its responsibilities to fulfill, and so do human beings. He pointed out that men were unaware of the formlessness of Heaven in spite of their knowledge of its successful fulfillment without seeking or any other effort; therefore, they could not and should not compete with Heaven in its work, for Heaven and Earth would not suspend winter because men disliked cold or reduce their vastness because men disliked remote distances. Similarly, men should try to change the things in their own world rather than give up their effort and count on Heaven for help. When men made their efforts, Heaven would not interfere with them; therefore,

> If you reinforce the foundation and cut expenditures, Heaven cannot impoverish you. If you are perfectly provisioned and your actions are timely, Heaven cannot afflict you with illness. If you conform to Dao and do not deviate from it, Heaven cannot bring you misfortunes. Accordingly, neither flood nor drought will result in famine, neither cold nor heat can cause sickness, and neither natural disasters nor anomalies can bring you danger and make you suffer (On the Way of Heaven).

Here is an important point put forward by Master Xun: the distinction between Heaven and man should be clarified. No one could become sagely till he reached such an understanding. This is his important judgment on and opinion of the relationship between man and nature.

Nevertheless, this does not mean that men had nothing to do with Heaven at all. As mentioned above, Master Xun believed that an important characteristic of men is the capacity of participation in generating and nourishing all things by their government. Therefore, a clear and deep understanding of the functional characteristics of Heaven and Earth is necessary before playing their part in this process. And before Heaven or nature, they should take actions rather than passively expect its interference:

> To exalt Heaven and admire it—How can it compare with raising it as an animal and putting it under control? To obey Heaven and praise it—How can it compare with grasping its sequence of change and putting it to use? To observe the seasons and wait for blessings—How can it compare with obeying the seasons and exploiting them? To wait for things to increase of themselves—How can it compare with exerting your talents to transform them. To long for things to serve your purpose—How can it compare with managing and never losing them? To long for the source from which things are born—How can it compare with finding the means to bring them to completion? Hence, if you do not put in effort but only long for blessings from Heaven, you will lose everything (On the Way of Heaven).

This is another important point made by Master Xun in discussing the relationship between Heaven and man: to control the mandate of Heaven for human purposes.

However, does it mean that men are permitted to do what they please and do not have to respect Heaven if they put the sequence of nature under control for their own benefit? Of course not. On the contrary, men should respect Heaven. Only by giving due respect to nature can they achieve the perfection of human affairs and the harmony between Heaven and man. This is what Master Xun meant by saying:

> These are the regulations of a sagely king: When plants blossom and bear fruits, axes are prohibited in the wooded mountains so that the trees and grasses are not cut prematurely and their growth is uninterrupted. When turtles, crocodiles, fish, and eels are breeding, nets and poisons are prohibited in the lakes and ponds, so that they are not killed prematurely and their growth is uninterrupted. By plowing in spring, weeding in summer, harvesting in fall, and storing in winter, the four activities are kept in their right seasons, so that the five grains are produced ceaselessly and the common people have more than enough to eat. Fishing in the ponds, lakes, marshes and streams is prohibited in certain seasons so that fishes and turtles are plentiful and the common people have more than they can consume and use. Cutting and felling, growing and nurturing are done in right seasons so that mountains and forests are never laid barren and the common people will have more than enough timber. This is the part played by a sagely king: He is watchful of Heaven above, settles all things on land, links Heaven and Earth and acts on all things in between. His role is both subtle and evident, brief yet long-lasting, narrow but extensive, divine and profound but to the point (On Kingcraft).

Basing on the distinction between Heaven and man and the dissuasion of man from competing with Heaven, Master Xun persuaded people to be aware of the way of government and the initiation and capacity of participation to turn the power of Heaven to their own use. However, men must be conscious of what they should or should not do, otherwise they would fail to take advantage of Heaven and Earth so as to make all things in their service and achieve harmony with nature. This view is still inspiring to us today and worthy of pondering.

III. The Origin, Role, Meaning and Spirit of Ritual

Ritual is the core of traditional Chinese culture, a comprehensive culture that maintains harmony between people so that social stability and order are built. It is inclusive of belief, morality, system, rules of speech and action, customs, rules of etiquette, and so on. According to legend, it was King Wen and Duke of Zhou who established and perfected ritual and music. Ritual was based on men, emphasizing their subjectivity and conscious self-discipline. By the Spring and Autumn Period of the Eastern Zhou Dynasty, ritual and music were being corrupted. For this reason, Confucius worked hard throughout his life to promote the doctrine of benevolence and expected that the people would exert self-restraint and therefore the culture of ritual and music might be restored and social order reformulated. While Confucius asked people to deny themselves and observe proprieties, he did not explain much about ritual itself probably because in his time the rules were so still deeply rooted in the society and known to everyone that demonstration was redundant. By the end of the Warring States Period, however, ritual and music were virtually abandoned. There was only a superficial knowledge of ritual among people. Under such circumstances, Master Xun made a systematic and profound study of it with repeated emphasis on its importance in defining the codes of conduct, developing social harmony, and maintaining national stability. He pointed out that "men cannot survive if they do not have the sense of propriety, the things they do will not succeed if they neglect rites, and a country cannot remain in peace without promotion to ritual" (On Self-Cultivation).

His essay On Ritual is a comprehensive exploration of the origin, function, meaning and spirit of ritual. The essay begins with a definite and detailed answer to the question "What gave rise to ritual?":

> Man is born with desires which, if not satisfied, cannot but seek some means of satisfaction. If there is no measure or limit to his seeking, there will inevitably be contentions. Contention causes disorder which in turn leads to difficulty. The Former Kings hated this and established rite and morality in order to divide people according to their roles and duties and regulate their desires before satisfying them, so that no desires are left dissatisfied because of the deficiency of goods and goods are not exhausted by the desires. In this way both desires and goods are restricted and well-coordinated over the course of time. This is the origin of ritual (On Ritual).

From here we can see that our previous understanding of ritual was only associated with ethics, behavioral norms, etiquette and ceremonies, and so on. Actually, Master Xun traced the cause and aim of ritual to the coordination of social distribution and the compromise between natural resources and social needs. With ritual, desires are regulated before they are satisfied without leaving any demand unmet because of the deficiency of goods or good being exhausted by demands so that "both desires and goods restricted and well-coordinated over the course of time." Such an important social function is the basis on which morality is built. For a long time, however, men ignored or avoided it when they talked about ritual, so that in the minds of the public this culture was only an empty moral sermon divorced from social reality. In fact, the reason why people should consciously self-discipline themselves and abide by ritual and morality was also related to the maintenance of a reasonable social distribution and the compromise between natural resources and social needs that concern people's livelihood. Therefore, Master Xun's causal analysis of ritual has very profound and important theoretical and practical significance.

Master Xun's exposition on ritual has very rich contents. He emphasized its formulation on the principles of nature: "ritual embodies principles that can never be changed." (On Music) It is the road people are required to follow in their practice: "Ritual is the foundation on which men behave themselves. Without it they would stumble and fall into the mire of errors." (Quotes from Master Xun). It is a sign that leads people in the right direction: "He who wades into water should mark out deep spots so that others might not fall in. Similarly, he who governs men should mark out the dividing line between order and disorder so that they might not fall into error. Ritual principles are markers." (On the Way of Heaven) It is also an embankment not to be broken through at random: "A gentleman must suit his words to certain occasions, his conduct to certain standards, and his principles to what he exalts and focuses on." (On the Influence of Confucianism) It serves as a way for self-improvement or perfection: "Ritual is established to rectify man's behaviors." (On Self-Cultivation)

There are four more points of reference concerning Master Xun's thought of ritual.

First of all, he insisted that difference in status was indispensable to a society and should be regulated by establishing rites, since it was natural that "two men of equal eminence serve neither; two men of equally humble station command neither," "With the same power and status as well as similar likes and dislikes, men would fight with each other over things which satisfy neither. Their fighting naturally leads to chaos and ends in difficulty." Therefore, the great kings of former times "established rite and morality to make distinctions between rich and poor, eminent and humble, and enable those above to dominate those below. This is the basis upon which all under Heaven is nurtured." (On Kingcraft) This is referred to in *The Book of History* when it says "Equality is only possible when there is inequality." Therefore, the ritual that nurtures is reflected in the distinctions it makes, i.e., "the ranks between noble and base, the superiorities between old and young, the degrees between wealth and poverty, and the differences between power and insignificance."[15]

Secondly, he attached great importance to the function and meaning of ritual in nurturing people's dispositions. He remarked,

> Who is aware that by observing rite and morality one's dispositions are nurtured? So, he who seeks only to preserve his life will lose it sooner, he who strives only for profit will surely suffer loss, he who feels contented in being slack, idle and comfortable for the time being will surely face danger, and he who chooses to indulge himself will surely meet his doom. Therefore, he who controls himself with ritual and moral principles will be fulfilled in his desires and improved in moral integrity; If he is overcome by his inborn desires and emotions, he will be lost in both (On Ritual).

This means that one may guide and regulate his own dispositions according to ritual principles instead of indulging them and consequently causing harm to himself. While stressing the necessity for men to nurture their dispositions and rectify their behaviors with ritual, Master Xun also emphasized the part played by penal law from the perspective of government, since ritual and law complemented each other, they "elucidated ritual and moral codes to transform them, established laws and standards to correct them, and enforced penalties to restrain them so that all under Heaven could achieve order and conform to goodness" (On the Evil of Human Nature).

Thirdly, he thought that ritual involved an external form of decoration which represented internal human emotions and reverence. "Ritual generally serves the living in making them happy and the dead in sending them off mournfully. It expresses the feeling of reverence in sacrificial offerings and displays the awe-inspiring majesty in military operations." (On Ritual) Therefore, ritual education and practice is an important approach to developing the inner emotions and respects of men. The fundamental spirit of ritual is respect[16]; "All things originate from heaven, and men originate from their ancestors ... In the sacrifices at the border there is an expression of gratitude to the source."[17] Master Xun importantly traced ritual to three sources that should never be forgotten:

---

[15] *The Book of Rites.*

[16] *The Book of Filial Piety.*

[17] *The Book of Rites.*

> Ritual has three roots. Heaven and Earth are the root of life. Ancestors are the root of tribes and clans. And kings and emperors are the root of order.

This is the theoretical source of the belief and worship of Heaven, Earth, monarch, parents, and masters as the most highly respectable and should therefore be remembered. In a word, Master Xun insisted that ritual be taken as the criterion in learning, self-cultivation, personal behavior, and actions, because it was most capable of evaluating the conduct of man.

Lastly, it is necessary to mention his important observation on ritual. In his opinion, ritual was something constantly changing with the times and people's hearts rather than something rigid; therefore, it would not do to follow the beaten track. He emphasized learning from the more recent system of rites and morality or from the kings of later times. He made it clear that "Ritual is based on complying with the aspirations of the people; therefore, behaviors that are not recorded in *The Book of Rites* but comply with the people's wishes are in accordance with ritual principles." (Quotes from Master Xun) In addition, he formulated a principle on how to inherit the traditional culture of ritual, that is, choosing the good old ones and putting them into practice (On Governance). This point is very important. If ritual principles are modified with the times and adjusted according to people's hearts, and if the good ones are retained and put into effect, then the construction and education of ritual culture can still be regarded as the essence and foundation of personal self-cultivation, interpersonal coordination, as well as the overall harmony of society.

IV. The Importance, Necessity and Content of and Approach to Learning

Master Xun stressed the importance of learning at the very beginning: "A gentleman says, 'One must never stop learning.'" (On Learning) His advice implies that there is no end to learning, so learning should not be limited in time. Since there is not much difference in men when they are born, why is there in reality the distinction between Yao or Shun and Jie or Zhou, and the difference between gentlemen and petty men? In Master Xun's opinion, this was chiefly due to different extents to which they received education, the environment they were exposed to, the company they kept, and the amount of effort they made. Learning involves the mastery of the correct way to behave oneself, as is described in *The Book of Rites*: "As the jade uncut will not serve as a vessel, so a man without learning will be ignorant of the way." The purpose of learning is to constantly improve and perfect oneself. Confucius said, "In ancient times, men pursued learning for themselves; the men of today do it for others."[18] Master Xun moved a step forward, saying, "A gentleman learns in order to ennoble himself, while a petty man regards learning as a gift which he can use to please others." (On Learning) It is preferable to demand oneself with the learning

---

[18] *The Analects*.

of a gentleman so that the learning is "received through his ear, stored in his mind, displayed in his appearance and behavior, and reflected in his actions" instead of going in through his ear before coming directly out of the mouth and that "Each word he says and every action he takes, no matter how usual they are, serve as an example for others to follow." That is, learning should be put into practice, so that one's words and deeds are in line with the rules and a model is set up for others to imitate.

What is involved in the self-ennobling learning of a gentleman and where does it start? According to Master Xun, "its courses start with the recitation of the classics and conclude with the learning of rites." The classics include *The Book of Rites*, *The Book of Music*, *The Book of Songs*, *The Book of History*, and *The Spring and Autumn Annals*. Master Xun saw as essential "reverence and order in *The Book of Rites*, the fairness and harmony in *The Book of Music*, the breadth and profundity in *The Book of Songs* and *The Book of History*, and the sublime words with deep meanings in *The Spring and Autumn Annals*." (On Learning) Rites were particularly important, for "learning concludes the rites that represent the culmination of moral integrity." With the content of learning determined, the key lies in following a good master: "Ritual is established to rectify man's behaviors, and a master is needed to properly interpret these customary codes. How are behaviors corrected if there were no rules? Without a master, how can we be sure what these practices are?" (On Self-Cultivation) In addition to a good teacher, external environment exercises its influence, neighbors and friends play an important part, and good conditions and atmosphere also count. In the eyes of Master Xun,

> Erigeron growing in the midst of hemp plants stands upright without propping. Snow-white sand becomes invisible when mixed up with black soil. Angelica is known for its aroma; but when its root is dipped in dirty water, a gentleman will keep away from it and ordinary people will refuse to wear it. It is untrue that it smells inherently unpleasant; it is made so by soaking in waste water. Therefore, a gentleman must be careful in taking up his residence and keeping his company, for this is the right way to protect himself against evil and draw near what is appropriate (On Learning).

Furthermore, Master Xun informed of a few crucial points in learning. Firstly, concentration, for "without quietly immersing oneself in hard work, there will be no brilliant accomplishment; without determined silent efforts, there will be no illustrious achievement." (On Learning) Secondly, accumulation, since "without the accumulation of small steps, no one can travel a thousand *li*; without the confluence of little streams, there can be no big rivers or seas." "Pile up earth to make mountains and wind and rain will arise up there. Accumulate water to make a deep pool and dragons will be born in it. Likewise, keep doing good to cultivate virtue and one will gain supreme wisdom and become a sage." (On Learning) Thirdly, a profound learning plus consciousness of where or when to stop, because "It is human nature to possess the cognitive ability; it is the law of things to be known. Yet with the inborn power of cognition, it is impossible to understand all the laws without any restraint even if one spends his whole lifetime doing it. One may learn hundreds of millions of principles of things, but they are insufficient to exhaust the complete cycle of transformation of all things. Then one is no different from a foolish person." (On

Removing the Obstacle of Limitations) What can be learned is infinite, so a limit is necessary. Otherwise, with a huge amount of knowledge but without the ability to be adjusted to changes, one is no different from a fool. Two proposals are of help to those who are fond of learning: to practice what is learned and to constantly examine oneself with what is learned. Master Xun said,

> Hearing is better than ignorance, seeing is better than hearing, comprehension is better than seeing, and practice is better than just comprehension. Learning does not end till knowledge is put into practice (On the Influence of Confucianism).
>
> Having observed a good conduct, you should make a careful self-examination to see if you behave likewise. On the other hand, when you see a bad behavior, you must feel afraid and examine yourself against it. When you find goodness in you, firmly cherish it; otherwise, if you spot badness in you, abandon it as if you were inflicted with the dirt it carries (On Self-Cultivation).
>
> A gentleman may become wise and faultless with broad learning and daily self-examination (On Learning).

These suggestions on learning still have profound meaning of enlightenment and practice for teaching and learning nowadays.

V. Removing the Obstacle of Limitations in the Way of Thinking

Master Xun said, "It is the common fault of men to be blinded by one-sidedness and therefore ignorant of great truth." (On Removing the Obstacle of Limitations) While this remark targeted the social reality when the Different Schools of Thought contended with one another, each person insisting on his own opinion and thinking himself right and others wrong, so that there was political confusion with each contending for domination, it also exposes the way of thinking among people in general. Human cognition has its own one-sidedness and limitations. It is restricted by the times and environment one lives in. It is also affected by external interference, point of view, preconceived ideas, to name only a few. As Master Xun pointed out, "What causes limitations? Some are caused by desire or hatred, some by views confined to beginning or end, some by what is distant or near, some by knowledge profound or shallow, others by matters of the past or present." In short, "All things are different and the comprehension of these differences result in the limitations. This is the common fault in the way of thinking." (On Removing the Obstacle of Limitations) Bias in thinking brings about errors in understanding, leading to mistakes in dealing with practical affairs. With positive and negative cases in history, Master Xun explained the failures caused by bias and prejudice that led to misfortunes and infamy throughout the ages, as well as successes brought about by immunity to bias and prejudice and the good reputation passed down to later generations. In Master Xun's mind, a perfect sage should be "benevolent, wise and free from prejudice."

Then how can one be free from bias and prejudice? Master Xun suggested that a clear mind should be kept in the careful government. To avoid the disasters brought about by bias and prejudice, it was necessary to know Dao, a complete mastery of which would guarantee a comprehensive understanding so that one could respond to and deal with matters when they should occur, adjust himself to changing circumstances in agreement with principles, and manage all things perfectly (Criticism of the Twelve Masters). Master Xun said,

> He who is expert in a specific thing is suitable to do it only; he who is well versed in Dao may place all things under control. A gentleman concentrates on Dao and uses it to inspect things. His concentration leads to the right way of thinking, and when he inspects things with Dao, his perception will be clear. To examine the clear perception of things with the right way of thinking, he is able to control all things (On Removing the Obstacle of Limitations).

Therefore, a mastery of Dao is essential. The way to its mastery is found in the mind since "The mind is the lord of the body and master of the spiritual intelligence. It issues commands instead of being commanded" (On Removing the Obstacle of Limitations).

Thus, Master Xun proposed the approach to removing bias and prejudice: starting from the cultivation of the mind, through its concentration and tranquility, to the understanding of Dao. To put it specifically, "the mind is also somewhat empty because it never prevents the collection of new information with what is already in storage," the power of concentration "does not prevent the understanding of one thing against that of another," and the quality of tranquility "does not allow dreams and fantasies to interfere with understanding." How could one be free from bias and prejudice or other types of interference if the mind should intend to be partial and keep from concentration and tranquility? Therefore, only by removing the influence of preconceived ideas, being concentrated in handling matters without other distractions, and settling down with tranquility in mind could one "lay out all things and weigh them according to certain standard" rather than seeing "desire or hatred only, beginning or end only, what is far or near only, what is profound or shallow only, and past or present only," so that "the differences will not be able to blind one another and lead to disorder," there will be "great clarity and brilliance" characterized by emptiness, concentration and tranquility in mind, and "None of the myriad things has a form that is imperceptible. None perception is not assigned a proper place. And none perception with a proper place fails in its function" (On Removing the Obstacle of Limitations).

These are only a few hints for those who read *Essays of Master Xun*, and the readers are expected to discover more inspiring ideas and viewpoints.

Xunzi Xin Zhu ("Essays of Master Xun with a Fresh Annotation") cannot be regarded as a completely new version since it was revised on the basis of the previous edition, the outcome of collective effort with Fuling Zhuang, Shaomeng Ma and I in charge of the drafting, published nearly forty years ago in 1979. As many readers felt that although this annotation bears a lot of viewpoints and vocabulary of that era, its interpretation of the original text of Master Xun is generally recommendable, easy to understand and suitable for general readers, the editors of Zhonghua Book Company suggested that I arrange for it to be revised for republication. I sought help from Yunhua Liang, a senior editor of Zhonghua Book Company who participated in and was in charge of this book, and he carefully checked and revised it from beginning to end. Then there was a delay of four or five years for various reasons till now when Zhonghua Book Company has decided that it be published by the end of this year. I invited a reading group from among my doctoral students, including Lei Xiao, Jizhong Wu, Jiaxi Xu and Jing Bian. Everyone took part in the reading, discussion, and revision (some of my other doctoral students also joined in from time to time). They completely rewrote and modified the thirty-two synopses and corrected some of the notes. Editor-in-charge Xu Zou also reread the whole draft carefully and offered many valuable and specific suggestions for revision. Therefore, the current version is also an achievement of collective effort.

Beijing, China
November 2017

Yulie Lou

Contents

1	**On Learning**	1
	Synopsis	1
	Text	2
2	**On Self-cultivation**	9
	Synopsis	9
	Text	10
3	**Doing Nothing Improper**	15
	Synopsis	15
	Text	16
4	**On Honor and Disgrace**	21
	Synopsis	21
	Text	22
5	**Criticism of Physiognomy**	29
	Synopsis	29
	Text	30
6	**Criticism of the Twelve Masters**	37
	Synopsis	37
	Text	38
7	**On the Relationship of a Monarch with His Subjects**	43
	Synopsis	43
	Text	44
8	**On the Influence of Confucianism**	47
	Synopsis	47
	Text	48
9	**On Kingcraft**	59
	Synopsis	59
	Text	60

xix

10	**On the Wealth of a State**	71
	Synopsis	71
	Text	72
11	**On Governance**	83
	Synopsis	83
	Text	84
12	**On the Way of a Monarch**	95
	Synopsis	95
	Text	96
13	**On Being a Minister**	107
	Synopsis	107
	Text	107
14	**On Attracting the Men of Learning**	113
	Synopsis	113
	Text	114
15	**On Military Affairs**	117
	Synopsis	117
	Text	118
16	**On Building a Powerful State**	129
	Synopsis	129
	Text	130
17	**On the Way of Heaven**	137
	Synopsis	137
	Text	138
18	**On Correct Judgement**	145
	Synopsis	145
	Text	146
19	**On Ritual**	157
	Synopsis	157
	Text	158
20	**On Music**	169
	Synopsis	169
	Text	170
21	**On Removing the Obstacle of Limitations**	175
	Synopsis	175
	Text	175
22	**On Rectifying Names**	185
	Synopsis	185
	Text	186

23	**On the Evil of Human Nature**	195
	Synopsis	195
	Text	195
24	**On Being the Son of Heaven**	203
	Synopsis	203
	Text	203
25	**Work Songs**	207
	Synopsis	207
	Text	208
26	**Allegories**	219
	Synopsis	219
	Text	220
27	**Quotes from Master Xun**	225
	Synopsis	225
	Text	226
28	**The Vessel of Warning**	241
	Synopsis	241
	Text	241
29	**On the Way of a Son**	247
	Synopsis	247
	Text	247
30	**On Self-Examination**	251
	Synopsis	251
	Text	251
31	**Conversations Between Duke Ai of Lu and Confucius**	255
	Synopsis	255
	Text	255
32	**Sidelights**	261
	Synopsis	261
	Text	261

Chapter 1
On Learning

Synopsis

This is an important essay on the method of learning.

It is comprised of two parts: (1) the nature and importance of learning; (2) the content and purpose of learning.

It is pointed out at the very beginning that there is no end to learning, the importance of which is demonstrated through two vivid metaphors: from indigo, a green plant, cyan, or greenish blue, is obtained; at a lower temperature, water changes into ice.[1] The secret of success in learning lies in constant self-examination, taking current reality into consideration, and the combination of learning with practice. Only in this way can one become wise and free from errors. The reason why men are born with the same cries but grow in different ways is due to the education they receive and the environment they live in. Therefore, men are advised to learn to make use of things and for self-protection be careful in choosing the community they live in and the company they keep. They are also warned to be cautious of the language they use in verbal communication and the positions they take in actions. Since with perseverance and concentration one can accumulate good merit and become a sage, one should start doing what is good and right here and now, no matter how trivial it might be.

Learning involves the Confucian classics. It begins with their recitation and finishes with the mastery of ritual principles with a view to transforming ordinary men of learning into sages. The classics are characterized by their breadth and profundity, encompassing all knowledge of human life. *The Book of Rites* is of particular importance. The purpose of learning is distinguished between the moral self-cultivation of a gentleman and the ingratiation of a petty man. In the process of learning, a teacher's role is emphasized, for he is qualified to show the connections between the classics and reality so that learners may put what they learn into practice. Emphasis is also

---

[1] Greenish blue (*qing*) is a favorite Chinese color and ice (*bing*) is regarded by the Chinese as representing purity and cleanness—Tr.

given to the part played by propriety in learning, which should be honored so that a scholar may be trained to behave himself in accordance with the codes of moral conduct and communicate with people with caution and that teachers and students may benefit from one another. At the end of the essay, it is clearly pointed out that the highest standard of learning is concentration and perseverance with which one may be well-versed in all things, benevolent and righteous all the time, stand firm and succeed in handling anything and thus he realizes the ultimate goal of becoming a perfect man – a gentleman who prizes perfection in moral integrity.

Text

The gentleman says, "One must never stop learning." The pigment cyan is extracted from the plant indigo and it produces a deeper color; ice is water frozen and yet it is colder.[2]

A green piece of wood straight as a plumbline, may be bent, by roasting, into the rim of a wheel round as drawn with a compass; however, it never recovers its original straightness when allowed to dry out in the sun, because it is no longer pliable. Thus, wood may be straightened against a carpenter's ink-line and metal may be sharpened on a grindstone. A gentleman may become wise and faultless with broad learning and daily self-examination.

One does not realize how distant Heaven is till he climbs up a lofty mountain, or how deep Earth is till he looks down into a canyon, nor is he aware of how profound learning is till he hears the instructions passed down from the Former Kings.[3]

Children from the states of Gan[4] and Yue or from the tribes of Yi and Mo[5] cry with the same voice at birth but follow different customs when grown up. It is education that brings about the difference. It is advised in *The Book of Songs*:

> Oh, you gentlemen, listen please,
>> Stay not always idle and at ease.
>> Fulfill your trusted duty in earnest,
>> Pursue moral integrity and be honest.
>> When divinities learn of what you do,
>> They'll bestow great bliss on you.[6]

Nothing divine is higher than the education with Dao[7]; no happiness is greater than freedom from sufferings.

---

[2] These comparisons are used to show that progress promises a higher quality.
[3] The famous wise monarchs in ancient times.
[4] A small kingdom in the Spring and Autumn Period, later replaced by the State of Wu.
[5] Minor ethnic groups in the north and east.
[6] Minor Court Hymns, *The Book of Songs*.
[7] Also known as Tao or the Way, general principles of philosophy and politics.

I kept thinking hard the whole day sometime before, but gained much less than what was learned in a moment. I once attempted to look into the distance on tiptoe and found I could not see farther away than by watching from a high position. Ascending a height to wave my hand, I can be seen farther away, but it is not because my arm becomes longer. Shouting downwind, I can be heard more clearly, but it is not because my voice becomes louder. Those who go traveling with the help of a carriage and horses may reach a thousand *li* easily not because they are good walkers. And those who cross a great river by a boat and oars make it without difficulty not because they are champion swimmers. A gentleman is not necessarily extraordinary by birth; he is just good at taking advantage of things.

In the south there is a bird called wren. It builds its nest with feathers woven together with hair and attaches it to the tassels of a tender reed. When a gust of wind breaks the plant, the eggs are destroyed and therefore the baby birds are killed. It is not that the nest is imperfect; it is due to the frailty of the plant to which the nest is attached. In the west there is a plant called blackberry lily. It is merely four *cun*[8] long, but being on the top of a high mountain, it overlooks the ravine a hundred fathoms deep. It can never grow so tall, but it is able to reach such a height by the location it finds itself. Erigeron growing in the midst of hemp plants stands upright without propping. Snow-white sand becomes invisible when mixed up with black soil. Angelica is known for its aroma; but when its root is dipped in dirty water, a gentleman will keep away from it and ordinary people will refuse to wear it. It is untrue that it smells inherently unpleasant; it is made so by soaking in waste water. Therefore, a gentleman must be careful in taking up his residence and keeping his company with men of education, for this is the right way to protect himself against evil and draw near what is appropriate.

All things happen on account of something else. Honor or disgrace is brought by a man's corresponding conduct. Meat breeds maggot when it rots. Fish produces worms when it gets dry. Disaster befalls a man when he is overcome by negligence. That which is rigid tends to break; that which is flexible is easily constrained.[9] Wickedness and nastiness accumulating in oneself result in grievances. Firewood looks the same when it is spread out, but fire seeks out the driest pieces first. Ground may look flat and even, but water seeks out the dampest spots first. Plants of the same species grow together. Birds and beasts flock together. And all things follow their own kind. For the same reason, as soon as a target is erected, bows and arrows will be drawn. Where woods grow in abundance, axes and saws will be attracted. When trees become tall and shady, birds will roost in them. And the moment vinegar turns sour, gnats will gather around it. Sometimes words court disaster and actions invite shame; therefore, a gentleman can never be too careful about what he says or what standpoint he adopts.

---

[8] A unit of length equivalent to less than 3 cm.

[9] An alternative interpretation is: That which is rigid is likely to be used as a support while that which is flexible as a cord.

Pile up earth to make mountains and wind and rain will arise up there.[10] Accumulate water to make a deep pool and dragons will be born in it. Likewise, keep doing good to cultivate virtue and one will gain supreme wisdom and become a sage. Therefore, without the accumulation of small steps, no one can travel a thousand *li*; without the confluence of little streams, there can be no big rivers or seas. Even though a thoroughbred can cover no less than ten paces in one leap, a nag may succeed all the same by traveling a thousand *li* in ten days. The success lies in its perseverance. Stop carving midway and even a piece of rotten wood cannot be cut through; carve with perseverance and stone or metal can be engraved. An earthworm has neither sharp claws or teeth, nor strong muscles or bones, but it is able to eat from the dirt above and drink from the spring below because of concentration in its pursuit. In contrast, a crab has six legs and a pair of pincers but would have no place to lodge unless it can find an empty hole dug by a snake or an eel. This is because it is restless in mind. Thus, without quietly immersing oneself in hard work, there will be no brilliant accomplishment; without silent determined efforts, there will be no illustrious achievement. He who wanders at the crossroads arrives nowhere; he who serves two masters pleases neither. The eyes that watch two different objects at once cannot be sharp; the ears that listen to two different things cannot be sensitive to both. A winged snake[11] has no feet but it can fly. A hare-like rat has five skills but it fails to find a way out.[12] It is sung in *The Book of Songs*:

"In mulberry trees the turtledove[13] stays,
   With seven younglings she has to raise.
   Behold the gentleman over there;
   He's always attentive and fair.
   He's always firm and kind,
   With a strong will in his mind."[14]

Thus, a gentleman concentrates on what he does.

In ancient times, when Huba[15] played the zither, fish down in the stream would come up to enjoy the music; when Boya[16] played the lute, the six royal horses raised

---

[10] The ancient Chinese believed that mountains inhale clouds and exhale mist and therefore both wind and rain are formed in the mountains. Master Xun made use of this belief to show that perseverance leads to achievement.

[11] A snake that flies according to an old legend. This is proved to be true by modern scientific observation.—Tr.

[12] A legendary animal that is able to fly but fails to get up to the roof, to climb a tree but fails to reach its top, to swim but fails to ford a mountain stream, to dig holes but fails to take shelter in them, and to walk but fails to outwalk any other animals.

[13] The bird is intralingually translated into cuckoo, which is incorrect, since cuckoo is best known to lay its eggs in the nests of other species to be incubated and fed by the foster parents.—Tr.

[14] Ballads from the States, *The Book of Songs*. The bird is said to be busy feeding its younglings the whole day—from top to bottom in the morning and from bottom to top in the evening. This song is used to stress that a gentleman should be attentive to his office and fair to the people around him.

[15] The best-known zither-player according to legends.

[16] A famous lute-player in the Spring and Autumn Period in ancient China.

their heads to listen, forgetful of their fodder. It can be seen from here that no sound is so faint as to be inaudible, nor is any action so well concealed that it cannot be detected. Where jade is buried in the mountains, the plants there display a special luster; where pearls are found in the deep sea, the cliff shores shine with uncommon glow. Are good deeds not constantly accumulated? If they are, how can they ever remain unknown?

Where does learning begin? Where does it end? I say its courses start with the recitation of the classics and conclude with the learning of rites. The objective is to get trained as a man of learning at first and as a sage in the end. Down-to-earth efforts over a long period of time promise great depths in comprehension; learning does not stop till death. Thus, there is an end to the courses; however, there is no end to learning. It is human to pursue learning; it is beast to give it up.

For the courses, *The Book of History*[17] keeps a record of governmental affairs, *The Book of Songs*[18] has a collection of verses that can be set to music, and *The Book of Rites* contains a general outline of rules and regulations as well as the codes of conduct by analogy. Therefore, learning concludes with rites that represent the culmination of moral integrity. All principles between Heaven and Earth are integrated into reverence and order in *The Book of Rites*,[19] fairness and harmony in *The Book of Music*,[20] breadth and profundity in *The Book of Songs* and *The Book of History*, and the sublime words with deep meanings in *The Spring and Autumn Annals*.

The learning of a gentleman is received through his ear, stored in his mind, displayed in his appearance and behavior, and reflected in his actions. Each word he says and every action he takes, no matter how usual they are, serve as an example for others to follow. In contrast, the learning of a petty man goes in through his ear and comes straight out of his mouth. It is only four *cun* from ears to mouth, and how can such a short distance serve to turn an ordinary man noble?

In ancient times men learned for self-improvement; nowadays they learn for the sake of others. A gentleman learns in order to ennoble himself, while a petty man regards learning as a gift which he can use to please others.

To volunteer information that is unsought is called officiousness; to offer information that is more than necessary is garrulity. It is as inappropriate to be officious as garrulous. A gentleman should respond like an echo.

In learning, no manner is of more advantage than to associate with the right people.[21] *The Book of Rites* and *The Book of Music* provide regulations and standards without detailed explanations; *The Book of Songs* and *The Book of History* present

---

[17] Also known as *Shangshu*, a collection of official statements and political documents in the Shang and Zhou dynasties.

[18] Also known as *Shijing*, the earliest collection of poems in China from the early Western Zhou to the mid-Spring and Autumn Period, adding up to 305 in number.

[19] A book recording the hierarchical moral codes and rites. Master Xun provided here a fresh interpretation of ritual and gave it new meanings.

[20] A book now lost.

[21] The right people refers to good teachers and helpful friends.

ancient matters that are not in line with current reality; *The Spring and Autumn Annals* is obscure and cannot be soon understood. Follow the right people in learning the doctrines of gentlemen and a noble character will be cultivated, profound knowledge gained, and world affairs comprehended. This explains why no approach is of more advantage than to associate with the right people.

Of all approaches to learning, none is quicker than consulting with the right people. The next best route is to honor ritual. To spend the whole life learning the jumbled doctrines of various schools in addition to the interpretation of *The Book of Songs* and *The Book of History* can only make a shallow scholar out of a man if he fails to consult the right people and lacks a strong sense of ritual. The learning of ritual propriety gives hints about and shows the right way to what is advocated by the Former Kings and the essence of benevolence and righteousness. It is just like holding a fur coat by the collar and shaking it with the five fingers curled: in that way, countless hair will be turned in order. To behave and act only in accordance with *The Book of Songs* and *The Book of History* without a sense of propriety and rules leads one nowhere; it is as hopeless as trying to measure the depth of a river with fingers, to pound millet with a long-handled spear, or to pick up food from a pot with an awl. Therefore, he who has a strong sense of ritual can be a disciplined man of learning even if he fails to achieve a full understanding; he who has keen perception can only make a corrupt scholar if he has a poor sense of ritual.

Offer no answer to improper questions. Take no heed of improper information. Pay no attention to improper talks. Keep from arguing with those who are arrogant and unreasonable. A man coming for advice according to Dao will be received; otherwise, he will be shunned. If he behaves with the utmost propriety, you may show him the orientation of Dao. If he speaks with modesty, you may inform him of the substance of Dao. If he shows his willingness to follow, you may go into the details of Dao with him. Therefore, discussing with someone at the wrong time is regarded as being officious; failure to speak to someone in good time is understood to be secretive; speaking to someone regardless of his reaction is taken as being blind. A gentleman is neither officious, nor secretive, nor blind; he is cautious in dealing with other men. This is the advice given in *The Book of Songs*:

> Don't give way to impatience and neglect
> And the Son of Heaven will come to protect.[22]

He who misses one shot out of a hundred cannot be called an expert archer; he who fails the last step of a 1000-*li* journey cannot be called a good carriage driver; he who fails to be well-versed in all things and benevolent and righteous all the time cannot be regarded as good at learning. Learning involves concentration and perseverance. An ordinary person now quits learning this and then picks up something else. With little merit but much fault, he may grow into a villain like Jie the tyrant or Zhi the robber. Only he who has a comprehensive learning and thorough understanding becomes a really good scholar.

---

[22] Minor Court Hymns, *The Book of Songs*.

A gentleman is aware that an incomplete and impure learning cannot be regarded as perfect. With this awareness, he reads widely in order to achieve mastery through comprehensive studies, ponders and explores for the purpose of complete understanding, follows the example of the right people in practicing what he learns, and abandons what is harmful in his practice in order to nourish what is beneficial. He trains himself in such a way that his eyes are guarded against what is ugly, his ears reject what is not proper, his mouth refuses to say what is wrong, and his mind desires only to deliberate over what is right. By the time he is really fond of learning, his eyes will take pleasure in the five colors,[23] his ears will gain pleasure in the five tones,[24] his mouth will get pleasure in the five flavors,[25] and his heart will experience pleasure as great as possessing the entire world. Hence, he is not to be moved by power, influence, wealth or position, or overwhelmed by numerical strength, or shaken by the idea of possessing the whole world. He lives by these principles and dies for them. This is what is called moral conduct and personal integrity. With such qualities, he stands firm. Gaining a firm foothold, he is able to deal with various complicated situations. Standing firm and successful in handling any situation, he is called a perfect man. Heaven reveals its brilliance, Earth shows its expanse, and a gentleman prizes perfection in moral integrity.

---

[23] Red, yellow, blue, white and black.
[24] *Gong, shang, jue, zhi* and *yu*, corresponding roughly to the notes of 1, 2, 3, 5, and 6 in today's numbered musical notation.
[25] Sweet, sour, bitter, pungent and salty.

Chapter 2
On Self-cultivation

Synopsis

This is an important essay on the rules of conduct emphatic about self-cultivation. Based on this emphasis, the central target and basic approach are demonstrated. The former may be summarized as doing good: both tireless pursuit of what is good and constant effort to lead others with what is good, ready acceptance of healthy advice, constant guard against evil, and effort to achieve harmony with what is good.

Concerning the relationship of self-cultivation with experience and circumstances, it is pointed out that he who has a noble aspiration makes light of wealth and status, he who possesses moral integrity despises the nobility and he who carefully examines himself looks lightly upon external things. A gentleman makes things serve him instead of being made to serve them. The thing that really counts in cultivating oneself is neither wealth nor status but justification and contentedness in the mind. Thus, an educated gentleman keeps along the right road in spite of poverty. External factors will not determine self-cultivation either, for even if a gentleman fails to be employed anywhere, he is still honored if he has respect on the outside, loyalty in mind and love for others. In a word, self-cultivation is reflected in every word one says and every action he takes; it is self-disciplined rather than imposed. A gentleman training himself to do good provides liberal relief to the public, shows respect to old people, and does not despise or humiliate those who are in difficulty. He is not fame-oriented in doing good; nor does he expect return for the help he offers. With these qualities, he is guarded by Heaven and free from disasters.

The fundamental approach to self-cultivation lies in the observation of the principles of propriety, which plays an essential role in one's physical and spiritual well-being and is intimately associated with his routine life, his speech and his actions. Without these principles, a man cannot survive in the true sense, the things he does will fail, and a country cannot remain stable. The key point in following these principles is the inner control of *qi* or vital force and the nourishment of mind. This further demonstrates their physiological, psychological and mental significance to men. In learning, the first important point to make clear is to be conscious of a limit, for an aimless trip leads nowhere. Therefore, a scholar approves of moral standards and acts according to them; with further understanding on this basis, he becomes perfectly confident. He has the rules of conduct as the limit of his learning in order to behave himself and follows a good teacher to guarantee that the principles of propriety he learns are correctly comprehended. A gentleman is required to be upright, careful, modest, quick-witted, fond of learning and respectful to his seniors. He must learn to cautiously avoid humiliation, bravely does what is reasonable, and overcome personal desire in favor of fairness and justice no matter he is poor and humble or rich and honored.

Text

Having observed a good conduct, you should make a careful self-examination to see if you behave likewise. On the other hand, when you see a bad behavior, you must feel afraid and examine yourself against it. When you find goodness in you, firmly cherish it; otherwise, if you spot badness in you, abandon it as if you were inflicted with the dirt it carries. For this reason, he who rightly points out my errors is my teacher, he who fairly considers me to be in the right is my friend, and he who flatters me is my victimizer.

A gentleman respects his teachers, he is on good terms with his friends, and he extremely hates those who do harm to others. He tirelessly pursues what is good, willingly accepts admonitions, and is constantly on the alert. This being the case, how is it likely that no advancement might be made even if he does not desire it! A petty man is just the opposite. He commits all manners of evil, but hates other men who criticize him; he is completely unworthy, yet expects others to consider him worthy. He is a tiger or a wolf in the heart and a brutal beast in behavior; however, he resents it when others consider him a villain. He shows favor to those who flatter him and keeps at a distance from those who offer him good advice. The words of correction sound like ridicule to him while the words of true advice are mistaken by him for persecution. Since he is like this, how is it possible that he will not perish even though he does not want it? These lines in *The Book of Songs*:

> He chimes in easily with persuasions;
> > He takes a dislike to dissuasions.
> > How deplorable it is!
> > Good counsels he refuses to obey,
> > Bad ideas he follows in every way.[1]

refer precisely to such men.

---

[1] Minor Court Hymns, *The Book of Songs*.

These are the rules that fit in on all occasions: harness qi[2] to nourish life and you can live as long as the Peng progenitor.[3] Cultivate your moral character to make yourself strong and you may become as famous as Yao and Yu.[4] Things that really count either in favorable circumstances or in difficulty are ritual propriety and good faith. When courage, uprightness, will, wisdom and strategy are concerned, a sense of propriety promises success while its absence leads to absurdity, disorder, negligence and sluggishness. When it comes to food, drinking, clothing, residence, actions and movements, harmony is achieved when they accord with rites; otherwise, everything goes wrong at any time. As for appearance, attitudes, bearing and paces, refinement is shown when rites are observed and arrogance, stubbornness, evil and vulgarity are divulged if otherwise. Hence, men cannot survive if they do not have the sense of propriety, they will not succeed in doing anything if they neglect rites, and a country cannot remain in peace without promotion to ritual. This is what it refers to in *The Book of Songs* when it sings:

> When rules of etiquette are observed,
> > It is proper whether you speak or smile.

To lead others with what is good is termed education. To achieve harmony with what is good is called compliance. To lead others and to achieve harmony with what is not good are considered flattery and toadying. To approve of what is right and disapprove of what is wrong are recognized as wisdom; to treat what is wrong as right and what is right as wrong is regarded as stupidity. To speak ill of good men is slander and to do them harm is persecution. To call what is right right and what is wrong wrong means honesty. To steal goods is an act of theft. To conceal an action is suspected of cheating. To speak readily of things is untrustworthy. To hesitate between pros and cons is inconstancy. To guard profit at the cost of righteousness is categorized as a major crime. Being well-informed is erudite while being less-informed shallow. Being much experienced involves profound learning; being less experienced means meagre knowledge. Tardy is he who has difficulty in progress; oblivious is he who has a leaky brain. Much order achieved through fewer measures shows good governance. Disorder in spite of plentiful measures is confusion.

What follows is the art of nourishing qi and mind: if a man is impetuous and easily given to passions, soothe him through the peace of mind. Tell him to be frank and straightforward if he is abstruse and non-committal in his thought. If someone is bold, fierce and ruthless, complement him with disciplines. If he is indiscreet in actions, regulate him with the sense of timeliness. If he is narrow-minded, broaden his mind and make him generous. If he is base, slow and greedy for profit, stimulate lofty aspiration in him. If he is mediocre and careless, have him transformed by teachers and good friends. If he is inattentive, frivolous and hopeless, warn him of

---

[2] The essential life force whose existence and properties are believed to form the basis of much Chinese philosophy and medicine.—Tr.

[3] He is said to have lived the longest in the ancient times.

[4] Both are legendary monarchs in ancient China, who represent the beginning and end of a golden age in the past.—Tr.

the imminent disasters. And should he be simple, honest and pure, bring him in line with ritual and music and enlighten him with reflections. Of all arts in controlling *qi* and cultivating the mind, no approach is more direct than following the ritual, nothing is more important than learning from good teachers, and no way is more efficient than concentration and whole-heartedness. This is how *qi* energy and mind are nourished.

With a lofty aspiration, a man overlooks both wealth and rank. With the cultivation of morality and justice he disregards the nobility. With introspection, he looks lightly upon external things. This is better expressed by a famous quote: "A gentleman is in control of things; a petty man is in the control of things."

When something ends with exhaustion in body but peace in mind, do it. If anything ends with little profit but much justice, do it. Rather than win eminence in serving a tyrant, it is better to follow moral principles by serving a monarch in difficulty and having your plans implemented. For this reason, a good farmer does not give up farming because of flood or drought, a good merchant does not quit business because of an occasional loss, and an educated gentleman does not stray away from Dao because of poverty.

Being modest and respectful on the outside, keeping loyalty and trust in the heart, adhering to rite and morality, and showing affection for others, a man will be honored even if he fails to win any position in any part of the four remote borders. If he is ready to do exhausting jobs, leaves ease and enjoyment to others, obeys the rules of conduct, and has an acute sense of perception, a man of honesty, faith and reason will be trusted even though he fails to be employed anywhere in the barbarian quarters of the world. However, if he looks stubbornly arrogant and is sinister and crafty at heart, spiritually polluted by the doctrines of Dao Shen[5] and Di Mo,[6] he is sure to be despised by all even if he succeeds anywhere under Heaven. If he is evasive before toilsome jobs and afraid of being involved but is fluent in speech and quick in action before pleasure, evil, dishonest, indulgent and unregulated, he is bound to be disdained and rejected even though he is successful anywhere in the world.

A man is respectfully cautious when walking not because he is afraid of stepping into mud. He walks with his head bent not because he is afraid of tripping over something. And he lowers his eyes after exchanging glances with another not because of fear. He behaves himself in such a manner not because he is afraid of offending the ordinary people but only because he desires self-cultivation.

A thoroughbred can run a thousand *li* a day and a nag may reach that distance in ten days. But what if the journey is endless with an indefinite destination? In this case, neither a fine horse nor an inferior one can make it even if it wears out its bones and tendons. However, if the journey has an end, in spite of its distance of a thousand *li*, they will sooner or later reach the destination one following the other, one being slow and the other fast. And what about those who walk along the road of life? Do they intend to travel an endless distance and reach the indefinite destination? Or do they have the intention of setting a limit to it?

---

[5] A legalist in the Warring States Period.

[6] Also known as Mo Di or Mo Ti, Founder of Mohism.

Investigations into the separation of hardness and whiteness,[7] unity of similarity and difference,[8] and things with and without thickness[9] are not without insight; nevertheless, a gentleman never engages in such debates because he sets his learning within a certain boundary. Unusual feats are never easy in performance; however, a gentleman refuses to do them because he considers them unreasonable. Therefore, a man of learning says, "Seeing that I am slow, my fellow traveler pauses to wait me so that I may start to catch up. Then whether slow or fast, either early or late, are we not able to reach our destination all the same?" Thus, a lame turtle can move a thousand *li* if it keeps going one step after another, a hill may be formed if we keep piling up earth bit by bit, and a river like the Yangtze or the Yellow River may be drained if we try to block its source or break down its banks. If they go forward now and backward then, or sometimes leftward and at other times rightward, the six thoroughbreds of a royal chariot will never reach their destination. As for the natural abilities of men, how could they be as widely different as between those of a turtle and six thoroughbreds? However, if a lame turtle reaches the goal while the six horses fail, there is no other reason than that one keeps on going while the other does not. The road may be short, but you can never reach the destination if you do not travel along it. A job may be trivial, but it will never be fulfilled if you do not work at it. And he who stays idle most of the time will never excel others quite much.

He who approves of moral standards and act according to them is a man of learning. He who has a firm will and practices it is a gentleman. And he who is sharp in mind and inexhaustible in wisdom is a sage. Without moral standards as a reference, men are at a loss. Without a full understanding of their principles, they are restless. And with further comprehension based on their mastery, they become perfectly confident.

Ritual is established to rectify man's behaviors, and a master[10] is needed to properly interpret these customary codes. How are behaviors corrected if there were no rules? Without a master, how can we be sure what these practices are? They are set up as such and are followed in such a manner; we take delight in them. When we say as our master does, we are as wise as he is. If we are contented with these social norms and wise as our master, then we grow into sages. Therefore, violation against ritual is defiance of its principles; disobeying the master means defiance of him. Flouting the rules set up by the master and having our own way may be compared to asking a blind man to distinguish colors or relying on a deaf person to differentiate tones—nothing will come of it but nonsense and recklessness. Therefore, the object of learning is rites and regulations. A master sets himself an example for others to

---

[7] A proposition by Long Gongsun who held that hardness and whiteness are independent attributes of stone and therefore there is a distinction between universality and individuality.

[8] A proposition by Shi Hui who held that similarity and difference are relative attributes of things, that there may be the distinction in specific cases but, basically speaking, all things are both similar and different.

[9] A proposition by Shi Hui who held that what has no thickness could not be increased in thickness, yet it could extend a thousand *li* in dimension. It is also said to be proposed by Xi Deng of the Spring and Autumn Period.

[10] Either a sovereign or a teacher.

follow and finds peace in his practice. This is what is meant by the lines in *The Book of Songs*:

> Being unaware of why we do the way we do,
>   Yet we're sure it obeys the Heaven's rules.[11]

A young man who is upright, cautious and respectful to his seniors can be called a good youth. Moreover, if he is modest, quick-witted and fond of learning, no one can surpass him, for he is already a gentleman. On the other hand, if a young man is lazy, evasive and shameless and loves food and drink excessively, he may be called a bad youth. Apart from that, if he is unrestrained, unreasonable, malevolent and treacherous, and shows no respect for his elder brothers, he is regarded as an ominous guy and may be punished, or even killed.

Respect old people and the young and adult will come to your rule. Do not despise or humiliate those who are in difficulty and the talented will gather around you. Do not seek fame for what good you do or expect reward for what help you offer and the worthy and unworthy alike will come to you. With these three qualities, you will be protected by Heaven against great misfortunes.

A gentleman takes profit lightly, escapes disaster before it occurs, avoids humiliation with awe, and bravely does what is in accord with reason.

A gentleman cherishes great aspirations although he is in poverty or difficulty, he remains respectful even when he becomes wealthy and noble, he is not sluggish or indolent even if he lives an easy and comfortable life, he does not appear tired even though he is exhausted. He is neither excessively harsh when angry nor unduly indulgent when happy. He has great aspirations even though he is in poverty or difficulty because he is determined to promote benevolence. He is full of respect even when he becomes rich and noble because he does not want to overwhelm people with his wealth and status. He shows no indifference or laziness even if his life is easy and comfortable because he upholds rite and morality. He does not appear worn-out when he is actually exhausted because he pays attention to the social etiquettes. He is not over harsh in anger or unnecessarily indulgent in good humor because he places principles before personal feelings. As is exhorted in *The Book of History*:

> Follow the right path of the kings rather than personal interest; walk along the right road of the kings instead of being misled by personal ill-will.[12]

This means that a gentleman is able to overcome personal desire in favor of fairness and justice.

---

[11] Major Court Hymns, *The Book of Songs*.
[12] Grand Rules, *The Book of History*.

Chapter 3
Doing Nothing Improper

Synopsis

A gentleman is advised to follow rite and morality and accumulate his merits if he wants to pursue self-cultivation. While he cannot follow mundane trends, he should not engage in deliberately different practices either if they are against the moral principles. Different from the previous essay which provides encouragement, this chapter offers exhortations, pointing out behaviors that are improper—tackling problems by violent means, offering sophisticated arguments, and winning antisocial fame—and showing behaviors that are proper—doing good for profit in conducting oneself in society, being good with or without talent in performance, and being morally different from the ordinary people but tolerant of them—so that a gentleman is able to adapt himself to circumstances and make progress all the while.

    The reason why a gentleman is able to do this is that he understands the general principle of self-cultivation and governance: to put in good order what is in line with rite and morality rather than chaos which should be removed in the first place. In governance as in self-cultivation, attention should be fixed on the positive side of ritual instead of the negative side of confusion, for things, whether well-organized or disorderly, tend to happen if they are borne in mind. Respect for good goes hand in hand with restraint on evil. Similarly, walking along the right route does not lead astray, having ritual propriety in mind ensures proper speech and action, while focusing on disorder certainly ends in confusion. Analogy like this is found frequently in this book (e.g., "those of his kind will do the same" and "find an echo in those of a like mind" in this chapter) and therefore attention should be given to such important inference. With this guiding principle in mind, a man in pursuit of self-cultivation should sincerely remain pure and talk according to rites, and in dealing with governmental affairs should know proper approaches and six decisive qualities. In both cases, being sincere is of fundamental importance to a gentleman.

The chapter is concluded with points of reference in the choice between the desirable and the undesirable as well as acceptance and refusal, giving earnest warnings once again.

Text

A gentleman does not choose to crack a tough nut by tricks that are against ritual, neither does he think highly of developing a sharp perception in academic pursuit unsuited to the rules of conduct or esteem the fame achieved by violating rite and morality. He values only words and deeds that are proper. For this reason, the behavior of drowning oneself carrying a big stone like what Di Shentu[1] did is despised by gentlemen because it is improper. Propositions like

> Mountains and canyons are on the same level.
> Heaven and Earth are near.[2]
> Qi and Qin[3] are adjacent.
> That which enters the ear comes out of the mouth.[4]
> Old women grow beard.
> There is hair in eggs.

and so on do not hold water; however, Shi Hui[5] and Xi Deng[6] could come up with explanations. A gentleman depreciates them because they are claims in disagreement with rite and morality. Zhi the Robber is on everyone's lips. His reputation is brilliant like the sun and moon and is passed on from generation to generation with that of Yu and Shun.[7] However, a gentleman does not value such fame because it is contrary to rite and morality. This serves to explain why, rather than prize improper means in handling difficult situations, or admire improper schemes in scholarly inquiry, or cherish improper hope of making oneself known, a gentleman would only treasure that which is in accord with the rules of conduct. This is also sung in *The Book of Songs*:

> "Many are fish on which to dine,
> Only in season they are deemed fine!"[8]

---

[1] A man in the last years of Shang, who committed suicide because of being unable to have his proposals adopted.

[2] An ancient cosmological hypothesis holding that heaven—the void up from the ground—starts where earth ends so that they always meet; therefore, both high mountains are as close to heaven as deep canyons, and hence mountains are as high as canyons are deep.

[3] Two powers of the Warring States Period far apart from each other, Qi being the present northern Shandong and southern Henan and Qin in the current Shaanxi.

[4] This is suspected to be a misplacement since it does not make much sense here.

[5] A famous nominalist in Song of the Warring States Period.

[6] A legalist of Zheng of the Spring and Autumn Period.

[7] Legendary sagely emperors of China.

[8] Minor Court Hymns, *The Book of Songs*.

A gentleman is easy to associate but difficult to get familiar with improperly. He is always on the alert and apprehensive and yields to no threat. He is afraid of troubles but will die in defense of justice. He desires what is beneficial but will do nothing he considers wrong. In personal relations he remains faithful but impartial. He is eloquent in speech without flowery language. How broad-minded he is! His manners are different from those of the rest world.

A gentleman is good whether he is talented or not, while a petty man is bad no matter he is capable or not. If a gentleman is talented, he is generous, tolerant, easygoing, upright, and guides others by enlightenment; otherwise, he is respectful, self-controlled, modest, and serves others with awe. On the other hand, if a petty man is talented, he tends to be haughty, depraved, dishonest, and would undermine others with jealousy, hatred and slander. It is therefore said that people count it as an honor to learn from a gentleman if he is good at something and a pleasure to inform him of other things if he is less talented, while they consider it cheap to learn from a petty man if he is skilled at something and shameful to inform him of other things he is incapable of. This is where the difference of a gentleman and a petty man lies.

A gentleman is generous but not negligent, disciplined but not acrimonious, eloquent but not argumentative, insightful but not going to extremes, upright but not overbearing, firm but not fierce, flexible and obedient but not drifting with the current, and respectful and cautious but not narrow-minded. This may be called perfect virtue. It is praised in *The Book of Songs*:

"How gentle and respectful are men!
   This forms the foundation of virtue."[9]

A gentleman highly praises the virtue and celebrates the merits in others. This is not to be taken as flattery or toadying. When he criticizes others with a fair mind and frankly points out his faults, it is not to be mistaken for calumny or fault-finding. A gentleman also talks of his own excellence, compares himself with Shun and Yu, or regards himself as a match to Heaven and Earth. It is not to be understood as boasting or self-importance. If he stoops or stands as the situation demands, flexible like rushes and reeds, it is not because of fear and cowardice. He yields to none and is full of valor and vigor. This does not mean that he is arrogant or brutal. This is because he accustoms himself to situations according to propriety and knows when it is appropriate to bend or straighten. It is chanted in *The Book of Songs*:

"He turns left when it needs,
   With skill he drives the steeds;
   He turns right if he will,
   Driving the chariot with skill."[10]

This means that a gentleman can bend and unbend and is capable of adapting himself to circumstances.

---

[9] Major Court Hymns, *The Book of Songs*.
[10] Minor Court Hymns, *The Book of Songs*.

A gentleman is the opposite of a petty man. With a lofty aspiration, he reveres Heaven and observes its law. With a limited aspiration, he is awe-inspired by the sense of propriety and capable of self-control. When wise, he is prudent and sensible, and understands by analogy the interrelationships between things on the basis of rites and regulations. When slow-witted, he stays honest, takes a correct attitude, and follows the rules of conduct. Being put in an important position, he will be respectful rather than reckless; otherwise, he will remain earnest and serious. When happy, he sets things in order peacefully; if worried, he copes with things calmly. When illustrious, his speech is refined and clear; in difficulty, his language is suggestive and composed. However, this is not the case with a petty man. With a high ambition, a petty man is rude and cruel; with a lesser ambition, he is depraved and subversive. If clever, he robs by force or by trick; if stupid, he is a cruel troublemaker. When placed in an important position, he becomes haughty and greedy, attempting to secure more gains; when left unappointed, he is resentful and dangerous. When happy, he is frivolous and flippant; when sad, he is frustrated and cowardly. Before success, he is haughty and biased; facing difficulty, he is self-abandoned and despondent. It is said in ancient times: "A gentleman makes progress in both conditions while a petty man falls in either." It refers precisely to this.

A gentleman puts in order what is orderly rather than what is chaotic. What does this mean? What is in accord with rite and morality is orderly and what is against rite and morality is chaotic. Accordingly, a gentleman brings peace and stability to that which is in line with ritual and moral principles instead of its contrary. But does this mean a state that is chaotic will not be put in order? No. Creating order in a state that is chaotic does not mean putting in order what is against ritual and moral principles. Rather, what is chaotic is replaced by what agrees with ritual and moral principles. Here is a man who looks dirty and is to be made good-looking. It is not to be done with the dirt he bears. The wish will not be made true till the dirt is cleared away. Therefore, eliminating chaos is not putting what is chaotic in order, just like removing someone's dirt is different from making him good-looking with the dirt on. Putting in order as an idiom is understood by gentlemen to bring order to what is orderly rather than chaotic, just like making someone good-looking without the dirt rather than with it.

When a gentleman keeps himself pure, those of his kind will do the same. If he speaks good words, he will find an echo in those of a like mind. Just as when one horse neighs, other horses respond with the same noise, or when one cow lows, other cows do the same as a response. This is not because they are wise; it is their natural inclination. For the same reason, he who has just had a bath has the inclination to shake out his robe and he who has just washed his hair is inclined to dust off his cap. It is human nature, for who could bear pollution from others when he is pure and clean?

For a gentleman, nothing is better than honesty if he wants self-cultivation. If he is honest, there is nothing more for him to do than to cling to benevolence and righteousness. If he adheres truthfully to benevolence, the principle will be simply manifested in his words and actions, and everything will be put in good order and transformed to goodness. If he develops the true sense of righteousness, everything he does will be properly arranged and thus clearly shown, and therefore bad habits will be converted. The alternation of transformation and civilization brings about the supreme virtue of Heaven. Heaven does not talk, but people worship it for its height and profundity. Earth does not talk, but people admire it for its depth and solidity. The four seasons do not talk either, but people anticipate their alternation. Each follows its own principles and thus shows its integrity.

When a gentleman gains perfect virtue, he will be understood even if he keeps silence, people will come close to him even though he has never offered them any favor, and he inspires awe without displaying anger. This is because he observes the natural law and truly clings to benevolence and righteousness. Taking benevolence as a principle, constancy will not be achieved without his being honest. Without being constant, his virtue will not be manifested. Without its manifestation, people will not obey him even if it is generated in his heart, shown on his face, and expressed in his words; even though they follow him, there will be suspicion.

Heaven and Earth are truly great, but they are not able to transform all things if they fail to be honest. Sages are truly wise, but they are not able to transform all men if they fail to be honest. Father and son are most intimate, but they will become estranged if they fail to be honest. A monarch is truly honorable, but he will be despised if he fails to be honest. Honesty is what a monarch guards securely; it serves as the foundation of government. As long as he is completely honest, those who are of his own kind will come to him as a matter of course. Maintaining his honesty, they will be attracted; abandoning it, they will be lost. With honesty, they are readily gathered. Easy gathering facilitates benevolent and righteous practices. Consistent concentrated practice of benevolence and righteousness ensures success. With success being guaranteed, the talent of every individual can be turned to good account and everyone seeks after the good and never reverts to his primary nature. Hence, they become civilized.

A gentleman may find himself in an honored position but he still keeps his modesty. He acts with caution and cherishes great aspirations. He listens to and looks at what is close at hand but he hears and sees what is far away. How so? It is the approach he adopts that makes the difference. To him, the dispositions of a thousand or ten thousand people are the same as those of a single person, the beginning of Heaven and Earth is like what they are today. And the way of all the Former Kings is the same as that of later kings. A gentleman examines the way of the kings of later times and then appraises the measures taken by all previous kings in a leisurely manner as though he were deliberating with arms folded in a formal stance. He analyzes the ritual and moral principles in order to clarify the boundary between right and wrong. With the guiding principle in his hand, he governs all the world as easy as controlling a single person. Therefore, the more limited number of principles, the greater achievements are made, just as with a carpenter's square only five *cun* big, one can measure all squares under Heaven. That is why a gentleman need not leave his own house, but with the approach he adopts, the information of how everything goes all over the country is gathered before him.

Some men of learning are successful, some are fair-minded, some are honest, some are sincere, while others are petty. Those who honor their monarch above, love the people below, deal with things that come, and settle matters that happen can be called successful men of learning. Those who neither collude with their inferiors to deceive their superiors nor accept their superiors without justification in afflicting the subjects below, hold a fair attitude in disputes and refrain from harming others for selfish interests may be called fair-minded men of learning. Those who neither complain against their monarch who fail to recognize their strengths nor seek honor through deception if their superiors are unaware of their shortcomings, neither conceal their good qualities nor gloss over their faults but rather present themselves as they truly are may be called honest men of learning. Those who are certain to be trustworthy in daily talk, prudent in ordinary behavior, fearful of following corrupt customs, and not self-righteous can be called sincere men of learning. Those whose words are rarely credible, whose behaviors are frequently unprincipled, who yield to whatever involving profit to themselves are properly considered petty men.

Fairness generates brilliance, prejudice causes darkness, honesty and sincerity promise success, treachery and hypocrisy lead to obstructions, sincerity and credibility work miracles, boastfulness and bragging result in delusion. A gentleman should be careful about these six qualities and their corresponding conditions. It is just these qualities that distinguish the sagely Yu from the tyrant Jie.

Below are reference points for the choice between likes and dislikes and between adoption and rejection: When you see something desirable, you must consider forward and backward what may be undesirable in it. When you see something beneficial, be sure to consider forward and backward what may be harmful in it. You must weigh both sides and consider each carefully before reaching the decision whether it is desirable or undesirable and whether to adopt or reject it. This will most frequently protect you against errors. In general, trouble results from being partial. When a man sees something desirable, he neglects its undesirable side; when he sees what may be beneficial, he overlooks what could be harmful. For this reason, whenever he jumps, he falls; whatever he does, it will end in disgrace. This is the harmful outcome of one-sidedness.

What other people detest, I detest it, too. To despise all the rich and honored and to yield to all the poor and humble—this is not necessarily the true disposition of those who are benevolent. Rather, it is the manner by which crafty and evil men deceptively steal a reputation for themselves in this benighted age. No intention is more dangerous than this. Hence it is said: Stealing a reputation is worse than stealing goods. Men like Zhong Tian[11] and Qiu Shi[12] might serve as an example: they were worse than robbers.

---

[11] Also known as Zhong Chen, a nobleman of Qi, who considered himself so lofty that he became independent of his wealthy elder brother and made a living on weaving straw sandals.

[12] Also known as Yu Shi, a senior official of Wei in the Warring States Period, who refused to be buried till his counsels were accepted and thus made himself famous.

Chapter 4
On Honor and Disgrace

Synopsis

A scholar both cultivates his moral character and learns the way of government in his pursuit of learning. This essay demonstrated the part Confucian scholars played in government through their human concern over honor and disgrace of individuals and society and a deep analysis of social disorders and human feelings.

One must be discreet in his words and deeds. Nevertheless, a lot of confusions and self-contradictions are found in what people say and do in their strife over fame and profit in the society. As a result, they get what is contrary to what they wish for, for they often overlook possible consequences. People engaging in fighting generally fight for but always forget about themselves, for they think positively about themselves and negatively about their opponents. If they are really gentlemen and their rivals petty men, their fight can be likened to the stupid action of "hacking cow dung with a prized dagger-axe." But it is often the case that they are unaware of the contradictions and confusions deeper within. Hence the presentation of the courage of dogs and pigs characterized by fierce and reckless struggles with malicious means.

A deep analysis of these self-contradictions reveals that people look for solutions to their problems from outside and never expect to find them from within themselves. Therefore, once the problem is traced, relevant measures will be taken against it, so that standards are established to distinguish between honor and disgrace, decision is made of what ensures security and benefit and what causes danger and harm, and understanding is reached that everyone is created and given a place by Heaven.

The essay stresses the feasibility of administration by means of the way taken by the Former Kings and the guiding principles of benevolence and righteousness in government. The first point of interest is that people are quite similar to each other in their desires but different from one another in the way to make their wishes true. A gentleman adopts the peaceful art of benevolence, righteousness and moral conduct while a petty man, being shallow, ignorant, without receiving education and unconscious of moral standards, sees only benefit and is therefore driven to danger. However, since men in disposition choose to go in different directions, their personal behaviors and social customs are decisive of their security and glory as well as honor and disgrace. Based on a scrutiny of human nature and intelligence, a sound approach may be found to prolonged progress of man with the way of the sagely ancient kings, the principles of benevolence, righteousness and the doctrines advocated in the four Chinese classics on poetry, history, ritual and music, with which more benefit is gained by cultivating personal taste, honor is won by making one famous, harmony is reached by communication, and happiness is gained by maintaining personal integrity.

Text

Pride and immodesty are both human misfortunes, but reverence and moderation ward off the five weapons.[1] There are such sharp weapons as lance and spear, but in keenness they are not to be compared with respect and restraint. Therefore, words of praise are warmer than cotton and silk while words of abuse hurt more deeply than spear and halberd. Thus, on a broad land one cannot tread, it is not because the ground is insecure. If he cannot find a place to set his feet on, it might be entirely due to his abusive language. Broad roads are full of people and narrow trails are full of peril. In such cases, one has no alternative but to be cautious.

It is great anger that leads to death because no consequence is considered in advance. It is jealousy that does one harm in spite of his perspicacity. It is slandering that places one in a dilemma for the great learning he has. It is improper talk that brings bad fame even if one desires a good reputation. Friends for wining and dining become less friendly because the way of association is wrong. Debate with skill concludes unconvincing because of dispute. Behavior that is honest goes unappreciated if one attempts to excel. Conduct that is upright wins no respect when it is offensive. Courage that causes no fear is corrupted by greed. Faith that receives no admiration is polluted with arbitrary preference. These are things a petty man does but a gentleman refuses.

A fighter[2] is forgetful of himself, his family and his monarch. Seeking an outlet for his temporary anger at the sacrifice of his life, he does it because he forgets all about himself. His family is instantly destroyed and his kinsfolk are unable to avoid the death penalty. He fights all the same, because he forgets all about them. He does what his monarch hates and is prohibited by law since he forgets all about him. He forgets himself, neglects his family, and ignores his monarch. These are cases not to be pardoned by penal law or tolerated by a sagely king. A nursing sow does not charge a tiger, nor does a nursing dog wander far from her pups, because they keep

---

[1] Knife, sword, spear, halberd and arrow.

[2] In the later years of the Warring States Period, there were freelance fighters fed by the nobility for their private purposes, e.g., bodyguard, assassination, and clan fights.

their family in mind. In contrast, a man who forgets himself, neglects his family and overlooks his monarch is even worse than a pig or a dog.

In general, a belligerent person is sure to think himself right and others wrong. If he is really right and others are resolutely wrong, then this is to consider himself a gentleman and others petty men. For a gentleman to attack and harm the petty men, is it a grave fault if he neglects himself, forgets his family and overlooks his monarch? What is done by a man like him can be compared to hacking cow dung with a prized dagger-axe made at Hufu. Is it to be considered wise? Nothing is more stupid! Is it to be regarded as beneficial? Nothing is more harmful! Is it to be treated as honorable? Nothing is more disgraceful! Is it to be understood as secure? No greater danger can be identified.

Why do men fight with one another? I would like to attribute their bellicosity to mental disease, but it will not do because a sagely king would kill them. I would classify them as birds, rodents, or beasts, but it is out of the question since they are of human form and share with men most of their likes and dislikes. Why are men bellicose then? I absolutely despise such behavior!

There are the courage of dogs and pigs, the courage of merchants and robbers, the courage of petty men, and the courage of the educated gentlemen. Fighting over food and drink, having no sense of honor or shame, ignorant of right and wrong, heedless of injury and death, fearless before numerical strength, and greedily aware only of food and drink—such is the courage of dogs and pigs. Seeking gains, struggling for goods, having no concern for polite refusals, daring and cruel, ferocious and fierce, greedily aware of profit only—such is the courage of merchants and robbers. Fearless of death and brutal—such is the courage of petty men. As far as anything is righteous, one will not submit to power, or care about his profit, or change his mind at the temptation of a whole state. He values life but upholds justice and will never surrender. Such is the courage of the educated gentlemen.

White hemiculter leusicus and ray are fishes fond of floating on the surface of water for sunlight. But once they are stranded on the sand, they will never reach water again even if they want to. Similarly, when a man is in trouble and wishes he had been cautious, it would not be of any help. Those who know themselves do not blame other people; those who understand fate do not complain against Heaven. Those who blame other people will find themselves in difficulty; those who complain against Heaven is unwise. Is it not far off the mark to condemn others when one has only himself to blame?

The following are the essential distinctions between honor and disgrace as well as the general conditions of security and benefit and those of danger and harm: Those who put righteousness before benefit are worthy of honor, while those who place benefit before righteousness bring themselves disgrace. Those who are honored always succeed; those who are disgraced invariably fail. The successful always exercise control and failures are always in the control of others. These are the great differences between honor and disgrace. Those who are sincere and simple always obtain security and benefit; those who are dissolute and rude always face danger and harm. Those who are secure and benefitted are always happy and easy while those who are endangered and threatened with harm are always worried and restless.

Those who are happy and easy always enjoy longevity. Those who are worried about danger and threat often die a premature death. Such are the general conditions which ensure security and benefit or cause danger and harm.

All men are created by Heaven and therefore have a place for themselves. The Son of Heaven obtains the whole world since he is perfect in thought and aspiration, strong in moral integrity, brilliant in wisdom and penetrating in insight. The feudal lords who are given their states since they issue orders according to law, take measures in accord with the proper season, hold hearings and make decisions with impartiality, obey the mandates of the Son of Heaven above and guard the people under their rule. The gentry are granted their lands and manor estates since they cherish good will and behave themselves well, put their governmental affairs in order, obey their monarch above and fulfill their official duties.

In the Three Dynasties,[3] laws and decrees, standards of measurement, penal codes, and maps of territory and census registers were rigorously observed, although their meanings might not be understood, and handed down from generation to generation without emendation or abolishment so that the princes and dukes were helped to sustain. For this reason, with the passing of these dynasties, the standards and rules were kept unchanged, and all the functionaries could gain their salaries and positions. The common people obtained warm clothing, plentiful food, and a long life, and were free of punishment and slaughter if they were filial to their parents, respectful to their brothers, honest, diligent, earnest in and never neglectful of their tasks and duties. Wicked men courted danger, invited disgrace, attracted punishment and death since they ornamented perverse teachings, beautified evil remarks, engaged in the absurd, and were boastful, rapacious, unrestrained, fierce, arrogant, and rude. They dragged out an ignoble existence in the chaotic society and created disturbances there. They were in danger because their reflections were shallow, their choices were not carefully made, and their decisions about what to adopt and reject were impulsive.

In endowment, nature, intelligence and capability, a gentleman and a petty man share similarities. In cherishing honor and detesting disgrace, in loving benefit and hating harm, a gentleman and a petty man are the same. They differ only in the way they seek or avoid these things. A petty man is eager to boast and expects others to trust him. He spares no efforts in deception, yet wants others to love him. And he behaves like wild beasts but desires that others think well of him. Such men reflect on questions hard to understand, do things difficult to carry out, and make proposals hardly tenable. In the end, they are certain to fail in their pursuit of glory and benefit and meet with disgrace and harm. Therefore, a gentleman both trusts others and wishes others to trust him. He is faithful to others and desires their faith in him. Being a man of integrity, he handles affairs properly and wishes others to be kind to him. Such people reflect on questions easy to understand, do things easy to carry out, and make proposals that are tenable. In the end, they are sure to win favor instead of causing hatred. For these reasons, a gentleman does not remain unknown when he is frustrated, turns eminent when he is successful, and becomes brilliant after his death. On the other hand, a petty man will jealously remark, craning his neck and

---

[3] Xia, Shang and Zhou dynasties.

standing on tiptoes, "In endowment, nature, intelligence and capability, they excel others in the first place!" He does not realize that they are not different from him. The only difference lies in the fact that a gentleman behaves himself properly while a petty man fails to do so. Thus, a thorough examination of the intelligence and capacity of a petty man reveals that he is capable of all that a gentleman does. For example, a native of Yue feels at home in Yue, a native of Chu feels comfortable in Chu, and a gentleman settles down in the Central Plains. This has nothing to do with their intelligence, capability, endowment, or nature. It is shaped by their different behaviors and customs.

Benevolence, righteousness and virtuous conduct often lead to security, but not necessarily to the absence of danger. Conduct polluted by filth, treachery and rapaciousness is often the source of danger, but not necessarily never secure. Therefore, a gentleman follows the conventional practice while a petty man chooses his unorthodox way.

Men generally have characteristics in common: they want food when hungry, they desire warmth when cold, they need rest when exhausted, and they pursue what is beneficial and hate what is harmful. Such are the innate instincts of man. They are inherent rather than learned; it is something the sagely Yu and the despotic Jie shared.

The eyes tell white from black and the beautiful from the ugly. The ears decide between sounds and tones that are pure or muddy. The mouth determines what is sour, salty, sweet or bitter. The nose tells apart fragrances and foul smells. And the skin distinguishes between hot and cold or pain and itching. These, too, are part of the nature that man is born with, that he does not have to develop, and that is true both of Yu and of Jie.

A man can be as famous as Yao or Yu. He may be as notorious as Jie or Zhi. He may also grow into a craftsman, a farmer or a merchant. This is the long-term accumulation of his behaviors and habits. If he becomes a Yao or a Yu, a man always enjoys peace and honor; otherwise, if he chooses to be a Jie or a Zhi, he has to frequently face peril and disgrace. To be a Yao or a Yu means joy and ease all the time; to be a craftsman, a farmer, or a merchant involves constant worry and toil. Nevertheless, people strive to be the latter rather than the former. Why? The answer is that they are shallow and ignorant. Neither Yao nor Yu was born with the virtue of a sage. Rather, they started by experiencing all troubles and difficulties and completed with long-term practice of self-cultivation. They did not become perfect men of integrity till their conduct was in line with moral standards.

A man is by nature a petty person. Without education and the restraint of rites and regulations, he seeks only benefit. Being a petty man by birth and living a life in troubled times, he acquires the chaotic customs. This is to add pettiness to pettiness and to get chaos from chaos. If no gentleman has the power and status to put him under control, there is no way to enlighten him. People nowadays know nothing but what their mouths and stomachs desire. How can they be aware of rite and morality? Or of decline and yield? Or of honesty and shame? Or of the part and whole of ritual propriety? They know only how to keep eating to their fill and satisfaction. Without education by a teacher and without the restraint of rites and regulations, a man has nothing in his mind other than the satisfaction and satiation of his mouth and stomach.

Let us suppose that a man is ignorant of the meat of livestock or rice and millet and that he has only seen beans, bean leaves, dregs and husks, he will be satisfied with such coarse food. Then suddenly someone comes to him bearing delicious meat and rice, he will be surprised and look at them with astonishment, exclaiming, "What are these strange things?" He will sniff at them and find they are pleasing to the nose. He will taste them and find them sweet to the mouth. After eating, he feels perfectly comfortable. He will abandon the old foods for these new ones ever since.

Is the way in which the Former Kings exercised their power followed together with the guiding principles of benevolence and righteousness so that people live together as communities, maintaining, protecting and supporting each other, and their security and stability are achieved? How sharply does it contrast with the way of Jie or Zhi the Robber? Does the difference merely lie between delicious meat and fine rice and dregs and husks? However, people make great efforts to follow the latter rather than the former. Why? The answer is that they are shallow and ignorant. Lack of cultivation and ignorance form the calamity of the world and the great tragedy of man.

For this reason, it is said that those who are benevolent delight in propagating the reasons of things and demonstrating them to others. With these principles publicized and shown, people may develop a good habit after trials and errors to observe and reaffirm them, the unenlightened will soon come to understand them, the uncultivated will be refined before long and the stupid will become wise in no time. If this is impractical, what benefit is there with a sage like Tang or Wu? And what harm is there with a tyrant like Jie or Zhou? With Tang and King Wu in reign, the world followed them and there was order; with Jie and Zhou in power, the world obeyed them and there was chaos. Seeing from this perspective, is it not true that people can be this or that in disposition?

It is human nature to desire the meat of livestock for food, silk with embroidery for dress, horse and carriage for transportation, and surplus money and goods for wealth. However, they are never satisfied in spite of their accumulation year after year or even generation after generation. Such is their natural disposition. Nowadays people living in this world raise chickens, dogs, pigs, as well as cattle and sheep, but dare not have wine or meat for their daily meals. They save more than enough knife-shaped money and have stores in granaries and cellars, but dare not wear silk or brocade for their clothing. Those who are thrifty have treasures deposited in chests and trunks, but they dare not travel by horses and carriages. Why are they doing so? It is not that they do not desire comfort. They have a long plan for the future, don't they? For they are afraid of not being able to keep going. For this reason, they economize further, continue to curb their desire, and accumulate more wealth for the time of need. Isn't this very considerate of themselves from the long-term point of view?

On the other hand, the shallow and ignorant type of men who live on just for the sake of remaining alive are unaware of such things. They waste their food, regardless of their future livelihood, and presently find themselves reduced to poverty. This is why they suffer from cold and hunger, and with a begging gourd and sack in hand, wind up as emaciated corpses in ditches.

Seen from this perspective, how much more important are the great ways of the Former Kings, the guiding principle of benevolence and righteousness, and the important doctrines advocated in *The Book of Songs*, *The Book of History*, *The Book of Rites*, and *The Book of Music*! They actually represent mature reflections on the world preserved for all the people under Heaven with a view of everlasting development. They form a rich collection of boundless achievements of everlasting importance. None but those gentlemen who have thoroughly cultivated themselves and meticulously studied them can understand the teachings. Therefore, it is said, with a short rope you cannot fetch water from a deep well; with people far less enlightened you cannot discuss the words of the sages. The main ideas of *The Book of Songs*, *The Book of History*, *The Book of Rites*, and *The Book of Music* are beyond the knowledge of ordinary people. Therefore, it is said, once they are put into practice, they will be carried on; once they are mastered, a nation will last long; once they are promoted, there will be success everywhere; every time they are considered, there will be peace; observe them often and everything will be handled properly; use them to cultivate your taste and there will be more benefit; employ them to make a name for yourself and you will gain honor; follow them in the company of others and there will be harmony; employ them to maintain personal integrity and there will be boundless joy. Am I right?

It is a natural desire shared by all men to be as honorable and wealthy as the Son of Heaven possessing the whole world. However, it is objectively impossible for such an attempt and physically impractical to satisfy their desires. Accordingly, the great kings in former times established ritual and moral principles to divide them into classes, so that there were differences between noble and base in status, old and young in age, wise and stupid in intelligence, and talented and talentless in aptitude. In this way, everyone had a place and everyone was in his place. Each gained according to the amount of work done. That was why they could live harmoniously together in communities.

Accordingly, when a man of virtue is in power, farmers will devote all their energy to growing crops, merchants will devote all their cleverness to increasing wealth, all craftsmen will devote their skills and intelligence to making tools and instruments, and the gentry and above as well as the feudal nobles devote their benevolence, honesty and ability to their duties and responsibilities. This is called the age of ultimate justice. In such peaceful and prosperous years, he who owns the land under Heaven feels easy and justified, and he who earns his living as a gatekeeper, receptionist, guard, or night watch never thinks he is paid low. Therefore, it is said: "Equality is achieved in inequality, straightness in what is crooked, and unity in diversity." This is the normal human relationship, as is said in *The Book of Songs*:

> "He receives jade large or small,
>   And becomes the protector of all."[4]

---

[4] Eulogies, *The Book of Songs*.

Chapter 5
Criticism of Physiognomy

Synopsis

It is a general tendency to judge people by their appearance, and men particularly praise those who can foretell someone's good luck or misfortune by his looks. However, looking into this phenomenon, one may find that the way of thinking dominates all, thus studying a person's mind is more important than reading his outer appearance. This essay offers quite a number of examples to reveal that the fundamental factor that determines a person's luck is his mind rather than his appearance. When his mind follows the correct method, a man becomes a gentleman in spite of his ugly appearance; otherwise, if the method is incorrect, he might become a petty man even if he is good-looking. Being a gentleman brings oneself luck; being a petty man may cause him trouble. The thing that gives one luck is his thought rather than his height, build or face. This accounts for the tragedy of Jie and Zhou, who were attractive in outer appearance but cherished ignoble thoughts.

There are three aspects in the way of thinking of a gentleman: bodily behavior, consciousness, and speech. First of all, he should avoid the "triple ill omens" and "threefold patterns" that cause him misery. Moreover, he should be aware of the importance of making distinctions because it is this ability that makes man different. Based on the differences being made, the social hierarchy of ranks and statuses is formed so that the rites and regulations established by the sagely kings, particularly the kings of later times, for scholars to follow. Finally, he should remember that everyone enjoys talking about what he thinks right. It is generally believed that a word of praise is more important than gold or jewelry, a piece of advice pleases more than decorative embroidery does, and a word of appreciation sounds more pleasant than music. However, proper speech is not easy, for a correct attitude and a proper method are quite necessary. Moreover, different speakers have different aims in their mind and their performance is often not on the same level. For instance, a gentleman usually promotes benevolence while a petty man spreads wicked ideas.

Text

In ancient times, there was no such thing as physiognomy and the men of learning never mentioned it.

Formerly, a man named Ziqin Gubu,[1] like Ju Tang[2] of Wei today, foretold people about their luck according to their physique and appearance and won public praise. In ancient times, no such thing happened and the men of learning never discussed it.

Hence, reading a person's build and appearance is not as reliable as reading his mind, and studying his mind is not as good as identifying his way of thinking, for body and face do not determine his thought which is dominated in some way by his method of thinking. When the method is correct and the mind follows it, nothing will prevent him from becoming a gentleman even though he has an evil countenance against his good mind. Conversely, if the method is wrong, nothing will stop him from becoming a petty man even if he looks good on the outside but has evil intentions. It is lucky to be a gentleman; it is unfortunate to be a petty man. Being tall or short, strong or weak, handsome or ugly, therefore, does not mean fortune or ill-fortune. In ancient times, people did not think this way, and the men of learning did not discuss it either.

Great men like Emperor Yao was tall, but Emperor Shun was short. King Wen of Zhou was tall but Duke of Zhou was short. And Confucius was tall but Zigong[3] was short. Formerly, Lü Gongsun, a minister of Duke Ling of Wei, was seven *chi*[4] tall with a face as long as three *chi* and a forehead as narrow as three *cun* but complete with two eyes, two ears and a nose, yet he was known all over the land. Ao Sunshu of Chu, a native of Qisi, was almost bald with sparse short hair. With a very long left hand, he stood lower than the crossbar on a chariot; nevertheless, he helped make the State of Chu a hegemon. Zigao the Duke of She was short, thin and feeble. When he walked, it looked as if he could hardly carry his clothes. However, during the revolt of the Duke of Bai,[5] when Prime Minister Zixi and War Minister Ziqi[6] were both killed, he took the state, killed the Duke of Bai and restored order as easily as turning his hand over. He was remembered by later generations for his benevolence, righteousness and other merits. So, in the judgment of others, it is useless to consider their height, reckon their strength, or measure their weight. You just look at their aspirations. Is it still worth while talking about whether they are long or short, strong or weak, and handsome or ugly?

And King Yan of Xu had such a protruded forehead that he could see it himself. Confucius looked like he were wearing an exorcist's ugly mask. The Duke of Zhou

---

[1] A native of Zheng of the Spring and Autumn Period, who was reported to have physiognomized Confucius and Wuxu Zhao, head of the Zhao clan.

[2] A famous physiognomist of the Warring States Period.

[3] Either Yong Ran, one of Confucius' disciples, or Zigong Hanbi, a man teaching *The Book of Changes* in the Warring States Period.

[4] A unit of length less than 25 cm.—Tr.

[5] Grandson of King Ping of Chu.

[6] Princes Shen and Jie, sons of King Ping.

was like a broken stump. Gaoyao[7] was greenish in complexion, like a pared watermelon. Hongyao[8] had hair all over so that his skin was not visible. Fuyue[9] was so hunchbacked that he seemed to have a fin on his back. Yin of Yi[10] had neither beard nor eyebrows. Yu was crippled; Tang had a limp in one leg, and Yao and Shun had overlapped pupils in their eyes. Are you followers going to discuss your will and compare your learning or judge other people by comparing their height, discriminating them between handsome and ugly, deceiving and despising one another?

In ancient times, outstanding figures such as Jie and Zhou were tall, strong-built, and handsome, their bearing surpassing all others. Nimble and powerful in action, they were a match for a hundred men. Nevertheless, they lost both their lives and their kingdoms and were put to the greatest shame in the world. When later generations talk about evil men, they would be taken as typical examples. Their tragedy was caused by their meagre knowledge and degraded ideal rather than by their appearance!

Nowadays, there are unruly men and frivolous villagers beautifully made up and looking seductively charming. They wear fanciful dresses with effeminate ornaments and imitate ladies in facial expressions and bearing. All married women wish they were their husbands. All girls expect them to be their fiancés. Ladies everywhere are found to abandon their parents and desire to elope with them. However, ordinary monarchs would be ashamed to have them as ministers, ordinary parents are ashamed to have them as sons, ordinary men are ashamed to have them as younger brothers, and ordinary people are ashamed to make friends with them. In no time they would be arrested by the local authorities and executed in large market places. All of them would cry to Heaven in bitter tears over their miserable end and regret their past too late. Their tragedy was caused by their ignorance and indecency rather than by their appearance. This being the case, which will you approve of?

The triple ill omens for a person's future: being reluctant to serve his elders when he is young, being unwilling to serve the honorable when he still remains unknown, and being disinclined to serve the worthy when he is still worthless. These are the three signs of a man's misfortune. A man's threefold patterns of behavior that lead to misery: Reluctance to take good care of his subordinates and preference to reproaching his superiors—this is the first type. Contradicting to the face of another and backbiting him—this is the second type. Failure to recommend men of virtue and respect men of learning, being superficial and far less competent—this is the third type. With the triple ill omens and the threefold patterns of bad behavior, a man will find himself in peril if he occupies a high position; he is on the road to ruin. The following lines in *The Book of Songs*.

> How heavily it snows!
>> Melt starts when the sun shows.
>> A post below is to him allowed,

---

[7] A legendary official in charge of criminal punishment in the reign of Yao.

[8] A minister under King Wen of Zhou.

[9] A minister under King Wuding of Shang.

[10] Prime minister of King Tang, who assisted in replacing Xia by Shang.

>   He refuses and remains proud.[11]

point against just such men.

What is it that makes a man man? It is his ability to make distinctions. The desire for food when hungry, the desire for warmth when cold, the desire for rest when tired, and the desire for what is beneficial and the hate for what is harmful—these are innate human characteristics rather than nurtured later in their lives. They are shared by the sage Yu and the tyrant Jie. However, the characteristic that makes a man different is not that he is bipedal and furless but that he is distinction-conscious. Now that an orangutan is also bipedal and furless, but men sip soup and eat meat made from the animal. Hence, what makes a man human lies not in his being a furless biped but in his power of discrimination. Birds and beasts have their affiliations but not intimate father-son relationship. There is the gender difference between male and female, but there is no distinction between sexes like that of humans. Hence, the way of man is characterized by his ability to understand distinctions.

No distinction is greater than the hierarchy of ranks; however, ritual is more important than the social structure. And the sagely kings are still greater than ritual. However, there are a hundred sagely kings; so, which of them shall I follow? They say: the rules of propriety established by the sagely kings long ago are lost, the rhythms of music established long ago are no more, the positions in charge of the rules established long ago are neglected. Consequently, if we want to trace the principles of the sagely kings, we should observe those most clearly preserved by the sagely kings of recent times, who were monarchs over all under Heaven. To abandon these sages for those in antiquity is just like rejecting our own monarch and serving the monarch of others. So, I think we must examine today if we wish to learn the history of a millennium, we must scrutinize one or two if we want to understand hundreds of millions, we must study the way of Zhou if we need to know the ages of antiquity, and we must carefully observe the gentlemen valued in Zhou if we are to learn the way of Zhou. Therefore, we have similar sayings such as

>   From what is nearby one gets to know what is far away.
>   From one instance one infers all else.
>   From one small clue one can see clearly what is coming.

The conceited and ignorant men say, "The conditions of ancient and modern times are different; therefore, different measures are taken accordingly to put things in order." And people are bewildered. Those ordinary men are stupid and therefore speechless before arguments; they are ignorant and therefore powerless in thinking. They may be deceived about what is happening before their eyes, not to mention the tales a thousand ages ago. The conceited and ignorant men may deceive about what is happening at the gate or in the courtyard, to say nothing of the hearsays over a thousand years ago!

How is it that the sages are not deceivable? Because they make judgments on past things basing on their experience. Hence, to judge an individual according to

---

[11] Minor Court Hymns, *The Book of Songs*.

his present conditions, to understand the feelings of someone according to his own, to evaluate something according to other things of the same kind, to measure the achievement of someone according to views and opinions, and to observe everything according to Dao, it is the same in ancient times and at present. Things of the same kind follow the same rules no matter how long they last as long as they do not contradict each other. Hence, they are not puzzled by the various hearsays and false reasoning or confused by the jumble of things because they measure all with one and the same principle. Nothing has passed down to us about any important person before the Five Emperors.[12] It is not because there were no people of virtue but because too long a time has passed for us to know. No record of remarkable government achievements prior to the Five Emperors has handed down to us. It is not because there were no great achievements but because they were made too long ago to trace. Yu and Tang had great accomplishments but they are not as concrete as those of the Zhou. This is not because there was nothing material but because they happened too long ago to remember, for reports long ago tend to be in general outlines of important matters and recent accounts may be in concrete descriptions of small details. The stupid cannot work out the details after hearing the broad outlines; they fail to make generalizations after hearing the minute details. For this reason, the rules established by sagely kings long ago are forgotten and the rhythms of music established long ago are no longer there.

Opinions that are neither in accord with the moral principles of the great kings of past dynasties nor submit to rite and morality are called vicious talks. Well-argued they may be, a gentleman will not listen to them. Following the principles of the Former Kings, observing ritual and moral principles, and getting close to scholars do not constitute a sincere man of learning if he is not fond of or take delight in discussions. A gentleman is fond of truth in his heart, consistent with it in his action, and takes delight in talking about it. Hence, he must be an eloquent speaker. No one is not fond of talking about what he advocates, a gentleman being particularly so. Therefore, a good word presented as a gift is a more valuable than precious metals or gems, a good piece of advice is more beautiful than decorative patterns embroidered on official costumes, and a good talk sounds more pleasant to the ears than the harmony of percussion and string music. For this reason, a gentleman never tires of beneficial talks. A shallow and ignorant person is just the opposite of this. He cares only substance and ignores the beauty of appearance. This is why he is lowly and vulgar all his life. The explanation of Diagram Kun in *The Book of Changes*—"A tightly closed bag refuses both fault and praise." is also fit for scholars behind the times.

The difficulty of persuasion lies in motivating the extremely base with the most profound principles and persuading men to transform utter confusion with the principles of peace and prosperity. It is never to be brought straight to the point. However, distant cases might be groundless and absurd while recent ones flat and unconvincing. He who is good at persuasion finds his way between the two. He has to cite distant examples that are not preposterous and recent cases that are not commonplace. He

---

[12] They are usually said to be Huangdi (or Yellow Emperor), Zhuanxu, Ku, Yao, and Shun.

modifies them to suit to occasions and changes them with the passage of times. He does the job calmly or imperatively, with much talking or few words, just like channeling the flow of water by dams or straightening a piece of wood by a bender. By hook or by crook, he turns every point convincing without offending anyone.

Thus, with himself a gentleman is as strict as checking the straightness of wood against the plumbline; yet he receives others like a boatman meeting his customers with the oar in his hands. Being strict with himself, he sets a good example for others to follow; receiving others like a boatman, he is generous to all and with their assistance he may accomplish great causes under Heaven. Hence, a gentleman is virtuous and yet is able to tolerate the unworthy. He is wise but tolerant of the foolish. He is knowledgeable but patient with those who are shallow and ignorant. And he is pure but tolerant to the impure. This is called all-embracing. The following lines in *The Book of Songs*

> The men of Xu express their fidelity
> Owing to the merit of His Majesty.[13]

may serve as a proper description.

Below are the proper methods of persuasion: be solemn and sincere in appearance before your listeners, upright and earnest in attitude toward them, and helpful with strong confidence, illustrate questions with analogies, enlighten the audience through analysis, and pass your knowledge on to them with friendliness and ardor. Hold precious your view, attach importance to it, cherish it, and trust it and it will not fail to be accepted. Even if you do not intend to please, no one will fail to give it attention. This is called being able to make what one values valued. It is described in an ancient book as "Only a gentleman can make what he values valuable."

A gentleman must be eloquent in argument. No one is not fond of talking about what he advocates, a gentleman being especially so. A petty man argues to spread wicked ideas whereas a gentleman does to advocate benevolence. If an opinion runs contrary to benevolence, it is more advisable to keep silence about it than to discuss it and it is better to be dull-witted than intelligent in its argument. If a view coincides with the principle of benevolence, its promotion is highly recommended and its poor discussion is held in contempt. Hence, great is the argument that is congenial to benevolence! That which is established by a ruler and used to guide his subjects below is called a government decree; that which is expressed by officials below for their devotion to or counselling for their monarch is termed remonstrance or dissuasion. Therefore, a gentleman never grows weary of practicing benevolence. He is fond of the idea of benevolence in his heart, consistent in practicing it, and delightful in promoting it. Hence, he must clarify the concept of benevolence. Argument over trifles is not as helpful as the discovery of clues; discovering evidence is not as important as making distinctions. Argument about small matters may reveal problems, attention to clues may lead to the solution to problems, and distinctions help to materialize the organizations. And thus, the distinction between the sages and the educated gentlemen are fully made.

---

[13] Major Court Hymns, *The Book of Songs*.

There is the argument of petty men, the argument of the educated gentlemen, and the argument of sages. No prior consideration or planning is necessary, appropriateness is self-assured when expressed, there is a proper definition and clear classification, and there is an endless variety of measures and variations—these are characteristic of the argument of sages. With prior consideration and planning, few but effective words, good organization, extensive knowledge, straightforward and proper expressions, and in conformity with reality—these are characteristic of the argument of the educated gentlemen. However, if his speech is eloquent but not to the point, his action is deceitful and inefficient, he is not ready to follow a wise king above and incapable of bringing harmony to the ordinary people below, but he is self-important, haughty, smooth-tongued and measured in speech, such a man may be called a champion villain. A sagely king coming to power chooses such men before robbers to mete out punishment, because thieves and brigands may be transformed but such men are incorrigible.

Chapter 6
Criticism of the Twelve Masters

Synopsis

Ideology is intimately related with the criteria according to which right and wrong are distinguished and is crucial to order or chaos. Having realized its importance, the author provided a general survey of the contemporary schools of thought. Basing his discussion on Confucianism, he emphasized the right path of the doctrine, described its current conditions and pointed out its shortcomings with a view to establishing a good social order.

It is important to note that this essay attempts to divide into three groups of six types represented each by two typical figures the doctrines with insufficient value of reference for social order. The first group of men drifted along with their poor teachings, yielding to their instincts and doing whatever they pleased, just like beasts; some of them might restrain their natural instincts, but they talked unintelligibly to show they were extraordinary, did little that was of benefit to the society, and detached themselves from other people. The other two groups were concerned with the management of society. One consisted of the Mohists and Legalists and might be labeled ignorant while the other was made up of Logicians and the Zisi-Mencius branch of Confucianism and labeled knowledgeable. The former promoted pragmatism and stressed economy, but some were ignorant of the way to the unity of the world and the importance of rites to a country. Some overlooked the role played by social hierarchy and slighted the difference among human beings; others exalted the rule of law but did not observe the principles or divorced themselves from reality. The latter were smart people, but they did not follow the principles established by the Former Kings or favor rites and regulations; they were insightful but their teachings were useless; they talked much but achieved little. And Zisi and Mencius approximately observed the principles of the great Former Kings without understanding their role of guidance. They were eccentric and without sense or order, they used words so vague that no clear explanation was made; they talked about things so profound that they were unintelligible.

Based on the above analysis, the summary of six schools of thought being aware of the real world but insufficient for its government is logically perfect. Some later researchers claimed that Master Xun criticized only five schools of their ten representatives, excluding Zisi and Mencius, probably because they did not realize the internal logical completeness of the Six Schools of Twelve Masters, for even though this sixth school were not represented by Zisi and Mencius, such a doctrine would exist all the same. The essay sharply pointed out that the insufficiency of these doctrines lay basically in their ignorance of the system, garrulity, lack of propriety and righteousness against which corresponding measures were taken by the Confucian sages: combination of principles and strategies of government, coordination between words and deeds, and integration of guiding principles with laws and orders.

Text

There were men taking advantage of the present turmoil to disturb the world by whitewashing perverse doctrines and embellishing evil ideas. They attempted to throw the people under Heaven into confusion so that they were ignorant of the fundamental differences between right and wrong and between order and chaos.

Some men indulged their instincts and felt contented in unrestrained passions. They behaved like beasts, neither following rites nor contributing to the order of society. Nevertheless, their doctrines were well-grounded, their arguments were well-presented, so much so that the foolish people were deceived and confused. Xiao Ta and Mou Wei[1] were their representatives.

Some men repressed their instincts, talked of the most profound and stood aloof from the world. They intended to be wise by extraordinary attempts, failed to become one with the masses, and ignored the fundamental distinctions in society. Nonetheless, their doctrines were well-grounded and their arguments well-presented, so that it was sufficient to deceive and confuse the foolish people. Zhong Chen[2] and Qiu Shi were their representatives.

Some men were ignorant of the way to unify the world and establish standards and norms for their country. They advocated the principles of merit and utility, emphasized frugality and economy, and neglected the gradations of rank and status. They did not tolerate interpersonal differences and the discrimination between monarch and ministers. Nevertheless, their doctrines and arguments were so well-grounded and well-presented that it was enough to deceive and confuse the foolish masses. Mo Di[3] and Song Xing[4] were their representatives.

---

[1] Both were Daoist scholars in the Warring States Period.—Tr.

[2] See note 33 in Doing Nothing Improper.

[3] Founder of Mohism.

[4] Also known as Jian Song or Songrong or Master Song, a native of Song in the Warring States Period.

Some men highly praised the rule of law but failed to observe the law themselves. They disdained the virtuous and the wise and chose what suited themselves. They followed the orders from above and the social customs below. They cited the articles of law every day and investigated them repeatedly, but kept away from the reality and failed to fulfill them. They never used them in managing state affairs and establishing the order of status and position. In spite of that, their doctrines and arguments were well grounded and presented so that it sufficed to deceive and confuse the foolish masses. Dao Shen[5] and Pian Tian[6] represented such men.

Some men refused to follow the principles of the great Former Kings and disapproved of rite and morality. Instead, they were fond of unusual theories and playing with bizarre expressions. They were able to penetrate deeply into all things but their doctrines did not prove to be urgently necessary. They were skilled in debate but unrealistic. They did much but achieved little. And their doctrines could not be treated as guiding principles of good order. Despite everything, their doctrines and arguments were grounded so firmly and presented so effectively that it was sufficient to deceive and confuse the foolish masses. Shi Hui[7] and Xi Deng[8] were representatives of this type.

Some men roughly followed the Former Kings but did not understand their guiding principles, looking as if with a brilliant mind, great aspiration, wide experience and extensive knowledge. They converted claims of antiquity into a theory and called it the Five Virtues,[9] perverse and nondescript, vague and therefore without offering any explanation, and obscure and therefore unintelligible. However, they embellished their phrases and claimed with humble reverence, "This is really what our late master[10] said!" Zisi[11] made the proposal and Mencius chimed in with him. The foolish Confucian scholars of the ordinary world followed blindly and, being unaware of the fact that they were wrong, accepted what they were taught and passed it on, believing that Confucius and Zigong were sure to be esteemed by later generations because of their opinions. This was the fault of Zisi and Ke Meng.[12]

Other men combined the principles and strategies of governance, coordinated the words and deeds of people, integrated the guiding principles of government, and brought together the heroes under Heaven before informing them of the great imperial accomplishments of the past and teaching them the great principles of rule. Then sitting on the bamboo mats inside the great hall, with the rules and regulations of sagely kings all available, they initiated the customs of a time of peace and prosperity. The six doctrines were denied admittance and the twelve masters were refused a

---

[5] A native of Zhao in the Warring States Period.

[6] A Daoist figure in the Warring States Period.

[7] A key figure of the School of Logicians in the Warring States Period.

[8] A figure of the Legalist School in the Spring and Autumn Period.

[9] Benevolence, righteousness, propriety, wisdom and honesty.

[10] Confucius.

[11] Also known as Ji Kong, Confucius' grandson and one of the major representatives of Confucianism.

[12] Mencius.

place. Though they did not possess the tiniest plot of land, princes and dukes could not rival their fame. Even if they could only be offered the position of senior officials, no single ruler could keep them to himself, and no single state was broad enough for them to stay in. With their reputation greater than that of the feudal lords, no ruler did not wish them to be his ministers. They were sages without status and power. They were men like Confucius and Zigong.

Still others unified all under Heaven, put everything under control and used them to raise and nourish their people and benefit the whole world, so that none under their influence disobeyed them, the six doctrines instantly disappeared, and the twelve masters were converted accordingly. Such were sages with position and power. They were men like Shun and Yu.

Now what do the men of virtue and goodwill occupy themselves with? If they observe the laws and regulations of Shun and Yu, follow the moral principles of Confucius and Zigong, and curb the teachings of the twelve masters, the world will be free from disasters, the cause of the benevolent will be fulfilled, and the accomplishments of sagely kings will be made manifest.

To trust what is trustworthy means honesty; to doubt what is doubtful involves honesty, too. It is benevolent to esteem the worthy; it is also benevolent to despise the unworthy. It is wise to speak when it is appropriate; so is it to keep silence when it is necessary. Thus, knowing when to remain silent is as good as knowing when to speak. Therefore, he who talks much but whose words conform to propriety and righteousness is a sage. He who talks little but conforms to propriety and righteousness is a gentleman. And he who is absorbed in much talk without propriety and righteousness is a petty man in spite of his eloquence. Hence, much toilsome labor about nothing to the satisfaction of people is regarded as a wicked thing. Exhaustive mental efforts leading to nothing in line with the principles of the great Former Kings is regarded as a wicked idea. Skillful debate filled with analogies and complemented with instant response is regarded as a wicked talk if it does not accord with rite and morality. These are the three types of wickedness prohibited by the sagely kings.

Being cunning and insidious, lawless and capricious, hypocritical and treacherous, and crafty in personality, eloquent but pointless in speech, close but unnecessary in urgency—these are traits disastrous to good government. Stubborn perverseness, readiness with clever excuses, tactful schemes with sophistication, eloquence contrary to common sense—these were severely prohibited in ancient times. Being smart but not law-abiding, courageous but reckless, insightful but deviant in behavior, short of resources but extravagant, and wicked with numerous accomplices, going astray in seeking a shortcut, and falling into the abyss after grabbing an important position—these are behaviors detested by the whole world.

To convince all under Heaven: You should not be arrogant to others because you are high in position and status, make things difficult for others because you are intelligent and farsighted, fight to gain precedence over others because you are brilliant and quick-witted, or bring harm to others because you are resolute and bold. Ask others if you do not understand, learn from others if you cannot do something, be modest if you are talented—these are regarded as behaviors of virtue. Fulfill your obligations as a subject before your monarch, pay attention to seniority in the community before your fellow men, satisfy the requirements for juniors before your seniors, observe ceremonial rules and show courtesy when you meet friends, and remember to give guidance to or be tolerant of those who are lowly and still young. Love everyone, respect all, contend with none, be magnanimous like Heaven and Earth to all things, and the worthy will honor you and the unworthy will be friendly with you. Those who refuse to accept you can be classified as perverse, weird and crafty; they deserve punishment even if they are among your brothers. This is portrayed in *The Book of Songs*:

> Not that to Shang God was unkind,
> > But that the old rules were not in your mind.
> > None like the grand old man was found,
> > But the laws were there running aground.
> > Since you refused to obey them all,
> > That may serve to account for the downfall.[13]

The so-called officials in ancient times were honest, sincere, friendly and easygoing. They paid attention to moral cultivation, were ready to share what they had, and had a methodical mind. They kept far away from offences and were ashamed of being wealthy alone. Their counterparts today are deceptive, reckless, self-indulgent, unlawful, and defiant. They commit all sorts of evil and lack any sense of rite and morality. They are greedy for profit and have a taste only for power and influence.

The so-called recluses in ancient times were noble-minded, sensible and upright. They were reconciled to their contemporary situations, subordinated to great truths and exalted correct opinions. Their counterparts today are not talented but claim that they are, ignorant but claim that they are knowledgeable, insatiably greedy but pretend to desire nothing, and sinister and dirty but boast of their prudence and honesty. They take uncommon customs as common and deviate from the right path to show that they are extraordinary.

The following are what the educated gentlemen can or cannot do: They can be noble-minded but cannot insist that others be respectful to them. They can be trustworthy but cannot demand that others trust them. They can be qualified for a certain position but cannot ensure that they be thus employed. Hence, a gentleman is ashamed if he is morally uncultivated, but not if he is slandered; he deems it a shame to break his promise, but not if he is untrusted; he feels it a humiliation to be ungifted, but not if he is unused. For these reasons, he can resist the temptation of honor and glory and is not daunted by slanders. He follows the Dao, behaves himself well and is not swayed by external things. Such may be called a true gentleman. And the lines in *The Book of Songs*:

> He is so modest, gentle and polite;
> > Such is the core of virtue bright.[14]

---

[13] Major Court Hymns, *The Book of Songs*.
[14] Major Court Hymns, *The Book of Songs*.

praise precisely men like him.

An educated gentleman looks like this: He wears his hat high and his robe loose. He appears mild, solemn, serious, composed, happy, broad-minded, tolerant, unequivocal and frank. Such is the proper bearing of a father or an elder brother. He wears his hat high and his robe loose. He looks simple, honest, nice, sincere, upright, diligent, respectful, obedient and cautious. Such is the proper behavior of a son or a younger brother.

Let me tell you the unseemly manners of those scholars: They wear their hats low over their foreheads with the chin-straps loose, their belts slack and with an air of self-importance. They walk unsteady, slack their pace, peep right and left and stare blankly. They are shallow, dispirited and self-contained. They indulge in wining and dining and enjoying music. When attending ritual ceremonies, they assume an air of disgust and are full of complaints. When engaged in difficult work, they are lazy and sluggish. They shun this and evade that and are content with temporary ease and comfort. They are shameless and not afraid of insults and abuses. This is how those scholars behave themselves.

They wear their hats improperly. They talk tastelessly. They walk with steps unsteady imitating those of Yu[15] or quick and short copying those of Shun.[16] Such are the manners of mean Confucian scholars like Zizhang[17] and his type. They are properly dressed, look serious and are taciturn. Such are the manners of mean Confucian scholars like Zixia[18] and his type. They are lazy and afraid of being involved, timid and overcautious, shameless and fond of good food and drink, claiming that a gentleman naturally does not have to engage in manual labor. Such are the manners of mean Confucian scholars like Ziyou[19] and his type.

A gentleman is not like them. He may be at leisure but he is not indolent. He may overwork himself but he is never sluggish. He observes principles but adjusts himself to changing circumstances. He can manage all affairs perfectly. And thus, he makes himself a sage.

---

[15] Emperor Yu could not walk firmly because he fell sick in his legs and feet from the long-term endeavor to regulate the rivers and watercourses all over ancient China.

[16] When he was young, Emperor Shun used to walk in this manner before his parents to show his filial respect.

[17] A student of Confucius, also known as Shi Zhuansun, a native of Chen in the Spring and Autumn Period.

[18] A student of Confucius, also known as Shang Bu, a native of Jin in the Spring and Autumn Period.

[19] A student of Confucius, also known as Yan Yan, a native of Wu in the Spring and Autumn Period.

Chapter 7
On the Relationship of a Monarch with His Subjects

Synopsis

With the assistance of Zhong Guan, Duke Huan of Qi succeeded in rallying the other states around him nine times and achieved the leadership of an overlord. This is regarded as a historical model of the monarch-subject relationship. Based on the discussion of the hegemony achieved by Duke Huan, this essay briefly demonstrated how a sagely king achieved the unity and how a worthy minister behaved himself in the eyes of Confucians.

Despite the fact that Duke Huan achieved his leading status among the warring states by his great wisdom, determination and political integrity, even the young learners under Confucius felt it a shame to discuss about him, because he achieved victory by fraudulence, he was aggressive but pretended to be modest, and he pursued gains in the name of humanity, which characterized a typical petty man only. On the other hand, a sagely king was worthy but could offer help to those who were unworthy, he was strong but treated the weak generously, and he was ashamed to fight but willing to demonstrate propriety to all. In a word, a sagely king followed principles and exercised little punishment and therefore could unify all under Heaven in spite of his limited territory of only a hundred *li*.

In treating his monarch and colleagues, a wise minister adopts the universal approach to success and follows the universal principle of service; therefore, he could retain favor and a high position, have an important power in a powerful state, keep his office secure for great responsibilities, and protect himself against trouble in future.

Text

Someone asked, "Among the disciples of Confucius, even teenagers considered it a shame to talk about the Five Hegemons.[1] Why?".

My answer: "Because these men indeed make one ashamed to praise them. Of the Five Hegemons, Duke Huan of Qi was the most famous. Before he became an overlord, he murdered his elder brother and seized the power. Under his rule, he failed to marry off seven of his aunts, sisters and cousins.[2] Life within the inner gates of his palace was so indulgent and extravagant that a half of the taxes of Qi could not meet his demand. In dealing with external affairs, he deceived Zhu, attacked Ju, and annexed thirty-five other states. With such sinister, filthy, licentious and extravagant conducts, how could he have won the praise of the followers of the great gentleman?".

"Since he was like that, how could he have become a hegemon instead of being destroyed?"

My answer: "Well, it was because he was fully aware of the fundamental principles of government. So, who could have destroyed him? Without any suspicion, he foresaw Guan's abilities to be entrusted with the entire state. This was the greatest wisdom in the world. Secure at home, he forgot his anger toward Guan; out in the public he forgot his hatred for him. Eventually he respectfully addressed him as uncle. This was the greatest decision ever made under Heaven. He established Guan as his uncle so that none of the nobility or royal relatives dared to be jealous of him. He appointed Guan a position as honorable as that of Gao and Guo[3] so that none from the court dared to show his hatred. And he bestowed Guan a fief with 300 *she*-communes[4] so that none of the rich dared to defy him. All people, both the noble and the lowly, whether old or young, were in good order; they obeyed and honored him. This is a basic rule under Heaven. A feudal lord who takes hold of one of these keys can be destroyed by none. Duke Huan had all of them in his control, so how could he have been brought to ruin? He was bound to be a hegemon! He made it as a matter of course rather than by chance."

"Since this was the case, why was it that even the teenage followers of Confucius considered it a shame to talk about the Five Hegemons?"

My answer: "They did not take governmental enlightenment as the foundation, exalt propriety and righteousness, systemize the rules of etiquette, and make themselves admired from the heart. They regarded strategy and tactics as important, paid attention to the balance between labor and rest, and saw that necessary materials were accumulated and preparedness against war was solidified so that they could defeat their rivals. They won by schemes, disguised their bellicosity with modesty,

---

[1] Duke Huan of Qi, Duke Wen of Jin, King Zhuang of Chu, King Helü of Wu, and King Goujian of Yue.

[2] IT was regarded as the duty of a family's head to marry off his female members on coming of age.—Tr.

[3] Both were senior ministers of Qi.

[4] Equivalent to 75,000 households.

and sought profit in the name of benevolence. They were merely outstanding petty men, and how could they be worthy of praise by the great gentleman's followers?

"A true ruler[5] is not like this. He is able and virtuous but ready to help those who are unworthy; he is powerful but he may be lenient with the feeble; he is victorious in fighting but ashamed to launch a battle. He will perfect the rules and regulations before making them public so that savage nations are automatically transformed and malignant and deceitful forces destroyed. Thus, a sagely king causes destruction as little as he can. King Wen of Zhou wiped out four states, King Wu defeated two, and when Duke of Zhou helped to complete the great cause, there was no state left for King Cheng to destroy. Surely this does not mean that the principles of rule were no longer observed. King Wen followed them and, with his rule over merely a hundred *li*, could achieve unification of all under Heaven; Tyrants like Jie and Zhou abandoned them and, with the power to rule all under Heaven, both ended their lives more miserable than ordinary men. Hence, for a small state, a successful application of the principles of rule guarantees independence while a poor use of them results in being ordered about just like the State of Chu with its six thousand *li* of land. Thus, it is dangerous for a ruler to seek great power and influence instead of mastering the principles of governance.

"These are approaches to retaining favor, staying in office and freedom from being detested and rejected: If your monarch honors you, be respectful and modest. If he trusts and takes care of you, be prudent and humble. If he gives you sole authority, be careful and familiarize yourself with all the conditions of your assignment. If he is friendly with you, be cautiously obedient and do not let yourself go astray. If he keeps you at a distance, be whole-hearted in office and never betray him. And if he demotes or dismisses you, be fearful but not resentful. Do not assume great airs when you are honored. Do not engage in dubious acts when trusted. Do not think you are a law unto yourself when given important tasks. Do think you do not deserve it when wealth or profit is offered to you and do not accept it till your declination fails. Receive it properly when good fortune comes and treat it with calmness if misfortune strikes. Give favors widely when rich; economize on expenditures when poor. Be satisfied whether highly placed or lowly and no matter rich or poor. But you would rather commit suicide than commit wicked things. These are the approaches to retaining favor, staying in office and freedom from being detested and rejected. You may be poor and lonely, but you will be lucky if you follow these rules, as is sung in *The Book of Songs*:

> He is loved by all
>> For he observes ancestral laws.
>> He always cherishes his forefathers
>> And carries on their cause.[6]

"This is the art of seeking to retain a high position, taking charge of great responsibilities, holding an important power in a powerful state and remaining free from

---

[5] The ideal ruler who, in the mind of Master Xun, can unify all under Heaven.

[6] Major Court Hymns, *The Book of Songs*.

future trouble: You had better be ready to cooperate with your colleagues, recommend the worthy to proper posts, grant favors broadly, eliminate grudges, and do no harm to others. Carefully do it if you are qualified to the responsibility; otherwise, if you are incompetent and afraid of losing favor, you had better be cooperative and recommend those who are worthy to the post and follow them willingly. In this way, it will be glorious to gain favor and remain blameless if you lose it. This is the magic key to the service of your monarch and the art of avoiding disasters. For this reason, those who are wise make allowances for the time of inadequacy when their supply is adequate, keep mindful of trouble when things are smooth, and take account of danger when they are secure. They take great precautions lest misfortunes should happen; therefore, there will be no fault in doing anything. Just as Confucius pointed out, 'He who is clever and follows moral standards can definitely regulate his actions; he who is courageous and cooperative will surely be competent at great tasks; he who is learned and modest is certainly virtuous.' The stupid do exactly the opposite. When they occupy important positions and hold absolute power, they are a law unto themselves and jealous of those who are virtuous and capable, they repress those who are meritorious, and push aside those who commit errors. They are complacent and take lightly old grudges against them. They are stingy and unwilling to give favors when they hold high office; they assume great airs and seize power when they are subordinates so as to inflict harm on others. Is it likely that such type of men would succeed if they want to be free from danger? For this reason, such men will surely face danger if they hold high office, lose their power if entrusted with heavy responsibilities, and end in disgrace if they are trusted. You can simply stand by and wait for them to happen: it will take time for a meal. How so? Because those who would throw them out are many while those who would support them are few.

"This is a universal rule to be successful in serving your monarch and to be sagely in behaving yourself: Establish rites and regulations as the highest standards and stand firm with them. Begin with a respectful mind, command them with honest and faith, implement them with caution, guard them with sincerity, and try to reaffirm them repeatedly in times of difficulty. Your monarch may be unaware of your efforts, but cherish no hatred in your heart. Your merit may be remarkably great, but do not flaunt it. Seek little, but contribute much. Tirelessly show esteem for your monarch. In this way things will always go smoothly for you. Serve your monarch with them and you are sure to succeed; Be benevolent and you are sure to be a sage. This is the universal approach to success.

"It is a universal principle for the junior to serve the senior, for the humble to serve the noble, and for the unworthy to serve the worthy. However, there are cases in which some men are ashamed to remain inferior when their positions are not high. Such is the frame of mind of villains. They keep the intention of opposing rite and morality in their minds and engage in actions against these principles, yet they desire the reputation of a gentleman or a sage. This would be like the attempt to lick the sky on one's stomach or to save a person from being hanged by pulling at his feet. It is obviously impossible because the efforts lead to opposite directions. Therefore, a gentleman suits his action to the current situation: he bends when necessary and straightens out if possible."

Chapter 8
On the Influence of Confucianism

Synopsis

This essay chiefly discusses the social role played by Confucianism in the system of a state.

In Confucianist ideals, great thinkers are called sages and politicians are called great scholars. Duke of Zhou, both a sage and a great scholar, was a model of the Confucian learning and governance. Taking the form of a conversation between King Zhao of Qin and Master Xun, this essay demonstrates the core meaning of being a Confucianist to be following the example of the great kings of former dynasties, promoting rite and morality, carrying out his responsibilities and bringing honor to his monarch. Therefore, Confucianism was always of benefit to the country no matter if a scholar was employed and whether he was in an inferior or superior position.

In learning, Confucian scholars were supposed to practice the principles of the great Former Kings as well as rite and morality in such a way that they could reinforce their personal cultivation, accumulate their virtue, learn to be thoughtful of others, be able to manage situations according to the guiding principles and therefore win honor. Their status and position were determined by their moral integrity and ability and each one of them was put in a proper place in the government. Everything they would say or do should contribute to good order characterized by proper arrangements above and proper divisions below, whose realization could prevent disorder and overcome difficulties.

Basing on Confucianism and starting from the perspectives of learning and governance, Master Xun classified people of different virtues and abilities according to two relative orientations: the rite and morality of the Former Kings and human nature. As far as learning was concerned, people could be divided into commoners, the men of learning, gentlemen, and sages according to the degrees to which they practice the rite and morality of Former Kings and accumulate moral virtues. From the viewpoint of governance, they can be divided into ordinary men, shallow scholars and virtuous and great scholars. The essay focuses on the virtues of great scholars and their roles in the government.

Men are divided into gentlemen and petty men in relation to their education and inborn nature and according to the extent to which they are transformed. On another level, they are divided into ordinary men and lesser and great scholars. No matter in learning or in government, gentlemen should talk properly in different situations, regulate their conduct, and practice self-cultivation in accord with relevant principles. These were the necessary prerequisites of cautious behavior, good habit, and long-standing training.

Text

The role of a great Confucian scholar: When King Wu of Zhou died, King Cheng was only a child. Duke of Zhou left the kid aside and succeeded King Wu in order to keep the world under control, because he was afraid of a possible general revolt against Zhou. He took over the position of the Son of Heaven and managed the affairs of the kingdom as if they were his in the first place; nevertheless, no one under Heaven considered him greedy. He killed Prince Guanshu and deserted the capital of Yin by transferring its people elsewhere, but no one under Heaven regarded him as ruthless. He placed the world under control and established seventy-one vassal states of which fifty-three were in the hands of the Jis; however, no one under Heaven thought that he was partial to the royal clan. He educated and guided the boy king and made him understand the fundamental principles of rule so that he was able to follow in the footsteps of King Wen and King Wu. Then Duke of Zhou handed over the world to King Cheng. The empire did not stop its service of Zhou Dynasty although Duke of Zhou turned north as a subject to pay his respects. The Son of Heaven as a post cannot be occupied by a young child or taken by someone else as regent. If the child has the abilities, the world is restored to him; if otherwise, the world will abandon him. That was why King Cheng as a child was put aside by the duke who succeeded King Wu so as to control the world since he dreaded the prospect of a general rebellion against the dynasty. When the young king came of age and had his capping ceremony held, Duke of Zhou handed back the throne and power to show that he dared not destroy the rule of inheritance. The duke was now no more in control of the world under Heaven. He used to own all under Heaven but now it did not belong to him; he did not abdicate it in favor of his nephew. King Cheng formerly did not own the world but now he had it; he did not seize the power. It was a matter of change in status and order. In this case, the substitution of a branch for a trunk[1] could not be understood as arrogation, the execution of a man by his younger brother could not be regarded as cruel, and the change of positions between a monarch and his subject could not be considered improper. Depending on the peace under Heaven, Duke of Zhou fulfilled

---

[1] Compared with the crown prince, Duke of Zhou was seen as being from a branch of the family tree.

the cause of King Wen and King Wu. This indicated morality and justice between a subject and his monarch, which were not without some variations but guaranteed unity and peace under Heaven. None but a sage could have done this. And this shows the role a great Confucian scholar can play.

King Zhao of Qin asked Master Qing Sun, "Is Confucianism of no help to the state?".

Master Qing Sun replied, "The Confucian scholars learn from the Former Kings, exalt ritual and moral principles, fulfill their duties as subjects, and make their monarch honorable. When a king employs them, they serve as competent subjects in the royal court and behave properly; if they are not used, they go down to live among the ordinary people and remain honest and obedient. In misery or difficulty and in hunger or cold, they are not avid of profit by dishonest means. Even though they lack a tiny spot of land to place their awls on, they are still clear in sense of maintaining the altars of soil and grain. Their loud calls receive no response, but they are fully aware of the discipline in controlling all things and nurturing the ordinary people. Assigned a high post, they are as capable as princes and dukes; placed below others, they are the pillars of a state and the treasures of a country. Even though they retire into out-of-the-way lanes or shabby cabins, no one fails to respect them because they are still respectable with good virtues. For instance, when Confucius was to become Minister of Justice in the State of Lu, Shenyou dared not overfeed their sheep in the morning,[2] Gongsheng[3] divorced his wife, Shenkui[4] fled across the border, and the horse and cattle traders of Lu abstained from forcing up prices of their animals. They would check all their unhealthy tendencies to meet Confucius. When Confucius lived in Quedang, young people there would offer their parents and elder brothers a bigger share because they were influenced by Confucius' idea of filial piety and brotherly love. With Confucians serving in the court, the government becomes refined. When they are among the ordinary people, popular customs are improved. Such are Confucians as subjects of a ruler!".

"What are they like when they are placed in high positions?" asked the king.

"They will play a more important part," answered Qing Sun. "They have high aspirations and strong wills. They are good at regulating the royal court by means of ritual and having laws, standards, rules and regulations implemented among the officials. They promote education so that people may develop the virtues of loyalty, faithfulness, love, and beneficence. They refuse to do a single thing that is against justice or kill a single person who is innocent for the purpose of conquering all under Heaven. Thus, the moral principles of the monarch will be trusted among the people, spread to all corners of the land and be followed unanimously. Why is it so? It is because he enjoys an honorable reputation and is admired by all under Heaven. Hence those who are close to him sing his praises and receive him warmly and those who are far away will take the trouble to come to him, so that all within the four seas

---

[2] A native of Lu, who drove his sheep to the market and cheated the buyers by giving the animals much food and water in advance.

[3] A native of Lu of the Spring and Autumn Period, a hen-pecked husband of a licentious wife.

[4] A native of Lu, who was incorrigibly wasteful.

will become like one family and all those who are within reach do not fail to submit to him. He can be called an example for people, as is sung in *The Book of Songs*:

> From the east to the west
> And from the north to the south,
> No one but obeys him.[5]

Since a Confucian scholar is like that when he is arranged in a subordinate post and like this if he is appointed to a supreme position, how could we say that he is of no use to the country?"

"You are right!" King Zhao exclaimed.

The way of the great Former Kings is benevolence sublimed and is implemented along the most proper road. What is the proper road? It is rite and morality. The road is neither the way of Heaven nor that of Earth; it is the way of man. It is the principles a gentleman follows.

When a gentleman regards someone as worthy, it does not mean that he is capable of all that men can do. When he thinks of someone as wise, it does not imply that he can learn all that is known to man. When he finds someone eloquent, it does not mean that he can discriminate all that every dialectician can. When he holds someone to be perceptive, it does not mean that he is skilled in perceiving everything that all others can comprehend. Rather, a gentleman is limited in his abilities. In surveying the rises and falls of field, deciding whether the soil is fertile or barren, and planning the cultivation of the five cereals, a gentleman is not as good as a farmer. In putting commodities into circulation, judging the quality of goods and comparing their prices, a gentleman is less capable than a merchant. In designing with a compass or a square, applying the ink box and line, and handling other tools with skill, a gentleman is not equal to a carpenter. In mutual bullies and humiliations regardless of right and wrong or true and false, a gentleman is no match for Shi Hui and Xi Deng. When it comes to the determination of hierarchy and appointment of official positions according to abilities so that both the worthy and the unworthy get their proper posts, both the capable and the incapable have their own places, everything is reasonably used, and all changes are properly accommodated so that Dao Shen and Di Mo find no chance of spreading their views and Shi Hui and Xi Deng dare not tout for their quibbles, then things will be discussed in accord with reason and done according to command and requirements. This is what a gentleman is expert in.

Generally, if something contributes to reason and order, do it; otherwise, if anything is of no benefit to reason and order, quit it. This is called the proper response to things. If a learning or a doctrine contributes to reason and order, accept it; otherwise, if it is of no benefit to reason and order, refuse it. This is called the proper attitude to learning. Any undertaking or doctrine that is improper is described as wicked and is therefore abandoned in an ordered society and followed in a chaotic age. When it comes to the mutual transformation of fullness and emptiness, the

---

[5] Major Court Hymns, *The Book of Songs*.

separation of hardness and whiteness[6] or that of identity and difference,[7] they are beyond the power of those who have a keen sense of hearing, a sharp sense of sight, or a silver tongue and those who have the intelligence of a sage to come up with an answer soon. Being ignorant of them does not prevent a man from making himself a gentleman; their knowledge will not diminish the chance of becoming a petty man. A craftsman may be skillful all the same without that knowledge; a gentleman without such knowledge does not stop him from contributing to good order. If princes and dukes are fond of them, it will cause confusion in the laws. If the ordinary people are fond of such things, it will disturb their work. Nevertheless, those wildly arrogant, muddle-headed, and stupid men attempted with their disciples to justify their doctrines and argue over their analogies and examples till they were old in age or their children grew up without realizing that they should despise them. This may be regarded as utter stupidity. These men are not as good as those who appraise chicken or dogs in making them a fame. A poem collected in *The Book of Songs* says:

> If you were a ghost or a monster,
>> I could not describe how you look.
>> But you have human face and eyes,
>> And I will see your true appearance.
>> I have composed this good song
>> To expose your inconstancy.[8]

It refers precisely to such men.

"I am humble but I want to be noble, I am foolish but I want to be wise, I am poor but I want to be wealthy—is it possible?"

"My answer is that you can make it perhaps only through learning! Learning is like this: one becomes a man of learning by practicing what is learned, a gentleman by trying his best with what is learned, and a sage by a thorough mastery of what is learned. I may become a sage or choose to be an educated gentleman at least, and who can stop me from doing that? Should an ignorant ordinary villager in the past suddenly become equal to Emperor Yao and Emperor Yu, would it not be a case of change from humility to nobility? Sometime ago, he might wonder about the difference between a door and a house, but soon he could trace the source of benevolence and righteousness, distinguish between truth and falsehood, handle matters under Heaven as easily as turning them in his palm and telling between black and white. Is it not a case of change from folly to wisdom? A while ago, he might have nothing at all, but now suddenly he is in control of the power over all under Heaven. Is this not a case of change from poverty to wealth? Now here is a man going begging with a variety

---

[6] A proposition made by Long Gongsun of the Warring States Period, who attempted to distinguish between universality and individuality by demonstrating that hardness and whiteness are separate attributes of stone but are independent of each other.

[7] A proposition made by Shi Hui of the Warring States Period, who held that the similarities and differences between things are relative. All concrete things may be similar or difference; however, fundamentally speaking, all things are either similar or different.

[8] Minor Court Hymns, *The Book of Songs*.

of great treasures concealed at home, and people will still say that he is rich. Those of his treasures can neither be worn as clothes nor eaten as food, and they cannot be sold presently. Nevertheless, he is regarded as rich. Why? Is it not because the resources of great wealth really lie here? A man with great learning is also wealthy. So, is it not a case of change from poverty to wealth?"

Hence, a gentleman is noble without a position and wealthy without a salary. He is trusted without persuasion, awe-inspiring without displaying anger, honorable although living in poverty, and cheerful although living in isolation and without help. Is it not because all that is most respectable, most wealthy, most solemn, and most awe-inspiring is accumulated here? Therefore, it is said that an honorable reputation is not won through cliquish malpractices, or made by boasting, or established by coercion. It is surely obtained through really hard working. It is lost when contended for, gained when declined with modesty, solidified when proper principles are observed, and falls through as a result of boasting. Therefore, a gentleman must strengthen his personal cultivation and be thoughtful of others; he must be intent on accumulating his virtue and handle things according to correct principles. In this way, his fame will rise as surely as the sun and moon, and the people under Heaven will respond to him as loud as thunder. Thus, it is said: a gentleman may be in seclusion but still prominent, lowly but honorable, and yielding but triumphant. The two lines in *The Book of Songs* below sing in praise of him:

> The crane in far-off marshes does cry,
>> Its voice is heard to the heavens high.[9]

The mean and low are just the opposite. They gang up for private interests but their reputation continually diminishes. They contend with each other contemptibly but grow more notorious. They risk their lives for comfort and gains but sink deeper in peril. The following lines in *The Book of Songs*

> Plain and mean was that guy
>> Who kept blaming others.
>> With a noble rank he deemed not high,
>> He fought till he was fatal with disasters.[10]

refer precisely to such men.

Thus, he who is less capable but assumes a great responsibility can be likened to a man who is weak but shoulders up a heavy load: he will get nothing except a crush or fracture; he who is unworthy but claims himself to be so can be compared to a hunchback who desires to be higher: more and more will point at his head and laugh at him. Hence, a wise ruler appoints men to certain positions according to their moral integrity so as to avoid disorder; an honest and loyal minister who is truly competent accepts the commission so that he will not find himself in difficulty. Both arrangements on the higher level that prevent disorder and divisions on the lower level that do not run into difficulty symbolize supreme order. *The Book of Songs* has these two lines:

---

[9] Minor Court Hymns, *The Book of Songs*.

[10] Minor Court Hymns, *The Book of Songs*.

Fair is felt on the left and on the right,
  And all men adhere to him all right.[11]

They may serve to describe the interrelationship between a ruler and his subjects that fends off disorders.

Following popular customs as moral excellence, taking goods and money as treasures, and regarding nourishing of life as supreme objective—these are the virtues of common people. If a man observes the customary rules, has a strong will, and refuses to distort what is learned because of personal desires, he is properly called a man of firm will. If he observes the customary rules, has a strong will, chooses to modify what is learned to correct his dispositions, expresses himself appropriately in most cases but fails to make himself understood, behaves himself well most frequently but not perfectly, deliberates properly on most occasions but not thoroughly, highly praises those he admires, and gives guidance to those who are not as good as himself, he is properly called a simple and honest gentleman. If he studies the laws of all the kings in the past and is as clear about them as telling black from white, adapts himself to current changes as readily as counting numbers, accustoms himself to rites and regulations in routine responsibilities and feels it as easy as moving his limbs, is as familiar as learning seasonal changes in seizing right opportunities for meritorious service, and is able to help stabilize the political situation, bring harmony among the common people, and unite hundreds of millions of men as one, he is properly called a sage.

How orderly he does things! Well, he is so methodical. How dignified he is! Well, he is strict with himself. How firmly he stands! Well, he is consistent from beginning to end. How calm he is! Well, he remains the same all along. What perseverance! Well, he adheres to moral principles without any tiring. What brilliance! Well, he puts his wisdom to intelligent use. How upright he is! Well, he adjusts his conduct to moral integrity. How composed! Well, he talks with grace and color. How affable! Well, he is happy that other people are virtuous, too. And how sad he is! Well, he is worried that some men may behave themselves improperly. A person of this kind is properly called a sage because the Dao he follows is generated in oneness.

What does oneness mean? It means sticking to that which is divine and firm. What does it mean to be divine? It means putting a country into good order with complete and perfect method. What does it mean to be firm? It means the quality of not wavering or faltering before anything. A person who is both divine and firm is called a sage. A sage reflects all that accords with Dao. All great principles under Heaven are unified in him, including those of all great kings of past dynasties. Accordingly, *The Book of Songs, The Book of History, The Book of Rites,* and *The Book of Music* all find their sources in him. *The Book of Songs* expresses his aspirations, *The Book of History* records government affairs, *The Book of Rites* prescribes the standards of conduct, *The Book of Music* promotes harmony, and *The Spring and Autumn Annals* conveys deep meaning with sublime words. Hence, the style of *feng* ('ballads') is characterized by self-restraint and innocence because the poems were composed for

---

[11] Minor Court Hymns, *The Book of Songs.*

the purpose of control; the style of *xiaoya* ('minor hymns') differs from *daya* ('major hymns') because the former intends to impress by means of adornment while the latter aims at glorification and enhancement; the style of *song* ('eulogy') marks perfection because it involves complete understanding. All great principles under Heaven are found here. He who follows them will prosper; he who turns away from them will perish. There has never been a single case in which one does not prosper by following them or does not perish after turning away from them. Never! From antiquity to the present day.

A man quoted from Confucius, "What a great man of virtue Duke of Zhou was! He was noble in status but more respectful, rich but more economical, and victorious but more vigilant."

This is my response: "This is neither how Duke of Zhou was like, I am afraid, nor how Confucius commented on him. For when King Wu had passed away, King Cheng was still quite young. So, Duke of Zhou had to put the child aside and succeeded King Wu. When he was on the throne and seated himself against the royal screen, the feudal lords politely hurried into the hall. On this occasion, to whom was he respectful? Having all the country in control, he established seventy-one fiefs and fifty-three of them were occupied by the royal Ji clan. All the royal descendants, as long as they were not mad or stupid, became eminent feudal lords under Heaven. So, who would say that Duke of Zhou was economical? The day King Wu launched the punitive expedition against the tyrant Zhou was inauspicious for military affairs, since eastward maneuver offended star-god *Taisui* ('Jupiter').[12] So, when the troops were stopped by flood at River Fan, bothered by the collapse of city walls at Huai, and upset by a landslide at Mount Gongtou, Prince Huoshu was frightened into crying, 'In the past three days we were interrupted by five disasters. Does it imply that we should not do so?'.

"'Why not?' replied Duke of Zhou, 'since the tyrant Zhou disemboweled Bigan, imprisoned Jizi[13] and allowed Feilian and Wulai to hold the governmental power.'

"Then all the battle steeds advanced together. The troops had their breakfast at Qi, lodged for the night at Baiquan and approached the outskirts of Mu the following morning. At the signal of drums, the king's soldiers turned around to rebel, and the tyrant was killed with the power of the Shang people themselves. It was thus clear that the tyrant Zhou was killed by the Shang rather than by the Zhou people. Accordingly, there were no captives or other heads chopped off and no rewards for triumphant charges. On their return, the troops of Zhou put their three types of armors[14] away and laid their five kinds of weapons[15] down. Since now it was united under Heaven, songs and music were established with the rise of *Wu* and *Xiang* and the abolition of *Shao*

---

[12] Jupiter marked the twelve-year cycle and was thus found at a certain position in Heaven every year. In ancient times it was believed that military campaigns in the direction of the yearly star would cause disasters.

[13] Both Bigan and Jizi were tyrant Zhou's uncles, who were so punished because of their remonstrances.

[14] Armors made of leather from cattle and rhinoceros.

[15] Knife, sword, spear, halberd and arrow.

and *Hu*.[16] Within the four seas, none refused to change their minds and pledged their allegiance. Therefore, the outer gates were never closed and no boundary was found under Heaven to obstruct the traffic. At this time, against whom was he vigilant?

"Fu Zao was a master charioteer under Heaven, but without a chariot and horses he would have had no way to show his talent. Yi was a champion archer in the world, but without bows and arrows he would have had no way to display his feat. A great Confucian scholar is good at coordinating all under Heaven, but without a land extending as far as a hundred *li* he has no way to demonstrate his outstanding accomplishments. With a strong chariot and select horses, if a man fails to cover one thousand *li* and reach far, he is not a Fu Zao the charioteer. With a bow ready and arrows straight, if a man fails to shoot from afar and hit the target, he is not a Yi the archer. With a land extending as far as a hundred *li*, if a man fails to coordinate all under Heaven and put the ferocious adversaries under control, he is not a great Confucian scholar.

"A great scholar finds no match in reputation among princes and dukes even though he is hidden in an impoverished alley or a leaky house and without a tiny bit of land of his own to place an awl in. Trust him with a land extending as far as a hundred *li* and you can find no rival among those states extending as far as a thousand *li*. In castigating ferocious adversaries and coordinating all under Heaven, none could overthrow him. Such are the qualities of a great Confucian scholar. His words conform to conventions. His actions accord with ritual principles. He does not regret doing anything. He can handle dangers properly and respond to emergencies promptly. He keeps up with times and accustoms himself to the rises and falls of the world. Although there may be myriads of changes, his principles remain the same. These constitute the criteria for testing a great Confucian scholar. When he is in frustration, shallow scholars laugh at him. When he is successful, heroes are influenced by him, deceitful guys evade him, those who advocate immoral doctrines are afraid of him, and others are regretful. If successful, he coordinates all under Heaven. When frustrated, he establishes a noble reputation independently. Heaven cannot cause his death; Earth cannot bury him. He is not corrupted in an age like that of Jie the tyrant or Zhi the Robber. None but a great scholar can get on in the world. Confucius and Zigong belong to this category.

"Thus, there are ordinary men and Confucian scholars who are further divided into shallow, virtuous and great ones. Those who pursue wealth and profit rather than learning and lack the sense of justice belong to ordinary men. Those who wear a broad-sleeved large robe with loose girdles and a plug hat follow the ways of the Former Kings roughly enough to disturb the social order. They pursue a mixture of absurd doctrines, fail to learn from the kings of later times so as to unify the rules and regulations, overlook rite and morality, and disdain *The Book of Songs* and *The Book of History*. They dress and behave themselves the same way as the ordinary folk but are not disgusted with it. They are hardly different from Master Mo[17] in talks and discussions but are not wise enough to make distinctions. They invoke the kings of

---

[16] Names of music for King Wu, Emperors Shun and Tang.

[17] DI Mo, founder of Mohism.

former times in order to deceive the stupid and seek food and clothing from it. They are overjoyed once they gain enough to feed themselves. They choose to follow the eldest sons,[18] wait upon the favorite subjects, flatter the distinguished guests, and are willing to serve all their lives without any other aspiration. Such are shallow Confucian scholars.

"On the other hand, there are those who learn from the kings of later times, unify the rules and regulations, observe rite and morality and disdain *The Book of Songs* and *The Book of History*. Their discourse and conduct are both disciplined, yet their wisdom does not outreach what law fails to cover or they fail to hear or see, or, in a word, they fail to reason by analogy. They admit what they really understand and do not pretend to know if otherwise. They do not deceive themselves as well as others, and therefore respect the worthy, fear offenses against the law, and are never negligent or arrogant. Such are virtuous Confucian scholars. And there are those who learn from the kings of later times, integrate rite and morality, and unify rules and regulations so that what is profound may be observed from what is shallow, the present may be managed according to past experience, and the myriads of inferences may be drawn from one instance. They can identify those that are conscious of benevolence and righteousness, even if they are among birds and beast, as easily as telling between white and black. With principles and laws, they are able to handle strange things and bizarre transformations never witnessed or heard of once they emerge suddenly somewhere. They have nothing to wonder about. They promote rites and regulations and consider things according to them so that everything is in perfect agreement as though the two halves of a tally were joined together. Such are great Confucian scholars.

"Hence, if a ruler employs ordinary men in his government, a state of ten thousand chariots will perish. If he employs shallow Confucian scholars in his administration, a state of ten thousand chariots will manage to survive. If he employs virtuous Confucian scholars in his court, a state of a thousand chariots will be secure. If he employs great Confucian scholars on his staff, a land of one hundred *li* will be in order within three years, all under Heaven will become one and the feudal lords will submit themselves to the rule. And in a state as powerful as with ten thousand chariots, proper measures lead to peace and stability, and the country will become influential very soon.

"Hearing is better than ignorance, seeing is better than hearing, comprehension is better than seeing, and practice is better than just comprehension. Learning does not end till knowledge is put into practice. He who puts knowledge into practice is reasonable and therefore becomes a sage. A sage takes benevolence and righteousness as his fundamental principles. He has a clear sense of what is right and what is wrong. He suits his action to his words. Everything he does is without the slightest error. There is no other way to this than simply to put his knowledge into practice. For this reason, if one hears something but does not see it, even though he hears extensively, there are surely errors; if he sees something but does not understand it, even if he learns it by heart, it is empty and useless; if he has the knowledge but does not put it

---

[18] The eldest sons enjoyed the right of succession.—Tr.

into practice, he will be at a loss even if he is rich in knowledge. It is not benevolent neither bothering to listen nor bothering to look, even if it is appropriate. Following this route a hundred times leads to hundred-percent error.

"Hence, without being taught by a teacher and ignorant of customary rules, it is certain that a clever man will develop into a robber, a daring man will become a thief, a man of abilities will make trouble, a man of insight will generate fantastic ideas, and a man of eloquence will produce absurd arguments. On the other hand, being taught by a teacher and observing laws and moral standards, an intelligent man will grow illustrious in no time, a courageous man will establish his prestige presently, a talented man will succeed soon, an intelligent man will reach a thorough understanding of things quickly, and a man with a silver tongue will be able to deliver prompt judgments. Therefore, the education by teachers and the consciousness of moral standards are a man's great treasures. It is his greatest misfortune to be without them.

"Without the education by teachers and moral standards, a man will place his inborn nature in the dominant position. With them, he will be able to put the accumulation of learning in the first place. Education and morality are both obtained from accumulation rather than inborn nature, for inherent qualities are inadequate to establish a state of good order independently. Nature is something I cannot create, but I can change it. Habit is not something I am born with, but I can develop it. Actions and habits may change one's nature; concentration and wholeheartedness help in their formation. Customs may transform one's will; enduring influence of customs will change his qualities. Concentrated and whole-hearted, one will develop the divine power and match both Heaven and Earth.

"Hence, heap up earth and a mountain is shaped, accumulate water enough and a sea is formed, and assemble mornings and evenings and a year is made. The highest is named Heaven, the lowest is called Earth, and the six directions in between are called the extremes. A man in the street who accumulates goodness to the perfect extent is called a sage. One seeks something before getting it, practices before success, accumulates before reaching a height, attains perfection before becoming a sage. Hence, a sage is made after a long-term effort of accumulation. A man who keeps hoeing and plowing will grow into a farmer. A man who keeps chopping and hewing wood will turn into a craftsman. A man who keeps selling goods will become a merchant. And a man who persists in observing rite and morality will prove to be a gentleman. None of a craftsman's sons fails to continue his father's trade; the inhabitants of a city are comfortably accustomed to their careers. Those who reside in Chu follow the style of Chu, those who live in Yue follow the style of Yue, and those dwell in Xia[19] follow the style of Xia. This is not due to their inborn nature but to their long-standing accumulation of practice.

"Hence, one may become a gentleman if he is conscious of cautious behaviors, gives careful attention to customs and habits, and places emphasis on constant practice and training. However, if he indulges his dispositions and fails to devote his

---

[19] A collective term for the states in the central plains, including Zhou, Lu, Wei, Ji, Jin, Song, Cao and others.

efforts to learning, he will be reduced to a petty man. Being a gentleman means constant peace and honor; being a petty man involves frequent danger and disgrace. No one but desires security and honor and hates danger and disgrace. And only a gentleman is able to obtain what he likes whereas a petty man invites daily what he detests. The following verse in *The Book of Songs*:

> Here are good men you avoid;
>> They are never employed.
>> There are men hard-hearted and cruel,
>> And they are arranged to rule.
>> So, men want to rebel very much,
>> For who can tolerate things as such?[20]

refers to what is discussed above."

Here is a classification of people: Some are invariably selfish in mind but expect that others will consider them to be public-spirited, they are always dishonorable in their conduct but hope that others will think them cultivated, and they are extremely stupid and ignorant but wish that others will consider them wise. Such are the qualities of the common people. Some may overcome the selfishness in their intentions and be public-spirited; they may curb the natural inclinations in their conduct and be virtuous. They are clever and are ready to consult others and develop their practical abilities. Being just, nice and capable, they may be called lesser Confucian scholars. Being public-spirited in mind, virtuous in conduct, wise enough to comprehend all fundamental principles and laws, they may be regarded as great Confucian scholars. Great Confucian scholars may serve as Three Chief Ministers of an emperor, lesser Confucian scholars may serve as the scholar-officials of feudal lords, and the common people are craftsmen, farmers and merchants. Ritual principles may be compared to *cun*, *chi*, *xun*, *zhang* and other measurements of length. They are used by a ruler to evaluate his subjects. Such are the ranks and types of men.

A gentleman must suit his words to certain occasions, his conduct to certain standards, and his principles to what he exalts and focuses on. When discussing government affairs to be executed, he must set the target at stability and peaceful existence. When talking about aspirations to be achieved, he must point to the requirements of a man of learning. When conferring on the code of ethics, he must stress devotion to the kings of later times. The governance of a state overtaking that of the Three Dynasties is uncertain; laws that deviate from the kings of later times are incorrect. All things, whether high or low, small or great, do not go beyond them. A gentleman keeps his will from galloping beyond these bounds. Therefore, a feudal lord inquiring about government affairs without touching upon security, stability and peaceful existence should not be given a reply; a commoner asking about learning without the wish of becoming a man of learning should not be offered instructions, and any doctrine of the Hundred Schools without touching upon the principles of later kings should not be heeded. This is what is meant by saying that a gentleman must suit his words to certain occasions and his conduct to certain standards.

---

[20] Major Court Hymns, *The Book of Songs*.

Chapter 9
On Kingcraft

Synopsis

This is an important essay reflecting the political ideas of Master Xun.

Adapting to the needs of the times, Master Xun made an argument for the establishment of a unified and powerful country from the politico-economic perspective and drew an ideal blueprint for a unified kingdom.

A true ruler is characterized by respect for the worthy and employment of the capable, while the standard of judgment is rite and morality instead of family background. In managing people, it is essential to cherish love for them and bring them wealth and education. In case some refuse education and remain stubborn, punishment should be imposed. In diplomacy, a ruler should promote benevolence and righteousness in the first place. Even if military conquest is necessary, it should still be made for the sake of justice. Economically speaking, it is necessary to reduce people's taxes and guide them to settle their duties and play their part. In the meanwhile, they should be encouraged to follow the laws of nature in exploiting natural resources.

"Equality is only possible when there is inequality" is a core idea of the Confucians in governing the society. The equality here is one based on respect for differences rather than absolute equality without distinctions, so the basic connotation of rite and morality is "distinctions." The Former Kings formulated ritual and moral principles according to the different characteristics of people and things in order that their position and status are determined. The reason why people can accept these principles and behave properly is that they have a sense of justice and the ability to tell between right and wrong, which set them apart from beasts and serve to explain why they are the most honorable under Heaven.

Based on the idea of governance, this essay divides the way of government into three types: rule of benevolence, rule by power, and rule by force. It is superior to be a true ruler, inferior to be an overlord, and dangerous to be a strongman. Therefore, one cannot never be too careful in choosing the right way.

Text

Someone asked me about the way to run a state. My reply is as follows: The worthy and capable should be promoted without considering their status or rank; the weak and incompetent must be dismissed without hesitation. The chief offenders ought to be executed without attempt to reform them; the ordinary masses can be transformed before any administrative measures are necessary. In this way, order will be in shape before the establishment of a hierarchy. Anyone who fails to observe rite and morality should be relegated to a commoner even if he is a descendant of a prince, a duke or the gentry. Anyone who builds culture and knowledge and observes rite and morality should be promoted to the post of ministers or the gentry even though he is only a descendant of an ordinary person. Hence, those who are inconstant and crafty and who flee hither and thither spreading evil ideas, advocating perverse doctrines, and engaging in treacherous affairs should be arranged to work and meanwhile educated with the expectation that they be transformed. They should be encouraged with commendations and rewards or disciplined with penalties. If they settle down to their work, keep them; otherwise, dismiss them. The disabled five types of people[1] should be accepted and fed by the rulers or employed by the authorities according to their abilities and provided so that they are all taken care of and none is left out. Those who act or use their talents against the times should be condemned to death without mercy. This is called the virtue of Heaven. It is the government of a true ruler.

The key to handling government affairs: Receive with due respect those who come with good will and punish those who come with evil intentions. With this distinction being made, the worthy and the unworthy will not be jumbled up and what is right and what is wrong distinguished. With the worthy and the unworthy being discriminated, men of outstanding characters will arrive; with right and wrong being told apart, the state will be put into good order. When this is done, your reputation will grow every day, all under Heaven will admire you, your orders will be carried out without fail, and the duties of a true ruler will be fulfilled.

In the supervision of administration, excessive dignity, harshness, meanness, and reluctance to guide others estrange the subordinates because of the fear they engender, precipitate concealment and prevent them from telling the whole truth. In such situations, important matters are likely to be neglected and minor things to fall through. On the other hand, ready compromise, willingness to guide others, and unchecked generosity attract all wicked ideas and swarms of tentative doctrines. In such cases, there will be too much to listen to and things will be annoying. This will be harmful, too. Thus, if laws and orders are established but not reviewed in their implementation, what they fail to cover is bound to fault; if functions and powers are set up but communication fails in their exercise, there is surely flaw in what they cannot reach. For this reason, for laws and orders established to be reviewed in their implementation and communication to be maintained between functions and powers set up so

---

[1] Those who are deaf, dumb, and lame, as well as who lose their limbs or anomalous.

that no schemes are concealed, no goodness is overlooked, and nothing goes wrong, only a gentleman is capable of them.

Fairness is the measurement of functions and powers; mean and harmony are the standards of government affairs. Where laws are available, carry them out; otherwise, use analogy. This is the optimal solution to government affairs. On the other hand, favoritism and defiance of principles are deviated routes to the treatment of government affairs. Hence, there have been cases in which chaos broke out in a country in spite of its good laws, but from ancient times to the present I have never heard of a single case in which chaos arose in a country with gentlemen. This is just like what is said in an ancient book: "Good order of a state is brought about by gentlemen while chaos is caused by petty men."

There can be no partiality among men of the same rank or status, no uniformity among men of the same power and influence, and no possibility of dominance among men who are equal to one another. Just as there is the difference of superiority between Heaven and Earth, a sagely king starts his reign with the establishment of a hierarchical system. Two men of equal eminence serve neither; two men of equally humble station command neither. This is quite natural. With the same power and status as well as similar likes and dislikes, men would fight with each other over things which satisfy neither. Their fighting naturally leads to chaos and ends in difficulty. The Former Kings abhorred such disorder; therefore, they established rite and morality to make distinctions between rich and poor, eminent and humble, and enable those above to dominate those below. This is the basis upon which all under Heaven is nurtured. The saying "Equality is only possible when there is inequality"[2] in *The Book of History* refers precisely to this rule.

If horses harnessed to a chariot are frightened, then a gentleman cannot ride the chariot in safety; If the common people are frightened of the government, then a gentleman will not feel secure in his position. If the horses are frightened of the carriage, the best thing to do is to calm them in the first place; if the common people are frightened of the government, the best thing to do is to grant them some favor. Select men who are worthy and good for office, promote those who are kind and respectful, encourage filial piety and brotherly love, take in and feed orphans and widows and aid the poor. If you do these things, then the common people will feel at ease with the government. When the common people feel at ease with the government, a gentleman will feel secure in his post. It is said in an ancient book:

> A ruler is a boat and the common people are the water. Just as water can bear the boat up, so can water capsize it.

This may serve as the best summary of the discussion above. Therefore, if a ruler desires security, nothing is better than a well-ordered government and love for the people; if he desires honor, nothing is better than exalting ritual and treating men of learning with respect; if he desires merit and fame, nothing is better than promoting the worthy and employing the capable. These are the major aspects in being a ruler of men. When these three points are handled properly, all the rest will be appropriate

---

[2] Marquis of Lü on Punishment, *The Book of History*.

as a matter of course. Otherwise, if these three points are treated improperly, all the other efforts are futile even if they are appropriately managed with an effort. Confucius pointed out: "Correctness in both major and minor matters guarantees a superior ruler; correctness in major matters and some minor ones makes a common ruler. As to correctness in minor matters but not in major ones, the outcome is evident without my further explanations."

Marquis Cheng and Lord Si[3] were rulers both skilled in amassing wealth by heavy taxation and meticulous in calculation, but they failed to win the support of their people. Zichan[4] won the support of his people but failed in governmental affairs. Zhong Guan was successful in governmental affairs but failed to promote ritual. Hence, he who promotes ritual becomes a true ruler, he who governs well builds a powerful nation, he who wins over the people makes peace, and he who accumulates wealth for himself perishes. Hence, a true ruler makes his people rich, a ruler by force makes the men of learning rich, a ruler barely manages to survive makes his officials rich, a ruler who fills only his own coffers and stuffs his own storehouses is doomed to lose his state. With his coffers filled and storehouses stuffed, the common people are impoverished. This is what is described as overflowing above and leaking out below. Such a state can neither defend itself at home nor triumph abroad. One has only to stand by and expect its imminent overthrow and destruction. Hence, collecting wealth means destruction to me but more power to my enemies. He who pays attention to the collection of wealth invites bandits, fattens his enemies, destroys his state, and threatens himself. Therefore, an enlightened ruler does not follow this route.

A true ruler contends for people, a ruler by force for allies and a ruler by power for territory. He who wins the support of the people may make the feudal lords swear allegiance to him; he who wins allies makes friends with them; he who grabs land makes an enemy of them. He who makes servants of the feudal lords becomes a true ruler, he who makes friends of them becomes a hegemon, and he who makes enemies of them finds himself in peril.

He who seizes land by force must use his military power to conquer the firmly-defended cities and the death-defying men dispatched to counterattack. He wins by inflicting great injury upon the people of other states. Extreme casualties on these people incur their great hatred which will be turned into the desire of continual fighting against him. In using his military power to conquer the firmly-defended cities and the death-defying men dispatched to counterattack, he inevitably inflicts great injury upon his own people and the heavy casualties on his own men will cause their great hatred which will be transformed into the increasing desire not to fight for him. With the people of other states growing daily more eager to fight against him, and his own people growing daily less eager to fight for him, a powerful force will naturally be weakened. The gain in territory and the loss of population result in more burden and less achievement. While there is more to defend and less for defense, the defensive force is on the contrary reduced. All the other feudal lords

---

[3] Both were monarchs of Wei in the Warring State Period, the latter being a grandson of the former.

[4] A senior official and prime minister of Zheng at the end of the Spring and Autumn Period.

maintain their mutual communication and ally with the states harboring a grudge against the powerful enemy. They watch for any vulnerable spot in its strength and take advantage of its possible difficulties. This signals the imminent peril to the powerful state. He who knows the way to be strong does not triumph over others by military force. He would most probably take the rule over the world as a king's mission, preserve his strength and consolidate his moral integrity. With his strength kept intact, the other feudal lords are unable to weaken him; with his virtual integrity solidified, the other feudal lords are unable to reduce him to insignificance. If there is no feudal lord domineering over all others, he would be constantly triumphant. Thus, he is a ruler who truly knows how to be strong.

However, he who intends to assume hegemony is not like this. He opens up fields, fills up his granaries, and prepares future supplies. Then he carefully recruits and selects men whose fighting skill surpasses that of common men, encourages them with generous rewards and correct them with harsh punishments. He preserves the states facing destruction, permits the continuation of those whose lineage faces extinction, protects the weak, restrains the tyrannical but shows no intention of annexing the land of his neighbors so that the other feudal lords will draw close to him. He treats his coordinate feudal princes with friendliness and the latter are pleased with him. The reason why the other princes draw close to him is because he does not intend to annex them. If he shows his intention of occupation, they will turn away from him. The reason why the other feudal princes are pleased with him is because he treats them friendly as equals. If he displays his inclination to treat them as subordinates, they will desert him. Hence by making it clear in his actions that he has no intention of invasion and by inspiring trust in his friendship and his sense of equality with them, he will always be victorious if there is no feudal lord domineering over all others. Thus, he is a ruler who truly understands how to be a hegemon.

The reason why King Min of Qi was defeated by the allied five forces and Duke Huan of Qi was taken as hostage by Duke Zhuang of Lu[5] was none other than this: they desired to rule over all but failed to follow the correct road.

Unlike this, the true ruler places benevolence, righteousness and power higher than do other states under Heaven. He holds benevolence higher and none under Heaven does not draw close to him. He regards righteousness higher and none under Heaven does not honor him. He attaches more importance to power and none under Heaven dare oppose him. A government observing these convincing principles coupled with an authority not to be opposed guarantees victory without battle, gains without being offensive, and submission without resorting to military forces. Such is the one who knows the correct way of a true ruler.

He who has a mastery of these three ways may rule supremely if he aspires, lord it over if he chooses, or become powerful if he wishes.

---

[5] Both cases happened in the State of Qi in the Warring States Period. King Min (r.301–284) was defeated by the allied forces of Yan, Zhao, Han, Wei and Qin and died at Ju. In 680 BC, when he was negotiating with Duke Zhuang of Lu (r.683–662) on a coalition, Duke Huan was forced by Mo Cao, an official of Duke Lu, to return the land of Wenyang.

A true ruler restrains his actions with rite and morality and makes decisions according to laws and regulations. His brilliance enables him to perceive the minutest detail and suit measures to endless changes. This is called the mastery of the fundamentals. Such is the one who can truly rule.

The system of a true ruler is characterized by his principles no earlier than the Three Dynasties and his laws and regulations undeviating from the kings of later times. The principles earlier than the Three Dynasties are described as distant and indistinct; the laws and regulations deviating from the kings of later times are not standard. There are regulations of dress, standards of dwellings, number of attendants, and proper articles and utensils for different funerary and sacrificial rites. All music that is impure should be abolished; all colors that are different from the conventional designs should be abandoned; all articles and utensils that are unlike the old ones should be destroyed. This is called reversion to the ancients. It is the system of a true ruler.

This is a true ruler's principle of human relations: he who is without virtue is not honored, he who is without abilities is not employed, he who is without accomplishment is not rewarded, and he who is innocent is not punished. No position at the court is to be taken by chance. No common people can manage to survive by luck. The worthy is honored, the able is employed, and each rank corresponds with its position without any fault. The deceitful are punished, the brutal are repressed, and punishments imposed are appropriate. The ordinary people are all assured that their good deeds at home will be rewarded in the royal court and their evil doing in secret will be exposed to punishment in public. This is called the constant rule. It is the policy adopted by a true ruler.

These are the laws of a true ruler: taxes shall be collected according to ranks, government affairs shall be regulated, and all resources shall be exploited to nourish the myriads of people. The tax on the fields shall be one tenth. Goods shall be examined at customs passes and in markets but no impost shall be levied. Mountains, forests, lakes, and weirs shall be closed or opened for use according to seasons and no taxes shall be imposed. Taxation on land shall be set according to its quality. Tributes shall be determined with distance taken into account. Goods and grain shall be freely circulated without delay so that the exchange of need is guaranteed. Thus, all people within the four seas are like one family. Thus, those who are nearby will not hide their abilities, and those who are distant will not complain about their toil. Whether close at hand or far in the distance, none will not hasten in his service with pleasure. This is called exemplary virtue. Such are the laws and regulations of a true ruler.

In the north there are fast horses and hunting dogs. Some are driven to the Central Plains where they are raised and put to their service. In the south there are feathers, ivory, rhino hides, copper ores, and cinnabar. Some are transported to the Central Plains where they are put to various uses. In the east there are fine and coarse cloth, fish, and salt. Some are sent to the Central Plains and turned into clothing and food. In the west there are leather and colored yaktails. Some are brought to the Central Plains and find their applications. Thus, those who dwell near the marshes have plenty of lumber, those who live in the mountains have adequate supplies of fish, farmers do not have to carve and chisel or fire and forge but have sufficient tools and instruments, and craftsmen and merchants do not work the fields and yet have enough food supply. Tigers and leopards are fierce, but a gentleman may strip off their hides for his use. Thus, all that Heaven shelters and Earth supports display their strengths and find their usefulness: they are employed to adorn the worthy and good above and nourish the common people below so that they live in peace and happiness. This is called perfect order. It is just like what is praised in *The Book of Songs*:

> Heaven created the mountain grand,
> > Grandpa made it a famous land.
> > With it being known far and wide,
> > King Wen brought it peace and pride.[6]

As a general principle is applied to various things, so one standard[7] is used to command all affairs, from beginning to end and back to beginning, endless like a circle. Abandon this principle, and all under Heaven will fall into decline. Heaven and Earth generate life, rite and morality create good order, and gentlemen bring ritual and moral principles into being. The establishment, implementation, accumulation and perfection of these principles constitute the foundation of being a gentleman. Thus, Heaven and Earth give birth to gentlemen who in turn bring order to them. Gentlemen form a triad[8] with Heaven and Earth. They serve as managers of all things and parents of the common people. Without gentlemen, Heaven and Earth would not be brought into good order, rite and morality would not be initiated, and there would be neither respect for rulers or teachers above nor good relationship between parents and children. This is called great chaos. The correct relationships between rulers and subjects, fathers and sons, elder and younger brothers, and husbands and wives have their beginning and end and vice versa. They share the order of Heaven and Earth and last for all generations. This is called the great foundation. Hence, in mourning and sacrificial rites, in court and diplomatic ceremonies, and in military organization the same principle is observed, so is it in giving honor or disgrace, ordering execution or absolution, and offering reward or imposing punishment, in behaving oneself well whether it involves a ruler or a subject, a parent or a child, an elder or a younger brother, and in professional ethics relating to farmers, scholars, craftsmen or merchants.

Fire and water possess *qi* but are without life. Grasses and trees possess life but are without consciousness. Birds and beasts have consciousness but are without the sense of justice. Humans possess *qi*, life, consciousness and the sense of justice; therefore, they are the most honorable beings under Heaven. They are no match for oxen in strength or horses in speed, but they make the animals work for them. How so? Because humans can form communities while the other animals cannot. Why are humans able to form communities? Because they are divided into classes. And how

---

[6] Eulogies, *The Book of Songs*.

[7] Namely, rite and morality.

[8] In traditional Chinese culture, Heaven represents time, Earth represents the wealth it offers, and gentlemen are able to create order by taking advantage of both.

can such divisions be put into practice? Because they promote justice. Hence, social divisions based on morality and justice lead to harmony that promises unity. Unity means power means strength means triumph over all things. For this reason, humans can dwell in buildings. They make a plan for the four seasons, place all things under control and bring benefit to all under Heaven. This is made true for no other reason than their divisions on the basis of morality and justice.

Therefore, men cannot survive without forming communities. With communities but without social divisions, there will be conflicts leading to chaos. As a result, there will be separation followed by weakening so that no victory can be secured over things. Consequently, there will be no houses to live in. This means that man cannot give up rite and morality even for a moment. On the basis of these principles, the quality of being able to look after one's parents is called filial piety, the quality of being able to serve one's elder brothers is called brotherly love, the quality of being able to attend to one's superiors is called obedience, and the quality of being able to use one's subjects is called a monarch.

A monarch is one who is good at organizing men in society. When a society is properly organized, all things will find their proper places, the six domestic animals will increase in number, and all other living beings will fulfill their allotted span of life. When bred and raised according to the seasons, the domestic animals will reproduce themselves. When planted and cut in the right time, trees and grasses will flourish. Similarly, if government orders are timely, the common people will act in concert and the worthy and good men will be obedient.

These are the regulations of a sagely king: when plants blossom and bear fruits, axes are prohibited in the wooded mountains so that the trees and grasses are not cut prematurely and their growth is uninterrupted. When turtles, crocodiles, fish, and eels are breeding, nets and poisons are prohibited in the lakes and ponds, so that they are not killed prematurely and their growth is uninterrupted. By plowing in spring, weeding in summer, harvesting in fall, and storing in winter, the four activities are kept in their right seasons, so that the five grains are produced ceaselessly and the common people have more than enough to eat. Fishing in the ponds, lakes, marshes and streams is prohibited in certain seasons so that fishes and turtles are plentiful and the common people have more than they can consume and use. Cutting and felling and growing and nurturing are done in right seasons so that mountains and forests are never laid barren and the common people will have more than enough timber.

This is the part played by a sagely king: he is watchful of Heaven above, settles all things on land, links Heaven and Earth and acts on all things in between. His role is both subtle and evident, brief yet long-lasting, narrow but extensive, divine and profound but to the point. Therefore, it is said, he who commands all according to rite and morality is a sage.

The duties of officials are:

> *Zaijue* ('Minister of Reception') is in charge of affairs involving the reception of guests, religious ceremonies, banquets, and sacrifices.
> *Situ* ('Minister of Culture') is in charge of affairs involving clans, scale of city walls, and quantity of utensils and instruments to be displayed.

Sima ('Minister of War') is in charge of military affairs, including the number of soldiers, chariots, armor and weapons.

Taishi ('Grand Master') is in charge of revising government decrees, examining poetry, prohibiting lewd music, and revising other inappropriateness without delay, so that the standard music is not corrupted by barbarian, vulgar and aggressive tones.

Sikong ('Minister of Public Works') is in charge of matters like repairing dikes and bridges, dredging irrigation channels, draining off overflow waters, reinforcing dams, opening or closing sluice gates at the appropriate time, so that farmers could reap what they grow against bad weather, flood or drought.

Zhitian ('Director of Agriculture') is in charge of matters like inspecting the physical features of fields, examining the fertility of soil, deciding the order in which the five crops are grown, inspecting the accomplishments of farmers, supervising the storage of harvests, and arranging repairs without delay so that farmers are bent wholeheartedly on farming and do not divert their attention to other skills.

Yushi ('Supervisor of Resources') is in charge of formulating provisions of fire prevention in order to conserve the resources of mountains and woods and the fish, turtles and various vegetables of lake areas and marshes, opening and closing these areas in right seasons so that the whole nation is sufficiently supplied without exhausting the wealth.

Xiangshi ('District Preceptor') is in charge of matters like coordinating rural communities, demarcating the homestead, stimulating the raising of six domestic animals, learning arboriculture, encouraging education, promoting filial piety and brotherly love, and attending to all matters at the appropriate time so that the common people will obey government orders and live peacefully in the countryside.

Gongshi ('Supervisor of Craftsmen') is in charge of matters like passing judgment on various craftsmen and their products, determining the time for their activities, encouraging quality and practicability, and facilitating the use of necessary implements so that articles with carvings or patterned designs are not manufactured in private.

Yuwu ('Hunchback Sorceress') and *Boxi* ('Lame Sorcerer')[9] are in charge of matters like observing the changes between Yin and Yang, telling fortune according to atmospheric variations, predicting future events by burning punched turtle shells, foretelling good and ill luck or omens by means of the Five Signs,[10] exorcising evil spirit and summoning lucky ones.

Zhishi ('Minister of Trade') is in charge of duties like cleaning cemeteries and latrines, repairing roads, taking precautions against theft and robbery, evaluating and controlling prices, and attending to these matters without delay so that there is security for guests, merchants and other travelers and an unobstructed flow of goods.

---

[9] In ancient times, the crippled were charged with divination if they were skillful in these tricks.—Tr.

[10] Five weather conditions in which a divination is undertaken: raining, clear, overcast, cloudy and other conditions in between.

Sikou ('Minister of Justice') is in charge of duties like penalizing the deceitful and repressing the brutal, preventing against debauchery, eliminating evils, and imposing the five punishments[11] so that the brutal are reformed and the wicked desist from evil-doing.

Zhongzai ('Minister of State') is in charge of revising laws and regulations on the basis of government education, listening to all proposals and reviewing them regularly, measuring accomplishments, deciding on rewards and commendations, and attending to these matters without delay so that all officials exert their best efforts and the common people are not careless and lazy.

Pigong ('Feudal Prince') is in charge of establishing the principles of rite and music, correcting personal conduct, promoting transformation based on education, refining popular customs, and granting favors far and wide so that all are turned into a harmonious unity.

Refining moral principles, promoting ritual propriety, perfecting the rules of etiquette, unifying all under Heaven, perceiving the minutest detail in everything, and convincingly making all people under Heaven obey his rule. This is the job of a monarch over all under Heaven.

Thus, if the affairs of government are in disorder, it is the fault of the *Zhongzai*. If the customs of a nation are corrupted, it is the error of the *Pigong*. If the world fails to be unified and the feudal lords desire to rebel, then the monarch is not the right ruler.

When one meets all the qualifications of a king, he can be a king; when one fulfills all the requirements of a hegemon, he can become an overlord; one survives with the existence of living conditions and perishes without it. To govern a powerful state with ten thousand chariots, he establishes its authority and strength, wins a good reputation far and wide, bends his enemy states to submission, turns his own state from danger to safety and changes the portentous into the propitious. It all rests here with him, not with others. To be a true king or a hegemon, to live in security or be threatened by danger or even to die, it is all determined by a king himself rather than by others. If a state is neither powerful enough to intimidate its neighbors nor well-known to all under Heaven, this means that it cannot yet stand on its own. So how can it be free from trouble? When a brutal force poses threat to the world and if I do not want to follow the example, I am not prevented from making myself a Yao even if I have to work and live with a ruler as cruel as Jie. This is not the key to winning merit and fame, nor is it what accounts for the security or peril in which a nation finds itself. What determines the achievement of merit and fame and the situation of safety or danger is surely the foundation on which one aspires to and worries about when his country is powerful and prosperous. If one truly regards his state as a place for a true ruler, he may rule all under Heaven. Otherwise, if he mistakes his state for a dangerous place facing destruction, he will face danger and even be destroyed in the end.

---

[11] Tattoo, cutting off the nose, amputating the foot, castration, and death.

In times of prosperity, a state should stand neutral and show no favoritism to any side or enter into either vertical or horizontal alliance.[12] It should remain quiet, keep its troops immobilized and look on as those brutal forces fall upon one another. By the time peace is made through government and education, the ritual principles are clarified, and the common people are trained, the military force will be the strongest. By the time benevolence and righteousness are cultivated, rite and morality are elevated, laws and regulations are rectified, the worthy and good are selected and the common people are nourished, the best reputation will be established. By firmly exercising control, strengthening the military force and winning a fine reputation, Yao and Shun unified all under Heaven and nothing more could be added to this! When those who resort to all sorts of schemes and intrigues are dismissed, the men of worth, virtue, ability and wisdom will come forward of themselves. When punishments and government regulations are appropriate, the common people are in harmony, and national customs are moderated. The army of a state will be strong, its cities will be secure against attack, and its enemy nations will naturally submit. When attention is paid to farming, goods are accumulated, the habit of extravagance is overcome, and both the ministers and the common people observe rules and regulations, wealth will increase and the country will be rich as a matter of course. When these three conditions are realized and the whole world yield obedience, the tyrants will be unable to command their troops. Why? Because no one will follow them to war. Launching a military expedition involves using people. If their people love me as they do their parents and are fond of me as they are of the fragrance of orchids, they will be like being branded or tattooed in the eyes of their own people and be regarded as enemies. Even if they were as cruel as Jie and Zhi the Robber, how could they be willing to harm whom they love for the sake of whom they hate? Their people are won over. Thus, in ancient times there were men who won all under Heaven starting from one single state. They did not invade other states and grab their land. Rather, they enlightened their government so that no one under Heaven did not admire them and therefore the violent could be eradicated and the ruthless suppressed. For this reason, when Duke of Zhou launched his punitive campaign to the south, the states in the north complained, "Why does he not come here?" And when he marched eastward, the states in the west grumbled, "Why does he not come to us first?" Who could fight against such a ruler? He who can bring such good order to his state may become a true ruler.

In times of prosperity, it is essential to stop war and love the people by letting them recover. New fields should be opened up in order to fill the granaries and make ready future supplies. Men with outstanding fighting skills should be carefully recruited and selected before encouraging them with handsome rewards, guarding against them with cruel tortures and electing reasonable scholar-officials to command and supervise them. With this being done, it rests reassured to gather wealth and goods

---

[12] IN the latter period of the Warring States, Qin, the state in the west, was the most powerful. The other states east of Qin were located roughly from north to south. When some or all of these states joined their forces against Qin, a vertical alliance was in shape; when Qin attacked joined some of the other forces against another, a horizontal alliance was formed.

and repair weapons and other appliances so that there will be plenty of goods and materials to use. While others always expose their weapons, armor and implements of warfare to the sun and let them be destroyed, we mend and renovate ours, keep them in good repair and cover them in the storehouses. While others waste their wealth, goods and food supplies every day in open fields, we collect and store ours in the granaries. While others drive their men of talent, feat, strength and valor as well as capable ministers to battle to be crushed and exhausted daily, we offer them amnesty, accept them all and modify them at court. In this way, others will decline daily while we will be better off, others will be poorer while we will be wealthier, others will be worn out while we will remain at ease, and, between rulers and their subjects as well as between superiors and inferiors, there will be greater hostility and distance in other states while in ours there will be less distance and more friendliness. Thus, their decay is in expectation. And he who brings such good order to his state may become a hegemon.

To conduct oneself in society, it is advised to follow the routine customs. To handle matters well, it is advised to observe ordinary conventions. To recommend the worthy and employ the capable, it is advised to choose from ordinary people. To treat one's subordinates and the common people, it is advised to be tolerant, generous and kind. Those who do as thus advised will live in security.

Reckless and uncouth in conduct, suspicious and hesitant in handling matters, promoting those who flatter and are silver-tongued in recommendation, and taking from one's subordinates and the common people by force and deception—such behaviors lead one to great danger.

Arrogant and irritable in conduct, subversive and treacherous in handling matters, promoting the insidious and tricky in recommendation, and desirous of the utmost effort but neglectful of the contribution or expecting only taxes but regardless of the business in treating one's subordinates and the common people—such manners lead one to destruction.

One is never too careful in selecting from these five types of conduct because they respectively shape the road to a true ruler, a hegemon, existence in security, great danger and destruction. He who is adept at the choice may become a true king and will be in control of others; he who is poor in it will be in the control of others and will go to destruction. Great indeed is the disparity between a true ruler and a failure facing death or between being in control and being under control.

Chapter 10
On the Wealth of a State

Synopsis

This essay demonstrates the way to bring prosperity and strength to a state.

According to Master Xun, in developing the economy of a country and making it prosperous and strong, it was politically necessary to make clear social divisions and have them organized, to honor the worthy and employ the capable, and rigorously implement awards and punishments, and economically essential to tap resources, reduce expenses, strengthen the fundamental, restrict the incidental, and enrich the people. These measures were all based on rite and morality whose key was held by the ruler of men. The ruler above, with his wisdom and benevolence, offered his support and instructions to his people engaging in specific work of production. Only when a monarch and his people played their respective parts, when both superiors and inferiors performed their own duties, could the state become strong, the people grow rich, and stability be guaranteed.

Master Mo condemned music and proposed frugality in expenditure to solve the problem of insufficiency of things. In response to this, Master Xun pointed out that the trouble in the world did not lie in the insufficiency of things, but in the contentions among people, which could be accounted for by the ignorance of rite and morality. Mo's condemnation of music and proposal of being frugal in expenditure could only deal with the symptoms rather than the root causes and could only worsen the problems; therefore, Master Xun suggested that the Confucian learning be adopted in governance.

The ruler of men should avoid the extremes of either one or the other or bias toward one end. He should not abandon what should be done while specifically granting minor favors to the people, hoping in vain to gain their enduring support; neither should he be too eager for accomplishment and merit at the risk of his people's security, which promised no enduring support of the people either.

The essay concludes with the emphasis on rite and morality rather than trade with other states relying on goods, covenants and land.

Text

All things share the same space but are different in form. They have no set applications but are used by men. This is a natural law. Men of all grades and types live together. They have the same demands but differ in the way to meet them. They share the same desires but are different in intelligence. This is human nature.

On one hand, all people approve of certain things, no matter they are intelligent or foolish. On the other hand, they do not approve of the same things, and this serves to distinguish between wisdom and stupidity. With the same power and influence but difference in intelligence, if men seek personal gains without trouble and indulge in desires without control, then they will rise up in contentions and no one will be pleased. Thus, even the wise will not succeed in bringing order. And their failure in bringing order means no merit or fame is recognized. Consequently, there will be no discrimination among the people and therefore no distinction between the monarch and his subjects. With no monarch to command the ministers and no superiors to supervise the inferiors, there will be disasters under Heaven as a result of indulgence in desires. With the same desires and dislikes, people will fight with each other over the limited supply of what they all want. The achievements of various skills provide for one person, for it is impossible for him to be skillful in all fields or to engage in all jobs. Being isolated and independent of one another, men will be reduced to poverty. Living in a community without distinctions there will be conflict. Poverty is misfortune and conflict leads to disasters. To remedy misfortunes and eradicate disasters, nothing is better than to make clear social divisions and distinctions and have people organized. If the strong threaten the weak and the intelligent intimidate the stupid, the people below disregard their superiors and the young bully their elders, and the government fails to promote virtue, the old and weak will suffer the grief of losing their means of support and the strong will suffer from the disasters resulting from their contentions. If working and making achievements were what people dislike, merit and profit were what they like, and there were no division of labor, people would suffer the failure of achievement and the calamity caused by their contention over merit. If the union of man and woman, the role and duty of husband and wife, as well as marriage and wedding fail to observe the proprieties, people will suffer the grief of family disruption and the disaster of struggling over mates. For these reasons, the wise instituted the distinctions.

A state is made self-sufficient by means of reducing expenses, enriching the people, and forming the habit of storing up the surplus. Expenses may be reduced by observing the ritual principles and people may be enriched by government policies. With people being enriched, there will be surplus and popular wealth. When the public are wealthy, their fields will be fertile and well managed. With fertile fields and good management, the yield will be a hundred times greater. The ruler collects taxes according to laws and regulations and the people economize on their uses according to ritual principles. The surplus piles up like mounds and hills and there is not enough room to store it even if burning is adopted once in a while. Then, why should a gentleman worry about having no surplus? Therefore, the conscious effort to reduce expenses and enrich the people will gain a reputation for being benevolent, righteous, able and virtuous, and have an accumulation of wealth as substantial as mounds and hills as well. This is due to no other cause than reducing expenses and enriching the people. Failure to cut expenses and enrich the people will reduce them to poverty which in turn causes the infertility of soil and waste. As a result, with the fields overgrown with weeds, the yield will not reach even a half of what is normal. Even though the ruler manages to take away or simply seizes by force, he will not be able to get much. And if he does not use it frugally according to the rules of propriety, he will be known as greedy and corrupt but actually goes short and remains empty-handed. This is due to no other reason than his failure to control his expenditure and try to make his people rich. The Announcement to the Prince of Kang[1] says:

> Shelter all like Heaven and maintain your moral integrity and you will be wealthy.

It refers to such cases.

The rules of propriety differ between noble and humble, young and old, poor and rich, as well as major and minor. The Son of Heaven wears a red dragon-robe and crown, the feudal lords black dragon-robe and official hat, the officials second-class robes and hats, and the men of learning leather caps and clothes.

Virtue and status should match; status and salary should match; salary and performance should match, too. From the men of learning above, men should be controlled through ritual and music while the ordinary people must be controlled by means of laws and regulations. Establishing states according to the size of land, raising a population according to the amount of profit, and planning work according to manpower so that each person is qualified for the job he is assigned, each undertaking reaps profit sufficient to support the people, and in every case the income and expense of clothing, food and other daily necessities balance before storing up the surplus—such is called the agreement with laws and regulations. Thus, from the Son of Heaven down to the commoners, all things are handled in this way, whether great or small either in importance or in amount. This can be summarized as: no one may occupy a position by luck at the royal court and no one can survive by good fortune if he ignores his proper occupation.

Reduce taxes on the cultivated fields and open country, tax moderately at markets and passes, minimize the number of merchants, impose forced labor rarely and never take farmers away from their fields in the busy farming season, and the state will be rich. Such is called enriching the people through government policies.

Human beings cannot survive without living in groups. Living in a group without distinctions being made, they will fight with one another. Their fighting will cause disorder which ends in poverty. Therefore, without forming a hierarchy, it is a disaster to man; with distinctions being made, the basic interest under Heaven is guaranteed. And a ruler is the center of this administration. For this reason, to praise him is to celebrate the foundation of the world, to defend him is to secure the foundation of the world, and to honor him is to esteem the foundation of the world. The Former Kings divided people before organizing them into grades so that some were noble

---

[1] A chapter in *The Book of History*.

while others humble, some were treated liberally while others meagerly, some lived an easy life while others labored arduously. They did so in order to define the system of benevolence and implement it rather than to make a reputation of debauchery, arrogance, luxury and magnificence. They had various vessels carved with emblems and clothes embroidered with patterns so that their wearers were differentiated as noble or humble without making them much pleasing to the eye. They had bells, drums, flutes, chime stones, zithers and flutes manufactured so that the auspicious and the inauspicious were told apart and joy and harmony were enhanced without seeking any other purpose. They had palaces, mansions, terraces and halls built so that men could escape extreme heat and wetness, cultivate their virtue, distinguish between what was important and what was insignificant and pursued nothing beyond. It is said in *The Book of Songs*:

> Engraved are the ornaments;
>> Of metal and jade is their substance.
>> Diligent and tireless is our king
>> Bringing the four quarters under control.[2]

It refers precisely to this.

When it comes to the colorful attire to wear, dainty dishes to eat, plenty of materials to accumulate for use, and the whole world under Heaven to control, these are not intended to show luxury, arrogance and willfulness but rather the unity of all under Heaven, order brought to all transformations, management of all things, rearing of all the people and benefit to the whole world. No one is better here than a benevolent man of noble virtue, who is wise enough to put the world under control, adequately kindhearted to bring peace, and sufficiently virtuous to transform by means of education. With him, there will be order; without him, there will be chaos. Indeed, the ordinary people depend on him for his wisdom; therefore, they rush one after another to hard work so that he can stay at ease in order to nurture his wisdom. Indeed, they praise his kindheartedness; therefore, they run the risk of their lives to defend him in order to nurture his benevolence. Indeed, they admire his virtue; therefore, they carve various emblems on vessels and embroider different patterns on clothes for ornament in order to nurture his virtue. Thus, the ordinary people honor the man of benevolence above them like Heaven, love him like their own parent, and willingly risk their lives in his defense for no other reason than the good policies he determines, the great accomplishments he makes and the ample profit he brings in. In *The Book of Songs*, the following poem.

> I carry it on the shoulder, put it on my cart,
>> Driving my ox and wagon I depart.
>> When my trip of delivery is done,
>> I am told to return home.[3]

---

[2] Major Court Hymns, *The Book of Songs*.

[3] Minor Court Hymns, *The Book of Songs*.

portrays the scene of delivering tax grain to the state.

Therefore, it is said: a gentleman resorts to his virtue while a petty man uses his strength. A man of strength is driven by men of virtue. Tempered with the moral education given by gentlemen, the ordinary people are found to be effective with their physical strength, their collective life proves to be harmonious, their wealth turns out to be accumulated, their place in the society is steady, and their life span is expected to be longer. Without moral education, there will be no affection between father and son, no fraternal love between brothers, and no happy relations between man and woman. With it, the young grow and mature, and the old are looked after properly. This may be further illustrated as: "Heaven and Earth give them life while the sages help them succeed."

But today things are different. The rulers impose heavier levies in knife and spade currency to rob the common people of their wealth, increase taxes on the fields to snatch away their food, and raise tariffs at passes and marketplaces to make the transactions difficult. And that is not all. They deliberately find fault and wait for opportunities to cheat. They also engage in scheming after power and plotting overthrows to topple each other and ruin the morals of the time. The common people are clearly aware of the great danger and destruction to be brought about by the filthy, ugly and cruel. Thus, some ministers assassinate their monarchs, some subordinates murder their superiors, some are disloyal to their towns, betray moral integrity and refuse to die unworthily for their masters. This is due to no other reason than the fact that the rulers look for trouble themselves. It says in *The Book of Songs*:

> No word uttered finds no response;
> No favor granted has no return.[4]

It refers precisely to this.

The way to make the whole world rich rests with determining social divisions. Tilling the fields, marking off the boundary of farmland, clearing out weeds, planting grains, and fertilizing the fields frequently—these are the business of farmers and other common people. Observing the farming season, supervising and encouraging people to work, improving their efficiency and gains, bringing them in harmony, urging them to be diligent and hardworking—these are the duties of generals.[5] To ensure that the high-lying fields do not suffer from drought and the low-lying fields are free from waterlogging, to keep cold and heat harmoniously regulated, and to see that the grains ripen in their right times—these are the works of Heaven. When it comes to the responsibility of protecting the people in general, giving universal love, and keeping them all in order, ensuring that they are free from the misfortunes of cold or hunger even in years of crop failure because of drought or flood—these belong to sagely rulers and their worthy prime ministers.

Master Mo was upset and expressed his worry about the insufficiency under Heaven. Insufficiency is not a universal disaster after all. It was only the overanxiety of Master Mo. Now in this field grow the five grains. Managed well, a single *mu*

---

[4] Major Court Hymns, *The Book of Songs*.

[5] In the ancient times, generals were in charge of both civilian and military affairs.

of land will yield several *pen*[6] of grains twice every year. Melon crops and fruit trees will bear melons, peaches, dates, and plums measured in *pen*. There will be flavorings and vegetables measured in pools. Furthermore, there will be cartloads of the six domestic animals and wild beasts, ponds and schools of fishes and turtles, flocks of wild geese and other flying birds resembling a sea of smoke, as well as swarms of insects among them. Things that can be the source of food supply are countless. Among the myriad things produced by Heaven and Earth there are more than enough to feed people, and things like flax, silk, feather, and hide are more than enough to clothe them. Thus, insufficiency is not a universal trouble. It is something only Master Mo worried about too much.

The universal trouble is caused by chaos. Why don't we try to inquire together who causes the chaos? I think it is Master Mo who cast the world into disorder by his Condemnation of Music[7] and threw the world into poverty by his Moderation in Expenditure.[8] This is not an attempt to calumniate his person. But his doctrines will necessarily lead to such consequences. In the opinion of Master Mo, in reigning over a land big as all under Heaven or small as a single feudal state, a ruler would put on coarse clothes, eat poor food, carry the world on his back, and, being overcome with grief, get rid of music. In such conditions, the land would be very poor and fail to provide things enough to meet the people's desires. As a result, it would be impossible to offer rewards. With a land vast as the entire world or small as a state, Master Mo would reduce the number of attendants and government posts, highly praise merit, appreciate toilsome efforts and share both responsibility and credit with the common people. If things were like this, there would be no authority. Without authority, penalties would not be implemented. If rewards failed to be dispensed, the worthy would not be appropriately appointed. If punishments failed to be administered, the unworthy would not be dismissed from the posts they should occupy. When the worthy were not promoted and the unworthy were not dismissed, neither the competent nor the incompetent would be put in the proper office. In such a situation, nothing would be in its proper place, no change would be properly responded, opportune time would be missing, geographic advantage would not exist, and the unity of people would be destroyed. By then, it would be as though all under Heaven were boiled or burned. Even if Master Mo wore coarse clothes with a rope as his belt, ate beans and drank only water, how could he have all of the world adequately provided? Since the root is destroyed and the source is cut off, the wealth under Heaven is surely exhausted.

The Former Kings and the sages did not do things like this. They were aware that, as rulers or superiors, they would fail to unite the population without adorning themselves first, to rule over the people without being rich themselves, or to stop the fierce and violent and beat the cruel and tough without making themselves awe-inspiring

---

[6] A large unit of dry measure.—Tr.

[7] One of Di Mo's major arguments, which held that music should be abolished because it actually interfered with people's work and duties rather than did anything beneficial at all.

[8] Another major argument of Di Mo who insisted that both rulers and ordinary people should be economical.

and powerful in the first place. Therefore, it is necessary to satisfy the ears by striking large bells, beating loud drums, blowing reed pipes and flutes, and playing lyres and zithers, to please the eyes by vessels with carvings and inscriptions and clothing with color patterns and designs, to fill the mouth with fine meats and good grains with the five flavors, and to keep them mindful by increasing attendants, completing official posts, granting more rewards, and imposing more severe punishments, so that the common people under Heaven will realize what they desire or fear are all found there, so the rulers will be able to encourage by rewards and inspire awe by punishments. With the policies of rewards and punishments implemented, the worthy will be promoted, the unworthy dismissed, and both the competent and incompetent properly arranged. In this way, there will be harmony in all things and all sudden changes will be properly handled. When there are opportune times determined by Heaven above, geographical advantages offered by Earth below, and the unity of people formed in between, wealth and goods will rush out like gurgling springs, roll on like rivers or seas, pile up like mounds or hills and find no place to be stored without being burned once in a while. How could the world have the trouble of insufficiency? Hence, if the way of the Confucians does work, all under Heaven will be peaceful and wealthy, accomplishments will be made when the people are used, and harmony will be achieved when bells are struck and drums beaten, just like the descriptions in *The Book of Songs*:

> The bells peal and drums pound,
>> The flutes and stones blend their sound,
>> And abundant blessing is sent down.
>> In large measure blessing does come,
>> Impressive, dignified, composed and calm,
>> We have drunk and eaten to the full,
>> Our happiness and luck are plentiful.[9]

On the other hand, if the way of the Mohists did work, all under Heaven would promote frugality and become poorer. Fighting would be condemned but it would occur daily all the same. People would toil away but would appear haggard and their achievement would prove less and less. Weighed down with sorrow and wearing a grave expression, they would condemn music but would grow less harmonious every day, just like the descriptions in *The Book of Songs*:

> Heaven keeps spreading diseases,
>> Deaths and disorder multiply;
>> From the people are heard no praises;
>> What is heard is endless lament only.[10]

To neglect government affairs and nurture the people with petty favors in order to pacify and love them, preparing thick porridge for them in the winter and melons and

---

[9] Eulogies, *The Book of Songs*.

[10] Minor Court Hymns, *The Book of Songs*.

oatmeal in the summer in order to steal a brief moment's approval from them—this is a makeshift approach. It wins temporary praise from villains and does not last. By this approach, no achievement will be made in doing anything and no merit will be established. It is an immoral way of government.

To noisily drive people to labor against time in blind pursuit of development and merit regardless of their reputation or support, so that progress was made at the cost of causing people's hatred. This is an unacceptably careless and extreme approach, leading to corruption and decline without any accomplishment being made. Therefore, it is impractical to neglect government affairs and nurture the people with petty favors in order to get their support, so is it to achieve merit but forget the people. Both approaches are bad.

Consequently, the men in ancient times refused to do so. They protected the common folk against heatstroke in summer and cold in winter; they kept the ordinary people from overstraining themselves on hectic days or delaying their jobs in the farming season when relaxed. With things done, their accomplishments were made and people from all levels became rich. The common people loved their rulers. They were obedient to them like flowing water and affectionate to them as if they were their parents. They were happy to risk their lives for them. All this was due to no other reason than that their rulers were perfectly faithful, honest, gentle and fair-minded. Hence, if the ruler of men desires merit soon, it is better to be moderate and tolerant than anxious for success, and it is more pleasing to be faithful and fair-minded than granting rewards. He must correct his own faults before gradually pointing out the errors of others because this is more effective than imposing punishments. If a ruler possesses these three virtues, his subjects will respond to him like a shadow or an echo. He will be eminent and successful even if he does not intend to be so, won't he? Just as it is said in *The Book of History*:

> If a ruler is greatly brilliant, his people will try their best, and their work will be coordinated and quickly done.[11]

If punishment is imposed before the exercise of education, the evil cannot be vanquished even if there is a complex system of penalties. If education is not strengthened by punishment, villains will remain at large. With merely punishment and no reward, the diligent people will be left unencouraged. Punishment or reward not based on rules will lead to suspicion among the people, corruption in customs, and inconsistency in people's behaviors. For this reason, the Former Kings defined rite and morality in order to unify the people, tried to be earnest in taking care of them, honored the worthy and employed the capable so that they were all arranged, encouraged them with noble titles, official attire and awards, coordinated them by assigning tasks in due seasons and lightening their burdens, and gave comprehensive considerations in looking after and nurturing them as if they were infants. With these measures taken, evils would not rise, thieves and robbers would disappear, and those who sought after the good would be encouraged. Why were things like this? This was because their ways were easy, the ideas they instilled into people's mind were firm, their

---

[11] The Announcement to the Prince of Kang, *The Book of History*.

policies were consistent, and their rewards and punishments were clearly defined. Therefore, it is said: "When a ruler is whole-hearted, his subjects will be constant and steady; when he is double-minded, they will change their mind constantly. This can be likened to grass or trees: the leaves and branches are controlled by the roots.

Instead of getting benefit from the people before offering them benefit, it would be more beneficial to benefit them before being benefitted. Rather than refrain from showing the people love but make use of them, it would be more meritorious to show them love before making use of them. It is of more benefit to bring benefit to people without taking benefit from them than to take benefit from the people before giving them benefit. And it would be of more merit to show the people love without making use of them than to show them love before making use of them. He who gives the people benefit without taking it from them and loves the people without making use of them wins over the world. He who gives the people benefit before taking it from them and shows love to the people before making use of them defends the land. And he who refrains from giving the people benefit but takes benefit from them and refrains from showing the people love but makes use of them places the state in peril.

You cannot decide whether a state is in order or in chaos or good or bad till you come to its borders. If you see its guards on constant patrol and its passes in severe control, then the state is definitely in chaos. Entering its territory, if you find its fields deserted and its city walls dilapidated, then it has a greedy ruler. Inspect the royal court and you will find that the honored are unworthy. Observe the official posts and you will find that they are occupied by the incapable. Look at those who are trusted and you will find that they are dishonest. Then the ruler is a muddleheaded one. If the ruler and his ministers and other officials of all levels are very particular about wealth and goods in revenue and expenditure, and if they are ignorant, loose or careless about the ritual and moral rules, then the state is in disgrace. On the other hand, if the farmers take delight in working on the fields, the soldiers are ready to die for their country, the officials of all levels observe the law, the royal court exalts ritual, and the ministers are in concert, then the state is in good order. Inspect the royal court and you will find that the honored are worthy. Observe the official posts and you will find that they are occupied by the capable. Look at those who are trusted and you will find that they are honest. Then the ruler is an enlightened one. If the ruler and his ministers and other officials of all levels are lenient and simple with wealth and goods in revenue and expenditure, and if they are serious and careful about the ritual and moral rules, then the state is in prosperity and honor. Among those who are equally worthy, those who are close are given precedence in honors. Among those who are equally capable, those who are of old acquaintance are given precedence in the assignment of office. Among the officials of all levels, those who were corrupt are transformed into men of virtue, those who were rude are converted to kindness, and those who were treacherous become honest—these are the accomplishments of an enlightened ruler.

To decide whether a state is strong and prosperous or weak and poor, the following points of evidence are of good reference. If the ruler does not exalt ritual, his army is weak. If he does not love his people, his army is weak. If he breaks his promise, his army is weak. If he offers meagre rewards, his army is weak. And if his generals are incompetent, his army is weak. If the ruler is fond of accomplishment, the state will be impoverished. If he is fond of profit, the state will be impoverished. If he has a huge body of the gentry, the state will be impoverished. If he has a big population of artisans and merchants, the state will be impoverished. If he has no rules and regulations of expenditure, the state will be impoverished. If those below are poor, the ruler is poor. If those below are rich, the ruler is rich. Thus, fields and countryside areas are the roots of wealth. Warehouses and granaries are as the branches of wealth. The working of the common people according to seasons and the orderliness of production are the source of wealth. The gradations of tax rates and the treasury are the course of wealth. For these reasons, an enlightened ruler must be careful to keep all things in harmony, economize on expenditures, broaden the sources of income, and frequently take these questions into consideration, so that there is supply in surplus under Heaven and it is unnecessary for the ruler to worry about insufficiency. Then both the ruler and his people are so rich that there is no enough room to store up their wealth. This involves the ultimate knowledge of government. There were ten years of flood under Yu and seven years of drought under Tang; however, there was no famished look under Heaven then. A decade later, there was crop harvest and still an accumulated surplus of old grain. This was due to no other reason than that they had a comprehensive understanding of the relations between root and branch as well as source and course. Therefore, with the fields deserted and the granaries full and with the commoners poor but the royal treasury and storehouses full, the state is on the verge of destruction. With the roots cut off, the sources exhausted and the wealth gathered and collected in the treasuries, and the ruler and his ministers being unaware of the harm, the destruction of the state is around the corner. With the whole state to support him and yet he is not satisfied, this is called avarice. Such a ruler is the most stupid. He starts out seeking riches and ends up by losing his state. He starts out seeking profit and ends up by endangering his own person. In ancient times, there were ten thousand states, but now there are only a few more than ten left. This is due to no other cause than this same principle. All rulers ought to have realized this by now!

A state only a hundred *li* around is big enough to be independent. Generally, those who attack others do so either for fame or for profit; otherwise, their aggression might be provoked by hatred. In governing his state, a benevolent ruler will cultivate his will and aspirations, correct his conduct, exalt propriety and righteousness, keep his promise and observe laws and regulations. If a man of learning in plain cloth robe and coarse hemp-woven shoes is like this, princes and dukes cannot be his rival in fame even though he lives in an impoverished alley or in a leaky house. Trust him with the state and no one under Heaven can neglect him. If such is the case, those who seek fame will not come to attack the state. A benevolent ruler will open up fields and wasteland, fill his granaries and storehouses, and improve the weapons and farm implements. He and his subjects will be of one mind and his three armies[12] will pull together. In such conditions, a long-distance military expedition against another state is infeasible. Inside his territory, the forces are gathered in solid defense. With

---

[12] The main army and the left and right columns.

fair opportunities available, they will launch head-on counterattack and capture the enemy generals as easily as stirring cooked wheats with a stick. What little the enemy might gain would be inadequate even to cure the wounded and make up for the loss, while he has love for his soldiers and hatred for his enemy. Such being the case, those who seek profit will not come to attack. A benevolent ruler will carefully handle with justice the relations between small and big states as well as weak and strong states, with perfect ritual, great jadeware for sacrificial ceremonies and other rich gifts and with graceful, eloquent and intelligent gentlemen as diplomats. If the opposite side is quite reasonable, how could it bear any grudge against him? If things are like this, those who are angry will not come to attack. If those who pursue fame will not come, those who seek profit will not come, and those who give vent to their hatred will not come either, then his state is as firm as a rock and as long-lasting as stars. While other states are in chaos and peril, mine alone is in good order and security. When the others are on the decline, mine will rise and conquer them. Thus, a benevolent ruler does not defend his own state only; he will take other states into consideration. It says in *The Book of Songs*:

> The gentleman, a man of virtue,
>> Has done nothing improper.
>> He has done nothing against the ritual,
>> And may govern the states in all directions.[13]

It refers to such cases.

Below is the difficulty or ease with which a state is governed. It is difficult to serve a strong and brutal state, but it is easy to get served by that state. To serve it with goods and treasures, no alliance can be maintained when the resources are exhausted. To enter into a treaty of alliance with a pledge, the alliance may be broken in a few days. To bribe it with a half of the land, its desire is unlikely to be satiated when the other half is also ceded. The more obediently it gets served, the more aggressive it will become. It will not stop till goods and treasures are exhausted and the land is completely occupied. Under such circumstances, none could avoid the disaster even if he were assisted by Yao on the left and Shun on the right. To draw an analogy: let a maiden wear jewels around her neck, adorn herself with jade and carry gold. If she ran into a robber in the mountains, she would not be able to escape even if she should bend down or drop on her knees to beg like a servant rather than look him in the eye. Therefore, without a way to unite the people, it is impossible to defend one's country and keep oneself secure only by imploring with sweet words and serving with restlessness. For this reason, an enlightened ruler does not do so. He will establish ritual to consolidate his government, revise laws to control his officials, and to govern his people through political enlightenment before rectifying his court with rules of etiquette, requiring his officials to carry out their duties, and bringing the common people into uniform actions. Such being the case, those who are nearby will come closer, and those who are far away will pledge their allegiance to him. With those who are above and below being of one mind and the three armies making

---

[13] Ballads from the States, *The Book of Songs*.

a united effort, his reputation is influential enough to overawe all under Heaven and his force is sufficiently powerful to conquer all under Heaven. He gives directions with his arms folded and none of the brutal forces will refuse to obey him. It is just like a combat between the giant Wuhuo and the dwarf Jiaoyao. This may be briefly described, as a saying goes, that it is hard to serve a strong and brutal state but easy to bring it into service.

Chapter 11
On Governance

Synopsis

Since a state is the most powerful instrument and the ruler of men occupies the most powerful position under Heaven, he who rules must be aware of holding the position by following the fundamental principles that promise great security and prosperity, for otherwise there will be great danger and disaster, even a tragic ending like King Min of Qi who, facing threat of death, sought in vain to be a common man. It can be seen that the ruler of men might be high in position but might fail to stay secure unless he follows the right way. By analyzing the different results from different ways of government, this essay offers a profound demonstration of the correct road to order and the essential points involved.

Two key elements—the responsibility of a ruler to carefully choose his prime minister and the government according to rites and regulations—are shown in the three types of government: the true rule established by righteousness, hegemony achieved through trustworthiness, and destruction led by intrigues and schemes.

While it is true that all men desire happiness, an enlightened king should remember his duty and the principles he should follow to achieve order before finding happiness in it. Therefore, if a ruler should guard his state, he would have to appoint a prime minister after consultation as to his virtue and competence and use his officials well according to their abilities. This is in agreement with the essential requirements of ritual and laws. If a ruler should take over the world, he would have to be sure how to unify the people and find wise gentlemen for assistance, just as what he should do in safeguarding his state. It is particularly difficult to choose the worthy and capable since a ruler would often rely on his own bias and preference, and therefore exclude the worthy and promote men out of partiality, which is fatal to his honor, security and survival.

Following the four elements that reflect the efficiency of government, i.e., rule of law, worthy ministers, honest people, and refined customs, Master Xun concluded with a summarized analysis of the key of ritual and laws, the key for rulers of men, as well as the causes of difference in individuals and customs.

Text

A state is the most powerful instrument and the ruler of men the most powerful position under Heaven. Control the state and hold the position with Dao and there is great stability and prosperity. This is the source from which a good reputation is built up. To control the state and hold the position without following Dao involve grave danger and disaster. It would be better not to have them, for, in the worst situations, it would be impossible for one to choose to be an ordinary man as in the cases of King Min of Qi and King Xian of Song.[1] Thus, a ruler with the most powerful instrument and position of the world cannot guarantee security with nothing done; he must follow Dao for that purpose.

So, he who governs a state may become a true ruler if he observes the principle of righteousness, a hegemon if he honors his promise, and a loser if he engages intrigues and schemes. A wise ruler must be careful in choosing from the three alternatives. And a man of virtue should be clear about them.

Governing a state by promoting rite and morality rather than by doing them harm by any means, a man of virtue will never commit an act against righteousness or kill an innocent even if he could gain all under Heaven by doing so. He will restrain his thought and defend his state with rite and morality as firm as a rock! All those who join him in government abide by the principle of righteousness. All the penal codes for the nation are laws and regulations in accordance with justice. And all aspirations that a ruler shares with his ministers are righteous. Under such circumstances, the people admire their ruler on the basis of righteousness and the foundation is solidified. With a solid foundation, the state achieves its stability and therefore there is peace under Heaven. Without so much as a pinpoint of land to plant an awl in it, Confucius sincerely trained his thoughts, controlled his behaviors and harmonized his words with righteousness. And from the day of his success, his name went down to later generations instead of being hidden from the world. Now if all the powerful feudal lords under Heaven are made to cultivate righteousness in their thoughts, judge their laws and regulations with righteousness, apply it in their government, and repeatedly emphasize it by means of reward and punishment so that it remains consistent from beginning to end, in such conditions, their reputation will grow and spread between Heaven and Earth and become as bright as the sun and moon and as loud as thunder! Hence, it is said, if a state becomes one with righteousness, it will become famous in a single day. Cases in point are found in King Tang of Shang and King Wu of Zhou. With Bo and Hao as small as a hundred *li* around each, they brought unity to all under Heaven, made the feudal lords their subjects and all places within reach paid

---

[1] King Kang of Song (328–286 BC), the last ruler of Song in the Warring States Period, who was defeated by King Min of Qi and died on his exile in Wei.

their allegiance. It was due to no other reason than the fact that they were righteous. This is what I mean when I say "he who governs a state may become a true ruler if he observes the principle of righteousness."

A ruler's virtue and his sense of righteousness may not be perfect yet; nevertheless, he may have a general idea of the principles of government and have won popular trust in his system of rewards and punishments as well as permissions and prohibitions. And his ministers and subjects are clear that he is credible. When government orders are released, even if failure and loss are spotted, they are not concealed from the public. When agreements are settled, even though failure and loss are discovered, the allies are not cheated. If things are like this, the army forces will be strong, the city defense works will be solid, and the enemies will be fearful. If a state is uniform in action and clear about the treaty of alliance, its allied states will be trustful. Even though it is out of the way and backward, it is still able to inspire awe under Heaven. Such examples are found in the Five Hegemons. If governmental enlightenment is not taken as the foundation, propriety and righteousness are not exalted, the rules of etiquette are not systematized, and the people's admiration is not from the heart. However, if strategies and tactics are regarded as important, the balance between labor and rest is given attention, the accumulation of necessary materials is emphasized, the preparedness against war is solidified and mutual trust is secured, there will be no rival under Heaven. This is why Duke Huan of Qi, Duke Wen of Jin, King Zhuang of Chu, King Helü of Wu, and King Goujian of Yue, all of whom being rulers of remote and backward states, could inspire awe under Heaven and form a threat to the central states. There was no other reason than the trust they enjoyed. This is what I mean by saying, "he who governs a state may become a hegemon if he honors his promise."

Governing a state by advocating merit and profit rather than promoting righteousness and trustworthiness, a ruler hankers only after gains without being afraid of either cheating his people out of minor profits or deceiving his allies in pursuit of great profits and constantly desires the possessions of others at the cost of neglecting what is already in his control. Under such circumstances, none of his ministers, subordinates, and the ordinary people will not be prevented from deceiving him. With the ruler and his subjects cheating each other, there will be fall and split between superiors and subordinates. In such a situation, his rival states and allies will scorn and distrust him. Even with intrigues and schemes becoming prevalent, the state cannot avoid being endangered and weakened, and it is doomed to perish. Such was the case of King Min of Qi and the Duke of Xue[2] who, with the powerful state under their control, constantly engaged in dashing about different states and making allies rather than devoting to the cultivation of rite and morality, taking political education as the basis or aspiring for the unification of all under Heaven. When strong, the state could destroy Chu on the south, subdue Qin to the west, defeat Yan on the north and conquer the middle state of Song. However, when attacked by the joint forces of Yan and Zhao, the king and his state perished like the dead leaves shaken and falling from a tree and suffered the greatest disgrace in the world. When later generations speak

---

[2] Also known as Wen Tian, a prime minister of Qi in the reign of King Min.

of bad men, they would surely mention them! This was due to no other reason than that they resorted to schemes and intrigues instead of following rite and morality.

The three alternatives discussed above are what a wise ruler should carefully choose from and what men of benevolence should be clear about. He who is good at making the choice will be in control of others; he who is not will be in the control of others.

The state is the biggest implement and the greatest responsibility under Heaven; therefore, it is necessary to determine the right position and place it there, for a perilous position would throw it into danger. It is also important to determine the right way and guide it along, for a road polluted by dirt and weed will be blocked, and a state in danger and obstruction will perish. The position here means the way of government and the persons involved in it rather than a geographical one with a boundary. Therefore, the way of a true ruler and the right person for such a true ruler will guarantee a successful rule, the way of a ruler by force and the right person for such a ruler will make a hegemon, and the way of self-destruction and the right person for such a loser will lead the state to destruction. The three alternatives discussed above are what a wise ruler should carefully choose from and what men of benevolence should be clear about.

Thus, the state is the greatest responsibility and it will not establish itself without being sustained through accumulation. A state is renewed generation after generation. The change lies in its successor rather than its system, or only in the jade article being worn and the gait being taken in walking according to one's position.

A day is as short as a morning and life as brief as a day; however, how is it that there are states that have lasted a thousand years peacefully? I would say that this is because they are sustained by laws and standards a thousand years old as well as trustworthy men of learning in the thousand years who put them into effect. A man cannot live as long as a hundred years old, but how could there be trustworthy men of learning of a thousand years? I would say that those scholars who restrain themselves with laws and standards that last a thousand years make themselves trustworthy just as long. Therefore, he who governs with the gentlemen who have accumulated rite and morality will become a true ruler, he who governs with the men of learning who are upright, sincere, and trustworthy will become a hegemon, and he who governs with the men engaging in schemes and subversion is doomed. The three alternatives discussed above are what a wise ruler should carefully choose from and what men of benevolence should be clear about. He who is good at making the choice will be in control of others and he who is not will be in the control of others.

He who rules over a state surely cannot depend on himself only. Since this is the case, prosperity and glory or decline and disgrace are determined by the selection of his prime minister. If a ruler is able, with the assistance of a capable prime minister, he will become a true ruler. If he is incapable but he is aware of both his fears and the importance in seeking talented persons, he will be strong. Otherwise, if he is incapable himself and unaware of both his fears and the importance in seeking talented persons, and he employs only those who use flattery and ingratiate themselves to him, the state will be reduced to an *état faible* and ultimately perish. A state receiving effective macro-control will be strong and eventually rule over the world;

otherwise, if it is given attention only at the micro level, it will be weakened and ultimately perish. A state in control partially at the macro level and partially at the micro level manages to survive. The macro-control starts with morality followed by profit and makes use of those who are capable without regard to either closeness or distance in relationship and nobility or lowliness in status. Such is called macro-control. The micro-control starts with profit followed by morality and makes use of those who flatter and ingratiate themselves to their superiors regardless of right or wrong. Such is called micro-control. Governance at the macro level is like that, governance at the micro level is like this, while governance partially at the macro level and partially at the micro level is somewhere in between. The saying "He who has it pure is a true king for sure, he who has it impure a hegemon he may secure, and he who has none is fatally done." refers precisely to them.

A state without ritual will fall into disorder. Ritual is to the order of a state what scales to weight, the ink-line to straightness, and compass and square to circles and rectangles: once they are established, it is impossible for anyone to cheat, just like what is sung in *The Book of Songs*:

> They are like frost and snow, stern and fair;
>> Bright as sun and moon, whatever is laid bare.
>> Follow them and you thrive;
>> Without them, you are not to survive.[3]

There can be no joy for a monarch if the state is in peril. However, if the state is secure, there can be no worry to the people. Disorder leads to peril while order promises security. The rulers today urgently pursue pleasure but are sluggish in governing their states. Are they not absolutely wrong? This is analogous to one who loves colors and sounds but is content to go without eyes and ears. Is it not sad? Man is disposed to desire the most beautiful colors for the eyes, the richest sounds for the ears, the tastiest food for the mouth, the most pleasant smells for the nose, and the greatest ease for the mind. These are five inevitable extreme desires of man. To gratify these desires, there are conditions to be met. Without these conditions being satisfied, the gratification is unlikely. A state in possession of ten thousand chariots can properly be regarded as vast and rich. With the way to bring order and effect reinforcement, it will be fine and there will be nothing to worry about. The conditions will be available to satisfy those five desires. Thus, all joys arise in a state with good order, while all sufferings are produced by disorders of that state. Anyone who is in urgent pursuit of joys but is sluggish in governing his state does not truly know what joys are. Therefore, an enlightened ruler will bring order to his state first before deriving various joys from it. On the contrary, a stupid ruler will be quick in his pursuit of pleasures and slow in his attempt to govern well; therefore, he will have to face countless troubles, but he will not stop till the destruction of the state and his death. Is it not lamentable? He desires joy but it turns out to be sorrow, he expects security but is found in peril, and he intends to be happy but ends in death. Is it not pitiable? Alas! May rulers of men examine the discussions above!

---

[3] Not available in the extant Chinese versions.

There is a way to govern a state, and its ruler has his duties. As for governmental affairs that can be handled effectively and at length in quite a number of days but have to be done in a single day, it is the business of the officials and functionaries he employs so that his enjoyment of ease and relaxation is undisturbed. What the ruler has to do is to appoint a prime minister after consultation and places him in charge of the officials and functionaries so that they follow the correct way and right orientation. In this way, he will rule over all under Heaven and match the fame of Yao and Yu. Such a ruler has very simple responsibility, but the tasks are carried out in precise detail; he experiences the utmost ease but enjoys the greatest accomplishments, wearing his robe loose and never leaving his comfortable bamboo mat. However, none within the four seas is reluctant to have him as their emperor or king. This is called the ultimate simplicity from which no greater joy is derived.

The ruler of men is capable in that he makes good use of others, while the common people are capable in that they have the capacity to do things themselves. A ruler can employ others to do things for him but ordinary people cannot shirk their responsibilities. A commoner with a hundred *mu* of land to farm is exhausted by his duties a lifetime because he cannot transfer it to others. Now a ruler has a single person to handle all the affairs under Heaven for him so that he has time more than enough to deal with few affairs because he makes use of other men. In managing as big as all under Heaven and as small as a state, if a ruler chose to do everything himself, there would be nothing more laborious and exhausting. If things were like that, even a slave would be unwilling to exchange post and responsibility with the Son of Heaven. So, why should a ruler do everything in person in the management of a country and unification of the four seas? He who does it follows the route of menial laborers advocated by Mohism. And he who appoints men according to their virtue and abilities follows the way of the sagely kings rigorously observed by Confucianists. It is said in an old book, "If farmers get their share of land to plow, merchants get their commodities to trade, craftsmen get their business to do, the gentry get their assignments to fulfill, feudal lords get their land to manage, and the Three Councilors lead in the discussion of the state's major policies, all that is left for the Son of Heaven to do is to wait with his hands down." When everything within and without is like this, nothing is unfair or out of balance and nothing remains unregulated. This is something in common with all kings and is in agreement with the essential requirements of ritual and laws.

With the basis of a hundred *li* of land, all under Heaven can be put under control. This is not false. The key factor is that the ruler knows how. Placing all under Heaven under control does not literally mean that the people of another state follow him carrying their land on the back; it means that he knows how to unify them. If all people are of one mind with him, how could the land go to anyone other than him? Thus, with a land of only a hundred *li*, the state has a complete hierarchy of ranks with sufficient supply of dress to accommodate all the worthy men under Heaven, and enough positions and offices to embrace all men of abilities in the world. If he chooses the good old laws and put them into practice, they will be sufficient to make obedient and submissive men who love profit. With the worthy men united, the men of abilities employed and the men fond of profit being submissive, all under Heaven comes under his control and nothing is left outside. Hence, a territory of a hundred *li* is sufficient to win all power with; with loyalty and trustworthiness being honored and benevolence and morality promoted, all people are won. Both being fulfilled, all under Heaven is obtained. Under such circumstances, the feudal lord who pays allegiance the last will be the first to find himself in danger. The trend toward unification is described in *The Book of Songs*:

> From the east to the west
> > And from the north to the south,
> > No one but obeys him.[4]

Yi and Pengmen were both expert archers to those who learn archery. Liang Wang and Fu Zao were both expert charioteers to those who learned driving. An intelligent gentleman is good at making people obedient. If people obey him, he has the authority; otherwise, he loses it. Therefore, a true ruler can do nothing till his people submit to him. If a ruler wishes to get archers who can hit a small target from a distance, none is better qualified than Yi and Pengmen. If he wishes to get charioteers who can cover a great distance very fast, none is more skilled than Liang Wang and Fu Zao. And if he wishes to conquer the states of Qin and Chu and unify all under Heaven, none is wiser than the intelligent gentlemen, who apply less wisdom and try less hard but make great achievements and who are optimistic and easy to please. Hence, an enlightened monarch considers him a precious treasure while a stupid ruler regards him as a tough nut.

It is the common human desire both to be as noble as the Son of Heaven, rich as to possess all under Heaven, and famous as a sagely king to be in control but not in the control of others. A true ruler has all these. It is also the common human desire to wear colorful clothes, eat food with rich flavors, have plenty of things for use, and exercise control over all under Heaven. With rich food and drink to consume, grand music and dance performances to enjoy, lofty pavilions and high terraces to show, spacious parks and gardens to visit, feudal lords to command and the power to unify all under Heaven—these are also what people naturally desire. And the ritual principles of the Son of Heaven regulate in this very fashion. With regulations being promulgated and government decrees all-encompassing, an official who neglects his essential duties will be put to death, any one of the three dukes or feudal lords who neglect ritual will be incarcerated in solitary confinement, and any state within the four corners that displays a dissolute and rebellious spirit will be destroyed. To be brilliant as the sun and moon in fame, to be great as Heaven and Earth in accomplishment, and to have all the people under Heaven responsive like an echo or shadow—these are also what people naturally desire, and only a true ruler may enjoy them. Thus, it is the natural disposition of a person to have good flavors for his mouth and nothing is more delicious than what a true ruler may eat, to have pleasant sounds for his ears and nothing is greater than the music a true ruler may hear, to have rich colors and feminine charms for his eyes and nothing is more beautiful than what a true ruler may enjoy, to have ease and comfort for his body and nothing is easier and more comfortable than what a true ruler may feel, and to have good profit for his heart and

---

[4] Major Court Hymns, *The Book of Songs*.

nothing is more abundant than salaries a true ruler may have. To be in possession of everything that is desired by all under Heaven, to firmly control all under Heaven like his children and grandchildren, who could look upon this prospect and not be filled with delight if he is not utterly mad, deluded, stupid or ignorant? Rulers who desire all these are found everywhere and men who are capable of bringing these about have never been absent in any generation, but for the past thousands of years there has been no single case in which both come together. Why? The answer is that no ruler of men has ever been impartial and no subject has ever been loyal. The rulers of men have excluded the worthy to promote men out of partiality. Their subjects have wrangled over official positions and have been jealous of the worthy. This is why there has never been a case in which the two meet. Why not widely collect worthy men who are genuinely able without considering whether they are close or distant in relationship and regardless of whether they are noble or humble in status? In so doing, the ministers would consider official positions less important, yield to those who are more worthy and able and willingly follow them. If things were like this, there would be another Shun or Yu and the great cause of a true ruler would arise. Were there anything more pleasing and beautiful than the great achievement of unifying all under Heaven and the reputation matching that of Shun and Yu? Alas! May the rulers of men be able to see what these words mean! Coming to a crossroads, Zhu Yang lamented, "This is where one may take a half step in the wrong direction but will realize later that he has made a blunder of a thousand *li*!" and wept sadly. When it comes to employing people, it is also a crossroads leading to glory or disgrace, security or danger, and life or death. A mistake committed here would be more lamentable than traveling. Alas! How sad it is! For a thousand years the rulers of men have not been awakened to this.

No country but has laws that guarantee order or laws that lead to chaos, men of learning who are worthy and unworthy, people who are obedient or rebellious, and customs that are good or bad. When both situations coexist, a country survives; with the former conditions being dominant, a country is secure; with the latter cases getting the upper hand, a country is in peril. With the four former states available, one rules; otherwise, with the presence of the four latter states, one perishes. If its laws bring about order, its ministers are worthy, its people are honest, and its customs are refined, the uniform presence of these four makes supreme order. In such conditions, a country will win without fighting, gain without attack, and conquer without striking a blow. Basing on Bo and Hao, both being territories of a hundred *li* across, King Tang of Shang and King Wu of Zhou succeeded in unifying all under Heaven, so that all the feudal lords submitted to their rule, and all lands within reach swore their allegiance to them for no other reason than that these four factors were uniformly present. In contrast, even though King Jie of Xia and King Zhou of Yin were in control of all power under Heaven, they failed to realize the wish to be an ordinary man when defeated due to no other cause than that the former four factors were absent. Thus, kings may adopt such different approaches to government, but only one principle works in the final analysis.

No superior fails to show his love for his subordinates and govern them according to ritual principles. He treats them as if they were babies. Governmental ordinances, regulations, and standards are established to govern the population; therefore, they cannot be applied to the people if there were the slightest flaw, even to orphans, childless old couples, widows, and widowers. For this reason, the people were so close to their monarch that they look up to him as their parent. They would rather be killed than disobey him. Superiors and their subordinates, including a monarch and his ministers, both old and young, either noble or base, all the way down to commoners—all regard it as the highest standard and examine themselves to ensure that they devote their attention to their duties. This is what all the kings share up to now and the key of ritual principles and laws. Accordingly, farmers divide up the fields and plow them, merchants divide up commodities and trade them, craftsmen divide up tasks according to their skills and exert themselves, the gentry divide up government positions and shoulder their responsibilities, the lords of all the feudal states share the land and guard them, the Three Dukes take charge of fundamental policies and discuss them, while all that the Son of Heaven need to do is to look on with hands folded. With things like this both inside and outside the court, nothing in the world is left unbalanced or in disorder. This is the same for all kings. It is the essence of ritual principles and laws.

As for routine affairs of government, including weighing and considering balance, each thing is put to proper use, clothing is properly specified, palaces and other buildings are constructed according to proper measurements, attendants and servants are of set numbers, and articles and utensils for funeral and sacrificial rites and observances are sorted according to ranks. These regulations are applied to the myriad things with all measurements of length meeting the standards and are executed by officials of all levels without informing their monarch in detail. Thus, if the ruler of men establishes correct lofty principles of government for his court and appoints truly benevolent men to various posts, then he will be at ease, the state will be well-ordered, his accomplishments will be great, his reputation will be fine, and he can further make himself a true ruler or at least become a hegemon. Otherwise, if he fails to establish correct and lofty principles of government for his court and appoint benevolent men to various posts, he will have to toil himself but achieve nothing and fall into disgrace, and his state will be thrown into disorder and exposed to threat. Thus, here lies the key for the ruler of men. Therefore, the proper appointment of a single person will win all under Heaven while the improper use of a single person means danger to the state. There is no such thing as being unable to properly use a single person but being able to properly use thousands or hundreds of men. Since he can properly use a single individual, why should he toil himself? There will be peace under Heaven when ritual is observed. It was for this very reason that King Tang made use of Yin of Yi, King Wen of Shang Lü, King Wu of Duke of Shao and King Cheng of Duke of Zhou. Less wise were the Five Hegemons, among whom was Duke Huan of Qi, who spent his time in the imperial harem indulging in music and other extravagances and amusing himself. However, he was not regarded with contempt, for he succeeded in assembling the other feudal lords on many occasions so that unity was once achieved under Heaven and he himself became an overlord. It was due to no other reason than that he knew to entrust the entire government to Zhong Guan. This is the essential principle a ruler must observe if he wants to become the ruler of men. Those who are wise will find it easy to follow their examples so as to strengthen their power, and their accomplishments and reputation are extremely great. For them, what else is worth doing? So, in ancient times, those who made great accomplishments and enjoyed great reputations must have followed this route while those who lost their countries and endangered themselves must have done the opposite. That is why Confucius exclaimed, "Those who are wise certainly know much but they focus on the few things that are crucial. So how can they not be insightful? While those who are stupid know little but tend to so many things, how can they not turn things upside down?"

When those engaged in governing a state are determined in status, the monarch and his ministers and other officials each should carefully attend to what they should hear and give no heed to what they are not supposed to hear, pay attention to what they should see and neglect what they are supposed to overlook. If each of them hears or sees what they should do according to their positions in the social hierarchy, even the people living in far isolated places or out of the way will accept their positions and act dutifully in order to obey their superiors. Such are the characteristics of a well-ordered state.

In governing his state, a monarch controls what is nearby rather than what is far away and what is prominent rather than what is obscure. He seizes the key link instead of dealing with a miscellany of trivial matters. If he is able to properly govern what is close, then what is remote will be in good order. If he is able to properly manage what is prominent, then what is obscure will be transformed. If he is able to put under control what is most important, then all other matters will follow the right rules. To be able to govern all under Heaven and still have abundant time as if having nothing much to do, such is the height of good government. To be able to manage what is close but attempt to manage what is far off, to be able to deal with what is prominent but attempt to deal with what is obscure, and to be able to grasp the key but attempt to control all the trifles—this is going too far and going too far is as bad as not going far enough. It can be likened to seeking a crooked shadow by erecting a straight log. To be unable to manage what is close but still attempt to manage what is far off, to be unable to deal with what is prominent but attempt to deal with what is obscure all the same, and to be unable to grasp the key but attempt to control all the trifles—this is all erroneous. It can be compared to seeking a straight shadow by erecting a crooked log. Hence, an intelligent ruler emphasizes essential principles whereas a benighted ruler attempts to control everything. A ruler emphasizing essential principles has everything complete whereas a ruler attempting to control everything lies all things in waste. The duty of a ruler is to choose a prime minister, establish a set of laws, and set an aim. By these means he commands all, illuminates all and demonstrates his accomplishments. A prime minister, in turn, is supposed to choose officials for all offices and supervise the execution of all affairs so as to readjust the official responsibilities for ministers and other officials and functionaries in the royal court, to measure their achievements and efforts, to assess their appropriate commendations and rewards so that he can present their achievements and merits to the ruler at the end of the year. If qualified, they are retained; otherwise, they are dismissed. Hence, the ruler of men takes great pains to choose a prime minister but rests at ease when he is employed.

He who governs a state is wealthy when he gains the strength of his people, strong when he obtains their willingness to die for him, and honored when he wins their praise. If he gets all the three, he will have all under Heaven; otherwise, if he loses all of them, the world will abandon him. He to whom all the world comes is called the true ruler and he whom the whole world abandons is lost. Tang and Wu followed this principle, practiced what was righteous, did what was beneficial and eliminated what was harmful to the world; therefore, all the world came to them. So, a ruler should stress moral virtue so as to lead his people, clearly define rite and morality to guide them, be trustful and honest in order to take good care of them, elevate the worthy, employ the able, appoint them to proper positions, and grant titles, costumes and other rewards to emphasize the importance. He should make his people work according to seasons, lighten their obligations and make readjustments for coordination. He should look after them completely and nourish and support them as if they were newborn babies. In nurturing the people, he should be generous; in employing them, he should be reasonable. Governmental orders, regulations and standards are made to govern the people under Heaven, so they should not be applied even to widowers, widows, orphans and other solitary persons if they have the slightest bit against reason. Thus, the people worship their monarch as god, love him like their parent, and fight and even die for him willingly. This is due to no other reason than the fact that he is virtuous and enlightened and the benefits and advantages he brings them are genuinely substantial.

In a disordered age, things are different. People are guided by corrupted, neglectful, aggressive actions and robbery and exposed to political trickery and schemes against one another; the state affairs are disrupted by intercessions of court entertainers like actors, clowns and dwarfs and women of the harem; the foolish are arranged to instruct the wise and the unworthy are placed above the worthy; the ordinary people are made to live in utter poverty and labor extremely hard. For this reason, the common folk despise their ruler as a witch, hate him like a ghost, and wait each day for their chance to desert him, trample him under their feet, and banish him. Confronting unexpected invasions, they will not die on his behalf as expected and no persuasion will win them over to them. That is why Confucius said, "You will be treated by others in the same way you treat them."

What endangers a state? The answer is: to place petty men over the common folk and let them abuse the power they are granted, and to rob the ordinary people by improper means—these are great calamities that endanger a state. If the ruler of a big state is fond of securing petty profits, it is a danger to the state. If he develops increasing fresh desires when he is satisfied with such usual ones like women and songs, terraces and pavilions, as well as parks and hunting grounds, it is dangerous to the state. If he covets what belongs to others instead of engaging in a good management of what is already in his possession, it poses danger to the state. Cherishing the above three evil intentions in mind and choosing to commit governmental affairs to those who are interested in political trickery and schemes against one another, a ruler has little influence to exercise but much disgrace to his reputation and his country is surely in danger. Then he presents danger to the state. Being the ruler of a big state and being fond of deception and contrivance rather than exalting ritual and moral principles and observing laws of tradition, a ruler will be followed by the ministers at his court who will become accustomed to disregarding rite and morality and fond of trickery and schemes against one another. If the customs of the ministers at his court are like this, then the common folk will do the same and get used to ignoring rite and morality and coveting profit. If the customs of a ruler and ministers or the superiors and their subordinates are all like this, then even if the state possesses a broad land, it has little power of influence. Even though it has a big population, its armies are necessarily weak. No matter how numerous its punishments and penalties are, its edicts will not likely to be put into effect below. This is a state in peril and such a ruler represents danger to the state.

He who advocates Confucianism does not act this way. He surely takes every detail of things into consideration. At the court, he surely exalts rite and morality and makes certain the difference between the noble and the lowly. In such a situation, the gentry all regard their integrity as important and determine to die for the legal system, and the ministers observe the same system and pay attention to their responsibilities and emoluments. Under such circumstances, all the functionaries under them will fear the laws and abide by the rules and regulations; passes and markets will be monitored but no tax or duty is imposed, and price contracts as well as prohibitions and interdictions will be verified to ensure that they are enforced with impartiality. With these being guaranteed, none of the merchants will fail to be honest and harbor deceitful intentions; all craftsmen will fell and collect timber in proper seasons, be granted enough time for their work and give full play to their skills and techniques. In such cases, none of them will fail to be honest and trustworthy and turn out rough and shoddy work. Taxes on the fields in the countryside will be lightened, collection of money reduced, labor service rarely imposed, and farmers are never taken away from their fields in the busy farming season. In such conditions, no farmers will fail to work hard and undertake other endeavors. If the gentry emphasize their integrity and will die for the system, the army will be strong. If the functionaries are afraid of the laws and abide by the rules and regulations, the basic system of the state will not be turned into chaos. If the merchants are honest and harbor no deceptive intentions, trades and travels will be secure, goods and products well-circulated, and the needs of the state provided. If the craftsmen are trustworthy and do not make poor-quality products, utensils and other articles will be clever and handy and materials not in short supply. If farmers work hard on their land and spare little time for other things, nothing will be neglected because they do not fail to take advantage of the proper conditions of weather above, soil below and human cooperation in between. This is called the efficiency of government orders and the refinement of customs. When these conditions are met, there will be firm defense, powerful conquest, prestigious settlement in peace, and fruitful actions. This is what a Confucian scholar means by taking all details of things into account.

Chapter 12
On the Way of a Monarch

Synopsis

The way of a monarch is what should be followed by those who rule over a country. Two variables are analyzed here: the understanding of a monarch in governing his state introduced by a quote from *The Book of Songs* and the way to be followed by the rulers of men.

In contrast to the way of government and the persons involved in it as demonstrated in *On Governance*, the current essay further reveals that people are the more fundamental and critical factor in the government of a state. First of all, no law comes into force till someone competent carries it out, nor do regulations apply in specific cases till someone intelligent does it by analogy. Law has its origin in gentlemen since they have a total mastery of ritual principles whose essence lies in that everyone has his or her own identity, such as ruler and minister, father and son, brother, husband and wife, and so on. Furthermore, gentlemen are the root of good order and the tools of measurement are the branches. Therefore, it is essential for the ruler of men to understand that people follow the example of their superiors, and accordingly observe ritual and moral principles, honor the worthy, employ the capable and rid of the greed for profit; otherwise, his ministers and other officials will tailor the law to suit their selfish ends. So, self-cultivation is the fundamental principle of the ruler of men in bringing order to his country. "A monarch can be compared to the sundial and his people the shadow: when the sundial is straight, so is its shadow." That is, a ruler serves as the example of his people. In governing a country, it is man who plays a fundamental and decisive role in governing a country, which is constituted by cultivating oneself, loving the people, and honoring the men of learning.

The principles followed by a monarch includes love for his people by means of winning the allegiance of his subordinates and unifying the people, and honor for the men of learning by enlightening the government and refining the customs. When a ruler loves his people, he should be able to organize them and determine the social divisions with the highest goal of a full reflection of the ultimate Dao, "all under

Heaven follow him as though it were of a single body with him, just as the four limbs follow the dictates of his mind." The most direct way is the careful selection of a prime minister. He should observe certain principles in selecting the personnel and follow certain rules in using them. The principles he should observe in choosing men involve ritual requirements and the rules he should follow in employing them include restrictions according to rank, with consideration being taken into the need of the state and specific personal talents.

Text

There are monarchs who lead their states to chaos, but there are no countries that are necessarily chaotic. There are men who can bring about order, but there are no rules by which a state may create order of itself. Archer Yi's feats are not lost, but not every age has an archer skillful as Yi. Yu's laws have survived, yet Xia did not have a king like him in every generation. Thus, there is no law that comes into force spontaneously, nor can its regulations by analogy apply themselves in specific cases. With men who are competent, the law works; otherwise, it perishes. The rule of law is the foundation of good order and gentlemen are its origin; therefore, with gentlemen, laws may be implemented completely even if they are only sketchy. Otherwise, if there are no gentlemen who can put them into effect, laws may be applied in improper sequences, fail to deal with evolving affairs and are sufficient to create chaos even though they are formulated in detail. Making definite regulations without understanding the fundamental principles of law will necessarily cause confusion in dealing with specific matters in spite of their multiplicity. For this reason, an enlightened ruler makes haste to find the right men whereas a benighted ruler hastens to obtain power and influence. He who is eager to find the right men remains at ease and finds his country in good order, his accomplishments are extraordinary, and his reputation is great; he could either be a true king or become a hegemon. He who is eager to obtain power and influence rather than the right men will overwork himself but his state is still not in order, his accomplishments are undermined, his reputation is disgraced, and his country is gravely imperiled. Therefore, the ruler of men takes pains to find the right men for him and rests relaxed in employing him. *The Book of History* describes exactly this when it says, "Only King Wen was respectful and cautious in selecting a single man."[1]

Fitting together the halves of a tally[2] and the copies of a contract are means by which trust is established, but if a monarch is fond of schemes, then the ministers and functionaries of his ilk will take the advantage of this to engage in trickery. Drawing lots is a means by which impartiality is ensured, but if a monarch tends to be partial, his ministers and functionaries will take advantage of it to show favoritism.

---

[1] The Announcement to the Prince of Kang, *The Book of History*.

[2] Credentials with two halves, made of wood, bamboo, jade or metal, serve as a token by which authority if conferred.—Tr.

Steelyard and scales are means by which fairness is guaranteed, but if a monarch is interested in overthrowing justice, then his ministers and functionaries will take advantage of it to distort truth. Tools of measurement like *dou, hu, dun* and *gai* are designed for the purpose of uniformity in standards, but if a monarch is driven by greed for profit, then his ministers and functionaries will take advantage of them to take from the people without limit by collecting much but offering little. So, the tools of measurement are nothing but branches rather than the source from which good order comes; gentlemen are the sources. The officials watch over the measures and gentlemen maintain the source. When the source is clear, so is what flows out of it; otherwise, if the source is muddy, what flows out of it is dirty. Thus, if a monarch observes rite and morality, elevates the worthy, employs the capable, and is not greedy for profit, then his subjects will be extremely modest and loyal and will be diligent in serving as ministers. In such circumstances, even among the common folk, trust will be established without fitting together the halves of a tally or copies of a contract, justice will be ensured without drawing lots, fairness will be guaranteed without using steelyard or scales, and uniformity in standards will be achieved without a variety of utensils of measurement. In such conditions, people will be diligent without being encouraged and obedient without imposing punishment. Officials in charge will not have to toil before the affairs are done. Governmental edicts will not have to be numerous before the customs are refined. All the ordinary people will observe the laws of their monarch, follow his aspiration, work diligently for him and find peace and delight in it. When paying taxes, they are forgetful of the expenses; when working hard, they are forgetful of the fatigue; when confronting invasion, they are forgetful of death. The city walls will be solid without being reinforced, the weapons will be powerful without being sharpened, the enemies will submit without launching a punitive expedition, and the people of the four seas will be unified without waiting for a decree. This is called the utmost peace. It is described in *The Book of Songs* as.

> Under Heaven prevails the government by justice,
>> So that even Xu yields its surrender in the distance.[3]

Question: How to be a ruler of men?
Answer: He should govern by ritual principles and apply them everywhere without preference.
Question: How to be a minister?
Answer: He should wait upon the monarch according to ritual principles, be loyal and obedient and never relax.
Question: How to be a father?
Answer: He should be generous and kind, and follow ritual principles.
Question: How to be a son?
Answer: He should be respectful, loving, and extremely polite.
Question: How to be an elder brother?
Answer: He should be kindhearted and friendly.
Question: How to be a younger brother?

---

[3] Major Court Hymns, *The Book of Songs.*

Answer: He should be respectful, obedient and careful in doing things.

Question: How to be a husband?

Answer: He should be completely harmonious rather than dissolute and licentious; he should observe ritual principles and be clear about the distinction between husband and wife.

Question: How to be a wife?

Answer: She should be gentle and obedient and attend her husband when he watches ritual principles; be fearful, anxious and respectful all the same if he is otherwise.

Deviation from these ways of behavior leads to chaos; complete adherence to them leads to order. This has been fully proved.

Question: How can people behave themselves well all round?

Answer: They should thoroughly comprehend the ritual principles. In ancient times, the great Former Kings understood ritual completely before practicing it universally; therefore, they never failed to behave themselves properly. For the same reason, gentlemen are modest without being overcautious and respectful without being intimidated. They do not bow and scrape either in poverty or in frustration and are not arrogant with wealth and honor. They are able to cope with changes successfully. This is because they completely understand ritual. Thus, in regard of ritual, a gentleman observes and feels contented in it. In carrying out his duties, he is straightforward and without any fault. In respect to the manner of dealing with people, he is generous and tolerant, rarely complains and never stoops to flattery. As far as his own conduct is concerned, he is careful in self-cultivation and never pretends compliance. In dealing with unforeseen events, he is prompt, quick and full of self-confidence. In respect to Heaven, Earth and everything else, he devotes his attention to their ways in order to give full play to their potential for application rather than tracing their origins. When it comes to the relation with the affairs of officials and men with special skills and feats, he gives attention to the use of their accomplishments instead of attempting to compete with them. He is untiringly loyal and compliant to his superiors and fair and impartial to his subordinates. In social communication, he seeks those who cherish the same ideals and remains loyal to them. And dwelling in his home village, he is forgiving within the boundary of order. For these reasons, he enjoys a good reputation when in difficulty and surely accomplishes if successful. His infinite kindness extends to all under Heaven and his wisdom enables him to stay free from any doubt in confronting the myriad changes. Good-humored and broad-minded, he fills up the space between Heaven and Earth with moral integrity and righteousness and his benevolence and wisdom reach the limit. This is called a sage with a total mastery of ritual principles.

Question: How to run a state?

Answer: I have heard of the way to improve oneself, but I have never heard about how to run a state. A monarch can be compared to the sundial and his people the shadow: when the sundial is straight, so is its shadow. A monarch can be likened to a plate and his people water: if the plate is round, the water in it looks round, too. If a monarch is fond of archery, his ministers will attempt to be ready for shooting. King Zhuang of Chu likes slender waist; consequently, there were men starving themselves in his court. That is why I said, "I have heard of the way to improve oneself, but I have never heard about how to run a state."

A monarch is like the source of his people. If the source is pure, the flow is pure, too. Otherwise, if the source is muddy, so will be the flow. Hence, he who has a state but fails to love or benefit his people will not succeed in winning people and making them love him. If the people are not won to love him, it is impossible to have them serve or die for him. When it is impossible to have his people serve or die for him, it is unlikely that his armies will be powerful and his cities are firmly defended. Without powerful armies and well-defended cities, he will fail to expect that no enemies will invade his country. Consequently, it is beyond hope to escape danger, remain intact or survive when enemies come. Confronting danger, destruction and death but still seeking comfort and pleasure—this is what an arrogant ruler does and is done regardless of time. So, if he wants his armies powerful, his cities firmly defended, and himself comfortable and happy, the ruler of men had better return to his people. If he desires to win the allegiance of his subordinates and unify the people, he had better return to government. If he wishes good order and refined customs, he had better seek the right men for assistance. There are many such men and those who get them for their assistance are not absent in any generation. These men live in this age but aspire for the way of the ancient times. No prince or duke is fond of it; such men alone have interest in it. None of the people would follow it; only such men practice it. He who is fond of it is reduced to poverty and he who does it finds himself in difficulty. However, such men will still persist in their practice and do it without even a momentary pause. They alone are clear about what lies in the success or failure of the kings of former times; they can distinguish between security and danger or good and bad as easily as telling white from black. If such men are given important positions, all under Heaven is unified and all feudal princes become their ministers. If they are given minor roles to play, awe is inspired among their neighbors and enemies. Even if they are denied employment, the state suffers no disasters as long as they are not given permission to leave the land. Therefore, the ruler of men is secure if he loves his people and is honored if he likes the men of learning; he perishes if he chooses neither. It is just like what is sung in *The Book of Songs*:

The men of virtue are a fence;
 The broad masses are walls.[4]

Question: What is Dao?
Answer: It is the principle followed by a monarch.
Question: What is a monarch?
Answer: It is he who has the ability to organize.
Question: What does it mean to be able to organize?
Answer: It is to be good at supporting the people, govern them, employ them and ornament them. He who is good at supporting his people draws them close to him. He who is expert in governing his people guarantees security. He who is talented in employing his people is ensured happiness. And he who is skilled in ornamenting

---

[4] Major Court Hymns, *The Book of Songs*.

his people wins honor. If he possesses all these four skills, so that all under Heaven comes to him, he is said to be able to organize. Conversely, he who is incapable of supporting his people fails to draw them close to him. He who is inexpert in governing his people is not guaranteed security. He who is poor at employing his people fails to be ensured happiness. And he who is incapable of ornamenting his people is not honored. If he lacks all these four skills, all under Heaven will abandon him and thus he is called a bad ruler and will be forsaken by all. It is said, therefore, that with Dao a state survives and without Dao it perishes. Reducing the number of craftsmen and merchants, increasing the population of farmers, prohibiting thieves and bandits, eradicating treason and other evils—these are the ways to support the people. The Son of Heaven assisted by the Three Dukes and a feudal lord by a single prime minister, each senior official holding a position, the men of learning carrying out their duties and all being impartial and following the orders—these are the ways to govern the people. Awarding a rank by judging the virtue of a candidate and assigning an official position by assessing his ability so that everyone performs a duty that suits to his ability: the worthiest are made the Three Dukes, the worthier feudal lords, and the worthy the gentry—these are the ways to employ the people. Ornamenting clothes and hats by embroidering certain designs and engraving different patterns on various utensil so that they signify different ranks—these are the ways to ornament the people. Thus, from the Son of Heaven down to the common people, none fails to give full play to their talents, realize their aspirations, and find security and happiness in their duties. These are things they share in common. They wear warm clothes, eat their fill, live in security, and travel for pleasure. The government affairs are handled timely, governmental regulations are clearly understood, and daily supplies are adequate. These are the same wishes they share. As to decorative patterns in multiple colors embroidered on clothing and precious delicacies composed of various flavors, they are the reflection of abundance. A sagely king tailors abundance to make differences so that distinctions are drawn between the able and virtuous as well as the noble and base, and contrasts are made between the young and old as well as the close and distant. As a result, all under Heaven, from princes and dukes up in the royal court to the ordinary men down under, is clear why such differences are made: it is for the purpose of clarifying social divisions and securing order so that peace is guaranteed for all generations to come. Thus, the Son of Heaven and the feudal lords make no excessive or wasteful expenditures, the gentry are abstained from unrestrained conduct, officials of all levels are prevented from indolence or negligence in carrying out their duties, and the common folk are protected against evil or perverse customs and stopped from theft or robbery. This can be regarded as universal justice achieved. Therefore, it is said, "When there is order, abundance extends to the common folk; if chaos occurs, insufficiency reaches even princes and dukes." The contrast refers exactly to this.

The ultimate Dao is fully reflected when both ritual and laws are exalted and therefore the state is in good order, when the worthy are respected and the capable employed and therefore the people are conscious of the right direction to go, when all opinions are heard and judgements justly made and therefore any doubt is cleared up, when the diligent are rewarded and the indolent punished and therefore none remains lazy and idle, and when public consultations are held and a clear distinction is made between right and wrong and therefore all under Heaven is won. After that, people are distinguished in status and duty, things are done in the right sequence, men of talents and abilities are employed, and nothing is left undone. Then, business is done in the way of business and selfish approaches are stopped. The principle of public interest is highlighted and selfish intentions are put to rest. If things are like this, men of outstanding virtues will be recommended and those who are glib and cunning dismissed; those who are greedy for private gain will be checked and those of integrity and moderation raised. It is said in *The Book of History*,

> Those who anticipate the time should be put to death without mercy, so are those who are behind the schedule.[5]

Once formed, a habit is not to be changed; besides, each of the hundred tasks is done differently in the way our ears, eyes, nose and mouth are not to be substituted one for another. Thus, when duties are determined, none will neglect them. When ranks are established, the correct sequence will not be disturbed. When all opinions are given attention to and everything is clearly perceived, none of the hundred tasks will be delayed. If this is the case, none of those from the ministers and the hundred functionaries down to the ordinary people will hesitate to cultivate themselves and feel contented in their positions, and only those who are truly competent dare to accept responsibilities. The common folk are changed in their custom, the petty men are transformed in their thought, and those who are treacherous are converted to honesty. This may be called the summit of government by means of education. Thus, the Son of Heaven sees things clearly without looking, understands well without listening to explanations, becomes knowledgeable without thinking deeply, accomplishes while remaining at rest, and sits all by himself with all under Heaven following him as though it were of a single body with him, just as the four limbs follow the dictates of his mind. This is described as the full reflection of the ultimate Dao, just as it is sung in *The Book of Songs*:

> He who is mild and respectful
>   Has the foundation of virtue.[6]

The rulers of men are all eager for strength and averse to weakness. They long for security and hate danger. And they desire honor and hate disgrace. They share these inclinations whether it is the great Yu or the despot Jie. In what way is it convenient to realize the three wishes and avoid the three aversions? The answer lies in none other than the careful selection of a prime minister. Hence, a man intelligent but nonbenevolent is unacceptable, so is he who is benevolent but not intelligent. A man of both intelligence and benevolence is a treasure valued by the ruler of men who, with his assistance, makes a true ruler or a hegemon. It is unwise not to hasten to seek such a man; it is not benevolent not to put him in office when he is obtained.

---

[5] Punitive Expedition of Yin, *The Book of History*.

[6] Major Court Hymns, *The Book of Songs*.

There is nothing more stupid than to expect accomplishments by luck without the help of such a person.

The rulers of men today have six sources of trouble. They employ the worthy to do things but consult with the unworthy in making rules and regulations, make the wise deliberate on things but hold discussions with the stupid, and use those who are of good virtue to take actions but suspect them with advice sought from those who are corrupt and perverse. How can they be expected to succeed? The way in which they do things can be compared to erecting a straight log and worrying that its shadow might be crooked. None is more confused than this. A saying goes, "The charm of a beautiful woman is considered a disaster by those who are ugly, a fair-minded man is treated as a festering sore by many, and those who observe Dao are like a curse to the corrupt and perverse." Is it possible now to expect those who are corrupt and perverse to judge impartially whom they resent? Such eagerness is like raising a crooked piece of wood and expecting its shadow to be straight. Nothing is more confusing than it.

In ancient times, people did not do so. They observed certain principles in selecting persons and followed certain rules in using them. The principles they observed in choosing men involve ritual requirements and the rules they followed in employing them include restrictions according to rank. Their behavior and bearing were measured by ritual, their intelligence, thought and judgement were tested by the achievement they made, and their merit was assessed according to the accomplishments of their long-term effort. Thus, the inferior were not to be placed over the superior, the insignificant were not permitted to judge those in authority, and the stupid were not to make plans for the intelligent. In this way, no blunder would be made in myriad actions. Therefore, adopt ritual norms to observe a person and you see whether he could stay respectful, place him in constant change and you see whether he is able to adapt himself to the environment, let him be easy and comfortable and you see whether he could keep from being dissolute and abandoned, and expose him to music and women, power and profit, resentment and anger, worry and danger and you see whether he could refrain from deserting his post. In this way, it would be as striking as black and white whether he possessed those good qualities or not. Could there be any distortion or perversion of the truth? Just as Bole could not be deceived about whether a horse was good or bad, a gentleman cannot be cheated into believing whether a person is good or bad. Such are the principles observed by a wise ruler.

If the ruler of men desires to obtain expert archers who can hit the center of the target from far away, then he should attract them with the prospect of a noble rank and a substantial reward. He should neither favor his sons and cousins within the royal house nor neglect those from remote places. Those who can hit the target are chosen. Is this not surely a way to obtain them? Even a sage cannot alter it. If he desires to obtain expert chariot drivers who can cover a great distance at the highest speed, say three hundred *li* a day, he should draw their attention with the prospect of a noble rank and a substantial reward. He should neither favor his sons and cousins within the royal house nor neglect those from distant regions. Those who make it are chosen. Is this not a sure way to secure good drivers? Even a sage could find no better alternatives. If he desires to bring order to his state, get his people in control, and coordinate and unify superiors and subordinates so as to be able to defend the cities from within and ward off invasions from without. Good order in a state guarantees its control over others rather than otherwise while chaos invites imminent danger, disgrace, destruction and death. However, in seeking high ministers for assistance, he is anything but impartial. He employs only those whom he favors and who fawn over him. Is this not absolutely wrong? For this reason, a state turns weak soon although its ruler desires it to be strong, finds itself in danger soon although its ruler desires it to be secure, and perishes soon although its ruler desires it to survive. In ancient times, there were ten thousand states, but only over a dozen have survived. This is due to no other cause than that all other rulers were mistaken in this matter. So, a wise ruler may offer gold and jewelry to others in private, but he never gives official positions and responsibilities in this manner. Why is there such a difference? The answer is that the latter is fundamentally harmful to those he favors. If the man is incompetent and the ruler employs him, it means that the ruler is muddleheaded. If the man is incompetent but he pretends to be capable, it means that the man is deceitful. With a muddleheaded ruler above and deceitful ministers below, destruction and death are not far off. It is a way leading to harm for both. It was not the case that King Wen of Zhou was without noble relatives, children, brothers or favorites; extraordinarily he singled out Grand Duke of the common folk and used him. It was not at all because the old man was in his favor! Was he one of his relatives? King Wen was from the Ji clan while Grand Duke was surnamed Jiang. Was he one of the old acquaintances of King Wen? They had never met previously. Was he handsome? He was 72 years old then and already toothless. He was used nonetheless. King Wen did so to establish healthy principles and make evident a noble reputation for the benefit of all under Heaven. He alone could never make it true, no man other than Grand Duke was the right choice, and he chose and employed him accordingly. Thereupon, healthy principles were formulated, a noble reputation was made known, and all under Heaven came into his control. He established 71 states, 53 of which were under the control of the Jis alone, so that the sons and grandsons of Zhou all became feudal lords of the empire as long as they were not mentally mad or deranged. This was true affection for the ones he loved. Thus, following the great principles of the world to establish great merit under Heaven, he could show favor to those of his love, and those below might be turned into eminent feudal lords. It is said, therefore, that "Only a wise ruler is able to demonstrate true love for those he cherishes; a muddleheaded ruler will only do harm to those he loves." It means precisely this.

  Things outside a wall are beyond sight; voices beyond a village neighborhood are beyond hearing. However, it is a must for the ruler of men to know roughly what goes on in his territory whether it is far away beyond the horizon or close to him within the borders. Both the changes under Heaven and home affairs vary, and slackness and confusion may occur somewhere. However, the ruler of men has no way to learn of them. This means that he is restricted and hidden from truth. The ears and eyes are so limited in their power to gain a clear perception and the ruler of men has such a vast territory under his dominion. If he is unaware of some of these things, it will be dangerous. But how is he to be informed of them? The solution: he must have favorites and trusted attendants around him as soon as possible because they are doors and windows through which he can spy on what happens far away and supervise the masses. So, it will not do till the ruler of men has his favorites and trusted men around, who should be sufficiently wise in making plans and honest enough to make judgements. Such men are called the instruments of the state administration. The ruler of men cannot be deprived of the time for amusements and tours or leisure and comfort; nor can he escape from disease, death and other unpredictable changes. Such being the case with the ruler of men, things in a state come about like water rushing from a spring and trouble would arise if a single event fails to be responded properly. For this reason, it is said that the ruler of men cannot manage the state all by himself; he must be equipped as early as possible with an office desk to write on or a walking stick to lean on, whose roles are played by his ministers. Thus, it will not do for the ruler of men till he has for assistance competent ministers whose moral reputation is sufficient to convince the common people and whose intelligence is sufficient to suit to all changes. These men are called the instruments of the state administration. Interactions with the feudal lords all around should not be broken but need not be intimate; therefore, it will not do for the ruler of men till he has someone to fully convey his intentions and resolve any doubts that may arise in faraway places. This man must be eloquent enough to remove trouble, intelligent enough to resolve doubts, resolute enough to ward off dangers. He will not return to report to his monarch till he fulfills his mission. And he should be qualified enough to cope with emergencies and protect the state against disasters. This man is called the instrument of the state administration. On the other hand, the ruler of men is called muddleheaded if he has no favors or trusted men around him, he is described as lonely if he is not assisted by competent ministers, and he is regarded as isolated if he does not have the right men to send as messengers to his neighbors. A man solitary and muddleheaded is said to be in peril. His state might survive; nevertheless, the ancients would regard it as dead. It is praised in *The Book of Songs*:

> Numerous is the array of talented men
>
> By whom King Wen enjoys his repose.[7]

It refers precisely to such cases.

Suiting the talented to right purposes: those who are honest, diligent, calculating meticulously and attentive to minute details without any error of omission are suitable clerks for specific purposes; those who are well-cultivated, upright, law-abiding, status-conscious, free from improper intentions, devoted to their duties and assignments, and not daring to add to or delete from the rules so that they are passed down to later generations without any damage are suitable gentry and functionaries; those who are conscious of observing ritual and moral principles by which their monarch is honored, showing goodwill to the men of learning by which a good reputation is won, loving the people so as to create peace in the country, maintaining the law for the purpose of unifying the customs, honoring the worthy and employing the capable so that an enduring efficiency is achieved, devoting their attention to the

---

[7] Major Court Hymns, *The Book of Songs*.

primary occupation of agriculture and prohibiting the insignificant occupations like industry and commerce so as to increase the wealth of the nation, keeping from the fighting over minor profits with their subordinates so as to achieve expediency in affairs, and clarifying regulations and making evaluations with practical purposes taken into account rather than rigidly sticking to set rules are suitable high ministers for assistance. However, they are not conscious of the way of a supreme ruler. Those who are capable of judging these three grades of talent and placing them in proper positions without any fault may be said as knowing the principles of the ruler of men. With such men in office, the ruler may stay at ease with great merit and a good reputation, and his country is in good order. He can make a true ruler, or a hegemon at least. These are essential to the ruler of men. On the other hand, if he fails in the judgement of these three grades of talent and is ignorant of this principle, condescends to overwork himself, and gives up the pleasures of the eye and ear, intending to deal with both big and small matters before bringing them to a finish each day, and considering to compete in cleverness or specialized expertise with his subordinates over trifles, it inevitably leads to chaos, which has been proved since ancient times. It is described as an attempt to look at what is beyond sight, listen to what is beyond hearing and do what is impossible.

Chapter 13
On Being a Minister

Synopsis

This essay discusses the way to be a loyal and faithful minister of the government. First of all, a classification of ministers is made on several levels. According to the contributions made, there can be fawning, presumptuous, meritorious and sagely ministers. According to what have been done for the monarch, there can be obedient, flattering, loyal, and assuming ministers. According to the manner in which their devotion is expressed and the effect thereof, there can be remonstrant, admonitory, assistant, or rectifying ministers.

In serving as a minister, it is necessary to distinguish among a sagely monarch, a mediocre, and a tyrant when devotion is shown. When it comes to self-cultivation, it is a must to observe the fundamental principles of benevolence and reverence. Three special cases are mentioned at the end as a supplementary explanation, which are comprehensible only to an enlightened ruler.

Text

There are various types of ministers: some are fawning or presumptuous while others are meritorious or sagely. Fawning ministers are unqualified in helping to unify the people at home or defend the nation against troubles from abroad, unpopular with the ordinary people and untrustworthy in the eyes of the feudal lords. However, they are artful, quick-witted, and silver-tongued and therefore win favors from above. Presumptuous ministers are not loyal to their monarch above but are skillful in obtaining a good reputation from the people, disregard public principles and universal norms, form factions and cliques and engage in activities of deception against the ruler and for personal gains. Meritorious ministers are competent in helping to unify the people at home and guarding the nation against troubles from abroad, popular with the ordinary people, trustworthy to the men of learning, loyal to their monarch, and they care for the people tirelessly. And sagely ministers honor their monarch above and love the people below, serve as examples for the people to follow in promoting governmental orders and instructions of civilization, respond instantly to unexpected occurrences and changes like an echo, and draw inferences from the categories by analogy in handling cases without a precedent, so that everything is well-done with regulations represented. Accordingly, he who employs sagely ministers will be a true king, he who employs meritorious ministers will be strong, he who employs presumptuous ministers will be in danger, and he who employs fawning ministers will be doomed. With fawning ministers in office, the ruler is sure to lose his life. With presumptuous ministers in office, the ruler is sure to lose his throne. With meritorious ministers in office, the ruler is surely promised with glory. And with sagely ministers in office, the ruler is surely honored. Seen from this perspective, Qin Su[1] of Qi, Marquis Zhou of Chu, and Yi Zhang[2] of Qin may be called fawning ministers, Quji Zhang of Han, Prince Fengyang of Zhao, and Prince Mengchang of Qi may be called presumptuous ministers while Zhong Guan of Qi, Fan Jiu of Jin, and Shu'ao Sun of Chu may be called meritorious ministers and Yin of Yi of Shang and Grand Duke of Zhou may be called sagely ministers. Such are the various types of ministers and these men are typical examples of the auspicious and worthy and the inauspicious and unworthy. A ruler must be careful to remember these points in choosing his ministers, for they are of quite adequate value for reference.

To follow the orders of a monarch for his benefit—this is called obedience. To follow the orders of a monarch at the expense of his benefit—this is called flattery. To violate the orders of a monarch for his benefit—this is called loyalty. To violate the orders of a monarch at the expense of his benefit—this is called presumptuousness. To cater to a monarch for the sole purpose of salaries to support one's hangers-on, regardless of his honor or disgrace and indifferent whether the condition of the state is good or bad—this is called a threat to the state. When the monarch has faulty plans or erroneous actions that will endanger the nation and eventually might destroy the country, if a minister, a father, an elder brother or anyone else is able to offer his suggestions before him and stays when his advice is taken or leaves when it is refused—this is called remonstrance. If anyone is able to present his advice and works on when it is accepted or sacrifices himself if it is refused—this is called earnest admonition. If any official has the capacity to assemble the wise to work together and gather all the ministers and functionaries to correct the fault of a monarch so that the state is delivered from possible disasters and protected against great harm, dignity is maintained for the monarch and peace is kept for the nation in spite of his majesty's restlessness and reluctance to condescend—this is called assistance. If anyone has the ability to fight against the errors of a monarch by taking advantage of the royal

---

[1] A native of Wei during the Warring States Period, who succeeded in persuading Yan, Zhao, Han, Wei, Qi and Chu to be united against Qin and eventually was killed in Qi.

[2] A native of Wei during the Warring States Period, who served as prime minister of Qin when King Hui of Qin was in reign. He made each of the six countries form alliance with Qin so that the alliances against Qin among the other states established with the initiation and assistance of Qin Su fell apart.

authority and defying the royal orders for the purpose of guarding the state against danger and delivering the monarch from disgrace so that his accomplishments suffice to bring about great benefit for the state—this is called rectification. Thus, men who actively remonstrate, admonish, assist, and rectify are true ministers of the state and are therefore treasures to the monarch. An enlightened monarch honors them and treats them well while a stupid or muddleheaded ruler regards them as a threat to himself. Thus, those whom an intelligent monarch rewards, a stupid monarch punishes; those whom a stupid monarch rewards, an intelligent monarch eliminates. It can be said that Yin of Yi and Jizi were men who remonstrated, Bigan and Zixu Wu were men who presented admonition in earnest, Prince Pingyuan was a man who assisted his monarch of Zhao and Prince Xingling was a man who rectified the errors of his monarch of Wei. This is like what is precisely advised in an old book: "Follow Dao rather than a monarch."

Employ the ministers who are upright and just and no partiality will be tolerated at the court. Trust the four types of men mentioned above and the errors of the monarch will not last long. If brave warriors are employed, enemies will disappear; when efficient ministers are stationed in the outlying regions, no loss of land will be suffered at the borders. Thus, an enlightened ruler takes delight in effective cooperation while a muddleheaded ruler chooses to work alone; an enlightened ruler elevates the worthy, employs the capable, and rewards them for accomplishments whereas a muddleheaded ruler is jealous of the worthy, afraid of the capable, and neglectful of their contribution. It is utter stupidity to punish the truly loyal and reward the treacherous because it is the very reason why Jie and Zhou were destroyed.

In serving a sagely monarch, it is natural to follow orders without presenting remonstrances or admonition. In serving a mediocre monarch, it is necessary to remonstrate or admonish without attempting to flatter him. However, in serving a tyrant, it is important to repair his defects and eliminate his faults without any attempt to correct his errors. If forced by chaos, one has nowhere to escape and is obliged to live under a tyrant, it is sensible to praise what good virtue he has, promote what he does rightly, speak of his strengths, avoid what is bad in him, conceal his failures, never mention his shortcomings and follow this as an established custom. It is advised in *The Book of Songs*,

> When major events will happen to the state,
> > Never divulge them to anyone
> > In case it should bring you any harm.[3]

The danger lies right in here.

Taking obedience as an ideal by being reverent, modest, compliant and responsive without venturing to make decisions or choices like taking or giving according to selfish interests—this is the principle to follow in serving a sagely monarch. Being loyal and trustworthy without attempting to toady; daring to remonstrate or admonish but not given to flattery; being firm, resolute and upright without selfish ideas or personal considerations; saying yes if it is right and no if otherwise—these are the

---

[3] Not available in the extant Chinese versions.

rules to observe in serving a mediocre monarch. Being accommodating but not adrift with the tide, flexible but not submissive, forgiving and tolerant without violating the principles, informing him of the ultimate Dao with nothing unaccommodating so that he might be transformed and constantly mindful of getting him to accept advice—these are proper ways to serve a tyrant. It is just like taming an unbroken horse, raising a newborn baby, or feeding a starving person: correcting his errors by taking advantage of his fears, helping him trace the source of his worries, bringing him onto the right road when he is happy, driving away what he hates when he is furious, and converting him indirectly. There is a similar piece of advice in *The Book of History*,

> Obey rather than disobey the orders and admonish carefully and tirelessly, and the monarch will be wise and his ministers modest.[4]

Serving one's monarch without being obedient means sluggishness; being vigorous but disobedient means lack in reverence; being reverent but disobedient means disloyalty; being loyal but disobedient means being without accomplishment; having accomplishments but being disobedient means absence of good virtue. Thus, being neglectful of virtue, it means harm to one's keenness in action, destruction to one's accomplishment, and negation of one's labor. It is something a gentleman does not choose to do.

There are those with great loyalty, those with considerable loyalty, and those with a low degree of loyalty, while there are those who are threats to the state. He who guards his monarch with virtue and transforms him is greatly loyal, he who tempers his monarch with virtue and assists him is considerably loyal, and he who remonstrates with his monarch about his errors and enrages him is loyal but unwise, but he who caters to his monarch for the sole purpose of his salaries to support his hangers-on, regardless of his honor or disgrace and indifferent whether the condition of the state is good or bad is a threat to the state. The way Duke of Zhou served King Cheng may be an example of great loyalty, the way Zhong Guan served Duke Huan may be an instance of considerable loyalty, and the way Zixu Wu served Fuchai may be a case of loyalty that was of a lower grade and unwise. The manner in which Chulong Cao served Zhou may be regarded as an example of threat to the state.

He who is benevolent surely shows respect to others. As a general rule, if a man is unworthy, he is worthless.[5] Disregard for someone worthy is characteristic of birds or beasts and that for someone unworthy is equal to teasing a tiger. Being like a beast, one is likely to be aggressive; teasing a tiger, one is likely to suffer disaster caused by the danger. It is advised in *The Book of Songs*:

> Bare-fisted, they dare not fight a tiger,
>> Boatless, they dare not cross a river.
>> Of the reasons of fear they know one,
>> Of all the rest they are aware of none.

---

[4] Not available in the extant Chinese versions.

[5] An alternative interpretation is: If a man shows no respect to others, he is unworthy.—Tr.

> They proceed with caution and fear
> As though a bottomless abyss lies ahead,
> Or upon a thin stretch of ice they tread.[6]

The song refers exactly to such a situation. For this reason, he who is benevolent is surely respectful to others.

There is a proper way to show respect for all. He who is worthy deserves honor and respect; he who is unworthy demands fear and respect. You approach the worthy and honor them; you keep a distance from the unworthy and be respectful, too. Both are respected alike, but for different things. A benevolent person is characterized by loyalty, trustworthiness, integrity and honesty and bears no harm intention toward others, treating everyone the same. Being loyal and trustworthy by nature, he takes integrity and honesty as his guiding outline, follows rite and morality as codes of conduct, regards rank and order as principles, and the slightest words he says and the tiniest movement he makes may serve as a model for others. The pair of lines in *The Book of Songs*–

> Spread no slander, inflict no harm,
> Few will not follow you as their model.[7]

refers precisely to this.

Modesty and respect are representations of ritual, harmony and concord are the basis of music,[8] caution and care bring benefit, and wrangling and resentment lead to harm. So, a gentleman rests in ritual, enjoys music, remains cautious, keeps from fight or resentment, and there is no fault in whatever he does. A petty man is just the opposite.

Smoothness achieved through removing obstruction of loyalty, peace transformed from danger, and echo with disaster and chaos are three cases incomprehensible to an unenlightened ruler. Presenting earnest admonition before achievement in goodness, violating royal orders before establishment of merit, running the risk of one's life not for private interest, and being completely loyal and righteous—these are characteristic of the first case. A similar example may be found in Prince Xinling of Wei. Seizing power before being righteous, killing a tyrant before being benevolent, reversing the ruling order before being correct, with accomplishments matching those of Heaven and Earth and benefit extending to all the living—these are characteristic of the second case. Examples are found in King Tang of Shang and King Wu of Zhou. Chiming in with his monarch when the latter is found guilty, obeying his monarch regardless of principles, not caring whether right or wrong or straight or crooked, catering to his monarch for the sole purpose of his position, and being confused and ignorant—these are characteristic of the third case. Examples are found in Feilian and Wulai. It says in an old book,

---

[6] Minor Court Hymns, *The Book of Songs*.

[7] Major Court Hymns, *The Book of Songs*.

[8] Music, in the traditional sense, is inclusive of dance.

Order does not happen if there were no chaos, straightness is unlikely if nothing is crooked, and uniformity is impossible if there were no differences.

It is also sung in *The Book of Songs*:

He received the jade bars, small and large,[9]
> Which, like the pendants of a banner, bid the feudal states to follow.[10]

Both refer to this.

---

[9] Rank tokens of a state.—Tr.
[10] Eulogies, *The Book of Songs*.

Chapter 14
On Attracting the Men of Learning

Synopsis

This essay focuses on the way in which the ruler of men should do in order to recruit men of talents and use them well. First, in identifying such people, it is necessary for him to be impartial, selfless, aware of the ways of things, and good at distinguishing between good and evil, so as not to be fooled by rumors and gossip.

 Master Xun pointed out that the people would be won "where punishments and government regulations are fair and impartial" and the gentleman won "where rite and morality are perfected." Either the men of learning or the ordinary people would not obey till their state was enlightened in politics and emphatic on rite and morality. The land and the people as well as Dao and laws were the foundation of a state, and "gentlemen serve as the commander of Dao and laws and will therefore not be permitted even a brief moment of absence." The worthy gentleman were very important to the security of a state. Only when these gentlemen were employed could a long-term stability be guaranteed. A country without such gentlemen would be reduced to peril even if there were healthy laws. A monarch should sincerely keep his words and deeds consistent and put into practice his emphasis on employing the worthy.

 In governing a state well, measures should be taken step by step. Firstly, those in power must set a good example for the people to follow, treat the people generously, and implement rite and morality. Furthermore, proper investigations and sensible judgements should be made to contribute to coordination. Finally, the worthy should be honored, the treacherous dismissed, and awards and punishments implemented, with rewards being prevented from surpassing the limit of standard and penalties from abuse.

Text

What follows are the ways to listen extensively, discover men of worth in obscurity, honor the illustrious, dismiss the treacherous and advance men of virtue. A gentleman refuses to listen to the praises from those banding together in a party or a clique. He does not believe false charges against the able and virtuous. He will not approach those who become jealous of and attempt to obstruct or conceal the able and virtuous. He does not grant requests accompanied by goods, money, or gifts of animals. A gentleman is cautious in dealing with wayward sayings, perverse doctrines, unreasonable events, unhealthy plans, undeserved fame, and groundless accusations through unofficial channels. He listens carefully, examines what he hears, determines whether it is right or wrong before granting rewards or imposing punishment and takes immediate actions. When things are handled in this manner, no evil sayings, no evil teachings, no evil undertakings, no evil schemes, no evil reputations and no evil accusations will be ventured and honest sayings, honest teachings, honest undertakings, honest plans, honest reputations, and honest accusations will go unimpeded to the ruler. And this is called the way to listen extensively, discover men of worth in obscurity, honor the illustrious, dismiss the treacherous and advance men of virtue.

Where rivers and ponds are deep, fish and turtles gather there. Where mountain forests are luxuriant, birds and beasts assemble there. Where punishments and government regulations are fair and impartial, the common people make their home there. Where rite and morality are perfected, gentlemen settle there. Thus, when affected by ritual, a person is cultivated in conduct. When influenced by morality, a state is enlightened in its government. When ritual becomes universal and honorable reputation plainly evident, all under Heaven will show their respect. And when orders are executed and prohibitions enforced, the work of a true king is complete! This is sung in *The Book of Songs*,

> With benefit extending to the capital,
> All the four quarters find their peace.[1]

Rivers and ponds are the natural habitat of fish and dragons. Mountains and forests are where birds and beasts dwell. And a country is home to the people of all trades and professions. However, if rivers and ponds dry up, fish and dragons abandon them. If mountain forests are sparse, birds and animals flee them. And if a state loses proper governance, the people of all walks desert it.

People cannot settle in peace without land to live on; land is not secure without people to guard it. Without Dao and laws, people refuse to come. Without gentlemen, Dao and laws will fail to be implemented. Hence, the relationship between land and people and that between Dao and laws form the foundation of a state. Gentlemen serve as the commander of Dao and laws and therefore will not be permitted even a brief moment of absence. He who obtains them will succeed in creating order and correspondingly guarantee security and survival. He who loses them will be thrown

---

[1] Major Court Hymns, *The Book of Songs*.

into chaos and therefore found in peril and destruction. There have been cases of chaos in which good laws are in place; however, I have never heard of a single case from ancient times to the present in which chaos breaks out with the presence of gentlemen. An ancient book says,

Order is the creation of gentlemen while chaos is caused by petty men.

It refers exactly to this.

With the support of the masses, even Heaven may be moved. Full of joy, even the years are lengthened. Honesty and trust work wonders, while exaggeration and fantasy exorcise the spirit and soul.[2]

The problem with the ruler of men does not lie in talking about the use of the worthy, but rather in not sincerely using them. Speaking of employing the worthy is just by opening the mouth; dismissing them constitutes concrete action. When words and actions contradict each other, is it not difficult to understand how the ruler of men could really wish for the worthy to come and for the unworthy to withdraw? For those who hunt cicadas at night, the task rests in making their lamplight bright and shaking the trees only. If the light is not bright, even if they shake the trees very hard, it will be helpless. Now if any of the rulers of men could make his virtue brilliant, all under Heaven would be drawn to him just as cicadas are drawn to bright light.

In facing government affairs and dealing with the people, it is necessary to employ moral principles to adapt to changes, be magnanimous and tolerant toward people and guide them with respect—this is the beginning of government. Then proceed to help them by means of proper investigations and sensible judgements—this is the intermediate stage of government. After this, decide whether to promote or dismiss or reward or punish—this is the conclusion of governmental affairs. Thus, the first year is the start and the third year the end. If the order were reversed, government orders would fail to be implemented, the ruler and his subjects would resent each other, and there would be chaos as a consequence. It is said in *The Book of History*,

Even though the punishments and executions are just, they should not be implemented immediately. You can only say, 'I have not yet put things in order.'[3]

That is, education should be put in in the first place.

Measurements are the standard of things; ritual principles are the standard for moral integrity. Measurements are used to determine the relationship of quantity; ritual principles are adopted to establish the proper relationship among people. Virtue serves in granting social status and ability in appointing official positions. Generally speaking, standards and principles should be strictly observed while people should be nurtured with tolerance and care. Rigorous standards and principles promise civilization; tolerance and care lead to stability. When civilization is established above and stability is realized below, this is the summit of accomplishment and fame, and nothing can be possibly added to it.

---

[2] This part is inconsistent with its context. It is considered to be located somewhere in *Doing Nothing Improper*.

[3] The Announcement to the Prince of Kang, *The Book of History*.

A monarch is the top authority in a state; a father is the top authority in a family. With one person in authority, there will be order; with more than one held in authority, there will be chaos. From antiquity to the present day, there has never been a situation that lasts where two persons are exalted to contend for authority.

To be a teacher requires four qualities, a good training with profound knowledge being excluded. If he is dignified and rigorous and therefore awe-inspiring, one can be a teacher. If he is from 50 to 60 in age and therefore has public prestige, one can be a teacher. If he is able to read and interpret the classics without trespassing or violating against his master, one can be a teacher. And if he is well-versed in the subtleties and capable of their explanation, one can be a teacher. Such are the four elements required of a teacher, excluding a good command of profound knowledge as well as a good training. As water whirls back to its depth and leaves fall to fertilize the roots, a successful disciple gratefully remembers his teacher.

> No words are never properly responded;
>> No good virtue is never properly requited.[4]

These lines in *The Book of Songs* refer precisely to this.

Rewarding should not surpass the limit of standard and penalties should not be abused, for undeserved reward benefits petty men while excessive punishment harms men of good virtue. If, unfortunately, transgressions are unavoidable, it is better to confer rewards beyond what is warranted than inflict penalties to wrongful excess. Instead of harming the good men, let the wicked benefit.

---

[4] Major Court Hymns, *The Book of Songs*.

Chapter 15
On Military Affairs

Synopsis

This is an essay on military issues.

With the inheritance of the Confucianist tradition, Master Xun recommended King Tang and King Wu's art of war rather than the strength of offensive strategy advocated by others. He held that a true king should base his military actions on benevolence and righteousness for the purpose of suppressing violence, removing harm, and stabilizing the world instead of contending for profit. He believed that the key to using troops was to be good at unifying the people and winning their support rather than manipulate power and cheat. The military affairs of a benevolent ruler could gain the support and love of the people, so that he and his ministers were of one mind with the three armies and therefore were invincible.

Master Xun also believed that the fighting capacity of an army was intimately related with the government of the country and the people's hearts rather than isolated, and benevolence, righteousness, and ritual were the essentials of the matter. With ritual observed, order brought to the state and the people's attachment obtained, the foundation of a strong army was solidified, while strong armor and sharp weapons, high walls and deep moats, and strict orders and heavy penalties were insufficient.

Master Xun pointed out at the end, "he who annexes a state by virtue is a true king, he who does it by force will be weakened, and he who does it by wealth will be impoverished." If the emphasis was only on military conquests rather than moral education, the country would still go on the decline. If benevolence, righteousness and ritual were emphasized, the government was enlightened, the educated gentlemen were submissive and the ordinary people stayed in peace, then there would be consolidated strength of defense and great power of conquest. With strict enforcement of orders and prohibitions, the undertakings of a true king would be complete.

Text

General of Linwu and Master Qing Sun held a debate on military affairs in the presence of King Xiaocheng of Zhao.

The king asked, "May I ask about the essence of military affairs?".

"Taking advantage of the timeliness of Heaven from above and the topographical conditions of the Earth below," replied the general, "Observe the movements of your enemies, set out late but reach the battlefield before them. These are the essential points to remember in using the army."

"No," objected Master Qing Sun. "From what I have heard of the way in ancient times, the foundation of military undertaking and aggressive warfare lies in unifying the people. If the bow and arrow are not well adjusted, even Yi the master archer could not hit a tiny target. If the six-horse team is not trained to work in harmony, even Fu Zao the master driver could not get his chariot very far. Similarly, if the men of learning and the commoners did not attach themselves to their rulers, even King Tang of Shang and King Wu of Zhou could not be victorious. Thus, he who is good at winning the support of his people is the one who will be good at using the army. Therefore, what is essential in military affairs is to be good at winning the support of the people."

"I don't agree," said General of Linwu. "In military operations, what counts are situations, conditions and the strategies adopted, including expediency and trickery. He who is expert in using arms moves swiftly and secretly, and no one knows from where he comes out to attack. Wu Sun and Qi Wu adopted this method and met no rival under Heaven. So, why is it necessary to win the support of the people?"

"We are not talking about the same thing," replied Master Qing Sun. "What I am speaking about are the military affairs of a benevolent monarch and the aspirations of a true king. What you value are expediency and schemes; what you do involves attacking and seizing by means of trickery and deception. These are the business of the feudal lords. The army of a benevolent monarch is beyond deception. Those who can be deceived are indolent and negligent, or weak and worn, or not of the same mind between rulers and their subjects. So, let a tyrant like Jie deceive another Jie, he might win by chance if he is clever enough. However, let him deceive a ruler like Yao, it would be like throwing eggs at a rock or stirring boiling water with fingers, or jumping into big fire or deep water and getting burned or drowned. A benevolent monarch is of one mind with his generals and his three armies make concerted efforts. A minister in relation to his monarch, or a subordinate to his superior, is like a son serving his father or a younger brother serving his elder brother, or hands and arms serving to guard the head and eyes and protect the chest and belly. Trying to deceive and then attack him will be as useless as alerting him before launching an attack. Moreover, if a benevolent monarch rules a state ten *li* in size, he will be well-informed of the conditions a hundred *li* around. If he rules a state a hundred *li* in size, he will be well-informed of the situations a thousand *li* around. If he rules a state a thousand *li* in size, he will be well-informed of the circumstances within the four seas. He will surely have a thorough grasp of the situation and be alert, and his men will be united as one body. Thus, the soldiers of a benevolent monarch will become an army when organized, remain orderly when dissolved, turn into a long blade with a sharp edge of Moye sword when spread and dashed forward, and anything touching or blocking it will be cut off and shattered. Stationed in a circular formation or camping in the shape of a square,[1] his armies are immovable like a rock. Whatever butts against it will be smashed and utterly routed and have to flee in helter-skelter. As for the ruler of a violent state, who will help him in his aggressive expeditions? Those whom he brings along must be his people who are nevertheless close to me as though I were their parent and fond of me as if I were the fragrance of spices and orchids. Looking back at their own ruler, they will find him repulsive as if he were burnt, like a tattooed criminal or a sworn enemy. Even if they were by nature like Jie the tyrant or Zhi the robber, men would not like to hurt those they love for the sake of those they hate, would they? For if they did, it would be like the case of someone's children or grandchildren being forced to kill their parents or grandparents. They would certainly come to inform me instead. So how could there be any use of deception? Therefore, when a benevolent monarch rules, the state flourishes day by day. The feudal lords who pledge allegiance first gain security, those who lag behind will be in danger, those who contemplate resistance find their territory reduced, and those who turn against him will perish. *The Book of Songs* sings,

> King Tang raised high his banner,
> Held his battle-ax in a serious manner.
> He looked like a fiercely raging fire,
> And who dared to suppress his desire?[2]

It means exactly this.

"Well said," exclaimed King Xiaocheng and General of Linwu. "And may we ask what ways should a true king follow and what actions should he take in employing his forces?"

"Everything is up to Your Majesty," replied Master Qing Sun. "The generals are of less importance. Please let me explain why some of the kings and feudal lords are strong and therefore survive and settle in security while others are weak and consequently place themselves in peril and even perish. There is order in a state if its ruler is worthy; there is disorder if its ruler is incompetent. If a ruler honors rite and values morality, his state will be in order; otherwise, if he neglects rite and despise morality, his state will be in disorder. And the state in order is strong while that in disorder weak. This is the fundamental principle of strength and weakness. If a ruler deserves admiration, his subordinates are reliable; otherwise, if he is not admirable, his subordinates may not be reliable. If the subordinates may be reliably used, the state will be strong; if they may not, the state will be weak. This is a constant rule of strength and weakness. Honoring rite and determining merit according to achievement constitute the top policy; stressing salary and position and

---

[1] Implying the firmness like Heaven and Earth since in traditional Chinese view, Heaven is round and Earth is square.—Tr.

[2] Eulogies, *The Book of Songs*.

valuing integrity form the secondary approach; honoring merit and despising integrity are the last choice. Such are the general rules leading to strength or weakness. He who is fond of warriors will be strong; otherwise, he will be weak. He who loves his people will be strong; otherwise, he will be weak. He whose government decrees are trustworthy will be strong; otherwise, he will be weak. He whose people are of one mind will be strong; otherwise, he will be weak. He whose rewards are generous will be strong and whose rewards are meagre will be weak. He whose punishments inspire awe will be strong and whose punishments create contempt will be weak. He will be strong if his instruments, tools, weapons, and armor are solid, firm and easy to use; he will be weak if those types of his equipment are of bad quality and inconvenient. He will be strong if he is cautious in using his military forces; he will be weak if he is reckless in such actions. He will be strong if he has the sole authority and weak if the authority is shared by another. Such are the constant rules of strength and weakness.

"The men of Qi emphasize the art of attack and defense. He who kills one enemy by such art is rewarded with the amount of gold enough for redemption regardless of victory or defeat of the battle. Such policy may be adopted for minor battles or against weak enemies. If it were applied to major battles or against powerful enemies, there would be loss of morale in soldiers who would scatter like birds and the battles would be lost in no time. Such an army lead a state to destruction. There is no army weaker than this. It is hardly different from a group of men hired from the marketplace for fighting.

"The rulers of Wei choose their foot soldiers who meet these qualifications: they can wear a helmet and three sets of armor, wield the crossbow nearly a ton in strength, bear a quiver with 50 arrows on their back with a halberd placed on top of them and a sword at the waist, and run a distance of a hundred *li* half of the day carrying three days' provisions. Once they pass these tests, their families are exempted from *corvee* labor and are given special tax benefits on their lands and houses. In a few years when they go into decline, and these privileges cannot be taken away from them. With new soldiers selected, their benefits remain unaltered. For this reason, the income from taxes is meager though the territory of the state is large. Such an army poses a threat to the state.

"The rulers of Qin provide a narrow way of living for their people. They use them harshly, too. They coerce them with authority, reduce them to destitution, tempt them with awards and intimidate them with penalties, so that people under Heaven are made to realize that the only way to gain any benefit from their superiors is to fight for them. They are made poverty-stricken before being employed and given credit for the merit so that their accomplishments and rewards promote each other. Thus, success in taking the heads of five enemies means the control over five households in his neighborhood. This is a promise of the most numerous soldiers and the most powerful fighting capacity in an enduring period of time, as well as more land that yields taxes. For this reason, Qin has been victorious for four generations. It is not due to luck. Rather, it is a matter of course.

"So, Qi's skills of attack are futile before the foot soldiers of Wei, who in turn cannot resist the redoubtable warriors of Qin. However, the warriors of Qin are no rival to the highly disciplined troops of Duke Huan of Qi and Duke Wen of Jin, who are no match to the army of benevolence and righteousness of King Tang of Shang and King Wu of Zhou. Anyone who should try to meet them in battle would resemble something burnt being flung against a rock. The soldiers of the abovementioned states are in pursuit of awards and profits; they all follow the way of hired laborers who know nothing about honoring their monarchs, conforming to regulations, or maintaining their moral integrity. Any one of the feudal lords who could refine their soldiers with rite and morality would rise to defeat them!

"Thus, to stress authority and deception and value merit and profit in assembling troops and selecting soldiers involve cheating; to educate and transform the army by rite and morality promises coordination. In cheating those who are deceptive, cleverness and stupidity make some difference. To cheat those who are coordinated in action can be compared to destroying Mount Tai with an awl—none but the stupidest person under Heaven would dare to attempt it. A true king would refuse to make such an attempt. When King Tang and King Wu launched the expedition against Jie and Zhou, they only saluted their armies with hands folded in front. And even the powerful and violent states hastened to their service and punished them like tyrants, just as it is so recorded in *The Book of History*.

"When an army is highly coordinated, all under Heaven will be placed under control. If it is coordinated to a lesser degree, the neighboring states may be conquered. In assembling an army and selecting soldiers, if authority and deception are emphasized and merit and profit valued, constant victories will not be guaranteed. The troops will be strong sometimes and weak at other times; survival and destruction will alternate each other. This is an army of robbers and a gentleman will refuse it. That was why Dan Tian[3] of Qi, Qiao Zhuang of Chu, Yang Wei[4] of Qin and Ji Miao of Yan, who were generally believed to be skillful in employing soldiers, were slightly different in cleverness and strength but shared in their ways in military affairs. In spite of that, they all failed to bring harmony and coordination to their armies. They were only able to deceive others by taking advantage of their weaknesses and plotted overthrows and were therefore still no different from robbers. Duke Huan of Qi, Duke Wen of Jin, King Zhuang of Chu, King Helü of Wu, and King Goujian of Yue were all able to attain harmony and coordination in their armies and it may be said that they were in the right conditions both ritually and morally, but they never grasped the essentials of the matter. That was why they were able to become hegemons rather than true kings. And here lies the difference in strength."

"Excellent!" exclaimed King Xiaocheng and General of Linwu. "And may we ask how to be a good general?"

Master Qing Sun replied, "In terms of wisdom, nothing is greater than discarding doubts. In terms of conduct, nothing is more important than avoiding mistakes. In

---

[3] A general of Qi during the Warring States Period, who, when Yan attacked Qi, led his army to defend the city of Jimo. Afterwards, he defeated the Yan army with a fiery bull formation and recovered more than 70 lost cities.

[4] Generally known as Yang of Shang, a famous legalist representative in the middle of the Warring States Period.

terms of action, nothing is better than freedom from regrets. It is enough to be free from regret, for success is not necessarily guaranteed. Therefore, institutions, decrees and policies should be rigorous and awe-inspiring. Awards and penalties should be resolute and implemented. Encampments and depots should be carefully planned and well-guarded. Military maneuvers, whether to advance or to retreat, should be secure, steady, and swift. Scouting out the disposition and movements of the enemy should be done in stealth in order to penetrate and the information gained should be checked repeatedly for reliability. Decisive battles should be carried out on the basis of what is clarified rather than dubious. These are called the Six Tactics. Do not so desire to maintain your position as a general that you hate the idea of losing it. Do not so press for victory that you forget the possibility of defeat. Do not attempt to inspire awe inside and despise enemies outside. Do not choose to see profit and overlook harm. Considerations should be made comprehensively and rewards of money and goods should be generous. These are called the Five Deliberations. There are three cases in which the command of a ruler may be ignored: a general would rather be killed than station his troops in a dangerous location, engage in a battle that is doomed, and deceive or bully the common people. They are called the Three Top Principles. A general committed by the ruler to command the three armies is called the ultimate officer if he is neither to be pleased by his monarch nor enraged by the enemies when the troops are properly settled, the other officers under him are properly arranged, and everything is set in good order. Thoughtful deliberation is necessary before any action and care should also be taken of the conclusion to ensure that the end is as good as the beginning. This is called the great luck. As a general rule, success in all operations rests in treating them with care and failure always goes hand in hand with carelessness. Therefore, it is lucky when care prevails over carelessness and fatal if the other way around. It promises success when sober-mindedness prevails over impulse and danger increases when rashness prevails over stratagems. Be careful when launching an offensive attack as if you were defending yourself, as watchful when marching as if you were engaged in a battle, and as dissatisfied when successful as if you won merely by luck. Be prudent in planning without negligence. Be attentive in operations without negligence. Be mindful in dealing with officers without negligence. Be heedful in treating soldiers without negligence. Be watchful in meeting the enemies without negligence. These are called the five failures prohibited. He who employs the Six Tactics, heeds the Five Deliberations, observes the Three Top Principles, and deals with all things with caution and without failure is called a true general under Heaven who is in communion with what is divine."

"Excellent," exclaimed General of Linwu. "May I ask about the military system of a true king?"

Master Qing Sun said, "A general is to die at his war drum, a charioteer at the reins, the officials at their respective posts, and officers and soldiers in battle formations. The army advances at the sound of drum and retreats at the sound of gong. Obedience to orders is more important; military merit is secondary. Advancing without authorization is just like retreating before the order is given—the penalty is the same in both cases. Killing the old and weak is prohibited, damage to food crops is banned, those who retreat without fighting are not to be arrested, those who offer resistance are not to be let go, and those who surrender are not to be treated as captives. As a general rule, in punitive expeditions, those who lead the common people astray rather than the common people are punished. However, if any of the common people tries to protect such villains, he will suffer penalties too. For this reason, the enemy soldiers who retreat without fighting are to be let live, those who put up a stubborn resistance are to be killed, and those who surrender are to be brought to the superiors. For instance, when Prince Qi of Wei[5] surrendered, he was enfeoffed in Song. Chulong Cao was executed in front of the army. And the Shang people who paid their allegiance were nurtured the same way as the people of Zhou. Hence, those who were nearby sang praises of the troops of Zhou and rejoiced, and those who were far away braved hardship and rushed over to them. States remote and out of the way all rushed to their service happily, all within the four seas became like one family, and all people within reach willingly submitted. The ruler of such a nation is called a person of exemplary virtue just as it is sung in *The Book of Songs*:

> From the east to the west
> And from the north to the south,
> No one but obeys him.[6]

A true king does not make war; he only launches punitive expeditions. When a target town is being firmly defended, no siege is laid to it. When the soldiers of the other side resist, no attack is made against them. And when its generals and soldiers are happy with each other, they deserve a blessing. A true king does not massacre when a city is conquered. He does not launch a sudden attack, nor does he keep his troops longer in the field than is scheduled. Therefore, the people of the state in chaos will choose his government; they will feel uneasy under their own ruler and long for his arrival."

"Well spoken," said General of Linwu.

"When you talk about military operations," said Xiao Chen, "you always regard benevolence and righteousness as the foundation. Since a benevolent man loves others and a righteous man does what agrees with moral principles, what use does he have for military actions, which are generally for fighting and contention."

Master Qing Sun replied, "This is not something as you understand it. A benevolent man loves others. It is just because he loves others that he hates those who do harm to them. A righteous man does what agrees with moral principles. It is just because he does what agrees with moral principles that he hates those who violate these principles. Military actions are carried out to put an end to violence and to prevent harm to others but not for the purpose of fighting or contention. Therefore, wherever the army of a benevolent monarch is stationed, there is great order; wherever it passes, there undergoes transformation. It is like a timely rain that makes everyone happy. In the cases in which Yao punished Huandou, Shun punished Youmiao, Yu punished Gonggong, Tang punished Jie of Xia, King Wen punished Chong and King

---

[5] One of the cousins of Zhou the tyrant of Shang Dynasty.

[6] Major Court Hymns, *The Book of Songs*.

Wu punished Zhou of Shang, the four emperors and two kings[7] commanded armies of benevolence and righteousness throughout the world. So, the people who were nearby admired their goodness, and those who were far away longed for their justice. The victories gained were without much fight and the people far and near came and submitted to them. Their abundant virtue extended to the limits of all four directions. The lines in *The Book of Songs* precisely refer to such cases:

> The gentleman, a man of virtue,
> > Has done nothing improper.
> > He has done nothing against ritual,
> > And he may govern the states in all directions.[8]

"The state of Qin has been victorious for four generations," Si Li[9] told Master Qing Sun. "It has the most powerful military power within the four seas and its majestic authority holds sway over all other feudal lords. This is not made true by means of benevolence and righteousness. Rather, it just does what is to its advantage."

Master Qing Sun replied, "Things are not as what you understand them. What you call advantage is not advantage in its true sense. The benevolence and righteousness I speak of are truly of great advantage. The benevolence and righteousness I speak of are the means whereby government is run. If a government is run properly, the people will draw close to, love, and willingly die for their monarch. This is why I said in the beginning that everything is up to His Majesty and the generals are of less importance. True, Qin has been victorious for four generations. However, it is constantly seized with fear that all under Heaven might be united to overthrow it with their collective power. Its army is what is called the army of decadent times, for it is short of the foundation of benevolence and righteousness. Tang did not succeed in banishing Jie merely at Mingtiao when he drove him off, nor did King Wu succeed in punishing Zhou of Shang only at the dawn of *Jiazi*[10] on which day the latter was defeated. Rather, the success was initiated in their earlier practice of rite and morality and the transformation of a so-called army of benevolence and righteousness. Now, the answers you have are not sought in what is fundamental but rather in what is secondary, which account for the chaos of the current age.

"Ritual serves as the highest criterion of order in government administration, the root of strength in a state, the way to inspire universal awe, and the general principle whereby merit and fame are established. Princes and dukes who follow it win all under Heaven while those who do not lose their states. Hence, strong armor and sharp weapons do not suffice to assure victory; high walls and deep moats are not enough for security in defense; stern commands and manifold penalties are insufficient in inspiring awe. He who follows ritual will succeed while he who does not will end in failure.

---

[7] An alternative version is four emperors and four kings.—Tr.

[8] Ballads from the States, *The Book of Songs*.

[9] A disciple of Master Xun, one of the legalist representatives in the Warring States Period, who assisted Emperor Shihuang in unifying China.

[10] The first day or year of the sixty-year cycle in the Chinese calendar.—Tr.

"The men of Chu make armor out of sharkskin and rhinoceros hides, which is tough as metal or stone. Their spears made from iron in Wan are as sharp as the sting of scorpions and wasps. And their soldiers move as nimbly and swiftly as gales. Nevertheless, their forces were defeated at Chuisha and General Mie Tang got killed. And with the rebel of Qiao Zhuang, Chu was torn apart. Was it because it lacked tough armor and sharp weapons? No! It was because the government was not run according to these principles. For the state of Chu, the rivers of Ru and Ying serve as natural barriers, the rivers of Yangtze and Han as moats, the forest of Deng as a protective screen, and Mount Fangcheng as a shield. However, the Qin troops swept down and seized the Chu capital cities of Yan and Ying as easily as shaking down dry leaves from a tree. Was it because Chu lacked natural defenses and barriers to protect it? No. It was because its government was not run according to these principles. Zhou the tyrant disemboweled Bigan, imprisoned Jizi and devised a hot pillar to kill anyone alive at any moment. His ministers were terrorized and none could feel certain of his fate. Nevertheless, when the armies of Zhou came, his commands failed to be carried out by his subordinates. Was it because the commands were not stern or the penalties were not manifold? No! It was because the government was not run according to these principles.

"In ancient times, weapons were nothing more than halberds, spears, bows and arrows, but an enemy state might submit before they were tried. City walls and battlements were not kept in repair, moats were not dug out, solid fortifications were not built, schemes and tactics were not devised; nevertheless, a state might be peaceful, free from fear of outside aggression, and secure in its position. There was no other reason for this situation than that the ritual principles were observed, all ranks were properly apportioned, and the people were employed in the proper season and truly cared for, so that they got along well with their superiors as the shadow follows the form or the echo answers the sound. Only when someone refused to obey an order was punishment applied. Thus, when one person got punishment, the whole world became obedient. The punished bore no ill will against their monarch, for they realized that the fault lay in themselves. For this reason, the penalties were rarely used but they were powerfully effective. This was due to no other cause than that they followed the ritual principles. In ancient times, when Yao governed all under Heaven, he might kill one man and punish two others, and all the world would be in order. This is what an old book means when it says, 'The authority, though awe-inspiring, is not attempted; the penalties, though established, are not applied.'

"Men usually do something for the sake of rewards and commendations. So, when they recognize the possibility of harm or injury, they abandon it. Therefore, rewards or punishments and authority or deception are not sufficient to get the utmost effort out of people or make them risk their lives for the state. If the ruler of men governs his people by reward and punishment or authority and deception rather than treats them with rite and morality as well as honesty and trust, he may only demand their accomplishments and services. However, if a powerful invader came and the people were sent to defend a city in danger, they would surely betray him; if they were made to fight against the enemies, they would surely be defeated; if they were assigned toilsome and disgraceful tasks, they would surely flee away. In a flash, they would scatter and even turn to take the advantage of their superiors. Thus, rewards and penalties as well as force and deception are merely measures taken in dealing with hired laborers or tradesmen and therefore insufficient for unifying the common people and bringing order to the state. Therefore, the men of ancient times were ashamed to resort to such means. Hence, it is necessary to develop a great fame so as to lead the people, make clear ritual and moral principles so as to guide them, keep honesty and trust so as to take care of them, honor the worthy and employ the able so as to place them in their proper positions, use ranks and corresponding robes as well as awards and prizes so as to make them exert themselves, let them work in proper seasons and lighten their burdens so as to adjust and nourish them, just as if they were newborns. With government ordinances settled and customs unified, if anyone should depart from the custom and refuse to obey his superiors, the common people would have a grudge against him, detest him, regard him as inauspicious and therefore expect that he be got rid of. And the necessity of punishment thus arises. Such men deserve severe punishment, for is there anything more disgraceful? Will someone think it profitable? When heavy punishment is imposed on someone, will he fail to correct his behavior if he is not mentally deranged or ignorant? After this, the common people will all realize that they should follow the orders of the monarch, yield to his will, and find rest and delight in it. Then there will be men who are capable of transforming themselves to goodness, cultivating themselves, rectifying their conduct, and keeping the practice of rite and morality, and people will all value and respect them, get close to them and praise them. Thus, awards come into practice. Such men deserve these awards, for is there anything of greater glory to them? Will someone think it harmful? When high ranks and abundant salaries are offered to support them, who among the living would not wish to receive the same benefits. With noble ranks and hefty rewards hanging before and clear punishments and absolute disgrace held behind, who could help himself even if he wishes to remain untransformed? Thus, the people turn to their ruler as naturally as water flows to the sea. Wherever such things happen, there is great order. Wherever such measures are taken, the common people are transformed and become obedient; the violent, brutal, daring and strong are transformed and turn honest; the prejudiced, perverse, selfish and dishonest are transformed and grow fair; the irritable and unreasonable are transformed and turn out polite and compliant. This is called the great transformation and perfect unity, which is described in *The Book of Songs* as.

> Under Heaven prevails the government by justice,
> So that even the state of Xu yields its surrender in the distance.[11]

"Generally speaking, there are three ways to annex a neighboring state: by virtue, by force and by wealth. When the people of another state honor my reputation, admire my moral integrity and wish to become my subjects, they throw open their gates and clear the roads to welcome me in, I will allow them to follow their old customs and remain in their native places, and they will all be at ease and follow the laws and orders I establish. In this way I gain new territory and grow more powerful. With the

---

[11] Major Court Hymns, *The Book of Songs*.

increase in population, I will develop more powerful forces. This is the way to annex a state by virtue. Instead of honoring my reputation or admiring my moral integrity, if the people of another state are afraid of my power and influence and dare not betray me even if they wish to get away. In such a case, with the increase in the number of soldiers, more resources will be necessary to support them. For this reason, there will be more territory with a bigger population but less power and weaker soldiers. This is the way to annex a state by force. If the people of another state neither honor my reputation nor admire my moral integrity but only intend to seek wealth and food because they are poor and hungry and come to me with empty stomachs and gaping mouths for something to eat. If things are like this, it is a must to distribute grains stored in granaries and cellars to feed them, offer them goods and money to make them rich, and appoint good supervisors to receive them. And these people may not turn trustworthy till three years later. For this reason, with the increase of territory, my influence will decrease; with a bigger population to feed, my country will grow poorer. This is the way to annex a state by wealth. Therefore, I say, he who annexes a state by virtue is a true king, he who does it by force will be weakened, and he who does it by wealth will be impoverished. From past to present it has always been the same.

"It is easy to annex new territory but hard to maintain a firm control over it. For example, Qi was able to annex Song, but failed to consolidate its grip, so Wei snatched it away. Yan was able to annex Qi but unable to consolidate its hold, so Dan Tian seized control of it. Shangdang of Han, a region extending several hundred *li* with a well-constructed city and ample stores, sought shelter in Zhao which was unable to hold on to it and ultimately was taken away by Qin. Thus, if one is able to take over another land but unable to hold it, it is sure to be taken away by someone else; if he is unable either to take over another land or consolidate his own, he is sure to perish. He who is able to firmly control his own land is surely able to annex new territory; with new territory consolidated, he will be able to go on annexing new land without a limit. In ancient times, for instance, Tang began in Bo and King Wu in Hao, both being territories extending merely a hundred *li*, unified the world and won the allegiance of all the feudal lords. There is no other reason for this than that they were able to consolidate their grip on their territories. It is important to bring the men of learning together with ritual and bring together the common people with government policies. With ritual well ordered, the men of learning will submit to your rule; with the government enlightened, the common people will be at ease. With the men of learning submissive and the common people easy, you achieved the great consolidation. In such conditions, your state will possess consolidated strength of defense and great power of conquest. With strict enforcement of orders and prohibitions, the undertakings of a true king will be complete."

Chapter 16
On Building a Powerful State

Synopsis

This is an essay on how to build a strong state and unify the world.

Master Xun believed that the government should exalt ritual, honor the worthy, emphasize the law and love the people in order to make a state powerful and prosperous. A country could not become stable and strong till the power of morality was promoted so that ritual and music were perfect, justice and law were rigorous, and the people's support was won.

Master Xun made a comparison between the two enlightened kings of Tang of Shang and Wu of Zhou with the two despotic rulers of Jie of Xia and Zhou of Yin. Both Tang and Wu were fond of doing what people approved of, for instance, rite and morality, modesty and courtesy, loyalty and trust; both Jie and Zhou were fond of doing what people hated, for example deception, contention and avarice. That was why the former were not forgetful of their people's support and eventually defeated the latter. With these cases, Master Xun urged Qi, Chu and other vassal states at that time to attach importance to rite and morality, love the common people and the men of learning, just as Tang and Wu did, so that they could be strong and survive long.

Analyzing the status quo of Qin, Master Xun found that its officials were respectful and cautious, its people were simple and honest, its government was simplified and economical, and its military force was strong. In a word, the state was powerful and prosperous with a vast territory and a perfect state of government. In spite of such advantages, it was often afraid of attack by the united force of other states and was therefore far from being a true ruler that could convince all under Heaven. This was because it was in want of great Confucian scholars to implement rite and morality. For this reason, he pointed out that the ruler of men must lay a solid foundation on which ritual and moral principles were observed and both faith and trust were maintained, and that the success of a true ruler could be achieved only by diligent routine management with justice valued and honored.

Text

If the mold is even and straight, the copper and tin are of top quality, the workmanship is brilliant, and the fire and alloying are properly controlled, then a Moye sword is successfully made when the mold is broken open. However, before trimming and sharpening, it cannot cut off even a rope. Trim the irregular and sharpen it, and the sword can slice a metal pan or bowl in halves and kill an ox or a horse in the blink of an eye. A powerful state is likened to the sword coming out of the mold: without education and unity, it can neither defend itself nor wage a war. Implement education and seek unity, and there will be a strong army and well-defended cities against the invasion of enemy states. A state has to be trimmed and sharpened, too, by rite and morality, as well as by laws and regulations. The fate of men lies with Heaven; the fate of a state rests in ritual. The ruler of men makes a true king if he exalts ritual and honors the worthy. He becomes a hegemon if he stresses the law and loves his people. However, if he cares only for profit and frequently resorts to deception, he will find himself in danger. And if he engages in intrigues and frames up the innocent, he will perish.

There are three types of powerful influence: that instilled by great virtue, that exerted by harsh punishment, and that realized through reckless and unruly means. Their examination can never be too careful. The first type is characterized by a perfect system of ritual and music, a clear hierarchy of social divisions and obligations congruent with them, a punctual implementation of policies and measures, and a manifest reflection of love and benefit for the people. In such circumstances, the common people will honor their monarch like the supreme ruler, regard him high as Heaven, cherish him as their parent, and stand in awe of him as deity. So, even though rewards are not offered, the people will try their utmost; even if punishments are not imposed, his power still exercises its influence. This is the powerful influence established by great virtue. The second type is characterized by the failure to apply ritual and music, to make clear social divisions and their inherent obligations, to implement proper policies and measures in time, to care for the people and to bring practical benefit to them. Nevertheless, the prohibition against violence is stringent and clearly enforced, the punishment for disobedience is prudent, the penalties are hefty and creditable, and the execution is severe, resolute, and sudden like the striking of thunder or the collapse of a wall. Under such circumstances, the common people will show their dread of authority because of threat and their disdain for their monarch when punishment is relieved. Under coercion, they may assemble. Whenever an opportunity emerges, they will scatter. And facing attack, they will be won over by the enemy. When people are not to be placed under control till they are forced by power or frightened by penalties or death to do so, this is called powerful influence exercised by harsh punishment. The third type is characterized by the presence of routine practice that creates chaos among people and the absence of care for and of effort to bring benefit to them, so that if the common people should grumble and complain, they would be tracked, arrested, and punished by scorching rather than mediated or harmonized. In such a situation, those below will definitely conspire together and run away from their superiors, and there will be imminent overthrow and destruction. This is powerful influence through reckless and unruly means. These three types of power and influence must be examined carefully, for influence instilled by great virtue brings stability and power, influence exerted by harsh punishment leads to weakness and peril, and influence through reckless and unruly means ends in destruction.

Master Gongsun said, "When Zifa launched an expedition northward against Cai, conquered it, captured the Marquis of Cai, and reported to the king on his return, 'The Marquis of Cai brought his land to Chu, and I have entrusted a few men there with its administration.' When he was rewarded later, Zifa declined, saying, 'The moment I issued the warnings and orders, the enemy troops withdrew—such was the power of His Majesty. When the army started the attack, the enemies withdrew—such was the power of the generals. When the soldiers were united in the battle with all their strength, the enemy troops withdrew—this was the power of the masses. So, I do not deserve the reward.'"

"In my opinion," I responded, "Zifa was respectful when reporting his mission but it was shallow of him to decline the reward, for the policy of honoring the worthy, employing the capable, rewarding the meritorious and punishing the guilty is not established for any individual: it is the principle of government inherited from the great kings of past dynasties and the basis on which people are unified. It is the proper response in approving the good and disapproving the bad. Good order comes out of it, either in ancient times or today. In ancient times, when the enlightened kings succeeded in undertaking great tasks or establishing great achievements, the monarch would enjoy the fruit, the ministers would share the credit, the gentry would be promoted in rank, the other officials would get higher salaries, and the soldiers would be provided with more pay and provisions. In this way, those who did good got encouraged and those who did otherwise were discouraged. With the ruler and his subjects being of one mind and with the three armies making concerted effort, everything would be successful, and great accomplishment and fame were a matter of course. Now, Zifa alone would not grant it. He acted against the way of the Former Kings, disrupted the laws of Chu, discouraged those who were meritorious, and humiliated those who were rewarded. Although he brought no disgrace to his family, he debased and humiliated his descendants. Yet he thought himself honest and upright in so doing. Was he not completely mistaken? That is why I say Zifa was respectful when reporting his mission but it was shallow of him to decline the reward."

Master Xun persuaded the prime minister of Qi, saying, "If one possesses the power of dominance over others and practices the way of domination, he will arouse no resentment under Heaven—such were the cases of Tang of Shang and King Wu of Zhou. However, if one possesses the power of dominance over others but does not practice the way of domination, he will fail even to find a place as an ordinary person even though he is sufficiently wealthy to own all under Heaven—such were the cases of Jie and Zhou the tyrants. Thus, it is far less in advantage if one possesses the power of dominance over others than if one practices the way of domination.

"Now a ruler and his prime minister dominate others by power of position. They approve of what is right and disapprove of what is wrong. They treat those capable as capable and those incapable as incapable, forsaking any selfish desires. They certainly observe the laws and the principles of justice that are mutually compatible and universally acceptable. Such is the way of domination over others.

"Now, you have won the trust of your monarch and the exclusive influence over the state below, and surely have the power of domination over others. Why don't you take this advantage to implement the way of domination, seek out gentlemen who are benevolent, honest, and sensible and recommend them to the king so that they may participate in the state administration and set straight what is wrong? In such circumstances, who in the whole country dare not practice what is righteous? When the monarch and his subjects, superiors or inferiors, noble or humble, old or young, all the way down to the common people, do what is righteous, whoever under Heaven would not want to conform to what is righteous? When men of worth are ready to serve in your court, men of abilities are willing to hold office in your court, and men in pursuit of profit choose Qi as their home, all under Heaven is unified. If you abandon all these efforts and choose what the common folks do, then the king's women will create chaos in the palace, treacherous ministers will throw the court into chaos, corrupt officials will cause chaos in the bureaus, and all the common people will be accustomed to seeking gains and fighting over profits. If things were like this, how could you maintain the state of affairs?

"Today the giant state of Chu hangs before us, the massive state of Yan presses from behind, the forceful state of Wei puts its hooks in us from the right, while the land in the west can be likened to a rope barely broken and Chu casts a greedy eye on our left from its Xiangfei and Kaiyang. In such an environment, if one of the states should devise a scheme against us, all other states would surely rise to take this advantage. If things were like this, Qi would be torn into four or three pieces and the state would be like a land borrowed from somewhere and we would be ridiculed by all under Heaven. Which of these two ways do you think is worthy of practice?

"Jie and Zhou were both descendants of sagely kings and heirs to those who possessed all under Heaven. When they were in reign, both were head of the imperial clans worshipped by all under Heaven. Each had a fief extending a thousand *li* with a population numbered into hundreds of millions. However, all the people abandoned them not long afterwards and rushed to the side of Tang and Wu, for they hated Jie and Zhou and honored Tang and Wu. How did this happen? What was wrong with Jie and Zhou and why were Tang and Wu successful? It was due to no other cause than that the former were fond of doing what people hated while the latter were fond of doing what people approved of. What did the people hate? Deception, contention and avarice. And what did they approve of? Rite and morality, modesty and courtesy, and loyalty and trust. We can compare the rulers of men today in this way: they desire to be ranked with the latter but their governance is no different from that of the former. In such a case, is it possible for them to make the reputation and accomplishment of the latter?

"As a general principle, he who succeeds must win the support of his people and he who wins the support of his people must follow Dao. What is Dao? It is the integration of rite and morality, modesty and courtesy, and loyalty and trust. Thus, a state with a military force of forty to fifty thousand soldiers is always strong and victorious not because it has the strength from its numbers but because it honors trustworthiness; a state with an area of several hundred *li* is peaceful and secure not because it has a vast territory but because it pays attention to its government. Now with a power of a few dozens of thousands of soldiers, attempt is still made to win allies through fraudulence and collusion; with a land extending several hundred *li*, attempt is still made to obtain more by robbery and other despicable means. This is equal to abandoning what brings one peace and strength and contending for what reduces one to peril and weakness or losing what one lacks and redoubling what one has in excess. Is it likely that such confusing and absurd attempt might lead to the accomplishment and reputation enjoyed by King Tang and King Wu? It is analogous to crawling on the ground in order to lick the heaven or pulling at someone's feet to save him from hanging himself. It certainly will not do; worse still, the more one tries, the further away one gets from the goal.

"As a subject of the king, if one is concerned only with personal benefit but does not care that his conduct is improper, then it is tantamount to driving a siege engine into a cave after treasures. A man of benevolence considers it a shame and refuses to do so. A man values nothing better than life and likes nothing better than peace. And among the things that nurture life and secure peace, nothing is more important than rite and morality. If men are only conscious of the value of life and fond of peace but forgetful of rite and morality, it may be compared to cutting one's throat for the purpose of longevity. Nothing is more stupid than that.

"So, the ruler of men is secure if he loves his people, honored if he cares for the men of learning but doomed if he does neither, just as it is pointed out in *The Book of Songs*:

> Good men are a fence
> And common people, a wall.[1]

"When brute strength reaches an impasse, the practice of justice works.[2] What does this refer to? The answer is that it refers to Qin. In terms of strength and power, Qin exceeds the times of King Tang and King Wu. In terms of breadth and vastness, it exceeds the land of Shun or Yu. Nevertheless, Qin suffers from an innumerable array of worries and troubles, fearing that all under Heaven might unite to crush it with their collective power. This is what I mean by saying that brute strength reaches an impasse. What does it mean by saying exceeding the times of King Tang and King Wu in strength and power? Both kings were able to bring those who were pleased with them into their service. Now the patriarch of Chu died there, the capital of Chu was captured, and the king of Chu fled to somewhere between Chen and Cai, carrying the three memorial tablets of the Former Kings. He is watching for an opportunity and determined to kick Qin in its belly when time comes. However, when Qin orders him to the left, he moves left, and when Qin orders him to the right, he moves right.

---

[1] Major Court Hymns, *The Book of Songs*.
[2] This is said to be the conclusive remarks of a dialog between Si Li and Master Xun.

This is taking one's enemy into service. This is what I mean by saying exceeding the times of King Tang and King Wu in strength and power. And what does it mean by exceeding the land of Shun and Yu in terms of breadth and vastness? In ancient times, when the hundred kings united all under Heaven and made servants of the feudal lords, their territories never exceeded the limit of a thousand *li*. Now Qin's territory extends to Shaxian in the south as far as the south bank of the Yangtze and borders the lands of the Hu and Mo tribes on the north. It occupies the land of the Ba and Rong tribes on the west and that of Chu bordering on Qi in the east. Its troops in Han have held Linlü over Mount Chang, its troops in Wei have seized Yujin 120 *li* from Daliang, the capital of the state, and its troops in Zhao have crossed the border forest of pine and cedar and occupied Ling. With its back against the west and guarded by Mount Chang, it has a territory extending in all directions under Heaven. That is why I say it exceeds the land of Shun or Yu in breadth and vastness. While its power inspires awe within the four seas and its strength poses a threat to the Central Plains states, it has innumerable worries and troubles and is constantly seized with the fear of being crushed by the combined forces under Heaven.

"What should be done then? The solution is to control its use of power and return to civilized means. Bring order to all under Heaven by employing those gentlemen who are upright, sincere, trustworthy, and competent. Let them engage in the administration of the state so that distinction is made between right and wrong or crooked and straight and the state affairs are managed in the capital city of Xianyang. Let those who obey do what they choose and punish those who are not compliant. If things are like this, orders will be executed anywhere under Heaven without dispatching troops out from the passes again. In such situations, even if a Brilliant Hall is to be built outside the passes to receive the feudal lords, it is virtually out of question. Nowadays, the expansion of territory is less urgent than the increase in trustworthiness."

The Marquis of Ying[3] asked Master Qing Sun, "What did you see in Qin when you were visiting there?"

Master Qing Sun replied, "It has mountain passes that are solidified and difficult of access and land features inherently advantageous. With mountains, streams, valleys and forests, it appears to be a wonderful place. Heaven offers manifold resources. This is its natural advantage. Entering its borders, I investigated its customs and found that the people there were simple, their songs and music were not indecent, and their clothing was not frivolous. They were very afraid of the superiors in charge and therefore obedient, just like the people in ancient times. When I reached the cities and their official bureaus, I noticed that their officials were all full of respect. None of them was not modest, thrifty, sincere, careful, loyal or trustworthy and never negligent, just like the officials in ancient times. In the capital city, I saw the gentry commute daily between their houses and offices without conducting any private matters. They did not form cliques or parties for selfish purposes. None of them was unreasonable or dishonest in performing their official duties. They were the same as their counterparts of ancient times. I observed its court and found that all matters were handled without delay. There was such a sense of leisure that nothing

---

[3] A native of Wei named Ju Fan, who served in the reign of King Zhao of Qin as prime minister.

had to be done at all, just like the court of ancient times. For this reason, it has been triumphant for four generations. It is not a matter of luck, but rather a matter of course. These are my observations. Therefore, we say that the perfect state of government is characterized by good order achieved with ease, brief rules that are comprehensive, and great accomplishments without much labor. Qin belongs almost to this category. But even so, it still has its worries and fears. With all the abovementioned conditions that it satisfies, Qin still has a long distance to cover before becoming a true ruler over all. Why? Probably because it has no Confucian scholars. Therefore, we say, 'He who has it pure is a true king for sure, he who has it impure a hegemon he may secure, and he who has none is fatally done.' This is something of which Qin falls short.

"In accumulating something that is minute, the yearly effort is less efficient than the seasonal, the monthly effort is better, and the daily effort is the best. As a general rule, men disdain minor assignments and do not try their utmost till major tasks arrive. If they are like this, they will invariably fall behind those who attend to minor matters. Why? Minor matters come frequently and it takes more time to deal with them, so their accumulation is efficient. However, major matters are rare and it takes less time to deal with them; therefore, their accumulation is insignificant. Therefore, he who sets a high value on each day will make a true king, and he who highly values his time of seasons becomes a hegemon, while he who confines himself to stopping a leak only when it is found is in danger, and he who wastes his time entirely is doomed. Accordingly, a true king takes every day seriously, a hegemon stresses the time of season, the ruler of a state barely surviving feels no distress till his state is in peril, and the head of a doomed state is ignorant of destruction or death till his state perishes and death happens. In history, there are too many cases of destruction and death to feel sorry about. The excellent records of a hegemon are kept according to seasons, while the accomplishments and merit of a true king are too many to be recorded every day. When it comes to material things like goods, wealth and treasures, the great ones count. However, in government and education, it is just the opposite: he who is able to accumulate what is minute succeeds soon. A vivid metaphor is found in *The Book of Songs*:

> Virtue is light as a feather,
> > But few can lift it over his head.[4]

"Generally speaking, there are villains because their rulers fail to value and honor justice, something that serves to prevent men from doing what is wicked. Nowadays, the rulers do not value or honor justice, all the common folks under Heaven have the idea of abandoning justice and the mind of wicked pursuit. As a result, villains arise. Furthermore, a superior serves as an example to his subordinates who follow him just as an echo responds to the sound or a shadow goes with its form. So, the ruler of men must be careful about it. Justice, or that which is righteous, serves to regulate the mind of men and all the things around the world. It brings peace to the rulers above and coordination among men below. Justice, in its essence, regulates

---

[4] Major Court Hymns, *The Book of Songs*.

all, inside or outside, above and below. This being the case, among the essential principles for the government of all under Heaven, justice is of primary importance and faith is secondary. In ancient times, Yu and Tang founded their conduct on justice and devoted to good faith, and there was order under Heaven. Jie and Zhou abandoned justice and turned their back on good faith, so the world was thrown into chaos. So, the superiors must carefully observe ritual and moral principles and maintain both faith and trust. This is the major foundation of the rulers of men.

"When the main hall is not yet cleaned, I cannot afford any spare time weeding in the countryside. If a sharp knife is about to pierce through my chest, it is impossible for me to notice a stray arrow. With a halberd suddenly brandishing over my head, I could not possibly avoid fending off the blow with my fingers at the risk of being cut. It is not because I do not regard these latter things as insignificant but because priority should be given to things of more importance or of more urgency."

Chapter 17
On the Way of Heaven

Synopsis

This is an essay on the relationship between Heaven and man. It tells their difference and also shows their unity. It is a reflection of the dialectical view of the ancient Chinese on this issue.

Master Xun developed this topic in two respects: how to treat Heaven and how to look at man himself. He pointed out that the evolution of Heaven follows its own rules instead of taking human factors into account. This opinion serves as the logical foundation of the whole essay. With this understanding, man will be aware of improving his environment by following the laws of nature, stop being fascinated by and dependent upon the personified Heaven, and clarify the distinction between Heaven and man. Compared with man, Heaven "succeeds without effort and receives without seeking." It is formless and intangible, and displays its achievement rather than its effort. Basing on this enlightenment, man will keep from competing with Heaven in its operation or going beyond the boundary of its knowledge.

Heaven has its own role to play and makes its own achievements; however, either order or disorder of human society is not caused by Heaven. Whether the falling of a star, the groaning of trees or the rainfall following a rain sacrifice is not the consequence of Heaven's effort. Unlike the ordinary people who regard it as supernatural, a gentleman would consider it merely as an outer form of something, try to understand its sequence of transformations and put it into use rather than obey Heaven and praise it, for he is aware that if men do not put in effort but solely long for blessings from Heaven, everything would be lost.

As for man himself, Master Xun loudly warned that violation against Dao would lead to misfortunes. He did not mean to set man against Heaven; rather, he persuaded men to obey its law and strengthen their government. When the work of Heaven is defined and its accomplishment made, man is created and his spirit given. As all things differ and vary, man is puzzled by the differences in his outward search and fails to command the incidental. Since man and all things are found between Heaven and Earth, he should start his search from himself and learn the way of Heaven from the way of man. With the understanding of Heaven, a man of intelligence and abilities entrusts experts with the observation of Heaven and he himself focuses on the fundamental principles of Dao. A gentleman observes ritual, cherishes what is within his power and does not long for what is within the power of Heaven.

Ritual is key to the fate of a nation. Social disorder is born out of evils of man, which are reflected in the absence of normal relations between ruler and subject, father and son, and husband and wife. Therefore, a ruler must promote ritual, adopt the principles of consistency passed down from kings of previous generations, and honor the worthy. The correct way is perfectly clarified when expressed out in ritual.

Dao must embody the principle of constancy and be "capable of exhausting all changes." It will not do "to use any single aspect to represent its whole." (On Removing the Obstacle of Limitations) As far as the relationship between Heaven and man is concerned, high intelligence is required to thoroughly examine their differences in addition to their similarities. This question should be studied comprehensively together with other chapters of this book so that an overall judgement may be made. It should be understood that Heaven in the true sense is short of a form or any other attribute in imagination. We cannot trace the cause of its cause to the infinity, thinking there is the first cause outside everything. It should also be understood that "The mind is the lord of the body and master of the spiritual intelligence. It issues commands instead of being commanded." (On Removing the Obstacle of Limitations). "Heart is the master of Dao," (On Rectifying Names) and Dao is learned by means of mind. Generally speaking, the disasters that beset mankind result from prejudices and the damage they cause (Doing Nothing Improper). If the mind is divided, it will fall into doubt and delusion (On Removing the Obstacle of Limitations). Only through a profound experience of such modes of thinking as comparison and analogy can prejudice and antagonism be prevented in an effort to understand (On Rectifying Names). In traditional Chinese thinking, Heaven has its seasons, Earth its resources and man his government. The coordination of the three forms the triple life forces of man with Heaven and Earth. The great vigor of Chinese culture is displayed in the humanistic spirit emphasizing humanity. With man's activity, independence and dynamic vigor, anthropocentrism might be prevented when the way of Heaven is understood and observed.

Text

Heaven evolves according to its own order. It does not exist for the sake of Yao or perish because of Jie. It is lucky to adapt to it with order and unlucky to respond it with chaos. If you reinforce the foundation[1] and cut expenditures, Heaven cannot impoverish you. If you are perfectly provisioned and your actions are timely, Heaven cannot afflict you with serious illness. If you conform to Dao and do not deviate from

---

[1] Farming or agriculture.

it, Heaven cannot bring you misfortunes. Accordingly, neither flood nor drought will result in famine, neither cold nor heat can cause sickness, and neither natural disasters nor anomalies can bring you danger and make you suffer. On the other hand, if you neglect the foundation and spend extravagantly, Heaven cannot make you rich. If you are inadequately provisioned and your actions are infrequent, Heaven cannot promise health. If you go against Dao and act absurdly, Heaven cannot give you good fortune. So, there will be famine before flood or drought hits, sickness before heat or cold attacks, and misfortune before disasters or anomalies invade. The seasons dominated by Heaven is similar to an orderly age below while catastrophes and calamities are incompatible with an age of peace and prosperity. You have no cause to curse Heaven, for disasters result from the way you follow. Hence, with an understanding of the difference between Heaven and man, you are a perfect person.

    It is Heaven that succeeds without effort and receives without seeking. Although this is profound, a perfect man will go and explore its profundity. Vast as it is, he will not exaggerate the role it can play. And ingenious as it is, he will never examine its mechanism. This is described as keeping from competing with Heaven in its work. Heaven has its seasons, Earth its resources and man his governance. This involves the coordination of the three. If man abandons what he relies on in this participation and expects to play the parts of Heaven and Earth, he is deluded. A star revolves with its planets; the sun and moon take turns shining, the four seasons succeed each other in proper order, the yin and yang interact with each other and transform things which are nourished by wind and rain. All things grow in harmony and develop with rich nutriment. We see only the achievement but not the effort. It is a miracle. We all know what it fulfills but none of us realizes its formlessness. Such is what is called Heaven. Only a sage does not transgress the boundary of its knowledge.

    When the work of Heaven is established and its achievement fulfilled, the form of man is given and his spirit arises therein. Love and hate, pleasure and anger, as well as sorrow and joy stored in it are called his heavenly emotions. Ears, eyes, nose, mouth, and body all have that which they perceive, but none of them can play the role of another. These are called their heavenly senses. The heart dwells in the center and governs the five organs, and hence is called their heavenly ruler. Using what does not belong to them as a resource for nourishment—this is called one's heavenly nourishment. To conform to the demands of his people in their service is called fortune and the contrary is called misfortune. This is called heavenly dictates. To darken his heavenly ruler, confuse his heavenly senses, reject the heavenly nourishment, defy the heavenly dictates, repress his heavenly emotions, and fails to complete his heavenly accomplishments—this is called great misfortune. A sage purifies his heavenly ruler, rectifies his heavenly senses, replenishes his heavenly nourishment, obeys his heavenly dictates and nurtures his heavenly emotions and thereby fulfills his great merit. Thus, he is aware of what he should or should not do, and he is able to take advantage of Heaven and Earth and make all things in his service. His actions are well-regulated, his nourishment is appropriate, and his life will not suffer. This is called understanding Heaven.

    Therefore, a truly capable person does not engage in anything beyond his power or sphere, and a truly wise man does not attempt to think about things beyond his intelligence or obligation. To know Heaven is to forecast its changes based on the natural phenomena that are witnessed. To recognize Earth is to multiply crops taking advantage of suitable conditions that are found. To learn the four seasons is to arrange farming affairs according to the regularity that is shown in seasonal changes. And to understand the variations of yin and yang is to bring order in line with the harmony that is revealed. A most capable and wise man entrusts experts with the observation of Heaven and he himself focuses on the fundamental principles of Dao.

Are order and disorder due to Heaven? Answer: The revolutions of the sun and moon and stars in constellations recorded in the calendar are the same for both Yu and Jie. There was time of order under Yu but chaos under Jie, hence order and disorder are not due to Heaven. Are they a matter of seasons? Answer: A multitude of crops germinate, grow and prosper in spring and summer and there is harvest and storage in autumn and winter. It is the same for both Yu and Jie. But there was time of order under Yu but chaos under Jie, and therefore order and disorder are not caused by seasons. Are they due to Earth? Answer: All lives with Earth; without Earth all dies. This is the same for both Yu and Jie. But there was time of order under Yu but chaos under Jie, which serves to show that order or disorder has nothing to do with Earth. This is what is meant in *The Book of Songs* when it sings:

> Heaven shaped the mountain grand,[2]
>> Great King made it a famous land:
>> A kingdom was built and blessed,
>> King Wen brought it peace and rest.[3]

Heaven does not suspend winter because men dislike cold, Earth does not reduce its vastness because men dislike remote distances, and a gentleman does not stop acting because petty men carp and clamor. Heaven has its laws, Earth has its rules, and gentlemen have standards for their conduct. A gentleman follows the conventions while a petty man is concerned for his gains. This is what *The Book of Songs* means when it says:

> If I have not done anything against rites,
>> Why should I care if anyone behind me bites?[4]

The king of Chu has a retinue of a thousand chariots, but it is not because he is wise. A gentleman chooses to eat coarse food grain and drink plain water, it is not because he is stupid. Both are coincidences. To be pure in will, honest in noble action, wise in thinking, living in the present and understanding the past—these are decisions within one's power. For this reason, a gentleman cherishes what is within his power and does not long for what is within the power of Heaven, while a petty man forsakes what lies within his power and longs for what is beyond him. A gentleman cherishes what is within his power and does not long for what is within the power

---

[2] Mount Qi, in present-day Shaanxi Province.

[3] Eulogies, *The Book of Songs*.

[4] Not available in the extant Chinese versions.

of Heaven; therefore, he makes progress every day. A petty man forsakes what lies within his power and longs for what is beyond him, so he slips back all the time. With the same motivation, the gentleman progresses daily while the petty man is left behind. And what separates the two wide apart lies just in this.

When a star falls or a tree groans, all the people are terrified. "What has happened?" they will ask. Answer: Nothing special happens. They are changes happening to Heaven and Earth due to the transformation of yin and yang and they are rarely observed. We may wonder at them, but we should not fear them. Solar and lunar eclipses, unseasonable rainstorms and occasional appearance of strange stars do occur all the time. If the ruler is enlightened and the country is politically stable, even if all these happen together, they cause no harm. If the ruler is stupid and the country is in danger, nothing of benefit happens by itself even if none of these things comes to pass. The falling of stars and the groaning of trees are brought about by the changes in Heaven or on Earth and result from the transformation of yin and yang. They happen only once in a while. We may marvel at them, but we should not be afraid of them.

Among the things that have happened, the ones really to be afraid of are monstrous human anomalies. Poor plowing makes crops suffer, incomplete weeding causes harvest failure, and political unrest results in loss of population. When fields are overgrown with weeds and crops are badly tended, food is expensive, people go hungry, the bodies of the dead lie along the roads—these are anomalies created by man. Governmental orders are unenlightened, the measures taken are untimely, the fundamental task is not properly attended to, the use of labor is against season, cows and horses interbreed and the six domestic animals produce monsters[5]—these are anomalies of man. Ritual and moral principles are neglected, internal and external affairs are confused, men and women engage in perverse and disorderly conduct, fathers and sons are suspicious of one another, superiors and inferiors estrange one another, and bandits and invaders come together—these are anomalies brought by men. And such anomalies are born from disorder. If these three types co-occur, there will be no security for the state. It is very easy to explain, but the misery they cause is great. They can be wondered at but should not be afraid of. It is said in an old book, "Odd occurrences among all creatures are never interpreted in the classics." Useless arguments and unnecessary investigations should be abandoned. But when it comes to relations like the obligations between a ruler and his subject, the affection between father and son, and the difference between husband and wife in their duties—these must be refined daily rather than neglected.

When you pray for rain and it rains. How do you explain this phenomenon? Answer: There is nothing special, for it often rains without the sacrifice being performed. When a solar or lunar eclipse happens, people attempt to save the sun or moon.[6] When there is drought, the rain sacrifice is held. When big decisions are to

---

[5] This clause is originally misplaced later in this paragraph.—Tr.

[6] In ancient times, when the sun or moon was eclipsed, people would attempt at its rescue, knocking plates and beating drums.

be made, a divination[7] is staged. Nothing is ever expected of the ceremony. It only gives an impressive appearance. Thus, a gentleman considers it as an ornament, but the ordinary people regard it as supernatural. Therefore, it is proper to consider it to be a form and it is dangerous to regard it as a miracle.

In Heaven, none is brighter than the sun and moon; on Earth, nothing is as bright or light as fire or water; of all things, no object is as dazzling as pearls and jade; for human beings, nothing can enlighten them better than rite and morality. If the sun and moon do not rise high in the sky, their light will not be radiant. If fire and water do not accumulate, their glow and moisture will not spread out. If pearls and jade do not shine on the outside, princes and dukes will not prize them. And if rite and morality are not advocated in a country, its merits and fame will not be known. Thus, the fate of men lies with Heaven and that of a nation with ritual. The ruler of men is a true ruler if he exalts ritual and respects the worthy, and a hegemon if he stresses the law and loves the people. He is in danger if he desires profit and schemes after power. And he is bound to perish if he engages in conspiracy, subversion and treachery.

To exalt Heaven and admire it—How can it compare with raising it as an animal and putting it under control? To obey Heaven and praise it—How can it compare with grasping its sequence of change and putting it to use? To observe the seasons and wait for blessings—How can it compare with obeying the seasons and exploiting them? To wait for things to increase of themselves—How can it compare with exerting your talents to transform them? To long for things to serve your purpose—How can it compare with managing and never losing them? To long for the source from which things are born—How can it compare with finding the means to bring them to completion? Hence, if you do not put in effort but only long for blessings from Heaven, you will lose everything.

What has remained unchanged through the kings of former generations can be safely regarded as principles of consistency. As one dynasty falls, another rises and consistent principles are adopted to suit the change. When the principles are consistent, there is order; otherwise, you will be ignorant of how to respond to the change. The essence of this principle has never ceased to exist. Chaos arises from deviating from it while order is born out of its perfect application. Thus, from the perspective of Dao, what is regarded as good should be done if it conforms to the principle; otherwise, if it deviates from the principle, it should not be done, for its violation leads to great confusion. When men cross waters, they mark the deep places; but if their markers are unclear, those who come after will drown. Similarly, when a ruler follows Dao as his principle, the country may fall into disorder if he does not make it clear. Ritual is such a set of principles. Its violation leads to a dark age with utter confusion. Hence, when Dao is perfectly clarified, internal and external affairs are handled differently, what is visible or invisible is constant, and people will be able to avoid the disasters.

All things form one aspect of Dao, and each thing constitutes only one aspect of everything. A stupid person mistakes one aspect of a single thing for Dao. This is

---

[7] A practice in ancient China using a tortoise shell or yarrow pieces to tell fortunes.

ignorance. Master Shen[8] has insight about that which follows but not into that which leads. Master Lao[9] sees the value of yielding but not that of leading. Master Mo[10] emphasized equality and was opposed to inequality. Master Song[11] held that men had few desires rather than many. If there were no one to take the lead, people would not find the gate open to advancement. To concede all the time without enterprise, there would be no distinction between eminent and humble. If there were universal equality and no hierarchy of distinctions, government orders would not be executed. And if men had few rather than multiple desires, there would be no way to educate and transform them. This is what *The Book of History* means when it advises,

> Do not choose personal preferences, pursue the royal way.
>
> Do not follow selfish desires, follow the royal road as you may.[12]

---

[8] Dao Shen, a legalist in the Warring States Period, whom Master Xun criticized for his counsel to obey the orders from above and follow the custom below, his promotion of rule by law but went short of guiding principles (*Criticism of the Twelve Masters*), believing it would be sufficient to follow the law like an ignoramus who preserved his nature and does not advance till he is pushed or follow till he is dragged (*All Schools of Thoughts*), and his ignorance of the role of the worthy (*On Removing the Obstacle of Limitations*).

[9] Dan Lao, also known as Laozi, a representative of Daoism, who claimed that men were helpless before nature and society and therefore were advised to obey nature passively without making active efforts.

[10] Di Mo, founder of Mohism, who advocated universal love and fought against inequality among men.

[11] Jian Song, a scholar of the Warring States Period, who claimed that men would be perfectly satisfied if only they were fed.—Tr.

[12] Grand Rules, *The Book of History*.

Chapter 18
On Correct Judgement

Synopsis

This essay is composed of two parts: dynastic system and human nature. The former concentrates on the doubts and misunderstandings of later generations about the sagely kings or the dynastic system from the present to the ancient times in chronological order, e.g., the world in the possession of Jie and Zhou was usurped and seized by Tang and Wu, the burial was frugal in remote antiquity, etc. The latter is related to public administration. By citing the views of Master Song, it points out that the fault of his theory lies in its failure to grasp the fundamental issues of human nature, human feelings, and human desires and to take the dynastic system as the highest standard. The fundamental of governing a country is to follow the way of the sagely kings, completely understand human nature, and guide men to rite and morality. The two parts demonstrated the relationship between human nature and conscious activity, two basic categories in the core theory of Master Xun on social administration.

The difficulty here is how to regard Yao and Shun's attempt of abdication in favor of others they deemed worthy. There are two points to consider. Firstly, it is necessary to truly understand the virtues of these sagely Sons of Heaven. To say that they were unmatched under Heaven does not necessarily mean that they had no rivals, but that they were of one with all things and that no opposition or boundary was set in their mind. Secondly, to fully comprehend the concept of all under Heaven and to think it the weightiest burden, the most extensive in coverage, and with the greatest multitude of people, no shape or form should be introduced as is done in understanding ordinary things since what is ultimate might be with form or formless. Abdication involves a grantor, a receiver and the object granted, i.e., there is a boundary between men and things. However, the Son of Heaven, having reached moral purity and perfection, was without such a boundary; all under Heaven was ultimate and formless and therefore could not be taken as an object to be given. The ordinary saying of Yao and Shun's attempt of abdication in favor of others is an improper comparison out of ignorance of the true meaning of the Son of Heaven and all under Heaven.

Text

One of the common views claims: "It is of most advantage for the rulers to keep truth from his subjects." It is not so. A monarch is an initiator to his people; he is an example for his subordinates to follow. The people listen to him and respond accordingly; the subordinates watch how he moves and act according to the rules. If the initiator keeps silence, the people will have nothing to respond to. If he hides the rules, those who are below will be ignorant of how to move. If people fail to respond and react, there will be nothing to depend upon mutually. That is equivalent to the situation in which there is no ruler at all. And nothing is worse than it. Thus, a monarch is the root for his subordinates. If he makes his policies public, his subject will be clear about what to do; if he is upright and straight, his subjects will be honest and trustworthy; if he is impartial and correct, his subject will be amenable and honest. Being clear about what to do, they are easily unified; being honest and trustworthy, they are readily employed; being amenable and simple, they are easily understood. Unification easily achieved means greater strength, employment readily accepted promises greater merit, understanding easily gained facilitates deeper knowledge. This is where order is born. Conversely, if a ruler keeps a secret of his policies, his subjects will be confused and hesitant; if he is treacherous, they will be deceptive; if he is biased, they will gang up for their private purposes. Being confused and hesitant, their unification is hard; being deceptive, they are not easy to be controlled; being cliquish, they are difficult to know. Strength cannot be gathered if people are difficult to unify, accomplishment cannot be increased if they are difficult to employ, and truth cannot be known if they are difficult to understand. This is where chaos arises. So, it is beneficial for a ruler to make his policies clear and public rather than obscure and hidden. If his policies are clear, security will be felt below; otherwise, if his policies are kept a secret, his subordinates will feel threatened. Feeling secure, people will esteem their ruler; feeling threatened, they will despise him. If he is easy to know, they will be close to him. Otherwise, if he is difficult to know, they will fear him. He is secure when his subjects draw close to him; he is in danger if they are afraid of him. Thus, nothing is worse if the way of a ruler is difficult to know, and nothing is more dangerous if a ruler engenders fear in his subjects. An old book says, "He who causes hatred in many is in danger." *The Book of History* praises King Wen of Zhou by saying, "He makes clear his brilliant virtue."[1] And *The Book of Songs* sings, "The light below is bright because of reflection."[2] The kings of former times showed their brilliant virtue. Did they do so merely to make it public?

---

[1] The Announcement to the Prince of Kang, *The Book of History*.
[2] Major Court Hymns, *The Book of Songs*.

One of the common views claims: "Jie and Zhou possessed all under Heaven; Tang and Wu usurped and seized it." That was not true. It is correct to say that Jie and Zhou once held the position of all under Heaven, but it is incorrect to say that they once owned the position of all under Heaven or that all under Heaven[3] belonged to Jie and Zhou.

In ancient times, the Son of Heaven had as many as a thousand officials but a feudal lord had only a hundred. He whose orders were executed in all the Xia states through these thousand officials was called a king; he whose orders were carried out in one of the states through these hundred officials so that he was not dethroned and his state not destroyed in spite of internal unrest is called a lord. The descendants of sagely kings inherited all under Heaven and held the power and position of the world. They had the supreme authority under Heaven. Nevertheless, if anyone of them lacked the abilities or behaved himself improperly, he would arouse resentment within his own state and even revolt in other states. There would be discord close to him in the state and refusal to cooperate far away from him among the feudal lords. His orders would not be executed within his own borders and the feudal lords would even attack and invade his territory. If things were like this, even though he had not yet perished, I would say that he had already lost all under Heaven.

With the death of the sagely kings, those who inherited their power and authority were so deficient in their ability to control all under Heaven that there was no monarch over the world at all. In such situations, if any of the feudal lords was illustrious in his virtue and great in prestige, people within the four seas would all want him as their monarch. If some state was ruled by an extravagant and self-indulgent tyrant, only he was able to punish it without harming the innocent common people and execute the tyrant like an autocrat forsaken by all. In such circumstances, it is proper to say that he could control all under Heaven and therefore could be called the true king.

It was not true that Tang of Shang and King Wu seized all under Heaven. They followed the proper way of government and carried out moral principles to establish whatever brought benefits for and remove whatever did harm to all under Heaven, so all the world offered their allegiance to them. Neither was it the case that Jie and Zhou the despots were deprived of all under Heaven. Rather, they turned against the virtue of Tang and Wu and disrupted the social divisions in agreement with rite and morality. It was because of their repeated beastlike behaviors and all sorts of crimes that they were abandoned by all the world. He to whom all under Heaven goes is called the true king; when all under Heaven abandons, it is called subjugation. So, the fact that neither Jie nor Zhou ever possessed the world and neither Tang of Shang nor King Wu of Zhou ever murdered his sovereign gets confirmed.

Tang and Wu were like the parents of their people while Jie and Zhou were like their enemies. However, a common view held that Jie and Zhou were monarchs and they were murdered by Tang of Shang and King Wu of Zhou, which means that the parents were killed and the enemies became masters. Nothing is more inauspicious than that! If one views as the monarch him to whom all under Heaven turns, then either Jie or Zhou had never had such experience. If one thinks Tang of Shang and

---

[3] An alternative interpretation is the position of the Son of Heaven.

King Wu of Zhou murdered their monarchs, no such statement has ever been made. It is straightforward slander!

The Son of Heaven must be someone who is qualified. The world under Heaven is the weightiest burden; only the strongest person can bear it. It is the most extensive; only the most insightful can deal with various things properly. It has the greatest multitude of people; only the most enlightened can harmonize them. And only a sage is capable of satisfying these requirements. Thus, only a sage is capable of making a true ruler. A sage is perfect in moral integrity and every other respect. He is the greatest standard under Heaven by which all is measured and judged.

Jie and Zhou were most vicious in their plans and strategies, darkest in their wishes and most confused in their conduct. Their own kin kept their distance, the worthy despised them, and their own people detested them. They were both descendants of Yu and Tang, but failed to get help from even a single person. Tyrant Zhou disemboweled Bigan, imprisoned Jizi, lost his life and his country, suffered the greatest disgrace under Heaven, and would serve as a typical example when the problem of evil was examined by later generations. And this was why he was unable even to protect his own wives and children. Therefore, those who are most worthy ensure the security within four seas and such were Tang of Shang and King Wu of Zhou, while those who are most incompetent fail to protect their own wives and children and such were Jie and Zhou the tyrants. Is it not utterly mistaken for some people to think that both tyrants of Jie and Zhou were in possession of all under Heaven and made Tang of Shang and King Wu of Zhou their subjects? Such men may be compared with hunchbacked and lame wizards who are so conceited as to think themselves bright.

It is possible to take a state by force, but it is impossible to conquer its world. A state may be usurped, but its world cannot. A man who resorts to force may grab a state but he cannot win the world in the same manner. A state may be obtained by stealing, but its world cannot be won in the same fashion. Why? A state is something small. It can be taken by petty men, grabbed through unjust means, and held by minor strength. However, the world is something big. It cannot be possessed by petty men, obtained through unjust means or maintained by minor strength. A state may be possessed by petty men who will not necessarily avoid losing it. The world is the greatest of all. Nobody except a sage is able to own it.

One of the common views claims, "In a well-ordered society in ancient times, symbolic rather than corporal punishments were employed: facial tattooing was replaced by black-branding, excision of nose by wearing a hat with grass-woven strap, castration by partial removal of apron, amputation of foot by wearing hempen shoes, and death penalty by wearing a collarless garment in reddish brown. Such were the punishments then." This was not the case. Did this symbolize good order? If so, nobody would have been guilty of any offense in the first place, and there would have been no need for physical as well as symbolic punishments. Or were the punishments thought to have been lightened? If some people were guilty of offenses and their penalties were lightened, that would mean those who killed others would not be put to death and those wounded others would go unpunished. With the greatest crimes being punished very lightly, ordinary men would not realize that they were crimes. Nothing would be more chaotic than that! As a general rule, penalties are established to prohibit acts of violence, instill hatred of evil acts, and prevent possible offences before they happen. If murderers are not put to death and those who wounded others go unpunished, it is called generosity to violence and liberality with villains. It is no hatred of evil. So, symbolic punishments were unlikely products of the well-ordered society in ancient times; they arise with the chaos of present age.

The ancient times of order were not like this. In most situations, titles and positions granted or awards and punishments given were regarded as a recompense accorded with the nature of the conduct involved. If a single case was treated improperly, it would be the start of chaos. If virtue was not matched by position, ability was not matched up to office, merit did not deserve award, and penalty failed to correspond to offense, nothing could be more inauspicious than that. In the past when King Wu of Zhou launched an expedition against Shang, he killed Zhou the tyrant, cut his head off and as a punishment suspended it from a red flag. The punishment of violent acts and the execution of fierce enemies represent the highest degree of order. It is a universal practice to put to death those who kill others and punish those who wound others. This has been the same for all kings who were ignorant of its origin. If punishment is balanced against offense, there will be order; otherwise, there will be chaos. Thus, heavy penalties lead to order and light ones to chaos. Punishment for offenses in times of peace is heavy and that in an age of chaos is light. This is referred to in *The Book of History* when it says, "The punishments and penalties are lenient in some ages but harsh in other ages."[4]

One of the common views claims, "King Tang of Shang and King Wu of Zhou were incapable of enforcing their prohibitions and commands." What was that? They say, "The states of Chu and Yue were beyond the restraint of their ordinances." This was not true. Actually, Tang and Wu were the best under Heaven at enforcing their prohibitions and commands. Tang dwelt in Bo and Wu in Hao, both places extending merely a hundred *li*, but the world was united around them, the feudal lords were their subjects, and wherever it was, as long as it was accessible by traffic, the people, being afraid of their power, became submissive, received their education and obeyed their rule. So, how could it be said that Chu and Yue were beyond their control? The way in which a true king establishes his rules and regulations varies: implements according to actual conditions and tributes according to distance. Why is it necessary that all of them should be identical? Thus, the people used bowls in Lu, jars in Wei, and containers of hide in Qi. Appliances and ornaments must be different in order to suit them to circumstances and customs. Accordingly, all states shared in their service to the king, but those on the Central Plains followed the same system while those in the barbarian regions in the four directions did not. Those who are within the royal domain do their service by tilling the land. Those who are immediately outside the royal domain do their service by scouting. Those who are farther away do their service by paying seasonal tributes. Those who are in the eastern and southern barbarian regions do their service by their obedience. And those who are in the northern and western barbarian regions do their service by nonregular tributes. Those who do service by tilling the land provide the daily offerings of royal sacrifice;

---

[4] Marguis Lü on Punishment, *The Book of History*.

those who do service by scouting provide the monthly offerings of royal sacrifice; those who do service by paying seasonal tributes provide the seasonal offerings of royal sacrifice; those who do service by obedience provide annual offerings of royal sacrifice; those who do service by acknowledging the domination of the Son of Heaven provide irregular offerings. Providing daily, monthly and seasonal offerings, paying annual tributes and acknowledging the domination are examples of provisions established according to different conditions and distances. These constitute the rules and regulations of a true king. Chu and Yue were the states providing seasonal sacrificial offerings and annual tribute and acknowledging the domination. Why were they not considered to be restrained till they were identical to those who provide daily and monthly offerings? Such view is based merely on conjectures made by the ignorant who are unqualified for the discussion of the system of a true king. A popular saying goes, "He who is shallow cannot be made to comprehend what is deep and he who is stupid cannot be invited to discuss wisdom, just as a frog in a deserted well cannot be expected to talk about the happiness in the Eastern Sea." It refers precisely to this.

One of the common views claims, "Yao and Shun abdicated and yielded their thrones." This was not the case. The Son of Heaven is the most honorable in power and position unmatched under Heaven. So, to whom should they yield their thrones? Being wise and kind and having reached moral purity and perfection, Yao and Shun faced south and made decisions of the world. The people, being afraid of their power, became submissive and received their education before being transformed and becoming fully compliant. By then, there were no talented men in hiding and no good deed being concealed. All that confirmed with them was right while all that diverged from them was wrong. Why was it necessary for them to give up all under Heaven in favor of someone else?"

One explanation was that "they did it at death." This was not the case, either. When they were in reign, the sagely kings awarded ranks according to one's virtue and filled offices according to one's abilities so that everyone was assigned the right job and all got what was proper for them. Those who were unable to control their selfish interests by moral principles or to transform themselves through efforts were all relegated to the status of common people. At the death of the sagely kings, all under Heaven was sageless and therefore there was none to whom the throne might be yielded. However, if there were sages, and they were found among the descendants of the sagely kings, all under Heaven would not depart from them, the positions in the court would be maintained, the system would remain unchanged, the world would be in order and nothing would be different. Since Yao was succeeded by another Yao, how could there be any difference? If the sages came from the Three Dukes rather than the descendants of the sagely kings, the world would turn to them as though they returned home. There would be a revival, the world would be in order and nothing would be different. Since Yao was succeeded by another Yao, how could there be anything different? It is hard to change a dynasty and its system. When the Son of Heaven lives, he is worshipped alone. There is order and stability. Ranks are assigned on the basis of virtue cultivated. When he dies, there will surely be someone who is able to carry the responsibility for all under Heaven. With distinctions made according to rite and morality, why should it be necessary to give up the throne?

Another explanation was that "they did it because of old age." This was not true. One declines in vigor, *qi* and strength, but not in wisdom, thinking and judgement. "They retired from it because they could not bear the toilsome labor," they explained. This is nothing but the contention of those who are afraid of work. The Son of Heaven exercises the greatest power and influence, remains perfect at ease, enjoys the greatest pleasures, and never gives in to his aspirations. He need not toil since he is supreme in position. For clothing, he is dressed in the five basic alternated with secondary colors, his garment being covered with repeated patterns, embroidered designs and ornaments of pearl and jade. For food and drink, he has beef, mutton, and pork, replete with rare and exotic delicacies, and with the most refined aromas and tastes. The food is presented with an array of dancers to the music. His feast begins at the sound of drum. The food is taken away to the strains of Yong for sacrifice to the kitchen god. A total of one hundred attendants are ready in the west antechamber for service. At the court, a canopy and screens are set up for him. He takes his position standing with his back to the throne to receive the feudal lords who hasten up to the foot of the steps for an audience.

When he goes out of the palace gate, witches and wizards exorcize the ill omens. When he goes out of the city gate, the master of sacrifices and the master of invocators pray for blessings. He rides in the Grand Chariot with rush mats to make him comfortable, with sweetgrasses on both sides to nurture his sense of smell, with a gilded crossbar in front to nurture his sense of sight, and the sense of hearing gets nurtured with bells on the crossbar and the frame tinkling to the rhythm of *Wu* and *Xiang* when the vehicle moves slowly and to the rhythm of *Shao* and *Hu* if the vehicle moves fast. The Three Dukes hold the shaft and the reins of the horses. The feudal lords guard the wheels, flank the car and lead the horses along. He is followed by the marquises of big states and senior officials who are in turn followed by the marquises of small states and other officials. Soldiers decked out in armor protect both sides of the road; the ordinary people dare not look around and hurry away to hide themselves. At rest, he is like a respectable deity; in motion, he is like a celestial ruler. He is taken good care of in old age and well-nurtured in infirmity. Could anything be better than this? An old man needs rest. But what rest has such peace, comfort, enjoyment and happiness? It is therefore said that a feudal lord retires on account of age but the Son of Heaven does not and that the throne of a state may be handed over to someone but the world cannot. This was the same in the past as it is today. "Yao and Shun abdicated and yielded their thrones" is a false statement. It is a rumor started by those who are ill-informed and spread by those who are shallow. These men are ignorant of the distinction between right and wrong as well as the difference between big and small or supreme and inferior. Therefore, one cannot discuss the great principles under Heaven with them.

One of the common views claims, "Yao and Shun were incapable of transformation through education." Why did they say so? "Because they failed to do so to Danzhu and Xiang, their sons." was the answer. This was not true either. Both Yao and Shun were best at transforming their people through education under Heaven. They faced south to make decisions for all under Heaven. The people, being afraid of their power, became submissive and received their education before being transformed and becoming fully compliant. The failure in transforming Danzhu and Xiang, their sons, was not their fault; it was Danzhu and Xiang themselves to blame. Yao and Shun were outstanding figures under Heaven while Danzhu and Xiang were merely deceitful and despicable petty men of their days. Is it not extremely unfair to blame Yao and Shun rather than Danzhu and Xiang as one of the common views did? So, this is sheer fallacy. Yi and Pengmen were expert archers under Heaven, but they could not hit the bull's-eye with a crooked bow and crooked arrows. Liang Wang and Fu Zao were champion charioteers under Heaven, but they could not succeed in traveling great distances with lame horses and a broken chariot. Similarly, Yao and Shun were masters in transforming through education, but they could not convert the deceitful and despicable petty men. In what world and in what age are there no such deceitful and despicable petty men? They have been in existence since Taihao[5] and Suiren[6] of ancient times. So, those who invented such sayings cherished no good intentions, those who learned from them suffered disasters and those who condemned them were lucky. The following lines from *The Book of Songs* express exactly this point:

> The calamities people suffer
> Do not come down from Heaven.
> They chatter and flatter
> Or gossip and backbite,
> Such are the behaviors of some men.[7]

One of the common views claims, "In remote antiquity, the burial was frugal with a coffin three inches thick and three sets of burial dress and coverlets. Because the burial sites did not impede the cultivation of land, the graves were not dug up. In the chaotic age of today, elaborate burials were in practice with ornately decorated coffins which invite grave robbers." This is a reflection of the ignorance of the way of good government and of the reason why graves are robbed. Generally, men engage in robbery for certain purposes. They intend either to make up for their deficiencies or top up their surplus. The sagely kings nurtured their people in such a way that they became wealthy and then conscious of satisfaction and were prevented from getting excessively rich. Thus, there was no theft or robbery, dogs and pigs refused grains, and both farmers and merchants were able to give away some of their products and goods. So fine were their customs that men and women did not meet on the road and people were ashamed of picking up lost articles. That was why Confucius said, "When Dao prevails under Heaven, robbers must be the first to be transformed!" The dead was strewn with pearls and jade and placed in an inner coffin filled with embroidered silk and brocade and an outer coffin painted with cinnabar and azurite and full of gold items, among which were trees fashioned from rhinoceros' horns

---

[5] Also named Fuxi, head of the eastern tribes in ancient China.

[6] A legendary figure who discovered the use of fire.

[7] Minor Court Hymns, *The Book of Songs*.

and elephant tusks with fruit made of semi-precious stones, yet no one attempted to rob his tomb. Why were things like that? It was because the robbers found the tricks for profit less effective and the shame derived from the offence more intense.

The chaotic age of today is just the opposite: the rulers fail to govern by law and their subjects do not observe the regulations. The wise are not invited to join in decision-making, the able are not permitted to run state affairs, and the worthy are not employed. In such conditions, opportunities endowed by Heaven, advantages given by Earth and harmony among the people are all lost. For this reason, all things are neglected. As a consequence, wealth and resources dwindle, and chaos arises. The princes and dukes far above are worried that they themselves have insufficient supplies, while the common people down below suffer from cold, hunger and emaciation. Consequently, men like the tyrants of Jie and Zhou gather together to steal and rob, posing a threat to the rulers. They are brutish like birds of prey and wild beasts and greedy like wolves and tigers. They even make dried meat out of adults and roast infants whole. Things being like this, why should we resent those who rob the graves of others and seek jewels or jade in the mouth of the dead? Even if a man is buried stark naked, how can he remain in peace underground since his grave will surely be dug up? Those cannibals will certainly eat his flesh and gnaw his bones. The claim that the burial in remote antiquity was frugal and therefore the graves were not dug up, while the burial today is elaborate and therefore is robbed is made by the wicked to confuse, mislead and deceive the foolish for illicit profit. Such is utter felony. An old book condemns such conduct by saying, "They threaten others for their own security and harm others for their selfish interests."

Master Song said, "If an insult is not understood as a disgrace, there will be no fighting. People fight because they regard an insult as a disgrace. So, no fighting occurs when an insult is not considered a disgrace."

"Does it mean that man does not hate being insulted?" someone asked.

"Yes," he answered, "but he does not regard it as a disgrace."

If that is the case, Song will be unable to make true what he wishes for. As a general rule, people fight because they hate it rather than they consider it a disgrace. Consider the court jesters, dwarfs and teasers. They insult but do not fight. Do they understand insult as something other than disgrace? They do not fight because they do not hate being insulted on such occasions. Now let a man get at the outfall of someone and steal his pigs, the owner will surely pull out his sword and pursue the thief at the risk of injury or even death. Is it because the owner considers the loss of pigs a disgrace? He is not afraid of fighting because he hates the thief. A man might consider it disgraceful to be insulted, he will not fight if he does not hate it. Although he is aware that it is not a disgrace to be insulted, he will surely fight if he hates it. This being the case, the reason he fights or not lies not in whether he feels or does not feel it a disgrace, but rather in whether he hates it or otherwise. So, is it not an attempt utterly wrong for Master Song to persuade others not to feel disgraceful when they get insulted since he fails to dissuade them from hating insult? It would be futile even if he had a glib tongue and wasted all his breath. It is unwise to be ignorant of its uselessness; it is inhumane to deceive others if he is aware of it. And nothing is more disgraceful than being neither humane nor wise. He believed that would be of benefit to others but actually it was of no benefit at all and he himself would have to leave in great disgrace. No doctrine could be more detrimental!

Master Song said, "It is no disgrace to suffer insult." My response is: a deliberation does not hold water till the highest standards are established on which it may start, for without such standards, it is impossible to distinguish between right and wrong, and discriminations and disputes cannot be settled. I have learned that "the highest standards under Heaven, the distinction between right and wrong, and the foundations on which status and its corresponding obligations as well as name and its corresponding descriptions are made constitute the system of a dynasty." Thus, argument and naming should follow the example of the sages and kings whose standards are established on the distinction between honor and disgrace. Honor and disgrace have two aspects respectively. Honor may come from moral cultivation or power and position. Disgrace may result from the lack of moral cultivation or be brought by power and influence. When one is fully-developed in inspiration and thought, well-cultivated in virtue and conduct, and brilliant in intelligence and wisdom, honor arises from within. This is honor derived from moral cultivation. When one holds a noble rank, receives substantial tribute and emolument, and occupies a position as high as the Son of Heaven or a feudal lord or at least an official or among the gentry, honor arises from without. Such honor is derived from power and position. If a man is filthy, abandoned, transgressive, rebellious, arrogant and cruel with a rapacious appetite for profit, disgrace comes from within. Such is disgrace from the lack of moral cultivation. If he is cursed or insulted, dragged about by the hair and beaten, cudgeled and flogged, punished by removing his kneecaps, decapitated, quartered, executed and laid unburied, torn asunder by five carts or tied by the hands from behind, it is disgrace brought by power and influence. Such are the two aspects of honor and disgrace. A gentleman may suffer disgrace brought by power and influence but not from the lack of moral cultivation while a petty man may enjoy honor deriving from power and position but not from moral cultivation. With disgrace brought by power and influence, a gentleman is not prevented from becoming a Yao; with honor deriving from power and position, a petty man is not stopped from becoming a Jie. Only a gentleman may enjoy both honors; only a petty man may suffer both disgraces. Such is the distinction between honor and disgrace. The sagely kings add it in their standards, the gentry take it as one of their principles, the other officials regard it as one of their rules, and the ordinary people consider it to be set custom. And this remains unaltered for thousands of years to come.

Now Master Song was different. Subjected to the humiliation, he expected a change one day in the concept of honor and disgrace. This was simply out of the question. It can be likened to filling rivers and seas with mud balls, or asking Jiaoyao the dwarf to carry Mount Tai on his back, which will crush him instantly. Several men who admire the doctrine of Master Song will bring harm to themselves if they do not quit.

Master Song said, "It is human nature to have few desires, but everyone believes that his desires are inherently numerous. This is wrong." Accordingly, he went about with many of his disciples, offering his doctrines, demonstrating his points through metaphors and examples, and persuading men to understand that their desires are inherently few. That being the case, I think one must also believe it to be human nature that the eye does not desire rich colors, the ear does not desire melodious sounds, the mouth does not desire delicious tastes, the nose does not desire pleasing smells, and the body does not desire the utmost comfort. Is it true that man does not desire these five great pleasures? Master Song admitted, "They are desires inherent in man." Then his theory will get nowhere, for he agreed that these five utmost desires were inherent in man but in the meanwhile claimed that man by nature had few desires. This is like believing that man wants to be rich and noble but does not desire goods or he likes beautiful women but hates to see Xishi the beauty.

In ancient times, people did not think so. They thought that man by his nature had numerous rather than few desires. For this reason, they rewarded men with plenty of wealth and punished them by reducing their salaries. This had been the practice of all kings. Hence, the worthiest received the official salaries of the world level, the next worthy of the state level, the least worthy of the fief level, and the honest common people were fully provided with food and clothing. Now Master Song believed that man by nature had few rather than many desires. If that were the case, it would mean that the kings of former times awarded men with what they did not desire and punished them with what they desired. Nothing is more confusing than that! Now Master Song, being complacent over his doctrine, gathered men about him as his disciples, established a school of learning, and composed writings on it. His theory would inevitably mistake good order for chaos. Was he not utterly wrong?

Chapter 19
On Ritual

Synopsis

This is a systematic demonstration of ritual.

Master Xun believed that ritual was formulated by the sagely kings to regulate men's desires and prevent them from disputes when their inherent desires were unsatisfied. It includes the system of hierarchy, moral norms, etiquette and ceremonies, and so on which can be divided into two categories: regulating people's needs before satisfying them by adjusting the distribution of property so that everyone's reasonable desires and demands could be met; differentiation between noble and lowly, old and young, rich and poor, power and insignificance for the purpose of individual differences and order.

Master Xun proposed the honoring of ritual since he believed that it was as fundamental to a state as the carpenter's plumbing line of ink to the straightness of wood. In his eyes, ritual principles were best in evaluating the conduct of man. Thus, when all the world should observe them, there would be order and security and therefore survival; otherwise, there would be chaos and danger that lead to destruction.

Master Xun traced ritual to three roots: Heaven and Earth the root of life, ancestors the root of tribes, and rulers and teachers the root of social order. Reverence for them was considered a quality of deep gratitude. The essay focuses on funeral and sacrificial rites, pointing out that the dead should be served as if they were alive and the absent as if they were present. There should still be love and reverence for those who had passed away. Burial served as respect for the physical form while sacrifice as respect for the spirit. On the contrary, if there was less love and respect for the deceased, it would be regarded as the way of a villain and the inclination to betray. The fundamental connotation of the funeral and sacrificial rites advocated by Confucianism is humanistic education, a development from the way of man to the way of Heaven. In the eyes of a gentleman, it is the way of man; in the heart of common people, it is service for the ghosts.

Text

What gave rise to ritual? Man is born with desires which, if not satisfied, cannot but seek some means of satisfaction. If there is no measure or limit to his seeking, there will inevitably be contentions. Contention causes disorder which in turn leads to difficulty. The Former Kings hated this and established rite and morality in order to divide people according to their roles and duties and regulate their desires before satisfying them, so that no desires are left unsatisfied because of the deficiency of goods and goods are not exhausted by the desires. In this way, both desires and goods are restricted and well-coordinated over the course of time. This is the origin of ritual.

Thus, ritual serves to nurture desires. The meat of domesticated animals, various grains, and the five flavors of seasoning serve to satisfy the mouth. The fragrance of spices and orchids serve to satisfy the nose. Carvings, inlays, embroideries and designed patterns serve to satisfy the eye. The sounds of bells, drums, flutes, chimes, lutes, zithers, pipes and organs serve to satisfy the ear. And spacious chambers, grand palaces, soft mats, comfortable beds, low tables and cushions serve to satisfy the body. In a word, ritual serves the purpose of satisfaction.

Having understood that ritual is a means of satisfaction, a gentleman also gives his attention to the distinctions determined by it. What are the distinctions? They are the ranks between noble and base, the superiorities between old and young, the degrees between wealth and poverty, and the differences between power and insignificance, i.e., everyone in his proper place. Thus, the Son of Heaven has the privilege of riding the Grand Chariot with rush mats to make himself comfortable, with sweetgrasses on both sides to satisfy his nose, with a gilded crossbar in front to satisfy his eyes, with the bells on the crossbar and the frame to satisfy his ears since they tinkle to the rhythm of *Wu* and *Xiang* when the vehicle moves slowly and to the rhythm of *Shao* and *Hu* if the vehicle moves fast, with the dragon banner of nine streamers to satisfy his airs, and with the insignias of recumbent rhinoceros, crouching tigers, sharkskin girth, silken carriage coverings, and dragon patterns on the chariot hooks to satisfy his sense of majestic authority. Thus, the horses for the Grand Chariot must be thoroughly reliable and perfectly trained before they are harnessed so as to satisfy his desire for safety. Who is aware that by risking life for moral integrity one preserves his own life? Who is aware that making expenditure is the way to the accumulation of wealth? Who is aware that being respectful, modest and courteous is the way to develop the sense of security. And who is aware that by observing rite and morality one's dispositions are nurtured? So, he who seeks only to preserve his life will lose it sooner, he who strives only for profit will surely suffer loss, he who feels contented in being slack, idle and comfortable for the time being will surely face danger, and he who chooses to indulge himself will surely meet his doom. Therefore, he who controls himself with ritual and moral principles will be fulfilled in his desires and improved in moral integrity. If he is overcome by his inborn desires and emotions, he will be lost in both. The Confucianists make it possible for a man to satisfy both while the Mohists cause him to satisfy neither. Such is the distinction between Confucianism and Mohism.

Ritual has three roots. Heaven and Earth are the root of life. Ancestors are the root of tribes or clans. And kings and emperors are the root of order. How could there be life without Heaven and Earth? How could there be clans without ancestors? And how could there be order without kings or emperors? There would be no security for anyone if one of these three was missing. Thus, ritual requires sacrifices to Heaven above and Earth below and respect for ancestors and monarchs. Such are the triple roots of ritual.

A king honors the founder of his family as Heaven, feudal lords dare not allow the temple of their first ancestor to fall into disrepair, senior officials and the men of learning worship their primogenitors. This reflects the distinction in their beginnings. It is the basis of virtue. The sacrifice to Heaven at the suburban altar is the privilege of the Son of Heaven, the sacrifice to Earth is the right enjoyed by the feudal lords and the rite for removing the mourning apparel is restricted to the gentry. These serve to distinguish between the noble who should serve the noble and the humble who should serve the humble, so that what should be great is significant and what should be small trivial. Thus, he who rules all under Heaven serves seven generations of ancestors in his sacrifice, he who rules a state does five, he who possesses a land of fifty *li* does three, he who has a territory of thirty *li* does two, and he who ekes out the barest of living is not permitted to set up an ancestral temple. This is the way to distinguish between great accomplishment that yields abundant benefit and little achievement that brings limited satisfaction.

At the Grand Sacrifice to all ancestors, a goblet holding pure water and a vessel holding raw fish are offered with unflavored broth to honor the basis of food and drink. At the seasonal sacrifice, a goblet holding pure water is offered as drink and followed by sweet wine, and food grains followed by rice and wheat are served as food. At the monthly sacrifice, unflavored broth is followed by various delicacies. These practices honor the basis and also cater to the practical needs. Honoring the base is called the proper form, catering to practical needs is called the rational use, and the integration of both constitutes the perfect form which corresponds to the primordial unity and is therefore regarded as the supreme ritual. Hence, it is considered the best for a goblet to be filled with pure water, a vessel to contain raw fish, and broth to be served flavorless. Such practices have been consistent. The impersonator of the spirit is not supposed to finish the wine offered by the server; the raw fish in the sacrificial vessel is not supposed to be tasted when the service is complete; the server offers food and drink three times but he himself is supposed to consume nothing. This is the same practice as it was in ancient times. Before fetching a bride for the grand marriage, before the arrival of the impersonator of the spirit in the ancestral temple, and before the dead is dressed in the graveclothes, the rites are the same as they were in ancient times. The plain silk covering of the Grand Chariot, the hempen cap worn at the suburban sacrifice, and the hempen sash worn loose at the beginning of the mourning ceremony—all these are one and the same today as they were in ancient times. The monotone wailing in mourning till the third year, the singing of the Pure Temple by one singer leading and three others joining in, and a musical band composed of a bell, a pair of percussion instruments named *fu* and *ge*, and a zither with red strings and holes in the bottom—this is the practice today as it was in ancient times.

Ritual is generally simple at the beginning. It is improved gradually in form and becomes satisfactory at the end. Perfect ritual gives full play to both emotions and forms. Less perfect is each surpassing the other. The least perfect is for emotions to return to the primordial unity. With ritual, Heaven and earth are in harmony, the sun and moon shine brightly, the four seasons proceed in order, the stars and planets move orderly, the rivers and streams flow regularly, and all things flourish. With ritual, love and hate are moderated, joy and anger are made to fit the occasion, those below are obedient, those above are enlightened, and all things change but nothing ends in chaos. Without it, all is lost. Is ritual not of the most importance? Establish and honor its principles and make them the highest standards, and nothing under Heaven can change it more or less. The root and branches are consistent; the end echoes the beginning. With its perfection and clarity as a system, it distinguishes between noble and humble as well as right and wrong. There is order, security and life when all under Heaven follows its principles; there is chaos, danger and death if otherwise. This is something beyond the comprehension of petty men.

Ritual is really profound in meaning. It is so deep that those who insist on the separation of hardness from whiteness or the unification of similarities and differences will be drowned in there, so great that those who intend to create institutions without authorization or hold shallow and perverse ideas will be lost in there, and so lofty in reason that those who are brutal, arrogant, and reckless, and who despise customs and consider themselves to be among the lofty will meet their downfall in there. When the plumb line is laid out, there can be no doubt whether a piece of wood is straight or not. When the balance is hung, there can be no doubt whether something is heavy or not. When the compass or T-square is available, there can be no doubt whether a certain shape is round or square or otherwise. Similarly, if a gentleman is thoroughly acquainted with the ritual principles, he can never be fooled by deceit or artifice. Thus, the marking line is most capable of telling straightness, the balance of achieving justice, the compass and square of judging squareness and roundness, and ritual of evaluating the conduct of man. Those who do not follow or stress ritual are called transgressors, while those who do are called disciplined men. Thinking within the scope of ritual is considered good at thinking, dwelling in ritual without vacillation is regarded as being steadfast. And he who is both good at thinking and dwelling in ritual without vacillation is a sage if he is perfected in ritual. Thus, Heaven occupies the loftiest position, Earth is the ultimate in depth, infinity is the limit of space, and a sage reaches the acme of virtue. Therefore, a man who learns should learn to be a sage instead of becoming a transgressor.

Ritual uses material goods as tribute for its performance, distinguishes between noble and humble in adornment for its ceremony, makes difference by different degrees of quantity, and determines the difference between lavishness and economy according to what is proper. If the ceremony is complex and consumption low, the ritual is grand; if the ceremony is simplified and consumption heavy, the ritual is economized. When ceremony and consumption run parallel, compromise and complement with each other, the ritual is moderate. Therefore, a gentleman is conscious of making a major ritual grand, a minor ritual economical, and an average ritual moderate. He never transgresses whether he walks or rushes or runs. This is where a gentleman remains in security. A man who conducts himself within this scope is an educated gentleman, anyone going beyond it is a commoner, and he who dwells in it, moves about and observes all its principles concerning sequences and gradations is a sage. Honesty involves the constant accumulation of ritual, generosity embodies the all-inclusive tolerance of ritual, loftiness reflects the exaltation of ritual, and perspicacity comes from the mastery of ritual. This is precisely what the following lines in *The Book of Songs* mean:

> All the rites are proper and moderate;
> Every smile and word are appropriate.[1]

Ritual is strict with matters of life and death, for life is the beginning of a man and death the end. When both beginning and end are good, he is perfect as a human being. Therefore, a gentleman is respectful of the beginning and careful about the end, treating both alike. Such is the way of a gentleman and such are the rules of rite and morality.

Respecting a man when he is alive but neglecting him after his death means respect for one with consciousness and contempt for one without it. This is the way of a villain and it reveals his inclination to betray. A gentleman would be ashamed to treat his servants or kids in such a manner, and how much more ashamed would he be to treat his monarch and his parents so! Death happens only once; it does not repeat itself. It is the last occasion on which a subject fully expresses his respect for his monarch and a son fully shows his love for his parents. It is boorish not to serve the living with honesty, generosity and courtesy. It is heartless not to bury the dead with honesty, generosity and courtesy. A gentleman despises boorishness and is ashamed of heartlessness.

Hence the inner and outer coffins of the Son of Heaven consist of seven layers; those of the feudal lords, five layers; those of the senior ministers, three layers; those of the men of learning, two layers. In addition, there are different rules concerning the amount and quality of grave clothes as well as the type of coffin ornaments for each rank, whereby reverence is expressed. In this way, life and death are treated alike, and what people all wish for is satisfied. This is the way of the kings of former times and the highest expression of a loyal subject and a filial son.

The funeral of the Son of Heaven creates a sensation everywhere within the four seas and is attended by the feudal lords. The funeral of a feudal lord affects the allied states and is attended by his senior officials. The funeral of a senior official disturbs a single state and is attended by the men of high orders whose funeral is known to his hometown and is attended by his friends. The funeral of a commoner gathers together his clan members and relatives and notification is sent throughout his community. However, attendance at the funeral of a punished criminal by his clan members and relatives is not permitted; his funeral is only attended by his wife and children. His inner and outer coffins are only three inches thick and undecorated,

---

[1] Minor Court Hymns, *The Book of Songs*.

with only three sets of grave clothes. The funeral procession is not allowed during the day, and the burial should be at dusk. In their routine clothing, the mourners go to bury the dead, return without ritual lamentations, mourning garments, or different lengths of mourning required, whether close or distant in relation, each returning to the usual routine. The funeral ends as soon as the dead is buried as though nothing had ever happened. This shows the greatest disgrace.

Ritual serves in carefully preventing auspicious and inauspicious matters from confusing each other. When fresh cotton is held up to the nose of the dying to see whether he is still breathing, loyal ministers or filial sons are aware of the imminent death; however, they are not supposed to consider about articles for dressing and encoffining the corpse. With tears and fear, they still hope he may survive and attempt to keep him alive. They do not start preparations for the funeral till it is certain that he is dead. The household with preparations made in advance does not encoffin the corpse till the following days and the mourning garments are not worn till the third day. Only then will the death announcement be sent out to those who are far away and in the meanwhile necessary articles are prepared for the burial. The period during which the dead lies in state in the coffin should neither exceed seventy days nor be less than fifty. Why? Because the mourners from far away may arrive, all articles may be prepared and everything will get ready by then. Besides, loyalty is fully expressed, ritual fully observed, and the ceremony complete. After this, divination is made in the morning to determine the date and in the evening the location of burial before the ceremony is conducted. On such an occasion, who could do what ritual forbids and who could stop what ritual demands? Hence, the three months of preparation for burial would make an impression for the dead to appear like what he is when living rather than keep the dead to bring comfort to those who are still alive. It is a way to express one's reverence and remembrance.

The general practice of a funeral rite: adorning the deformed appearance of the dead, with each move it is taken farther away, and with the passage of time, one returns to the usual state of mind. It is the way with the dead that if the corpse is not adorned, it becomes so hideous that no grief is felt. If it is kept close by, one will become casual with and then grow tired of it and consequently begins to neglect it and then no longer shows proper respect. If one day a person loses his monarch or parent but he fails to show his grief or reverence in his burial, he is no better than a beast. This is something a gentleman is ashamed of. Therefore, by adorning the appearance, the hideousness of a deformed corpse is disguised; by moving the corpse away, proper reverence is maintained; by returning to the usual state of mind with the passage of time, the life of the living is properly adjusted.

Ritual serves in restraining what is long and extending what is short so that excess is eliminated and deficiency made up. Thus, the form of love and reverence is extended and the good virtue of following moral principles is cultivated. Impressiveness and crudity, musical tone and weeping, joy and sorrow are pairs of opposites; however, ritual makes an alternative use of both on proper occasions. Impressiveness, musical tone and joy suit the purpose of peace and luck, while crudity, weeping and sorrow are kept for inauspicious occasions. In making it impressive, glamor or indulgence should be avoided. In keeping it crude, misery or damage should be avoided.

In performing music to bring joy, corruption or abandonment should be avoided. In expressing sorrow through weeping, distress or harm should be avoided. Such is the middle course of ritual.

Changes of appearance and facial expression should be sufficient to distinguish the auspicious from the inauspicious, to tell whether the rank is high or low, or to show whether the relation is close or distant. And that is all. Otherwise, it would be treacherous. Even if it is also hard to be like that, a gentleman would despise it. Just as it is proper to eat according to one's appetite and wear according to one's size, it is treacherous to seek a better fame by physically harming oneself. Being against the ritual principles, it is something other than the true feeling of a filial son and of other intentions. Thus, happiness and comfort make a beaming face and distress and worry a sad one. The expressions reflect auspicious and inauspicious events as well as happy or sorrowful emotions. Songs and laughter or weeping and lamentation reverberate auspicious and inauspicious events as well as happy or sorrowful emotions. The meat of livestock, rice and millet, liquor, sweet wine, thick gruel, and fish or beans, bean leaves, and soup serve to show auspicious and inauspicious events as well as happy or sorrowful emotions through food and drink. Ceremonial robe and the embroidery of white and black axes on it, colored silk with designs and patterns, or coarse cloth, mourning garment, hempen robes and straw sandals serve to demonstrate auspicious and inauspicious events as well as happy or sorrowful emotions through clothing. Spacious chambers, grand palaces, soft mats, comfortable beds, low tables and cushions or thatched huts, lean-to sheds, brushwood mats and earthen pillow serve to display auspicious and inauspicious events as well as happy or sorrowful emotions through dwelling. Both feelings are inherent in man. Cutting them short or recovering them, enriching them or making them simple, increasing or weakening them, developing them analogically and perfecting them, so that harmony is found everywhere—at the roots as well as the tips, from beginning to end—and rules are established for all generations to come. And this is ritual. It is comprehensible to none other than a gentleman who is obedient to and familiar with ritual and learns to put it into practice.

It is said that human nature is simple, like timber. Conscious effort renders it rich and orderly. If there were no human nature, there would be nothing for conscious effort to improve upon; if there were no conscious effort, human nature would have no way to refine itself. The integration of human nature and conscious effort makes a sage, who makes true the unity of all under Heaven. So, it is said that all things are born when Heaven and Earth unite, all transformations happen when yin and yang interact, and universal order is realized when human nature and effort are combined. Heaven can give birth to things but it cannot govern them; Earth can support people, but it cannot govern them. Of all things and men, no one is able to find one's proper place till the appearance of a sage. This is what it means in *The Book of Songs* when it sings:

> He can win over all beings that are divine
>   And appease all rivers and mountains.[2]

---

[2] Eulogies, *The Book of Songs*.

In the funeral rite, the dead are adorned as though they were still alive and sent off in a fashion roughly resembling the way in which they lived. Thus, death is treated like the living and absence like presence. Both end and beginning are given the same care. When a person has just died, the first things to be done include washing his hair and body, tying his hair in a knot, trimming his nails, and putting some food in his mouth, imitating what he did when living. If not washed, the hair is combed through with a wet comb and the body wiped with a wet towel three times. With jade plugged in the ears and uncooked paddy rice and white shells put in the mouth, the dead is treated in ways opposite to those in which the living is done. The corpse is dressed in underwear and three outer garments with a belt unbuckled. The face is covered with silk fabric, the hair tied up without a hairpin put in or a hat put on. The name of the dead is written on a banner and fixed to the wooden spirit tablet, which can only be seen clear on the front. Buried with the dead are articles including strapless hats, empty earthen jugs, bamboo mats without mattresses, utensils made of wood are without carvings, earthenware has just a rough shape, implements made of bamboo and reed are unusable, reed pipes and organs are not ready for use, zithers and lutes are strung but untuned, and the carriage is buried but the horses are taken back home, indicating that they are no longer of use. The articles of life are taken to the tomb as if it were a change of dwelling. Simple but unfinished, they look good but unfunctional, taken to the tomb with a carriage and buried while the bells, leather fixtures, reins and harnesses are not. This means that they are no longer to be used down there. It resembles a change of residence, so they are not to be used again but all serve as a formal expression of grief. Thus, the articles of life are no longer used; they serve only ceremonial purposes. The articles to be buried along appear quite normal but they are impractical.

Ritual generally serves the living in making them happy and the dead in sending them off mournfully. It expresses the feeling of reverence in sacrificial offerings and displays the awe-inspiring majesty in military operations. These are practices shared by all kings in ancient and present times but no one knows when they began. Thus, the tomb or grave resembles a house. The inner and outer coffins imitate the sideboards, top, and front and back boards of a carriage. The coverings and decorations for the coffins represent screens and curtains. The reed mats and wooden framework of the grave are the equivalent of walls, railings, doors and roof.

Thus, the purpose of the funeral rite is none other than to make clear the meaning of life and death, to send the dead off with grief and reverence, and to conclude by completing the burial. Interment is held to respectfully bury the corpse. Sacrifices are offered to respectfully serve the spirit. And inscriptions, eulogies, and genealogical records are prepared to respectfully transmit the name to posterity. Serving the living is the beginning and sending off the dead is the end. When both beginning and end are fully attended to, the duties of a filial son are fulfilled and the virtue of a sage is complete.

To deprive the dead for the sake of the living is what Mohism advocates; to deprive the living for the sake of the dead is called confusion; to kill the living and bury them along with the dead is savage. To send off the dead in a similar fashion that one would send off the living so that proper treatment is given to death and life and all is well from beginning to end—this is the standard of ritual and moral principles and such are what the Confucianists do.

Why does mourning extend into the third year? I believe it is a rule established according to feelings involved for the purpose of distinguishing between people near and far in relation or noble and humble in rank to ensure that their obligations are fulfilled and nothing is added to or deleted from them. Consequently, it is a practice not to be altered anywhere. It takes a long time for a great wound to heal and a great pain to disappear. The three-year mourning expresses the most intense grief as far as feelings are concerned. Wearing a mourning garment of coarse hemp, supported by a bamboo stick, living in a hut, eating thin gruel, and sleeping on firewood with one's head placed on a clod of earth—these represent the utmost grief. The three-year mourning period comes to an end with the twenty-fifth month when grief and pain are not yet over and thoughts of and longing for the dead have not been forgotten. The ritual permission to stop mourning marks the conclusion of ceremony for the dead and the return to normal life for the living, does it not? Of all creatures living between Heaven and Earth, those that have blood and feelings must be intelligent and therefore love their kind. Now consider the big birds or beasts: if any one of them gets lost and is separated from its group or mates, it is sure to follow the track back after a certain period of time, say a month. Passing its own place, it will wander around and linger about, call and cry, and pause hesitantly before continuing its journey. Even small birds like swallows or sparrows will give a plaintive cry before flying on. Among creatures of blood and feelings, none is more intelligent than man; therefore, man's feeling for his parents is not exhausted even on the day he dies.

Shall we follow those stupid, shallow and wicked men who have forgotten by evening their parents who died in the morning? If we should indulge in such a behavior, we would not even be as good as birds or beasts. And how could we live in the same community with such men and escape disorder? Or shall we follow the gentlemen who cultivate themselves according to rite and morality? If so, the twenty-five months pass as swiftly as a galloping horse glimpsed through the crack in a wall, and the mourning will continue without end. For these reasons, the Former Kings and the sages established a moderate standard so that those who have fulfilled the ritual requirements shall end the ceremony.

This being so, then how is the difference in mourning told between the close and the distant? For parents, the mourning is complete in a year. Why? Heaven and Earth have completed their cycle of change with the four seasons and all those in between have started afresh. And the Former Kings did the same as a symbol of a new beginning. Why then does mourning extend into the third year? It is for the purpose of increasing honor, so the mourning period is redoubled and another two years are added. Why does it last nine months or shorter sometimes? To show that it is not as grand as that for parents. Thus, the three-year period expresses the highest degree of honor, the three- and five-month periods are the lowest, and the one-year and nine-month periods fall in between. It follows the example of Heaven above, of Earth below and of men in between and represents the principle governing harmony and unity among men. Therefore, mourning into the third year is the highest expression of humanity and hence the loftiest in ritual. It is a custom followed by all the kings both in ancient times and at present.

Why does the mourning for a monarch last three years? A monarch is the ruler of order and good government and the source of rite and morality. He represents the ultimacy of feeling and form. So, is it not proper for all men to join together in paying him the greatest honor? *The Book of Songs* praises,

> Gentle and affable is the gentleman
> Who is the parent of the people.[3]

A monarch has always been regarded as the parent of his people. A father can give life to his children, but he cannot feed them. A mother can feed her children, but she cannot instruct or guide them. A monarch is able to nurture them and good at their education and guidance. So, it is complete for his mourning to extend into the third year. A wet nurse, feeding the child of another, is mourned three months. A foster mother who takes care of the clothing and bedding of another's child, is mourned nine months. And a monarch who makes all these possible is mourned into the third year. It is perfect! Following these principles, there will be order; otherwise, there will be disorder. Such is the perfect system of rites. This being done, there will be stability; otherwise, the state will be in danger, for it is the highest manifestation of feelings. With the accumulation of both, even though the three-year mourning is considered to be inadequate, there is no way to extend it. For similar reasons, there is sacrifice to the god of land and that to the god of grain, and there is also sacrifice to Heaven together with all deceased kings.

What is the purpose of lying in state for three months? It is to make the event magnificent and important so that great esteem and affection can be expressed. When preparations are made for moving the dead from the palace to his resting place in the grave, the Former Kings, being afraid that the burial standards might not be met, extended the period to make it sufficient. Thus, for the Son of Heaven the period is seven months, for the feudal lords five months, and for the senior officers three months, each was enough for the required affairs to be handled successfully so that the standards are fulfilled, all the required items are fully supplied, and the ritual principles are observed.

Sacrifice is a way by which man expresses his feelings of remembrance and admiration. A man is likely to be moved and correspondingly change in emotion. This happens involuntarily in due course. Thus, on occasions when people are happy together, loyal ministers or filial sons are sometimes overcome with such changes in feeling. Their feelings are so intense that, if the rite should be empty of content, they would be frustrated and unsatiated and ritual would seem lacking and incomplete. For this reason, the Former Kings established the ritual system so that their feelings of reverence and affection are fully expressed. That is why we say that sacrifice is a way by which man expresses his feelings of remembrance and admiration. It expresses the greatest loyalty, faith, affection, and reverence and represents the utmost courtesy and the fullest manifestation of ritual. This is comprehensible only to the sages. The sages

---

[3] Major Court Hymns, *The Book of Songs*.

understand it very clearly, the educated gentlemen feel at ease and carry it out, the officials in charge regard it as their duty, and the common people accept them as their custom. For a gentleman, it is the way of man. In the eyes of the common people, it is the service for ghosts. Hence, the gentlemen understand that musical instruments like bells, drums, pipes, chimes, lutes, zithers, and reed and reed organs and performances like *Shao, Xia, Hu, Wu, Zhuo, Huan, Xiao,* and *Xiang* both serve to express joy and sorrow and the change of feelings. Wearing a mourning garment of coarse hemp, supported by a bamboo stick, living in a hut, eating thin gruel, and sleeping on firewood with one's head placed on a clod of earth are considered by gentlemen to be the proper forms expressive of their feelings of grief and pain. There are regulations for military expeditions and gradations of punishments in the penal code that fit crimes. These are proper forms by which gentlemen express their unexpected feelings of loathing and hatred. When a sacrifice is to be conducted, divination is made to determine the appropriate day on which one purifies oneself, fasts, cleans and decorates the temple, sets out tables and mats, presents the ceremonial offerings, and informs the invocator as though someone were really going to enjoy the sacrifice. A bit of each of the offerings is taken and presented as if a ghost were really going to taste it. The provider lifts up the cup and the sacrificer presents the wine as though the divinity were going to drink it. When the guests leave, the sacrificer bows and sends them out before returning to change his clothing, resume his place, and weep as though the divine had really departed. How sad it is and how respectful they are! The dead is served as well as when he was living and treated as though he were still alive. He who receives the sacrifice has neither shape nor shadow, but the ceremony is properly held.

Chapter 20
On Music

Synopsis

This essay systematically demonstrates the idea of musical education.

The first half expounds the reason and strategy for the great Former Kings to create music. Music is derived from human emotions; therefore, it might lead to disorders without guidance. For this reason, the Former Kings formulated music to inspire kindness in men by means of the far-reaching effect of music of court hymns and eulogies to resist evil and stop strife. Music contributed to the harmony between the monarch and his subjects, father and son, brothers and sisters, and village chief and the fellow villagers, so much so that people became broad-minded and cooperative, observed rite and morality, and thus their manners and customs got transformed. As vocal music exercised a huge and rapid influence on men, the great Former Kings were very cautious in making the rules of music so that music suiting to rites was honored and corrupt music despised. The essay also criticizes Di Mo for his ignorance of the intention of the great Former Kings and his denial of the positive role of music.

The second half of the essay further expounds the importance of ritual and music for self-cultivation and government. In cultivating himself, a gentleman "guides his will with bells and drums and gladden his heart with lutes and zithers." Through music, his will would be purified; through ritual, his conduct would become perfect. Music helps unify and harmonize men and ritual helps to make distinctions. The combination of ritual and music would highlight their moral virtue and cultivation. In governing a country, when ritual and music were advocated, there would be clear distinctions between noble and humble or superior and inferior, and there would be harmony and joy without dissipation as well as ease and comfort without disorder. Thus, it would succeed in rectifying the individual, promoting the stability of a country, bringing peace to the world, and realizing the ways of a true king. Otherwise, if rites and music should go in decline, customs be corrupted, music be depraved, ritual and moral principles be replaced by boldness and strength, the world would fall into chaos.

Text

Music is joy, an emotion which man cannot help feeling. Man cannot do without music. If he feels joy, he cannot refrain from expressing it through his voice and giving it shape in his movement. The way of man—his voice, movement and emotional variations—is fully reflected here. Thus, it is impossible for him not to feel joy. His joy cannot be revealed apart from shape and form. The expression of his joy will inevitably be chaotic if it is not properly conducted. The Former Kings hated chaos, and therefore established the music of court hymns and eulogies as guidance so that the feelings of joy were fully expressed without becoming wild and abandoned, the musical composition was clearly discernible and not obstructed, and the intricacy or directness of melody, the elaboration or simplification of instrumentation, the purity or richness of sound, and the rhythm and meter of music were sufficient to arouse the kindness in man's heart and stop the wicked sentiments from approaching. Such were the principles followed by the Former Kings in establishing music. However, Master Mo objected to it. Incredible, is it not?

When music is performed in the ancestral temple of a ruling house and enjoyed by the monarch and his subjects, there is harmony and reverence. When it is performed at home and shared by father and his children or brothers and sisters, there is harmony and intimacy. And when it is performed in towns or villages and heard by both old and young, there is harmony and obedience. Hence, for musical performances the keynote is set in order to determine its harmony. With the coordination of various instruments, the rhythm is developed and the completion of form is achieved. It is sufficient to command unity and bring order to all transformations. Such was the approach the Former Kings adopted in establishing music. But Master Mo was against it. Incredible, is it not?

Hearing the music of court hymns and eulogies, men may heighten their aspirations and become broad-minded. Brandishing shields and battle-axes and rehearsing the motions of bending, stretching and straightening, men can grow dignified in appearance. Each dancing in his position and to the rhythm, the ranks and files are regular and the advances and retreats are orderly. Thus, music plays a role in conducting punitive military expeditions abroad as well as in creating a mood of courtesy and humility at home. In both cases, the function it performs is one and the same: in military expeditions, it serves to encourage obedience; in creating the mood of courtesy and humility, it cultivates the sense of deference as well. Hence music brings great uniformity to all under Heaven and conforms to rites and regulations. It is an integral component of human dispositions. It was the strategy of the Former Kings in establishing the function of music, but Master Mo was opposed to it. Unbelievable, is it not?

In addition, music was used by the Former Kings to exhibit their delight just as armies and weapons were used to give expression to their anger. In this way, their delight and anger were both properly expressed. Therefore, when they were delighted, all the world joined with them in harmony; when they were angry, the violent and unruly feared them. Ritual and music are precisely two major principles of the Former Kings in their way of government. Yet Di Mo opposed it. Therefore, it can be said that Mo's understanding of the principles of government can be likened to what the colors of black and white are to the blind and what sharp and dull sounds are to the deaf. It is just like someone who intends to go to Chu down in the south but moves up northward.

Music exercises a profound influence on men and transforms them soon. Therefore, the Former Kings were careful in their composition. When music is moderate and peaceful, the people become harmonious rather than abandoned. If it is solemn and majestic, the people will be coordinated rather than disorderly. When the people are harmonious and coordinated, the state's army will be powerful and its defense firm, and enemy states will not dare to invade. Under such conditions, the common people will live in security, delight in their home places, and serve their monarch wholeheartedly. Then the monarch's fame will be known abroad, his glory will be brilliant, and the people within the four seas will all have him as their leader. This is the foundation of a true ruler. But if music is seductive and depraved, the people will become abandoned and base. Abandonment leads to chaos and baseness to conflict. The army will be weakened and defense endangered as a consequence of self-abandonment and internal conflict, so enemies will come to attack. When this situation prevails, the common people will not rest secure in their dwellings and take no delight in their home places, and will fail to serve their monarch wholeheartedly. Thus, ritual and music will be cast aside and deviant tunes arise, which is the root to peril, decline, and disgrace. For this reason, the Former Kings honored ritual and music and despised evil music. In defining the duties of officials, it is said that "*Taishi* ('Grand Master') is in charge of the revision of government decrees, examination of poetry, prohibition of lewd music, and revision of other inappropriateness without delay, so that the standard music is not corrupted by barbarian, vulgar and aggressive tones."

"Music is something the sagely kings oppose," said Master Mo, "so the Confucians are wrong to encourage it." A gentleman does not think so. Music is something the sages take delight in. It has the power to create good will in people, exert profound influence on them, and facilitate the transformation of their customs; therefore, the kings of former times guided the people with ritual and music, and there was harmony among them. If the people with emotions of love and hatred had no way to express their joy or anger, there would be disorder. The Former Kings hated disorder; therefore, they cultivated their moral virtue and created proper music, and all under Heaven became obedient. A mourning garment of coarse hemp and the sound of lamenting and weeping make one sad in the heart. Donning armor, strapping on helmets, and singing while marching in rank cause the heart to be stirred to valor; seductive looks and the songs of Zheng and Wei drive the heart to grow licentious; wearing formal caps and court robes with broad sashes and dancing to the tunes of *Shao* and *Wu* bring dignity to the hearts of men. Therefore, a gentleman does not allow his ears to listen to licentious sounds, his eyes to gaze on female beauty, or his mouth to speak abusive words. A gentleman is very careful about these three matters.

Generally, when they are moved by wicked tunes, men display unhealthy tendencies as a consequence, and when such results prevail, there is disorder. When they are moved by decent tunes, men show their obedience, and when this trend develops, good order is formed. Just as one sings and others join in, so good or evil arises correspondingly. Therefore, a gentleman is careful about what he chooses or rejects.

A gentleman guides his will with bells and drums and gladdens his heart with lutes and zithers. Adorned with pheasant feathers and yak tails, the dancers wield their shields and battle-axes and follow the rhythm set by flutes and pipes. The music is clear and bright as Heaven, broad and great as Earth, and the dancers' movements and postures coordinate or alter like the four seasons. Hence, through music people's will is made pure, and through ritual they grow perfect in conduct, develop good sight and an exquisite sense of hearing, and become mild and moderate, so that their manners and customs are transformed, peace is found all under Heaven, good virtue is admired and happiness is all over. That is why I think music is joy. A gentleman enjoys music because he is thus morally cultivated. A petty man enjoys music because his desires are gratified. When virtue overcomes desires, one finds joy instead of disorder; when desires are fulfilled at the sacrifice of virtue, there is delusion but no enjoyment. Therefore, we say music is the means by which joy is guided. The instruments of metal, stone, silk, and bamboo serve to guide moral virtue, and when music becomes popular, people will march in the right direction. Thus, music is a major approach to the government of men. And yet Master Mo disapproved of it!

Moreover, music embodies harmony that can never be altered just as ritual embodies principles that can never be changed. Music brings unity and harmony among men and ritual distinguishes that which is different. Ritual and music work together as a restraint on the human heart. It is the essential nature of music to penetrate into the root and effect profound changes just as it is the principle of ritual to make clear integrity and do away with pretense. However, Master Mo wrongly accused music and his accusation is akin to crime. But all the enlightened kings had already died and there was no one to correct his errors. What is worse, those who are foolish learn from him. This is equal to bringing jeopardy to themselves. A gentleman promotes music, and this is his virtue. But goodness is hated in a chaotic age and no one listens to him. Alas! It is very sad that music cannot play its part! You disciples must exert yourselves in your studies and do not let yourselves be deluded!

What follows are the attributes and symbols of music: The drum is loud and violent. The bell is loud and clear. The chime stone is bright and rhythmic. The reed pipe and organ are solemn and melodious. The flutes are sonorous and inspiring. The ocarina and octal flute are low and atmospheric. The zither is soft and kind. The lute is gentle and sweet. The songs are clear and expressive. And the dances symbolize all things in nature. The drum is surely the lord of music, is it not? Hence, it resembles Heaven; the bell resembles Earth; the chime stone resembles water; the pipes, organs and flutes resemble the sun, moon and stars; the percussion instruments like *tao, zhu, fu, ge, qiang,* and *qia* resemble myriad of things. How do we know the meaning of dances? The dancers do not see themselves with their eyes, nor do they listen to themselves with their ears. Nevertheless, none of their gestures or movements fail to be distinct and rhythmic, whether they look up or down, bend or stretch, advance or retreat, quicken or slow down. They exert to the utmost the strength of their bones and sinews to match the rhythm of drums and bells without the slightest awkwardness or discord. How serious they are in their practice!

When I observe the drinking ceremony of local communities, I realize how easy the kingly way is. The host goes in person to greet the guest of honor and his attendants and all the other guests follow them. When they come to just outside the gate, the host bows his welcome to the guest of honor and his attendants; all the other guests simply enter on their own. This serves to make clear the distinction between eminent and humble. With three bows they come to the steps. After being offered precedence three times, the guest of honor comes up the steps to the hall. After bowing to all the guests, the host offers wine, to which the guest of honor responds with a toast. There follow many episodes of deferring and polite refusals between them, which are abbreviated for the attendant guests. As for the other guests, they ascend to receive the cup of wine, offer a sacrifice in their seats, drink the wine on their feet before descending without returning the cup to the host. In this way the distinction is made between rites for superiors and inferiors.

Then musicians enter and ascend to sing three songs before the host offers wine to his guests. The host does it again after the reed pipe players enter to perform three pieces of music. The musicians and players alternate with each other for three rounds before they perform in ensemble another three pieces. Then the musicians announce the completion of their performance before departure. After that, two of the host's attendants raise a goblet in a toast to the guest of honor's attendants and other guests, which means that two overseers of decorum are appointed. From this we see that they are harmonious and joyful without becoming dissolute. Following this, the guest of honor offers a toast to the host, the host offers a toast to the guest of honor's attendants who in turn offer a toast to the other guests according to their rank in age, ending with goblet washers. In this way we know that proper honor is given to all seniors without leaving anyone out. The formal ceremony being concluded, all participants descend to remove their shoes and ascend again to be seated. Now they may keep drinking according to the rules: drinking in the morning shall not prevent business before noon and drinking in the evening should not adversely affect business at night. When the guest of honor departs, the host bows and sees him out, and thus all ceremonies are brought to completion. From this we can see that it is possible to be easy and comfortable without being disorderly. Being clear about the distinction between noble and humble, distinguishing between superiors and inferiors, staying in harmony and joy without dissipation, giving honor to the seniors without leaving anyone out, remaining easy and comfortable without being disorderly—these five patterns of conduct are sufficient to rectify the individual and to promote the stability of a state. When there is stability in the states, there is peace under Heaven. That is why I say "When I observe the drinking ceremony of local communities, I realize how easy the kingly way is."

These are the signs of a chaotic age: Men wear glamorous clothing, make themselves up in a womanish manner, follow licentious customs, seek nothing but profit, engage in a mixed variety of activities, enjoy depraved music, compose deviant and ostentatious essays, pursue a life without restraint, send off their dead in a niggardly manner, despise rite and morality, value boldness and strength, rob when they are poor and do harm to others when they are rich. The age of order is the opposite of all this.

Chapter 21
On Removing the Obstacle of Limitations

Synopsis

This is a philosophical treatise illustrating the method of thinking.

Having witnessed the situation in which the feudal lords employed different principles of government and various schools of thought promoted their own doctrines, Master Xun attempted to find the epistemological origin of gain and loss, prosperity and decline, success and failure, order and chaos in politics through the analysis and comparison of historical experience with a view to providing theoretical guidance for the unity and stability of a country. He traced the cause of chaos on different levels to obscurity in cognition resulting from one-sidedness, and pointed out that the corresponding approach to removing such obscurity consisted in the mastery of Dao that runs constant through all things and events and exhausts all variations and changes.

How can Dao be understood? It is done through the mind which is found in a usual state of confusion and disorderliness caused by disturbances in cognition, including mutual oppositions and conflicts and which may be made orderly by means of emptiness, concentration and tranquility. These efforts were demonstrated to be able to achieve the ideal of great clarity and brilliance which in turn would help remove the biases and prejudices standing in the way of understanding.

Text

It is the common fault of men to be blinded by one-sidedness and therefore ignorant of great truth. When corrected, they will return to truth; but if they are of two minds, they will be doubtful and confused. There is no alternative Dao under Heaven; the sages are never of two minds. Nowadays the feudal lords employ different principles of government and the hundred schools advocate different doctrines, so that some of them are necessarily correct while others are incorrect, and some help create order while others lead to chaos. Those monarchs who led their states to disorder and the scholars who made their doctrines confusing all sincerely sought what was right and considered themselves to have made efforts in this direction. However, since they strayed from the correct road, they were enticed by other men with what pleased them. Biased in favor of their own knowledge, they were only afraid of hearing it criticized. Judging other doctrines on the basis of their own preferences, they were only afraid of hearing them praised. Therefore, they deviated from the right principles but were unconscious of putting themselves right and still considered themselves correct. Is this not what it means to be blinded by one-sidedness and therefore ignorant of great truth? Absent-minded, one will fail to see black and white right in front of him or to hear thundering drums close by. How much more so with a man who is limited in understanding! Is it not miserable for a man conscious of Dao to be criticized from above by a ruler who leads his state to disorder and denounced from below by men who make their doctrines confusing?

What causes limitations? Some are caused by desire or hatred, some by views confined to the beginning or the end, some by what is distant or near, some by knowledge profound or shallow, others by matters of past or present. All things are different and the comprehension of these differences result in the limitations. This is the common fault in the way of thinking.

Jie of the Xia and Zhou of the Yin dynasties are examples of rulers being so limited. Deceived by Moxi and Siguan, the former did not have confidence in Longfeng Guan. As a result, his mind became deluded and his conduct disorderly. Fooled by Daji and Feilian, the latter did not have trust in Prince Qi of Wei. Consequently, his mind became deluded and his conduct disorderly. Thus, all their ministers forsook loyalty and worked for their own personal gains instead, the common people hated and cursed them and refused to do their service, and the able and virtuous withdrew from the court and fled into seclusion. This was why they lost their lands and reduced their ancestral temples to ruins. In the end, Jie died on Mount Li and Zhou ended with his head dangling from the red pennon. Being unconscious of their fault in advance and having refused to accept remonstrances, they suffered from the disasters as a result of the limitations.

Tang of the Shang Dynasty took warning from the fate of Jie and kept a clear mind in the careful government. Accordingly, he was able to give enduring trust to Yin of Yi and kept Dao. This was why he could replace the king of the Xia and gain control over the entire nine provinces of China. King Wen took warning from the fate of Zhou and kept a clear mind in the careful government. Accordingly, he was able to give enduring trust to Wang Lü[1] and kept the right way. This was why he could replace the king the Yin and become the ruler of the entire nine regions of China. None of the distant regions failed to pay tributes of the rarest goods, so that they could see all beautiful colors, hear all great music, taste all good flavors, dwell in all splendid palaces, and receive all noble titles. When they lived, all under Heaven

---

[1] Better known as Shang Jiang or Grand Duke Jiang, a famous statesman in early Western Zhou, who assisted King Wen and King Wu in founding the dynasty.

sang their praises; when they died, all within the four seas wept. This may be called great prosperity. It says in *The Book of Songs*,

> Merrily, merrily dance the phoenixes
>
> Whose wings flap like shields
>
> And whose calls sound like flute in open fields.
>
> Male and female they both leap and dart,
>
> And the emperor is happy in the heart.[2]

The happiness is derived from not being restricted by limitations.

Among the ministers of ancient times who were blinded by limitations, Yang Tang and Qi Xi[3] served as examples. Haunted by his desire for power, the former expelled Master Dai[4] from the state. Obsessed with a desire for the throne, the latter framed Shensheng up. In the end, the former was killed in Song and the latter in Jin. One expelled a worthy prime minister and the other trapped a filial elder brother, but both were punished unawares. Such is the disaster of being blinded by limitations. Thus, from ancient times to the present there has never been a case in which someone who was greedy, despicable and treacherous and who struggled for power did not end in danger, disgrace and destruction. Shu Bao, Qi Ning, and Peng Xi were benevolent, wise, and free from prejudice; therefore, they could support Zhong Guan and enjoy a fame, fortune and title equal to those of the latter. Both Duke of Shao and Wang Lü were benevolent, wise, and free from prejudice; therefore, they were able to support Duke of Zhou and enjoy a fame, fortune and title equal to those of the latter. In an old book it says,

> It is enlightened to be able to identify the worthy; it is competent to be able to assist them. And he who is diligent and makes great efforts will enjoy long-lasting blessings.

This serves in explaining that happiness comes from not being blinded by any limitations.

In the past, some travelling scholars were blinded by their limited knowledge, among whom were those who advocated their confusing doctrines. For example, Master Mo was practically-minded and was ignorant of ritual, Master Song one-sidedly emphasized the importance of few desires but did not understand how they could be satisfied, Master Dao Shen only stressed the rule of law but was unaware of the part played by the worthy, Master Buhai Shen saw only the importance of power and influence but ignored the role of human intelligence, Master Shi Hui enjoyed playing with words and was ignorant of the truth behind them, and Master Zhuang focused on obedience to Heaven but overlooked the importance of human effort. Thus, from the practical perspective, Dao is the pursuit of profit. From the viewpoint of desire, it is wholly a matter of satisfaction. From the vantage point of law, it is a matter of regulations. In view of power and influence, it is a matter of expedience. From the angle of diction, it is a matter of arguments and logic. And

---

[2] Not available in the extant Chinese versions.

[3] A son of Duke Xian of Jin by his favored concubine named Ji Li.

[4] Huan Dao, a chief minister of the state of Song.

from the perspective of Heaven, it is a matter of letting nature take its course. These arguments focus only on one side of Dao. Dao is constant in itself. However, it is capable of exhausting all changes. It is insufficient to use any single aspect to represent its whole. Men with superficial knowledge observe Dao from just one side and fail to understand it truly. So, they think it sufficient and proceed to embellish it. Such men bring confusion to themselves and delusion to others. Those in high position deceive their subordinates; those who are subordinates foul their superiors. Such is the misfortune caused by limitations.

Confucius, on the other hand, was benevolent, wise, and free from prejudice. This was why his method of control over chaos sufficed to serve the purpose of the great Former Kings. He achieved an overall mastery of Dao and followed it instead of being blinded by one-sidedness. Hence his virtue is equal to that of Duke of Zhou and his fame matches that of the sagely kings of the Three Dynasties.[5] Such are the blessings of not being blinded by limitations.

The sages are aware of the trouble to be caused by improper ways of thinking and of the trouble caused by limitation in knowledge. Therefore, they do not see desire or hatred only, beginning or end only, what is far or near only, what is profound or shallow only, and past or present only. Instead, they lay out all things and weigh them according to certain standard. In this way, the differences will not be able to blind one another and lead to disorder.

What is the standard? It is Dao. It must be comprehended in the mind; otherwise, the right Dao would be refused and the wrong Dao accepted. When men can do whatever they please, who would like to keep to what they disapprove of and reject what they approve of? With a mind that refuses the right Dao, men will choose those who do not observe Dao rather than those who do. Such men will create disorder if they are joined by those who do not observe Dao in commenting on those who do, for how could they truly understand Dao? Only when Dao is truly understood in the mind can the right Dao be followed and maintained and the wrong Dao prohibited. On the other hand, with a mind that follows the right Dao, men will choose those who observe Dao rather than those who do not. When such men are joined by those who follow Dao in commenting on those who do not, they lay the foundation on which order will be created, for how could they not truly understand Dao? Therefore, the key to good social order lies in understanding Dao.

How do men comprehend Dao? I think they do it through the mind. How can the mind understand it? I think it does by being empty, concentrated, and tranquil. The mind is constantly adding to its storage, and yet it is somewhat empty. It never fails to learn both sides of a thing simultaneously and yet it is capable of concentration. It never stops moving and yet it may remain tranquil. Man is born with perceptive abilities and therefore has the power of memory, the faculty by which the mind stores information. However, the mind is also somewhat empty because it never prevents the collection of new information with what is already in storage. The mind is able to know from its birth. With this ability, it perceives differences. This means that it can understand different things at the same time and therefore gains the knowledge

---

[5] Yu of Xia, Tang of Shang, and King Wen and King Wu of Zhou.

of them. Nevertheless, it has the power of concentration. That is, it does not prevent the understanding of one thing against that of another. In sleep, the mind has dreams. In relaxation, it wanders off. In application, it reflects. Thus, the mind constantly moves. Nonetheless, it possesses the quality of being tranquil, which means it does not allow dreams and fantasies to interfere with understanding. He who seeks but has not yet attained Dao should be urged to take emptiness, concentration and tranquility as his code of conduct. He who seeks Dao and is empty in mind will receive it. He who applies Dao and is concentrated will have comprehensive understanding of it. He who reflects on Dao and is tranquil in mind will have a clear perception of it. He who perceives Dao clearly and puts it into practice has a true understanding of it. Being empty, concentrated and tranquil in mind is called great clarity and brilliance. None of the myriad things has a form that is imperceptible. None perception is not assigned a proper place. And none perception with a proper place fails in its function. With this ability, one may sit in his room and see all things within the four seas, live in the present and pass judgement on distant ages, observe all things and understand their true conditions, inspect orders and disorders and find their regular patterns, harness Heaven and Earth and put all things to use, master the great principles and become thoroughly familiar with all that is in the universe. Who knows the breadth and profundity of his wisdom, the brilliance and nobleness of his virtue, and the variations and adaptability of his form? His brightness is comparable to the sun and moon. His wisdom extends in the eight directions. Such is the Great Man. How could he be blinded by any limitations?

Mind is the lord of the body and master of the spiritual intelligence. It issues commands instead of being commanded. It is self-restrained and self-employed. It takes or gives up on its own free will. And it goes or stops automatically. Thus, the mouth can be forced to speak or to be silent; the body can be forced to crouch down or stretch out, but the mind cannot be forced to change its will. If the mind thinks something right, it will accept it; if it thinks something wrong, it will reject it. Therefore, the state of mind is said to be such that no prohibition may be placed upon its selections. Although the object it perceives may be many and diverse, it does not hesitate if it is perfectly concentrated. *The Book of Songs* says,

> I pick and gather the mouse-ear,
> > My small basket is yet with half load.
> > I am so eager to have my love here
> > That I forget my basket by the road.[6]

A small basket is easy to fill since the mouse-ear is found everywhere. However, one cannot stay on the roadside absent-minded. It is therefore said that nothing will be learned if the mind is distracted, understanding will not be thorough if the mind is not concentrated, and doubt and delusion will occur if one is absent-minded. Be concentrated on Dao in inspection and all things will be properly understood. If one does so, it means he has attained perfection. No principle of one type of things can

---

[6] Ballads from the States, *The Book of Songs*.

be observed if one is absentminded. Hence when a wise man chooses one thing, he puts his concentration on it.

A farmer is an expert in the work of the fields, but it may not be acceptable to make him a director of agriculture. A merchant is well-versed in the ways of the market, but it may not be acceptable to make him a director of commerce. An artisan is a specialist in manufacture, but it may not be acceptable to make him a director of the industry. But there are men incapable of any of these skills who could be appointed in charge of them. This is because they are well versed in Dao rather than specific things. He who is expert in a specific thing is suitable to do it only; he who is well versed in Dao may place all things under control. A gentleman concentrates on Dao and uses it to inspect things. His concentration leads to the right way of thinking, and when he inspects things with Dao, his perception will be clear. To examine the clear perception with the right way of thinking, he is able to control all things.

In ancient times, when he governed all under Heaven, Shun did not issue specific orders concerning each matter, yet all things were brought to completion. Thus, he who is concentrated on Dao and vigilant for dangers will be glorious on all sides, and he who brings his concentration to perfection will enjoy glory unawares. *The Classic of Dao* says,

> A mind that observes Dao is anxiously on guard; a mind that masters Dao is attentive to all the subtle manifestations.

Such minute distinctions are perceptible only to an enlightened gentleman. Hence, human mind may be compared to a pan of water. If it is set upright and not disturbed, the turbid will settle to the bottom and the clear will be on the top, so that if you look in it you can see your beard and eyebrows as well as the lines on your face. With a breeze passing over its surface, the mud will be stirred up and the clear water will be disturbed, so that you cannot see the correct reflection of your face in it. It is the same case with the mind. If you guide it with reason, nourish it with clarity, and do not allow external objects to unbalance it, it will be able to distinguish between right and wrong and resolve doubts. A small disturbance will change the external impression and upset the internal balance, and then the mind will fail to make gross distinctions. In the past, many men were fond of writing, but only Jie Cang enjoys the universal fame because he concentrated on it. Many men were fond of farming, but Houji alone is still remembered because he concentrated on it. Many men were fond of music, but only the name of Kui is passed down because he concentrated on it. And many men paid attention to righteousness, but Shun alone is honored by later ages because he concentrated on it. Chui invented the bow and Fuyou made the arrow, but it was Yi who had a mastery of archery. Zhong Xi invented the chariot and Du Cheng found ways to harness horses to it, but it was Fu Zao who perfected the art of carriage driving. Hence, from ancient times to the present there has never been a man who could be an expert without the concentration of his effort. Master Zeng once commented, "If anyone sees the baton and dreams he can swat a rat with it, how could he be permitted to sing with me!"

A man named Ji[7] lived in a stone cave. He was expert at guessing riddles and fond of reflection. Should he be stimulated by anything he desired to see or hear, he would be distracted in the mind. The noise of mosquitoes or gnats would interrupt his concentration. To succeed in thinking over a problem, he dwelled in quietude far away from the noise of mosquitoes and flies and other distractions to the eyes and ears. If one meditates on benevolence in such a manner, would it be considered to have reached its profundity? Mencius hated corruption and therefore divorced his wife. This could be said that he was anxious to outdo others, but it was not thoughtful deliberation. Master You hated dozing off, so he burned the palm of his hand in order to keep awake. This could be said that he was able to exercise self-endurance, but it failed to show that he was fond of reflection. To avoid the desires of eyes and ears and the disturbances of mosquitoes and gnats can be called the ability of self-warning, but it is not yet profound perception. Profound perception is possible only to a perfect man. Since he is perfect, what need has he for self-improvement, self-endurance and self-warning? A dull brilliance shines on the outside and a clear brilliance shines within. The sages do as they please to their hearts' content, but they are reasonable in the management of all things. So, what need have they for self-improvement, self-endurance and self-warning? The benevolent who practice Dao do not do so intentionally; the sages who practice Dao do not force themselves to do so. The benevolent think respectfully; the sages think joyfully. This is the proper way to govern the mind.

Generally, if there is doubt in one's observation and the mind is not inwardly settled, he will be unclear about external things. Failure of careful consideration will result in the inability to determine what is right or wrong. A person who walks in the dark will mistake a stone on the ground for a crouching tiger or a row of trees for men standing. This is because the darkness obscures his vision. A drunkard will try to leap a ditch a hundred paces wide as though it were a narrow gutter or stoop to go through a city gate as though it were a low doorway. This is because the wine has caused confusion in his spirit. Pressing against the eye while looking at an object will make it appear double; covering the ears when listening will make silence seem like a loud noise. This is because the external force has distorted the senses. Looking down at cows from a mountain top will make them appear like sheep, but he who looks for his sheep will not go down to fetch them. This is because the distance obscures their actual size. Looking up at very tall trees from the foot of a hill will make them appear like chopsticks, but he who looks for chopsticks will not go up for that purpose. This is because the height obscures their true length. When water is moving, its reflection wavers. So, people do not use it as a mirror to tell whether someone is beautiful or ugly because the flow of water stirs the reflection. Even if he looks up, a blind person cannot see the stars. But men do not determine in this way whether the stars are there or not because a blind has no sense of sight. Anyone attempting to determine the nature of things in such circumstances would be the biggest fool in the world. Such a fool who tries to settle one doubt with another in the determination of things will

---

[7] This is an allusion to Confucius' grandson.

never make a proper judgement. And if his decisions are inaccurate, how could he be expected to be free from any fault?

South of the mouth of the Xia River there was a man named Shuliang Juan. He was foolish and easily frightened. One night, the moon was bright and he went out for a walk. When he looked down and saw his own shadow, he took it for a crouching ghost. Then raising his head, he saw his own hair and took it to be a demon standing over him. He turned about and ran. He had hardly reached home when he was out of breath and died. Alas! Was it not sad? Whenever people believe they see ghosts, they surely make the judgements when startled, uncertain or confused. These are occasions when they mistake nothing for something or vice versa and make decisions accordingly. If a man is affected by dampness and contracts rheumatism, he beats a drum and offer a pig in hope of driving the evil spirit away and being blessed with recovery. He will surely wear out the drum and sacrifice the animal in vain. Thus, although he may not live on the south of the river mouth, it still makes no difference.

It is human nature to possess the cognitive ability; it is the law of things to be known. Yet with the inborn power of cognition, it is impossible to understand all the laws without any restraint even if one spends his whole lifetime doing it. One may learn hundreds of millions of principles of things, but they are insufficient to exhaust the complete cycle of transformation of all things. Then one is no different from a foolish person. If one goes on learning like this till his old age when his children grow up and still remains as foolish and ignorant of his error as ever, then he may be called an ignorant and presumptuous man.

Thus, learning should have a certain limit. What is the limit then? The limit is when one has perfect satisfaction. When is one perfectly satisfied? When he achieves the understanding of the sagely kings. A sage has a perfect mastery of all moral principles; a king has a perfect mastery of all regulations of a state. A perfect mastery of both is sufficient to be the ultimate standard of man under Heaven. Hence, in learning one should follow the sagely kings and observe their rules and regulations, seek out their guiding principles and follow their examples. He who strives in this orientation is a man of learning, he who comes close to this goal is a gentleman, and he who obtains a complete understanding is a sage. He who has intelligence but does not consider the regulations of the sagely kings can be described as unmethodical. He who has courage but does not defend the system of the sagely kings is called a treacherous coward. He who is capable of critical analysis but fails to differentiate the regulations of the sagely kings confuses public opinions. He who is multitalented but is not ready to enhance the principles of the sagely kings is wily, and he who has a silver tongue but refuses to propagate the principles of the sagely kings talks only rubbish. An old book says, "There are two things to do under Heaven: to perceive what is right through what is wrong and to identify what is wrong from what is right." Or to judge what conforms to the regulations of the sagely kings and what does not. If all the world fails to accept these regulations as the lofty standard of judgement, could they find any alternative to separate the right from the wrong or determine what is straight and what is crooked? If it fails to separate right from wrong, to determine what is straight or crooked, to tell good order from chaos, or to practice the way proper to human beings, the learning is of no benefit to man even though it is mastered, and it is of no ill consequence even if it is neglected. It is nothing other than the pursuit of strange arguments and bizarre claims or the playing on words for the purpose of confusing others. With a glib tongue, those who advertise such learning impose silence on others, endure disgrace without the sense of shame, abandon themselves without following the correct path, propose absurd arguments with an eye out for profit alone, dislike deference and yielding, and disregard ritual and moderation, but they like to jostle and hassle one another. Such are the ways of wicked men in promoting their doctrines and such are most of those who engage in the study of learning. This is what an old book means when it says,

> A gentleman despises those who play on diction and believe it to be clear perception or indulge in empty talks and believe it to be a controversial skill. A gentleman also despises those who have extensive experience and powerful memory but do not follow the principles of the sagely kings.

If any effort is of no contribution to success, if any pursuit is of no boost to attainment, and if any anxiety is of no help to easing a crisis, it should be abandoned completely. Do not allow them to thwart you or disturb your mind even for a moment. Do not long for what was and do not worry about what will be. Do not feel unhappy or sorry about anything. Act when the time comes. Respond to things when they arrive. Handle matters when they occur. Thus, everything will be very clear, whether it is order or disorder and no matter it should be confirmed or denied!

There has never been an enlightened ruler who succeeded by hiding truths or failed by making them public. Nor has there been a benighted ruler who succeeded by making truths public and failed by hiding them. If the ruler of men is too secretive, slanders will reach his ears while honest advice will be turned back, and petty men will draw near while gentlemen will be alienated. In *The Book of Songs*, it sings,

> If ink black is considered brilliant white,
>   A dark green fox would be all right.[8]

This is saying that when a ruler is ignorant, then his ministers will be treacherously deceitful. If the ruler of men is outspoken, honest advice will come and slanders will be turned back, and gentlemen will draw close while petty men will be kept at a distance. In *The Book of Songs*, it also sings,

> Those below are found in the light,
>   Since their monarch above shines bright.[9]

This is saying that if the ruler is as open as the day, his subordinates will be transformed to virtue.

---

[8] Not available in the extant Chinese versions.

[9] Major Court Hymns, *The Book of Songs*.

Chapter 22
On Rectifying Names

Synopsis

This essay attempted to clarify the relationship between name (concept) and reality (entity) and demonstrate the meaning in the rectification of names.

Master Xun believed that, rather than intrinsically appropriate, the names of things are conventional and are not established till contact is made with the objects of perception, and testing and verification are carried out in the mind so that both similarities and differences are available as the foundation on which judgments are made. For things whose names and realities are uncertain, old names may be kept or new names may be formulated according to objective changes. The key point in naming lies in investigating the content of things and determine the rules of designation. Names are definite and the realities to which they apply can be identified. When the basic principles of naming are observed, it will be possible to make clear the distinction between noble and base and discriminate between things that are different. As a result, there will be no trouble in making oneself understood or failure in any other undertakings.

Correct names are closely related with public morality and correspondingly with social order. When heresies are rampant and people are confused in their mind, the trouble is necessarily found in the confusion of names and the realities they designate. The right and responsibility of rectifying names rested with the sagely kings. In their absence, which might be worsened by the rise of evil doctrines, resort to gentlemen is necessary in order to clarify the ways of the sagely kings by powerful persuasion. The gentlemen should see to it that mind conforms to Dao, explanations conform to mind, and words and expressions conform to explanations so that names are used according to the convention and correspond to the facts and therefore understanding comes true. Master Xun introduced the persuasions and explanations characteristic of the sages and the educated gentlemen, and pointed out that gentlemen should employ correct names and proper expressions to guarantee that they were properly understood rather than seek to win over others.

He had one of his focuses on analyzing the relationship between social order and human desires and pointed out that order or chaos was determined by what the mind considered reasonable rather than by men's desires since human nature, emotions, and desires are inherent, irremovable and inexhaustible. He believed there could be no better principle than acting according to Dao, the proper standard from antiquity to the present, because it could bring one close to complete satisfaction or else place one's pursuit under control when conditions were unfavorable, so men should be aware of and go after Dao, see the value in oneself, and make oneself a master of things rather than vice versa.

Text

The established names[1] of the kings of later times: The terms of criminal law followed the Shang dynasty, the titles of rank were copied from the Zhou dynasty, and the terms of ritual were quoted from *The Book of Rites*. For the common names applied to all things, they followed the established customs and conventions of the various Xia states so that villages of distant regions with divergent customs could follow these practices in their cross-cultural communication.

The various common terms for man himself: What characterizes a man from birth is called $xing_1$ (性, "nature"), which represents the harmony of *yin* and *yang* as well as the interaction between sensory organs, natural rather than artificial. The likes and dislikes, delights and angers, sorrows and joys which constitute *xing* are called *qing* (情, "emotion"), which are natural and whose selections by the heart is called *lü* (虑, "consideration"). Actions taken on the basis of consideration is called *wei* (伪, "artificial or conscious activity") which is the outcome of accumulated consideration and repeated actions. Actions performed for legitimate profit is called *shi* (事, "cause; business"); actions performed for justice is called $xing_2$ (行, "virtue; moral conduct"). The inherent ability of man in understanding things is called zhi_1 (知, "knowledge"); zhi_1 in agreement with the objective world is called zhi_2 (智, "wisdom"). The inherent ability of man to do something is called $neng_1$ (能, "aptitude; instinct") or $neng_2$ (能, "talent; skill") when corresponding with the requirements of a situation. Injury to $xing_1$ is called *bing* (病, "disease"); an encounter by accident is called *ming* (命, "fate"). These are the various common names for man. They were the established terms of the kings of later times.

When a true ruler establishes the names, they become definite and the reality to which they apply can be identified. When the basic principles of names are observed, communication comes to be realized and he carefully leads his people in unified actions. Therefore, those who split words and coin arbitrary names for the purpose of confusing people in their use of correct names and arouse public controversy are called great villains whose crimes are as grave as forging credentials and tallies or tampering with weights and measures. Hence, none of his people dare attempt to

---

[1] Virtually equivalent to concepts or words.—Tr.

throw the proper terms into disorder; they all remain honest and are therefore easily employed to achieve efficiency. Since none dare bring confusion to the correct use of terms by making odd names, they are unified in following the basic principles and careful to follow orders. In such a situation, his rule will last. A long-lasting rule with great achievements is the epitome of good government, which is the outcome of carefully following the conventions.

Nowadays, however, there are sagely kings no more. Men are careless about the rules. As a consequence, strange words come into use, names and realities are confused, and the distinction between right and wrong is obscured. Under such circumstances, even if there are officials charged with preserving the codes of law and Confucians engaged in interpreting the rules and regulations, confusion still exists. If a true ruler rises, he will surely create some new names in addition to following the old ones. In such a case, it is essential to understand why names are necessary, how differently they are motivated and what crucial rules are to be observed in giving names.

Since things differ in form and structure and men hold different views about them, communication is necessary to make them clear. When different things are jumbled together and remain obscure in name and reality, it is impossible to distinguish between noble and base or to tell which are similar or different. In such a situation, there will be the problem of being unable to make oneself understood or failure in any other undertakings. For this reason, wise men make distinctions between them by adopting names to designate various realities so as to make clear the distinction between noble and base and discriminate between things that are the same and those that are different. When the distinction between noble and base is made clear and similarity and difference are recognized, there will no longer be the problem of making oneself understood or failure in any other undertakings. This is why names are necessary.

Then, how are names motivated so that there are similarities and differences? I would like to say that they are based on our sense organs. Generally, men belonging to the same community and having the same dispositions perceive and comprehend things in the same way; therefore, things most possibly copied by means of various comparisons will be understood. Thus, a common name is agreed upon for all things before it is expected for use when the occasion demands. Shapes, colors and textures are distinguished by the eye. Sounds are either pure or mixed and tones are harmonious or bizarre because of the ear. Sweet, bitter, salty, bland, hot, sour and unusual tastes are differentiated by the mouth. The rich variety of fragrance, aroma and other pleasant scents, the various types of foul odors like rankness, rancidness and putridness, and other variations of strange smells are discerned by the nose. Pain and itch, cold and heat, smoothness and roughness, lightness and heaviness are told apart by the body. Pleasure, worry, happiness, anger, sorrow, joy, love, hate, and all other desires vary because of heart. The heart has the power of testing and verification with which it comprehends various sounds through ears and understands different forms through eyes. However, it cannot play its role till it gets in touch with the objects of perception. If anyone coming into contact with a thing through the five senses fails to be aware of it and cannot explain it after testing and verification by the heart, then none will disagree that he is ignorant. This is the way in which one goes about distinguishing between things that are similar or different.

With the distinctions being made, names are assigned accordingly. Things that are the same should be given the same name; those that are different should have different names. Where a single character is sufficient to express the meaning, one character is used; where one character is insufficient to do so, a compound should be adopted. If the single character and the compound do not conflict, they may share a hyperterm without any harm being done. With the knowledge that different realities bear different names, it should be made clear that none of the different realities does not have a different name. Confusion must be avoided here. It is just like the case in which all the same realities share the same name. For example, the myriad things are great in number. On occasions we want to refer to all of them, we call them *wu* (物, "matter"). *Wu* is a great generalizing name shared by all physical substance. More generalizing names may be determined till no further hyperterms can be made by analogy. At other times, we want to refer to some categories of things, so we use words like *niao* (鸟, "bird") or *shou* (兽, "beast"). Both *niao* and *shou* are great classifying names. By analogy, particular classifying names can be decided till no further hyperterms are available.

Names are not intrinsically appropriate. They are established by convention. Once a name is made according to convention and becomes a matter of custom, it is appropriate; otherwise, if it differs from the agreement, it is inappropriate. Names are arbitrary. They are used to stand for certain realities by agreement. Once this relationship is established and the custom is formed, they become the names of those realities. There are clever names in the first place, simple and free from self-contradictions. They are good names. There are things similar in form but different in content; there are other things different in form but similar in content. They are distinguishable. Things similar in form but different in content may share a name but are still two different realities. Where form being changed into something else rather than content, this is called *hua* (化, "transformation"). Things transformed in form rather than in content are still called the same reality. This is why it is necessary to investigate the content of things and determine the rules of designation. It is the key to naming. So, we must be careful to examine the way in which the kings of later times established names.

Statements like

> It is no disgrace to suffer insult.[2]
> A sage has no love for himself.[3]
> Killing a robber is not killing a person.[4]

---

[2] Proposed by Jian Song.

[3] It is believed to be a Mohist view, holding that a sage does not love himself because he treats all men the same, including himself.

[4] A Mohism view, holding that robber and person are two different names.

are cases of confusion about the use of names that bring confusion to names. They can be prohibited by investigating why names are necessary and observing which statements are appropriate. Judgments like

> A mountain and a chasm are on the same level.[5]
>
> Man has few desires.[6]
>
> The meat of domestic animals is by no means more delightful in taste, nor is the sound of large bells more pleasant to the ears.[7]

are examples of confusion about realities that bring confusion to names. They may be rejected by examining the motivation of similar or different names and observing which judgments conform to reality. Self-contradictions like

> What are mutually exclusive are mutually inclusive.
>
> Oxen and horses are not horses.

are instances of confusion about the use of names that bring confusion to realities. They can be banned by testing according to convention and refuting what is opposed with what is accepted. All the fallacies and offensive statements departing from the proper way and fabricated intentionally by men are similar to these three types of errors. An enlightened ruler is aware of such differences and does not deign to argue with men over such claims.

It is easy to unify the people by means of Dao but it will not do to explain to them why. For this reason, an enlightened ruler governs them with influence, guides them with Dao, warns them with decrees, enlightens them with views and restrains them with penalties. And his people are naturally converted to Dao very soon. Why is it necessary to argue with them?

Nowadays with the death of all the sagely kings, the world is in chaos and evil doctrines arise. Without authority to exercise his influence or penalties to restrain the people, a gentleman is obliged to resort to persuasive speaking.

Naming is practiced when the understanding of reality fails. Convention is expected when the understanding of a name fails. Definition is made when the understanding of convention fails. Explanation is necessary when the understanding of a definition fails. Thus, convention, naming, definition and explanation are important forms of application that mark the beginning of a true ruler's business. A name plays its role if the reality it refers to is immediately understood when it is heard. The coordination of names comes true when these names are combined to form a discourse. Names are understood when they are properly used and coordinated.

Names are used to define different realities. Phrases are the names of different realities put together to express a single meaning. Explanation is a means by which

---

[5] Proposed by Shi Hui who insisted that that everything was relative and that there was no absolute difference between things.—Tr.

[6] Proposed by Jian Song who approved of the tolerance of mind.—Tr.

[7] This might be the view of the Mohists who attempted to make confusions between name and reality.

disputes are solved making use of the same names and realities. Names and conventions are means by which realities are explained. An explanation is a way to express the perception of Dao by the heart. Heart is the master of Dao, which constitutes the basic principles of good government. When heart conforms to Dao, explanations accord with the heart, phrases agree with explanations, and names are used correctly according to the convention, there is correspondence to the facts and therefore mutual understanding. When differences are carefully made without committing any error and analogies are drawn without violating any principle, anything heard will sound proper and the cause of everything will be made clear. Identifying what is evil by following correct principles is just like telling whether a piece of wood is straight or crooked with the carpenter's marking line. Only in this way can the confusion of unorthodox doctrines be prevented and the fallacies of various schools be exposed. With the wisdom and tolerance of all schools of thought and without the look of arrogance and self-righteousness, one's theory will be put into practice and there will be peace in the world. Otherwise, if his doctrine fails to be adopted, it is necessary to make Dao clear and live in seclusion. Such are the persuasions and explanations characteristic of the sages, as is praised in *The Book of Songs*:

> Being majestic and full of dignity,
> Like a jade vessel in perfect purity,
> With good fame known far and wide,
> A gentleman pleasant, simple and easy,
> In him men of the four quarters confide.[8]

In such conditions, he will succeed in cultivating the virtues of modesty and courtesy, and establishing harmony between old and young. He will avoid words of taboo and provoke no absurd arguments. He will reason with a benevolent mind, listen with an inquisitive mind, and judge with a fair mind. He is not to be touched by the praises of the multitude or the blames of many, nor does he try to bewitch the ears and eyes of other people. He will not seek the power and influence of the honored with bribes, nor does he take delight in the flattery of those around him. Therefore, he is able to abide by Dao wholeheartedly and hold on to his own views without being coerced. He is eloquent but does not make irresponsible remarks. He honors the impartial and upright and despises the vulgar and quarrelsome. Such are the persuasions and explanations of the educated gentlemen, just as what is praised in *The Book of Songs*:

> In this night that seems endlessly long
> I examine myself to see if I'm wrong,
> Whether I've neglected the principles of antiquity
> Or violated the rules of rite and morality.
> Why should I mind what others gossip about?[9]

---

[8] Major Court Hymns, *The Book of Songs*.
[9] Not available in the extant Chinese versions.

The discourse of a gentleman is profound, subtle, relevant, well-organized, and thoroughly developed from various points of view. He employs correct names and suitable expressions to ensure that his meaning is made clear. Those words and expressions are messengers of his thought and theory. If they are sufficient to convey his ideas, he makes no further demonstrations. However, if they are abused, his doctrine will be fallacious. Therefore, if a name is sufficient to represent the reality and expressions are sufficient to clarify his main idea, he need go no further. Deviation from this principle is called *ren* (, "deliberate hesitation in speech likely to be mistaken for difficulty in expression"), which a gentleman abandons but a fool picks up and makes it his treasure. For this reason, a fool's words are vague, groundless, discourteous, quarrelsome, irrational, overelaborate and noisy. He uses attractive names and fascinating expressions to express his meaning that lacks depth. He attempts all of them but fails to focus on the major idea; he takes great pains but achieves no result; he covets fame but remains obscure. The words of a wise man are easy to understand after some reflection, easy to practice properly and easy to establish if they are abided by. When successful, he will surely be able to obtain what he likes and avoid what he hates. While the words of a fool are just the opposite. It is just as what is sung in *The Book of Songs*:

> A monster or a ghost if you should be,
> What you are I certainly cannot see;
> But since you are with a shameless face,
> You will be revealed one of these days.
> I have composed this cheerful song
> To expose your inconstancy complete and strong.[10]

All those who hold that good order cannot be achieved till desires are removed are harassed by desires rather than correctly guide them. And all those who maintain that good order cannot be brought till desires are reduced are troubled by many desires instead of exerting control over them. Presence and absence of desires are two different types that distinguish between the animate and the inanimate; they do not account for peace or chaos. Many or few desires differ in extent to which emotions are aroused; they have nothing to do with order or chaos. Desire does not necessarily expect to occur when something is obtainable; a man who desires attempts it whenever he deems it proper. Desire is inborn; it does not occur when it is obtainable. He who desires tries to make it true when he thinks it possible, driven by the mind. The single desire endowed by Heaven is controlled in many different ways by the mind; therefore, it is difficult to identify it with the original desire. A man has the most urgent desire to live and the most intense hatred for death. However, some men abandon life for death, not because they desire death rather than life but because they are reluctant to drag out an ignoble existence and would rather die. Sometimes a man's inherent desires are intense but they are not followed by immediate actions. This is because the mind stops them. If what the mind permits is in agreement with reason, then even though desires are many, how could there be any harm to good

---

[10] Minor Court Hymns, *The Book of Songs*.

order! At other times, human desires are not so strong but stimulate excessive actions. This is because the mind drives them. If what the mind permits is against reason, then even though desires are few, how could they prevent chaos! Thus, order or chaos is determined by what the mind permits to be reasonable rather than the desires from a man's sentiments. If you trace the source of order or chaos where it is not found rather than where it exists and claims you have found it, actually you have missed it.

Human nature is endowed by Heaven. The sentiments are its substance. And the desires are the responses of these sentiments to things. It is inevitable for a man to pursue in sentiment what he desires when he believes it is obtainable. It is necessary for a man to practice what he desires with his wisdom when he believes it will do. Therefore, it is human nature not to be deprived of his desires even if he is merely a gatekeeper. Even though he is the Son of Heaven, he cannot completely satisfy all his desires; however, even though complete satisfaction of desires is impossible, it can be approached. Desires cannot be eliminated, but their pursuit can be put under control. Complete satisfaction of desires is impossible, but he who pursues it may get close to it; desires cannot be done away with, but he who is reflective can place his pursuit under control if what he is after is beyond reach. Act according to Dao and he can manage to get close to complete satisfaction if it is possible and place his pursuit under control when conditions do not permit. There is no better principle under Heaven.

As a general rule, no one fails to follow what he approves of and reject what he disapproves of. No one who is sure that nothing is comparable to Dao refuses to follow it. Suppose there is a man who desires to go south regardless of how far it might be and hates going north no matter how close it is. Is he likely to abandon the southward journey and turn north instead just because he may not reach his destination if otherwise? Today, people do not have too much of what they want, nor do they need less of what they hate. Would they just abandon the road to satisfy their desires and pursue the things they hate because they cannot completely satisfy what they desire? So, if they meet the desires of Dao, how could it lead to chaos just because the desires are increased? If they abandon the desires that are not in line with Dao, how could it adversely affect order just because the desires are reduced? Therefore, wise men just follow Dao in their actions and then all that is wished for by the heterodox doctrines of the minor schools will decline.

Generally speaking, what a man wants to get may not be completely what he wants; what he wants to get rid of may not be entirely what he hates. Thus, none of his actions should ever be taken without following any standard. If a balance is not properly adjusted, then the heavy side will rise so that men will assume they are light, and the light side will sink down so that men suppose they are heavy. This is how men get confused about light and heavy. Similarly, if men's standards are not correct, then misfortune may come in the guise of what they desire, and they will mistake it for good fortune, or good fortune may come in the guise of what they hate and they will mistake it for misfortune. This is how people become confused about fortune and misfortune. Dao is the proper standard from antiquity to the present. Turning away from it and depending on his own choice, one will be ignorant of where misfortune or fortune hides.

Text 193

In terms of exchange, if a man trades one object for another, people will say that there is neither gain nor loss. If he trades one for two, people will say that there is gain but no loss. If he trades two for one, people will say that there is loss but no gain. He who is skilled in calculation will trade less for more, and he who plans well does it according to what he thinks right. No man will trade two objects for one, because he knows well enough how to count. Acting in accordance with Dao is like trading one object for two, how could there be any loss? Turning away from Dao and depending on his own choice are like trading two objects for one, how could there be any gain? Anyone who trades the desires accumulated over a hundred years for the detest of the moment does it simply because he is not bright in calculation.

I used to observe and discovered a hidden truth hardly perceptible. There is no one who despises truth in his heart and does not desperately pursue material desires; nor is there anyone who desperately pursues material desires without any anxiety in his heart. There is no such person who acts contrary to the truth without being exposed to danger on the outside; nor is there is any such person who is exposed to danger from outside but does not fear in his heart. With inner anxiety and fear in the heart, even if one has fine meat in his mouth, he does not recognize the taste; even though he hears great music, he does not enjoy its sweetness; even if he sees costume with fine embroidered patterns, he is not aware of its beauty; even though he has soft and warm mattress as well as fine and smooth bamboo mat, he fails to feel the comfort they bring him. Thus, he has all the beautiful things of the world for him and yet he is unable to feel any satisfaction. And even if he feels happy for a while, he is still not free from anxiety and fear. Thus, with the beauty of all things of the world to enjoy, he is overwhelmed with worry; with the profit of all things to gain, he is consumed by suffering. For a person like this, does he pursue material desires for the preservation of life or its betrayal? He intends to satisfy his desires but actually gives free license to his sentiments. He means to preserve his life but actually brings harm to his body. He expects to nurture his pleasures but actually breaks his heart. And he aspires to improve his reputation but actually corrupts his own conduct. A man like this is no different from a thief or a robber even if he were enfeoffed as a feudal lord or hailed as a monarch. He may ride in a carriage and wears an official hat, but he is no different from the men who suffer hunger and cold. This is called making oneself the slave of things.

With peace and happiness in the heart, colors that are not beautiful may gratify the eye, sounds that are less than mediocre will satisfy the ear, poor food and vegetable soup can nurture the mouth, robes of coarse cloth and shoes of rough hemp thread may relieve the body, and a cramped room with reed blinds, straw mats, and worn-out tables and stools may conserve the physique. Thus, without enjoyment of all the beautiful things, one can still keep a pleasant mind; without position of power and eminence, one can still nourish his fame. If such a person is trusted with the world, he will think more for the interests of all under Heaven. This is called valuing oneself and making oneself a master of things.

A gentleman should be cautious of unfounded remarks, unusual behaviors, and untested strategies.

Chapter 23
On the Evil of Human Nature

Synopsis

This is an important essay on the question of human nature.

Master Xun held that man was evil by nature and the goodness in him was the outcome of conscious effort. In his opinion, man's nature was not something obtained by learning or fulfilled by application; it was generated as a matter of course. It favored profits and desires and might result in contentions or even riots if it were not properly guided; therefore, it was evil. But learning and application were conscious efforts and were acquired after birth.

In analyzing human nature, Master Xun highlighted the importance of rite and morality. He believed that the sages were familiar with what were artificial and made conscious effort by proposing ritual principles and moral codes in attempting to transform men and turn them to goodness.

Although evil by nature, it was believed likely that they might become sages. For instance, the reason why Yu made a sagely emperor was because he could keep practicing benevolence and morality and observing rules and standards, something everyone else is capable of. So, it was obvious that anyone could be converted to a sage like Yu.

In spite of his view of evil human nature, Master Xun gave his attention to its transformation through conscious effort, emphasizing the role of rite and morality in suppressing evil and promoting good. So, it is an important idea for transforming human nature and maintaining social order.

Text

Man is evil by nature. Whatever is good in man is the result of conscious effort.

Now, the nature of man is such that he is born with a love of profit. Following this nature, he grows aggressive and greedy and the sense of courtesy and deference in him disappears. He is born with feelings of envy and hate. Indulging these feelings, he becomes violent and dangerous and the sense of loyalty and good faith in him vanishes. He is born with the desires of the eyes and ears longing for beautiful sounds and colors. Indulging these desires, he turns dissolute and wanton and the sense of propriety, justice and order is lost. Thus, following his inborn nature and indulging his natural inclinations, a man is inevitably contentious and violent and therefore tends to disrupt the hierarchical social order, violate ritual and moral principles and end in riot. Therefore, a man must be transformed by the instructions of a teacher and restrained by rite and morality before he can be made courteous and cooperative, which contributes to social order. Thus, it is evident that a man's nature is evil and his goodness is the result of conscious effort.

A crooked piece of wood must await steaming and straightening on the shaping frame before it can be made straight. A dull piece of metal must be whetted on the grindstone before it can be made sharp. Now, since man's nature is evil, he must await the instructions of a teacher and the guidance of rite and morality before he can be put upright and orderly. Men without being educated by teachers and restrained by law will be deviant and dangerous rather than upright and easily corrigible. Without being restrained by ritual and moral principles, they are perverse, rebellious, and disorderly. In ancient times, the sagely kings were aware that man was evil by nature and was therefore deviant and dangerous rather than upright and readily corrigible. For this reason, they established ritual and moral codes with which a man's instincts were rectified and the man was transformed and guided in his behavior. In this way, man's behaviors began to follow order and conform to Dao. Nowadays, those who are transformed by laws and regulations and through education, accumulate culture and learning, and follow ritual and moral standards become gentlemen; those who indulge their inborn nature and give free rein to their emotions, do whatever they please, and violate ritual and moral principles become petty men. It is obvious that man's nature is evil, and that their goodness is a matter of deliberate effort.

Mencius held that man was good by nature because he could learn, but I do not think it is the case. It shows that he was ignorant of human nature and had failed to distinguish between basic nature and deliberate effort. Man's nature is what he is endowed with at birth by Heaven. It is something beyond acquisition by effort. Ritual principles and moral codes are established by the sages. They are things people can learn, practice and follow. What is beyond learning and mastery by practice but is endowed by Heaven is called nature; what can be obtained by learning and fulfilled by application is called acquired effort. This is the distinction between nature and acquisition.

Now it is a part of human nature for eyes to see and ears to hear. The ability to see clearly cannot be separated from the eye, nor the ability to hear acutely from the ear. Thus, it is obvious that the sense of sight through the eye and the sense of hearing through the ear are not acquired. Mencius claimed that man's nature was good originally and that evil arose because of the loss of his original nature. I think he is mistaken in saying so. Now, it is man's nature that as soon as he is born, he is separated from his original simplicity and naïve quality so that they are inevitably lost. It is apparent from this that the nature of man is evil. By saying man's inborn nature is good, it means that he is beautiful because of not departing from the original simplicity and that he is good because of not departing from the naïve quality. Naiveté and simplicity are to beauty what mind and wish to goodness, just like the clear sense of sight and the acute sense of hearing are inseparable from the eye and the ear. That is why we say clear eyes and acute ears.

It is the nature of man that when hungry he desires satiety, when cold he desires warmth, and when tired he desires rest. Such are their instincts. Now when a man is hungry, he dare not be the first to eat if he is in the presence of his elders, because he must yield precedence to them. When he is weary from work, he dare not demand rest because he should work for the sake of others. A son yields precedence to and works for his father. A younger brother yields to and works for his elder brother. Both cases are contrary to the inborn nature and against their inclinations, but they are the way of a filial son and constitute ritual principles and moral standards. Thus, following the instincts means flouting courtesy and deference to others. Courtesy and deference to others are at odds with inborn dispositions. It is clear to see from this that human nature is evil and their goodness is the result of conscious effort.

Someone may ask: "If the nature of man is evil, how did rite and morality come into being?" My reply is that they were the outcome of the conscious effort of the sages rather than the product of anything inherent in man. A potter mixes up clay and makes vessels out of it. Thus, the vessels are the artificial products of man rather than those of human nature. A craftsman makes a utensil out of a piece of wood. Thus, the utensil is the product of the deliberate activity of the craftsman rather than that of his nature. The sages kept thinking and got familiar with what were artificial. They proposed rite and morality and established laws and regulations. Thus, these principles, standards, laws and regulations were imposed by the sages instead of arising from human nature. As for things like the eye's fondness for beautiful colors, the ear's fondness for pleasant sounds, the mouth's fondness for delicious flavors, the heart's fondness for profit, and the body's fondness for pleasure and ease, they are all products of man's dispositions and sentiments; they respond spontaneously to stimulation rather than wait for human effort. However, if they do not respond spontaneously to stimulation and must wait for conscious effort, they are imposed. Such are the products of inborn nature and of conscious effort as well as their distinguishing characteristics. Thus, in attempting to transform man's evil nature, the sages conducted deliberate activities and their conscious effort produced ritual and moral codes. With the creation of these codes, they established laws and regulations. So, rite and morality as well as laws and regulations were produced by the sages. The sages are by nature identical to all other people rather than different from them. The reason they differ from and even surpass all other men is that they make conscious efforts to bring about changes. It is man's instinct to love profit and desire gain. Suppose there were brothers who had some property to divide. If they were to follow their instinct to love profit and desire gain, they will go into fighting. But if they are transformed by rite and morality, they will give precedence to others. Thus, following the instinct will lead to fighting even among brothers while transformation by rite and morality will guide men to yield even to strangers.

The reason why people want to be good is precisely because their nature is evil. Those who have little long for much, those who are ugly for beauty, those who live in cramped quarters for spaciousness, those who are poor for wealth, and those who are humble for eminence. Whatever a man lacks within he is sure to seek from without. The rich and noble do not wish for more wealth and power. Whatever a person has within he does not bother to seek from without. Seen from this perspective, people desire to do good precisely because their nature is evil. Now, by nature man is without rite and morality; therefore, he must study hard and seek to possess them. By nature, he does not understand these codes and therefore contemplates and seeks to comprehend them. Thus, as far as his nature is concerned, man has no sense of rite and morality and does not understand them. Without such principles, there is disorder; without the knowledge of these principles, man is offensive. Therefore, man is born with offense and disorder. It is evident from this that human nature is evil and his goodness is the result of conscious exertion.

Mencius claimed that man's nature was good. I disagree. All that is regarded as good by men under Heaven, past and present, is in accord with ritual and moral codes and social order; all that is regarded as evil is deviant, treacherous, offensive and chaotic. This is the distinction between good and evil. Now if man were by nature in accord with ritual and moral codes and social order, what could be the use of the sagely kings and rite and morality? And how could the existence of sagely kings and rite and morality add to human nature? However, it is not the case, for human nature is evil. The sages in antiquity became aware of the evil human nature. They believed that men were deviant and treacherous rather than upright and that they were offensive and trouble-making rather than orderly. Therefore, they demonstrated the authority of rulers to control them, elucidated ritual and moral codes to transform them, established laws and standards to correct them, and enforced penalties to restrain them so that all under Heaven could achieve order and conform to goodness. Such was the government of the sagely kings and the transformation brought about by rite and morality. Now let us suppose that there were no authority of a monarch, no education through rite and morality, no government by law, and no restraint of penalties, wait and see how the people under Heaven would treat each other. In such circumstances, the strong would inflict harm on the weak and rob them, the many would terrorize the few and control them, and the world would be thrown into chaos and perish in no time. It is obvious from this that man's nature is evil and that his goodness is the result of deliberate effort.

Those who are good at discussing things in ancient times must find their confirmation today and those who are good at talking about the way of Heaven must find its substantiation in the human world. That is to say, it is important to check and find verification for whatever in question. Consequently, they sit together for discussion before rising to arrangement and what is promoted will be put into force. Now, Mencius held that man's nature was good, but he failed to check and prove his view to be valid. He sat there propounding his theory, but failed to come up with a plan and put into action what he advocated. Was he not completely mistaken? Hence, if human nature were good, the sagely kings could be dispensed with and rite and morality put aside. Since human nature is evil, the sagely kings are supported and rite and morality honored. Therefore, as the press-frame is designed for the sake of bending wood and the ink line and marker is created for flat board, so are monarchs established and rite and morality elucidated for restraining the evil nature of man. It is clear from this that man's nature is evil and his goodness is the result of deliberate effort.

A straight piece of wood does not need the press-frame to straighten because it is straight by nature, while a crooked piece of wood does because it is not. Similarly, since human nature is evil, men must be governed by the sagely kings and transformed by means of rite and morality before the achievement of order and conformity to goodness. It is obvious from this that man's nature is evil and his goodness is the result of conscious effort.

Someone may say, "The accumulated conscious effort in establishing rite and morality is human nature; for this reason, the sages can create them." But I do not agree. A potter molds clay to make earthenware, but how can it be regarded as the nature of the potter? Similarly, a carpenter carves wood to produce a utensil, but can it be seen as the nature of the carpenter? The sages are to rite and morality what the potter to earthenware. How, then, can the accumulated conscious effort of establishing ritual and moral principles be considered their nature? As far as human nature is concerned, the sages such as Yao and Shun shared it with the tyrants like Jie and Zhi, so do gentlemen with petty men. Is the accumulated conscious effort of establishing rite and morality to be taken as the nature of man? If it is, then for what were Yao and Yu admired? For what were gentlemen respected? Yao, Yu and gentlemen were so regarded because they could transform the nature of people and the outcome of their conscious effort was the establishment of rite and morality. However, the sages are to rite and morality what the potters are to the earthenware. Viewed from this perspective, how can the accumulative effort of rite and morality be regarded as the nature of man? The reason Jie the tyrant, Zhi the Robber and petty men were despised is that they followed their inborn nature, indulged their emotions, did whatever they pleased, and contended for profit. Thus, it is clear that man's nature is evil, and that his goodness is the result of their enduring conscious effort.

Heaven did not favor Shen Zeng, Ziqian Min and Ji Xiao and rejected others. However, Zeng, Min and Xiao stressed actions and therefore won fame for their filial piety. Why? Because they gave full attention to rite and morality. Heaven does not favor the people of Qi and Lu and reject the people of Qin who are not as respectful and courteous as those of Qi and Lu in moral obligations between father and son or in the distinction between husband and wife. Why? Because the Qin people indulge their instincts, feel contented in unrestrained passion, and are careless of rite and morality. How could they be different in their inborn nature?

What does it mean to say that "a man in the street may become a Yu"? I say that what made Yu a sagely emperor was his practice of benevolence and righteousness and his observation of rules and standards. Since benevolence and righteousness as well as rules and standards can be learned and observed, an ordinary person is qualified to learn them and has the conditions to observe them in. Then it is obvious that he can become a Yu. If benevolence and righteousness as well as rules and standards could not be learned or observed, then even Yu could have failed in both cases. If an average man were inherently not able to learn or to observe benevolence and righteousness as well as rules and standards, he would be unable to know the moral obligation between father and son at home and the rules governing the correct relationship between a monarch and his subjects. Actually, it is not the case. The ordinary person knows the moral obligation between father and son at home and the correct relationship between a monarch and his subjects. It is obvious then that he has the quality to know and the condition in which he can follow these rules. Now if an ordinary person can learn and observe benevolence and righteousness as well as laws and standards which are knowable and practicable with his quality of knowing and with conditions in which he can follow them, it is obvious that he can become a Yu. Now let such an ordinary man engage in learning the ways to practice these principles and concentrate on it, with careful thinking and observation and the passage of time, he can accumulate goodness without stop and will ultimately live in close communion with Heaven and Earth. Thus, a sage is made with the constant accumulation of goodness.

Someone asked, "Since sageliness is the accumulation of goodness, why is it that everyone is not able to do so?" I think everyone is capable of doing so, but no one can be made to do so. Thus, a petty man is capable of becoming a gentleman but he is unwilling to do so just as a gentleman can become a petty man but he refuses to do so. It has never been the case that a petty man and a gentleman are incapable of becoming each other; the reason they do not become each other is that they cannot be made to do so although they can choose to do so themselves. Hence, it is correct to say that anyone in the street may become a Yu but it is not necessarily correct to say that everyone in the street can in fact become one. Even though one is unable to become a Yu, this does not stop him from becoming one. With a pair of feet, one may travel all over the world. However, no one can ever have done so. Similarly, it is not necessarily the case that an artisan, a carpenter, a farmer, and a merchant may not change their professions and each does the other's job; however, none of them actually can do so. It can be seen from here that one may do something but actually he cannot and his failure does not mean that there is no possibility of success. Nevertheless, there is a great difference between possibility and ability. And it is perfectly clear that they are not interchangeable.

Yao asked Shun, "How do you like human relations?"

"They are very bad," replied Shun, "and why do you ask? When a man has both wife and children, his filial piety is on the decline. When he satisfies his appetites and desires, his faith toward his friends withers away. And when he wins a noble title and good salary, his loyalty to his monarch diminishes. Oh, the relations of men! What relations they are in! They are very bad. So why do you ask?" Only the men of good virtue are an exception.

There is the wisdom of the sages, the wisdom of the educated men, the wisdom of petty men, and the wisdom of laborers. The wisdom of the sages is characterized by much talk with words of literary grace and in accord with proprieties and regulations, and a whole day's discussion on reasons for what they advocate, citing extensively, employing varied modes of expressions, but unifying all guiding principles and regulations. The wisdom of the educated gentlemen is characterized by less talk with words concise and straightforward and in accord with reason and standards as though drawing a line with the help of a marking line. The wisdom of petty men is characterized by absurd words, delusive behavior, and erroneous actions. And the wisdom of laborers is characterized by a glib tongue and agile limbs but both below moral standards, various skills that prove useless, quick analysis and fluent expression amounting to hardly anything, disregard of what is right or wrong and what is straight or crooked, and expectation of being triumphant over others.

There is courage of the superior order, courage of the middle order, and courage of an inferior order. When the proper road prevails under Heaven, he comes out courageously. When the great king of the former dynasty followed the right road, he carries on his will. He refuses to obey the ruler of a chaotic age or associate with the men of disordered times. He cares about neither poverty and hardship as long as there is benevolence nor wealth and eminence when benevolence is lost. If recognized by all under Heaven, he chooses to share the joy with them; he remains independent and fearless between Heaven and Earth if otherwise. Such is the superior courage. He is courteous, respectful, and modest. He places credit before wealth. He dare promote and elevate those who are worthy and single out and dismiss those who are unworthy. Such is the middle courage. He places wealth over personal security, takes comfort in actions leading to disaster, seeks widely to free himself from trouble, and relies on lucky escapes. He ignores what is right or wrong and what is just or unjust, seeking only to triumph over others. Such is the inferior courage.

Fanruo and Jushu were both the strongest bows of antiquity, but they could not come into shape without the work done by the bow-frame. *Cong* of Duke Huan, *Que* of the Grand Duke, *Lu* of King Wen, *Hu* of Lord Zhuang, and *Ganjiang*, *Moye*, *Juque*, and *Pilü* of King Helü were all the best swords of antiquity, but they could not become sharp without the whetstone and would be unable to cut anything without human power. *Hualiu*, *Qiji*, *Xianli*, and *Luer* were the finest horses of antiquity, but they could not travel a thousand *li* in a single day without the restraint of bit and bridle in front, the threat of whip behind and the driving of Fu Zao the master charioteer. Similarly, it is necessary for a man to seek a worthy teacher for guidance and good friends for company even though he has good qualities as well as the power of discrimination and comprehension. Guided by a worthy teacher, he will learn the correct ways of Yao, Shun, Yu and Tang; accompanied by good friends, he will witness behaviors of loyalty, trust, respect, and modesty. He will make progress every day in benevolence and righteousness without being conscious of it because his environment exerts an invisible influence on him. Now if he lives among men who are not good, then what he hears will be deception, calumny, treachery, and hypocrisy and what he sees will be conduct that is dirty, wanton, sinister and avaricious. He will soon be in danger of punishment and execution without his being aware of it because his environment shapes it. It is said in an old book, "If you do not know your son, observe the company he keeps; if you do not know your monarch, observe his attendants." Environment matters! Environment is critical!

Chapter 24
On Being the Son of Heaven

Synopsis

This is a political treatise on the authority and role of the Son of Heaven.

Master Xun pointed out that the Son of Heaven had supreme authority, which guaranteed the government of a country. To firmly establish and successfully maintain this authority, it was necessary to follow the example of the sagely kings, handle government affairs with justice, and create a hierarchy in which distinctions were made between noble and humble, close and distant, as well as old and young. He criticized the practices of excessive punishments, undeserved honors, judgement of an offence involving a whole clan, and promotion considering genealogic factors, all of which were the root of disorders. In his opinion, the Son of Heaven should follow rite and morality as well as laws and regulations and make sure that penalties fit the crimes and ranks fit the worth of individuals so that his authority was respected, government decrees were unimpeded, and an ideal political situation was formed with everyone playing his proper role.

Text

The Son of Heaven is the paramount head, that is, he is without peers. Within the four seas there are no ceremonies treating him as a guest. That means he does not visit as a guest. He can walk on his feet but does not do so till the master of ceremonies offers him guide. He can talk with his mouth but does not issue summons till his messenger official is ready. He sees without looking and hears without listening. He is trusted without making promises. He is well-informed without having to ponder over things. And he accomplishes without moving a finger. That is to say, everything is perfectly handled for him. The Son of Heaven has the greatest power and influence, enjoys the greatest physical leisure, and is perfectly contented in the heart. Nothing can frustrate his will, nothing causes him fatigue, and none enjoys greater honor than him. This is what *The Book of Song* means when it sings,

> Everywhere under Heaven,
> No land is not the king's land.
> From the land to the seas,
> None can disobey his command.[1]

Under the sagely king are the whole hierarchy of his subjects, each doing his duties proper to his title or rank and moral obligations. The gentry do not show unbridled behaviors, all other officials are not indolent or negligent in carrying out their duties, and the common people are free of evil and abnormal customs, do not commit the offenses of theft or robbery, or violate the prohibitions of their superiors. All people under Heaven are clear that wealth is not made by means of theft and robbery, longevity is not achieved by doing harm to others, and peace is not found in violating the prohibitions of their superiors. Following the correct way, they will get what they like; otherwise, they will suffer what they hate. For this reason, the penalties are rare, and the power of orders spreads like flowing waters. The world knows clearly that anyone committing a crime will not be able to escape punishment although he could flee or hide himself. Thus, none will fail to submit freely to his proper punishment. This is referred to in *The Book of History*: "Everyone admits his guilt."[2]

Thus, if punishment fits the crimes, it has the power of influence; otherwise, it will be neglected. If rank fits the worth of the individual who holds it, it inspires respect; otherwise, it will be despised. In ancient times, penalties did not exceed what fitted the crimes, and rank did not go beyond the moral worth of a person. Thus, in the government, if a father was executed, his son might be employed, or if an elder brother was killed, his younger brother might be employed. Punishments did not exceed what fitted the crimes, and ranks and honors did not go beyond the moral worth of the person. Each was allotted what was his due according to fact. In this way, those who did good were encouraged, and those who went wrong were discouraged. The punishments were rare, and the power of orders spread like flowing waters. Governmental decrees were perfectly clear, and education worked wonders. *The Book of History* means this when it says, "One man possesses moral integrity and billions of his people are benefited accordingly."[3]

Things are not like this in a chaotic age. Punishments and penalties exceed what fit the crimes, and ranks and honors go beyond the moral worth of the person. A whole clan is involved in the judgement of an offence while consideration is given to their genealogies in promoting those who are worthy. Thus, if one individual is judged guilty, his three generations will be executed. Even though one of them has the moral worth of Shun, he is punished all the same. Such is the penalty for offences judged with whole clans involved. If a grandfather is worthy, his descendants will be

---

[1] Minor Court Hymns, *The Book of Songs*.
[2] The Announcement to the Prince of Kang, *The Book of History*.
[3] Marquis of Lü on Punishment, *The Book of History*.

distinguished. Even though one of them behaves as bad as Jie or Zhou, he still enjoys the honor. Such is recommendation with genealogy being considered. If offences are judged involving the whole clan and the worthy are recommended with genealogy taken into account, how could there be no disorders as a consequence? This is referred to in *The Book of Songs* when it sings,

> All rivers rush and rumble,
> > High mountains collapse and tumble
> > And into deep valleys they turn,
> > Hills arise from valleys below.
> > Alack and alas for today's men!
> > Why do they not take warning from them?[4]

Discussion on following the example of the sagely kings means the awareness of what matters; handling government affairs with justice involves the awareness of what is beneficial. Awareness of what is important in discussion represents awareness of what is desirable; awareness of what is of benefit in dealing with matters is awareness of what to do. These two are the root of what is right and what is wrong and the source of gain and loss. Thus, between King Cheng and Duke of Zhou, there was never a case in which the former did not listen to the latter, for he knew what mattered. And between Duke Huan and Zhong Guan, there was never an occasion on which the former did not trust the latter with government affairs, for he knew wherein true profit lay. However, the state of Wu had Zixu Wu but could not put him to good use. As a result, it perished, because it deviated from the correct route and lost its worthy men. Therefore, he who honors the sages makes a true king, he who values the worthy becomes a hegemon, he who respects the worthy survives and he who slights the worthy perishes. This was true in ancient times as it is today. Thus, to elevate the worthy, employ the able, and place them in a ranked hierarchy so that there are distinctions between noble and humble, close and distant, as well as old and young—these are the principles of the kings of former times. When the worthy are elevated and the able are employed, the ruler will be honored and his subordinates will live in peace. With the distinction between noble and humble, government orders will be implemented rather than unheeded. With the distinction between close and distant, favor will be received without violating reasons. With the distinction between old and young, work will be fulfilled sooner with spare time for rest and leisure. Hence, benevolence embodies the proper relations among the people as mentioned above, righteousness is reflected in the divisions of the social hierarchy, moral integrity involves devoted service to both the living and the dead, and loyalty means sincerity and caution in doing these things. It is perfect when all these are fulfilled. To be complete and yet not boastful and to improve oneself in all these aspects—such is called being a sage. He is not boastful; therefore, he is able to give full play to his part without having anyone under Heaven attempting to compete with him in ability. He is talented but does not boast about his ability; therefore, he becomes the most honored under Heaven. This is what *The Book of Songs* means when it sings,

---

[4] Minor Court Hymns, *The Book of Songs*.

> The gentleman is benevolent and courteous,
>> No fault is found in his behavior and manners.
>> He observes both ritual and moral principles,
>> He can govern the states in the four directions.[5]

---

[5] Ballads from the States, *The Book of Songs*.

Chapter 25
Work Songs

Synopsis

Here is a group of three work songs composed by Master Xun in his later years in the style of ancient folk poetry to express his political thoughts.

The first song consists of two parts, dealing with the topics of chaos and order. Chaos happens if a monarch, self-willed and headstrong, alienates the worthy ministers and gives important positions to those who flatter him. This is shown by the deeds of the self-indulgent rulers and the treacherous ministers in history. There is order when correct government strategies are developed, the good examples of later kings like King Wen and King Wu followed, ritual and music advocated, good virtue promoted and penalties prudently imposed.

The second song continues with examples of successful government like Yao, Shun, Yu and Tang of Shang, describing the great order created by these sagely rulers who honored the virtuous and removed the treacherous. It strung up contrary cases citing the stupid rulers who, blinded by their biases, estranged the worthy, gave important positions to those who were skilled in flattery, and eventually brought ruin upon themselves and placed their countries in peril.

The third song expounds from five perspectives the principles of government necessary to a ruler: government ministers should carry out their duties; a monarch should be rigorous in following constant principles of government; both penal codes and judgement should be proper; in handling governmental affairs, no award and punishment should be given till truths are clarified; laws and regulations should be put into effect so that officials abide by them rather than act rashly.

With powerful examples of historical cases, these songs illustrate the ways that lead to order or disorder and may serve as a political warning against social realities.

Text

Let me sing a work song,
A song to tell what is wrong:
The able are framed up by the stupid in power,
The virtuous are ruined hour after hour,
So, the ruler gets no worthy men under
Just like the blind who helplessly blunder!

Let me tell you what foundation to lay,
You listen carefully to what I say:
When stupid yet willful, order is out of the question.
For a jealous ruler who desires to excel,
That disasters befall him it is out of question
Since no advice his ministers are likely to tell.

To know if a subject is in error,
You have to observe how he does his duty,
He is not if he honors the ruler,
Guards the state and promotes the righteous and worthy.
A remonstrance he turns down, his fault he conceals,
Foolishly he caters to the tastes above and the state faces its ordeals.

Who are said to leave virtue not adored?
Many who race after private gains.
Cliques are formed around their lord
So that he a fool always remains.
The worthy are kept at a distance wide,
Those who backbite get improved,
The loyal ministers are laid aside,
The authority of the ruler is removed.

Who are said to be men of worth?
Those who're clear they differ from their lord.
They honor the ruler and showed love for everyone.
When the ruler truly heeds what they say,
All under Heaven becomes one,
And all within the seas come to obey.

A ruler meets his misfortune
When slanderers have their fortune,
The worthy and able flee,
And the state will no longer be.

When an idiot becomes more stupid,
And an addle head more addlebrained,
A tyrant like Jie there will be.

A world suffers from calamities
Caused by the jealousy of men of abilities.
When Feilian seized the power of Shang
And gave office to Wulai and his gang,
Leaving their lord in his pursuit lower
Of large gardens and many a high terrace and tower.

King Wu, filled with outrage,
Led his army to the fields of Mu;
The soldiers of tyrant Zhou betrayed him.
Prince Qi was well-treated by King Wu
Since he yielded his allegiance
and given the feoff of Song for ancestral sacrifice.

When the age was on the wane,
Slanderers hung on tyrant Zhou,
Bigan's heart was cut out there and then
And Jizi got in jail and suffered so.
Then King Wu launched a campaign
Against the despotic rule of Xing,
With Shang Lü commanding the forces,
And the people of Yin their obedience rendering.

The evil of the world is shown
When worthy men are despised.
Zixu Wu was killed for his devotion,
Xi Baili for his counsel got exiled.
Duke Mu found Baili in the state of Chu
And put him in an important position.
With the institution of the Six Ministries
Qin was turned into one of the Five Hegemons.

The stupidity of this age is seen
In its hatred of great Confucian scholars
Like Confucius, who experienced frustrations
and failed to realize his aspirations.
Qin Zhan was thrice dismissed from his post,
Xie Huang was killed and his cause was lost.

Please listen, here are the fundamentals of affairs:
Remember the worthy and let them have their shares
As Yao did long long ago but we still see this day.
Those who backbite engage in all evils,
They are crooked and dangerous as devils,
They are suspicious of Yao's correct way.

Fundamental progress cannot be made
Till the worthy and the stupid are told apart.
In this King Wen and King Wu shared,
Who followed the example of Fuxi and prospered.
Order is thus secured and chaos appears if otherwise.
How can any problem or doubt arise?

In a word, what in this work song I sing
Is choosing the good way of governing.
The best way for perfect order to be achieved
Is to see that the principles of later kings are received.
Dao Shen, Di Mo, Zhen Ji, Shi Hui and other schools
Advertised their adverse thoughts only to fools.

Order is from oneness and unity derived.
Follow this principle and luck is assigned.
Gentlemen who are going to observe it
Are firmly determined in their mind.
Those men who should hesitate or slander
Are surely punished by law no wonder.

Water is perfectly fair,
Of this all should be aware.
Raise a bowl of water upright
And it remains level all right.
Anyone with a similar mind
Resembles a sage, wise and kind.
Powerful in influence and true of worth,
He may surely match Heaven and Earth.

In a world without a true king
To men of talent and virtue is no good thing.
Men of ill virtue feast upon fine meat,
And men of goodwill have poor food to eat.
Both ritual and music are cast aside,
The sages go hidden but Mohism will abide.

The guiding principle of a government
Is ritual complemented with punishment.
Gentlemen follow it in self-cultivation,
The common folk live in peace with its implementation.
If a state promotes good virtue and is careful of penalties
It will secure order and peace within the four seas.

A government may be managed with grace
When power and wealth are put in the second place.
Gentlemen should have sincerity
And keep their moral integrity.
This principle should be firmly observed
And far-reaching thoughts should be preserved.

What careful thinking brings
Is far-reaching aspiration.
When mind concentrates on things,
Divine thoughts are understood with admiration.
When careful thinking is concluded with divine thought,
Plus single-hearted devotion, a sage is surely wrought.

The way to good order is fine and will endure,
A gentleman following it will go, I'm sure,
From good to better and better to best.
All his men, young and old, will be blessed
With instructions to the young with love
And sacrifices to the ancestors above.

This first stanza is coming to the close
But it is not the end of what I intend to disclose.
A gentleman who listens to advice
Will go smooth and successful.
Remember to respect the worthy and wise
And discriminate against the crafty and evil.

I have a work song here I'd like to sing
To tell about many a sagely king.
Yao and Shun respected the worthy men
They intended to give the crown to You Xu and Juan Shan
Who placed morality before gain
And whose virtue was outstanding and brilliant.

Yao recommended a worthy man in his place

For the benefit of the populace.
He promoted the welfare of the population,
Showed it universal favor and affection.
Men were high or low in rank and noble or base in status,
There's a clear distinction between a ruler and his subjects.

Yao resigned in favor of someone capable;
Shun happened to meet with the right time.
Both respected the worthy and promoted the virtuous,
And the world was put in good order and prosperity.
The worthy and the sagely these days do appear
But remain unknown since the right time is not yet here.

Yao claimed no moral worth;
Shun did not decline the royal offer.
Yao made his two daughters as wives of Shun
And entrusted him with the government.
What a great man Shun was!
Facing south, he stood in position
And all things were properly arranged.

Shun handed the power over to Yu
For the benefit of the world.
He respected men of virtue,
Promoted men of worth,
And good order was maintained.
In the use of men he shunned no foes
And showed no favor to his kinsfolk,
He gave position only to the worthy.

Yao worked with virtue and his mind,
Without using shields and spears,
So, the Sanmiao became compliant.
He raised up Shun from the fields,
Entrusted to him the rule under Heaven,
And went into retirement himself.

Houji was put in charge of the five grains,
Kui was made Director of Music,
Even birds and beasts grew submissive.
With Xie being Minister of Education,
Men showed filial piety and brotherly love
And admire those who were of virtue.

Yu had achieved the great merit
In putting flood under control,
Eliminating harms to the people,
And banishing the tribe of Gonggong.
He channeled nine waterways in the north,
Joined the twelve islets together
To make the three rivers run unimpeded.

Yu divided the land into nine states,
And brought peace under Heaven.
He worked hard for his people,
And performed a valuable service.
He also had Yi, Gaoyao, Hengge and Zhi
Who worked efficiently to assist him.

Xie was the Swallow King[1]
Who begot prince Zhaoming.
He lived at Dishi before moving to Shang.
Fourteen generations had passed
Before Tianyi came into the world
To be known as the Successful King Tang.

First called Tianyi and later known as Tang,
He was the successful king of Shang.
He judged properly and employed right men,
He resigned in favor of Guang Mou and Sui Bian.
He followed the ways of the ancient sages
And laid a solid foundation for many ages.

I would like to express what I think
About the world in chaos and with stink.
It is caused by disorder, anarchy,
Hatred toward the good, jealousy of the worthy,
And prolonged trust for deceit and treachery.
Rarely is it free from disaster and calamity.

How disastrous! And how wicked!
The sagely and wise are not used,
But the stupid are trusted to make plans.
The chariot ahead is already overturned,
But those who follow keep going in its wake.

---

[1] According to legend, he was born by a black bird.

When are they going to awake?

He who is not awake
Knows not bitterness or ache.
He is so confused and forlorn
That he puts things upside down.
Good advice fails to reach the ears of the ruler
Who shuts both eyes, both ears and all doors.

When all the doors are closed tight,
He is utterly lost, mistaking day for night.
His men reverse wrong and right,
For selfish interest they band together to fight,
Deceive their superiors with their might
And hate those who are correct and upright.

The correct and upright are hated
By those who are perverse and wicked,
Stray away from the right road
And have no moral standard or code.
Do not complain against others
And think highly of yourself,
For who is without any fault?

He who takes no precautions
Will recommit the same errors.
He who refuses advice will feel no regret
Even if he should repeat the same mistakes.
Evil-doers are many and in power;
They backbite and cheat hour after hour.

If rulers do not guard against treachery,
Their men contend for favor, envy the worthy,
And become suspicious of one another.
Those who render their service cause jealousy,
The worthy are defamed by slanderers.
Cliques are formed for selfish interest
And the truth is hidden from the rulers.

When a monarch is blinded
And deprived of assistance,
He loses his power of control
Over the slanderers under his rule.

The revolt by the Duke of Guo Zhangfu
Forced King Li of Zhou to flee to Zhi.

The reasons for King Li and King You's downfall
Were that they refused to take counsel
And singled out and killed those who were loyal.
Alas! I am such an insignificant man!
But I am not the only one
To put up with these troubled times!

I would like to speak my mind,
But no one will give any heed.
Worse still, I might suffer the tragic death of Zixu Wu
Who offered his advice in vain
And was compelled to commit suicide
Before being thrown into the Qiantang River.

By examining past events,
We may keep alert and be aware
Of order or disorder and right or wrong.
(*missing*)
I'd like to sing this work song
To express what I have in my mind.

Here is a work song I'd like to sing
To tell the methods of governing.
For a king there are five principles here.
Both are expressed brief and clear.
If he observes them carefully,
His subjects will be upright and sincere,
And his state will surely prosper.

Each person should do his duties
Rather than roam about doing nothing.
Till the land, be economical
And there will be boundless wealth.
Listen to the lord in doing anything
And never order each other about
So that the strength of all is joined as one.

If everyone carries on his duties,
All will have enough food and clothing.
Each will enjoy his share for his grade

Or the rank and dress that agree with him.
The profit comes only from above,
And none will attempt to grant any favor,
So, who could reap any gains in private?

If the lord is clear and impartial in creating laws
And follows constant principles in his judgments,
When rules and regulations are made,
The people will be able to follow the right direction.
If promotions and demotions are given according to rules,
Eminence and humility are not determined at random,
Who would seek private access to the king?

If the law of the monarch is the standard,
The prohibited things are prevented,
And his teachings please everyone,
He will not lose his power.
Those who follow them are honored,
Those who deviate from them are severely punished
And who would dare go against the law?

If the criminal law is proper and made public
And its provisions are strictly observed,
There will be no punishment without authorization
And the private power of the nobility will be weakened.
When offenses and sentences are determined by rules,
No one will attempt to make them lighter or more severe,
And the majestic authority remains intact.

Let me tell you the foundation of government:
A ruler should clearly distinguish between right and wrong.
If he is fond of debates and deliberations,
He must give them careful considerations.
If the five principles[2] are observed and none fails in doing his duties,
The power of the ruler will be consolidated.
The key to handling political affairs
Is to clarify the facts after repeated investigations
And prudently implement rewards and punishments.
What is obvious should be further clarified
And what is hidden must be exposed

---

[2] The five principles mentioned above. An alternative explanation is the five approaches to hearing a case: listening to the statement, observing the facial expression, paying attention to the other details like breath, tones, and expressions in the eyes.

So that people may return to honesty.

All that is declared as order
Must accord with the law,
The reality of things must be examined,
Truth and falsehood must be distinguished,
Rewards and penalties must be implemented.
When all people speak the truth
Rather than deceive their lord,
All will be clear as the light of day.

If a monarch is enlightened and clear-sighted,
His eyes penetrate all that is distant or hidden.
He sees what law fails to cover or others fail to see.
He has bright eyes and sharp ears,
So, his ministers must respect the laws
And dare not do as they please.

Once royal decrees are made public,
There are codes of conduct.
The officials will act with caution
And dare not do anything wrong.
If none bends the law to suit private interest
And everyone plays his proper role,
All will abandon speculations and ingenuities.

The ministers diligently enforce laws and decrees.
The lord has the power over their modifications.
With sound investigations and careful deliberations,
There is the prospect of order and peace.
When all under Heaven is settled in this way,
There will be a model for the world to imitate.

Chapter 26
Allegories

Synopsis

Consisting of five descriptive proses and two poems, this composition reflects in literary form the political thought of the author. Concise and lively, it is a unique style of writing with rich implications.

Master Xun emphasized the importance of ritual and held it to be indispensable to affairs associated with life or death, military operations, the self-cultivation of gentlemen, the management of state affairs, and the creation of peace under Heaven.

Wisdom is the fundamental requirement in the practice and realization of ritual; however, it may be profound or shallow and serve good or evil purposes. For these reasons, it is necessary to be guided by ritual so that it grows into bright, reasonable, pure and faultless "wisdom of the gentlemen" and benefits the people under Heaven.

Master Xun made comparisons with ordinary things like cloud, silkworm, and needle in his understanding of the ways of self-cultivation and government. Cloud is often observed in the sky. It symbolizes the sagely kings because it is great like Heaven and Earth and shares great virtues with Emperors Yao and Yu. With its various shapes, the cloud brings moisture to all things but never claims its merit. Silkworms are expert in spinning silk which can be woven into cloth to adorn the people of all generations. Needle is used in sewing, providing coverings for the common people below and adornment for the rulers above. Their merits are great but they do not flaunt them. Like the worthy ministers and other officials, they make contributions to the world at the sacrifice of themselves.

The pair of poems at the end depict a dark world in which officials neglect their duties, villains take power, the virtuous become the target of attack, and the world is in chaos. The poems also convey the author's sense of self-encouragement and confidence in order in the future.

Text

Here is a great thing:
It is neither silk thread nor fabric,
Here is a great thing:
It is neither silk thread nor fabric,
Yet its grain is clear and its pattern right.
It is neither the sun nor the moon,
Yet it makes the world bright.
With it the living gain longevity,
The dead are buried with decency,
City walls are firmly defended
And the three armies are splendid.
He who has it pure is a true king for sure,
He who has it impure a hegemon he may secure,
And he who has none is fatally done.
I am so slow-witted that I do not know,
Can Your Majesty give me some clue?
The king asked if it is impressive but not so colorful,
Or concise, easily understood and well-organized,
If petty men despise it but gentlemen are deeply respectful,
If humans are beastlike without it but fully upright with it,
If commoners become sages and feudal lords unify all if they exalt it?
Since it is concise, clear, appropriate and reasonable,
Can I conclude it to be ritual?
(RITUAL)

Grand Heaven offers a thing
As a gift to the people below.
It may be plentiful or lacking,
And never evenly distributed.
It brought Jie and Zhou disorders
And made Tang and Wu worthy rulers.
Sometimes it is confused, sometimes clear,
Sometimes it is grand, at other times fine and tiny.
It extends to the four seas well within a whole day.
With it, a gentleman cultivates his mind.
But Robber Zhi used it to break into house.
It may be grand and high as Heaven
Or so tiny and fine that it cannot be seen at all.
With it, our conduct and deportment are rectified
And our undertakings may prove successful.
With it, the violent may be stopped, the poor become rich,
And the common people will live a peaceful life.

I am so slow-witted that I do not know.
Can Your Majesty give me some clue?
The king asked if it brings security and protects men against dangers,
If it brings people close to the virtuous and away from the corrupted,
If it is hidden deep in the mind to triumph over enemies when applied,
If it enables men to follow the example of Yu and Shun and advance along their road,
And if it brings propriety in people's behaviors and manners?
It is the essence of blood, vigor, thought and will,
With it, the common people may live in tranquility
And all under Heaven may become peaceful.
It is clear, reasonable, pure and without defect.
It is called the wisdom of the gentlemen.
(WISDOM)

Here is something:
It spreads silently on the fields when gathering,
It flies very high and scatters extensively when moving.
It may correspond to the compass when round,
If square enough it may correspond to the T-square.
It can be as great as Heaven or Earth
And virtuous as Emperors Yao or Yu.
The ethereal substance is more subtle than soft hair.
But it can be large enough to fill the vast space.
How swift it is when floating away into the distance!
How it swirls, like chasing or being chased, goes and returns again!
How it soars to form moisture and benefits all under Heaven!
It is so kind as not to abandon anyone,
Dark and dim, it travels to and fro,
And changes its shape all the time
As though it were with what is great and divine.
It emerges and vanishes very fast
And no one knows its entrance or exit.
Without it, all the world would die;
With it, all under Heaven will survive.
I am your slow-witted disciple
And would like to report this to you.
Would you please give me some clues
So that I could resolve this riddle?
The master asked if it is huge and unblocked,
If it fills up the entire space with no gap left and enter a crack without feeling squeezed,
If it travels so far and fast that it fails to send a message,
If it is dark and dim and cannot be fixed or blocked,
If it appears all of a sudden and brings ruins to all without hesitation,
Or if it accomplishes a great deal but does not claim it at all?

Dwelling on earth, it roams the space,
Wind is its friend and its children are the rains.
On winter days, it creates the cold
And on summer days, it brings the heat.
Extensive, enormous, essential and ethereal,
Let us conclude it to be cloud.
(CLOUD)

Here is a thing:
Looking naked and bare,
It repeats magical transformations.
Its merit benefits all under Heaven
And adorns a myriad generation.
With it, both ritual and music are complete,
The noble and the humble become distinct.
Cares for the old and nurtures for the young
Are not enhanced till it is available.
Its name is unpleasant[1]
Because it lives next door to Cruelty.
With merit achieved, its body is cast away;
When its work is complete, its home is broken apart.
When the old generation is discarded,
The new generation is preserved.
It delivers benefit to man,
But becomes the prey of birds.
I am too stupid to know what it is,
So, I request a divination from Wutai.
The wizard responds with these questions:
Does it have a body soft with feminine charm and a head like that of a horse?
Does it change so often that it may not live long?
Is it well-nurtured in its prime of life but slighted in its old age?
Does it have parents but is not told between male and female?
It lies in wait in winter and roams about in summer,
Living on the leaves of mulberry and spews out silk thread
Chaotic in the beginning but ordered in the end.
It grows in summer but fears heat.
It is fond of dampness but afraid of rain.
It believes the pupa to be its mother,
And the moth it takes as its father.
Three times it is in slumber and then up again
And its work then comes to a great conclusion.
Such is the lifestyle of the silkworm.
(SILKWORM)

---

[1] The name is a homophone of *cruelty* in Chinese.

Here is a thing:
It is born from the mountains and ends in the living chambers of men.
It is without knowledge or skill but useful in making clothes.
It breaks into things not for the purpose of robbing or stealing.
Day and night it joins together what are separate
Or creates beautiful designs and patterns.
It is capable of forming alliances broadwise or lengthways.
It provides coverings for the people and adornment for emperors and kings.
Its achievements are great but it does not flaunt them.
It appears when working and disappears if it has nothing to do.
I am too stupid to know what it is,
And come here to consult Your Majesty about it.
The king asks if it starts as something big and ends quite small,
If it has a long tail and a sharply-pointed tip,
And if its head penetrates and its tail shakes and winds around?
Since it goes and comes, starting by tying a knot at its tail.
Featherless and wingless, it moves back and forth with great speed.
It becomes busy when the tail grows long;
Another knot being tied, it is time to be gone.
A hairpin resembles its father,
A tube serves as its mother.
With it, the cover is stitched together
And the inner linings are joined and attached.
Such are the ways of a needle.
(NEEDLE)

When order was lost under Heaven,
Things were like what is described in this poem:
Heaven and Earth changed their positions and roles,
The four seasons were no longer in their proper sequence,
Stars perished or fell from their usual tracks,
So that darkness enveloped all day and night.
The dark and dim rose to prominence
While the sun and moon sank into obscurity.
Those who were fair-minded and selfless
Were accused of being quick to switch sides.
The pursuit for public good and interest
Was persecuted for desiring gorgeous buildings.
Those who meted out fitting punishment
Were guarded against as personal rivals or foes.
Those who were of pure and perfect virtue
Were attacked by gossipers and slanderers.

The benevolent were degraded and reduced to poverty,
While the haughty and violent threw their weight about.
It became threateningly dark under Heaven,
And the world would lose its best men entirely.
Dragons were treated like geckos
While owls were regarded as phoenixes.
Bigan suffered evisceration
And Confucius got detained in Kuang.
How brilliant was the light of their wisdom!
How lamentable it was that their times were unlucky!
How elegant was their desire to widely practice rite and morality!
But what a dark world they found themselves in!
The once-bright Heaven was forever gone
And their sorrow knew no bound.
A cycle of time is done with a thousand years gone,
From antiquity this is a constant rule.
Be diligent in your studies, my disciples,
For Heaven will not forget you.
The sages are waiting with their hands folded;
Your opportunity is around the corner.
We are foolish and full of doubt.
We wish you may pardon us and repeat.

Here is a short song:
I remember that faraway place.
How thwarting it is there!
The benevolent are degraded and reduced to poverty,
Ruffians are many and found free everywhere.
Those who are loyal are found in danger,
While slanderers are given important positions.
Beautiful jade and lovely pearls
Are not worn as ornaments,
And no difference is told
Between cloth and silk.
Beauties like Lüju and Zishe
Are not arranged a marriage.
Ladies and lads ugly as Momu and Lifu
Become everyone's favorite.
The blind is taken to be clear-sighted
While the deaf keen of hearing.
Danger is regarded as safety,
While good fortune as unlucky.
Oh, Heaven high above! Alas!
How could I get along with the men there?

Chapter 27
Quotes from Master Xun

Synopsis

This is a collection of quotes compiled by the disciples of Master Xun. It has a wide range of topics, including thoughts on promoting ritual, stressing law, honoring the worthy, employing the capable, education, learning, self-cultivation, teacher-student relationship and epistemology.

The topic of ritual occupies a major proportion with a description of its contents and principles, a display of its significance to both individuals and a state, and an emphasis on its compliance with the will of the people with the passage of time. Master Xun held that a state that exalted ritual, emphasized the rule of law, and honored the worthy would prosper while a state that chose profit before anything else and gained it by deception would be imperiled.

A demonstration is made of the crucial role played by a monarch with his power of judgement in employing the talented people and his moral virtue in bringing order to his state. A true ruler should be able to identify four types of people—those of treasure, vessel, instrument and curse—and treat them differently.

He observed that man had both the sense of righteousness and the desire for profit, which could not be got rid of. Such being the case, the superiors should place righteousness before profit and keep themselves from competing with the people for profit. In this way, the people would turn to goodness and the country would be in advantage. Facing natural disasters, the superiors should reflect on themselves and tend to state affairs with more diligence in addition to praying to Heaven for blessings.

Examples are cited of Emperor Shun, Confucius, Master Zeng, Zigong and others to show that a gentleman should pay close attention to his moral integrity and be good at following his masters and making friends in learning. This is also a reflection of Master Xun's own personality and moral pursuit.

Text

A general outline:

The ruler of men is a true ruler if he reveres ritual and honors the worthy and a hegemon if he stresses laws and regulations and loves his people; if he seeks only profit and keeps being deceptive, he is in great danger.

The best approach to the four sides is to start from the very center; therefore, a true ruler must dwell in the center of the world. This is one of the rules of etiquette.

The Son of Heaven has his screen wall outside the gate while the feudal lords have theirs inside. This is a rule of etiquette. An external screen wall blocks the view outside and an internal one prevents from being seen from outside.

When summoned by his feudal lord, a minister hurries out without being well-dressed and does not wait for his horses to be harnessed to the carriage. It is a rule of etiquette. This is portrayed in *The Book of Songs*:

> "Putting on my clothes upside down,
> I rush to my lord's urgent demand."[1]

When the Son of Heaven requests the presence of the feudal lords, they drag the carriages to the horses. It is a rule of etiquette. It is also described in *The Book of Songs*:

> "I must drag out my carriage
> To the pasture ground.
> From the Son of Heaven
> Came an order to me to be around."[2]

The Son of Heaven wears his crown to match the ceremonial robe emblazoned with mountains, a feudal lord is attired black, a senior official wears second-class formal robe, and a man of learning wears leather. This is a rule of etiquette.

The Son of Heaven carries a jade scepter, a feudal lord a jade tablet, and a senior official a bamboo tablet. This is a rule of etiquette.

The Son of Heaven uses an ornamental bow, a feudal lord uses a bow painted red, and a senior official uses a black bow. This is a rule of etiquette.

When feudal lords meet with one another, they are introduced by one of their senior ministers and escorted by all those well-versed in the rules of etiquette and entrust state affairs to the kind and generous ministers.

Gui ('a jade tablet') serves as a token of respect when sending an envoy to visit a feudal lord; *bi* ('a round flat piece of jade with a hole in the center') serves as a voucher when paying a state visit; *yuan* ('a huge ring of fine jade') serves as a voucher when a feudal lord summons his ministers and officials; *jue* ('a penannular jade ring') serves as a symbol of disconnection and *huan* ('a jade ring') of reconciliation.

---

[1] Ballads from the States, *The Book of Songs*.

[2] Minor Court Hymns, *The Book of Songs*.

A monarch must have a kind heart, for wisdom arises because of benevolence and ritual reflects its perfection. Therefore, a true ruler promotes ritual on the basis of benevolence. This is the arrangement of nature.

As is recorded in the *Rules of Etiquette*, "Too much money harms virtue and too many presents destroy ritual." Alas! Does ritual mean jade and silk? *The Book of Songs* sings:

> "Things show their beauty,
>   Because they're in harmony."[3]

When offered untimely, improperly and unhappily, the offering is against the ritual even if what is offered is beautiful.

He who wades into water should mark out deep spots so that others might not fall in. Similarly, he who governs men should mark out the dividing line between order and disorder so that people might not fall into error. Ritual principles are markers. The Former Kings used them to show what disorders were under Heaven. Today those who have cast ritual aside have removed those markers. That is why people are so confused that they fall into trouble and penalties are so numerous and complicated.

Shun said: "Only I can do whatever I desire to attain order." Thus, ritual is formulated for people from the worthy down to the commoners. It is not established for all men to be sages; however, it enables some men to become sages. One can never make it without learning. For example, Yao learned from Chou Jun, Shun from Zhao Wucheng, and Yu from Guo Xiwang.

At the age of fifty, one does not have to observe the mourning observances. At seventy, he may wear the mourning apparel only.

The ritual for escorting a bride to the wedding: The father, standing and facing south, offers the pledge cup to his son with the command, "Go and meet your helpmate and fulfill the great cause of our family line. Guide her to follow the example of your mother. She must be constant in her conduct."

"Yes," says the son, "I will try my best lest I should fail. How dare I forget your instructions!"

Proper conduct is conduct based on ritual principles which require that the honorable be revered, the aged be looked after, the elder be respected, the younger be cared for, and the humble be favored.

Rewards for family members should be given in the fashion they are bestowed by the state. Anger towards servants should be shown in the manner punishments are imposed on the common people.

A gentleman should treat his children this way: he loves them but does not show it in his countenance, he orders them about without a genial smile or a good word, and he guides them with reason rather than by force.

Ritual is based on complying with the aspirations of the people; therefore, behaviors that are not recorded in *The Book of Rites* but comply with the people's wishes are in accordance with ritual principles.

---

[3] Minor Court Hymns, *The Book of Songs*.

Ritual essentially serves to express happiness when waiting upon the living, sorrow when sending off the dead, and momentum of power when launching military activities.

To love one's parents, to remember one's friends, to award somebody's merits according to his accomplishments, and to appreciate someone on the basis of work done by him—these constitute the grades of benevolence. To honor the honorable, to respect the respectable, to value the worthy, to love the aged and to look up to the venerable elders—these constitute righteousness. Proper conduct makes up the order of ritual. Benevolence involves love; therefore, people get close to each other. Righteousness means morally right; therefore, it is reasonable. Ritual is characterized by moderation; therefore, it promises success. Benevolence has its proper habitat, and righteousness has its proper access. Benevolence is inhumane when it dwells elsewhere and righteousness is unjust if it proceeds through other channels. Favor done against reason does not constitute benevolence. Things in accord with reason are not righteous if they are left undone. Rules that are careful but inharmonious do not constitute ritual. Tones that are in harmony but are not expressed do not make music. Therefore, it is said that humanity, righteousness, ritual and music share the same purpose. A gentleman who practices benevolence on the basis of righteousness is humane. A gentleman who practices righteousness on the basis of ritual is just. A gentleman cannot succeed in formulating ritual till he provides specific rules on the basis of general principles. A complete comprehension of the three relations leads to Dao.

Money presented for funeral arrangements is called *fu*, carriages and horses for the same purpose are called *feng*, clothing *sui*, favorites of the deceased *zeng*, and jade cowry to be placed in the mouth of the dead *han*. *Fu* and *feng* are for the bereaved family while *zeng* and *sui* are for the departed. It is against the rite to send off the deceased without seeing the coffin and to offer condolences without an expression of sadness. Thus, going to a joyous occasion fifty *li* away or a funeral a hundred *li* away and offering funeral gifts in time are important points in ritual.

Ritual serves as a guide to government. Government without it goes nowhere.

When the Son of Heaven ascends to the throne, the Senior Minister comes forward and says, "Why has there been so much to worry about? It is good fortune to be able to remove troubles; it is disaster if otherwise." Thus, he delivers the first council. The Secondary Minister comes forward and says, "He whose virtue is as high as Heaven and possesses land below takes into account what is going to happen and anticipates troubles before they take place. Consideration in advance means being quick-witted, and a perfect completion is reached soon. Consciousness of any peril beforehand shows foresight, and he who has foresight may prevent trouble from happening. Consideration after a happening is called afterthought, which does not help the matter. Consciousness of trouble after it comes means difficulty in which misfortune is indefensible." Thus, he delivers the second council. The junior minister comes forward and says, "Be serious and vigilant, for when celebrators are in the hall, the mourners are already at the door. Fortune and misfortune are neighbors, but no one knows where their doors are. Be on the alert! Be cautious! All the people in the world are looking at you." Thus, he delivers the third council.

When Emperor Yu saw people plowing in pairs, he arose in respect, leaning on the crossbar of his chariot. Whenever he passed through a village of ten households, he would surely descend from his chariot.

It is against ritual either to hold hunting too early or to hold court too late. Any action in governing the people without observing the rites will fall into error.

A bow on knees with torso and head parallel to horizon is called *bai*, with hands touching the ground and head touching the hands is called *qishou*, with both head and hands touching the ground is called *qisang*. The servants of a senior official do not *qishou* to their master. This does not mean that the servants are respectable. The purpose is for the ceremony to be distinct from the manner of respect for a ruler and his subjects.

The order of seats for officials of the first rank[4] at village feast is arranged according to age; so is it for officials of the second rank at feast with clan members. However, for officials of the third rank, no precedence should be taken by those old clansmen even if they are seventy or older.

Upper senior officials belong to the third rank, middle senior officials the second rank, and lower senior officials the first rank.

The order of seats on auspicious occasions is arranged according to status; at funeral ceremony according to extent of intimacy.

Pin means extending greetings. *Xiang* means paying tributes. *Sidi* means private audience.[5]

The beauty in speech can be described as *mumu huanghuang* ('respectful and honest'). The beauty in the royal court can be described as *jiji qiangqiang* ('many a man of talents act in concert').

As a subordinate, a minister should remonstrate, but slander is not permitted. He may quit without showing hatred, and he may complain without getting angry.

A ruler inquires about the illness of his senior official three times when he falls sick and attends the mourning observances three times when he dies. A man of learning receives visit and condolence only once. A feudal lord does not visit his subordinates at home except to inquire about illness or offer condolences.

After the burial, the food given by the ruler or the father's friends may be taken. One need not avoid fine meals but he must decline if wine is offered.

Residence building should not surpass the ancestral temple in scale; daily wear should not be superior to mourning attire. This is a rule of etiquette.

The hexagram Xian of *The Book of Changes* tells the relation between husband and wife. The way a husband treats his wife must be correct, for it is the root to the proper relations between a ruler and his subjects and between father and son. *Xian* means response: proper response is triggered when the superior is placed below the inferior, the male below the female and the strong below the weak.

The invitation ceremony for a man of learning and the way a bridegroom meeting his bride both emphasize the beginning.

---

[4] The officials of the Zhou Dynasty are divided into nine ranks (called *ming*). The first rank is the lowest.

[5] These are terms used on diplomatic occasions.—Tr.

Ritual is the foundation on which men behave themselves. Without it, they would stumble and fall into the mire of errors. A slight deviation from it leads to great chaos.

Ritual is to the correct governance of a state what weight and beam of a steelyard is to the measurement of weight or what the ink-line is to the determination of straightness. Therefore, without ritual being observed, man cannot live, success is impossible, and a nation will not find peace. Without taking ritual principles as the code of their conduct, a ruler and his subjects cannot respect each other, a father and his sons cannot be on intimate terms with each other, brothers cannot get along well with one another, and husband and wife cannot be happy together. With these rules obeyed, the young will grow to maturity and the old get their support. Thus, it is Heaven and Earth that create man and it is the sages who help him grow up.

The tinkling of bells on the chariot chimes with the tunes of *Wu* and *Xiang* when the horses amble on and with those of *Shao* and *Hu* when the animals gallop. The gentlemen practice their manners and expressions to the rhythm before going out.

Wedding is not held before First Frost[6] or after the melting of ice. Intercourse takes place every ten days.

Look at your knees when you sit opposite another person. Look at your feet when you stand opposite another person. When you speak or reply to other people, look up at their face. Stand and speak with an interval between six and thirty-six (i.e., six times six) *chi*.

When appearance and emotions depend on and reflect each other as the inside and the outside, they are commensurate with ritual. Reflection on the basis of ritual is reflection in the true sense.

Ritual is characterized by the mutual agreement between the root and its branches and the mutual correspondence between beginning and end.

Ritual takes wealth and properties as its fund, nobleness and lowliness as its adornment, and abundance and scarcity as its differentiations.

An inferior minister serves his monarch with properties, an ordinary minister with his personal contribution, and a superior minister with men of talents he recommends.

It is said in *The Book of Changes*: "What is one to blame for if he reverts to the correct road?" *The Spring and Autumn Annals* praises Duke Mu as being worthy because of his conversion.[7]

If a man of learning has jealous friends, his worthy friends will not get very close to him. If a ruler has jealous ministers, worthy men will not come to him. He who blocks justice is described as stupid. He who hides men of virtue is said to be jealous. And he who does both is labeled as cunning and deceitful. Such crafty and treacherous men and jealous and stupid subjects are the filth and curse of a nation.

He who is expressive and capable of practicing his ideas is a treasure to the state. He who is not expressive but capable of practicing his ideas is a vessel for the state.

---

[6] One of the twenty-four divisions of the solar year in the traditional Chinese calendar, in late October.

[7] In the war between the states of Qin and Jin, Duke Mu of Qin did not listen to a senior minister's dissuasion and was therefore crushed by Jin. He drew lessons from the defeat and began to accept the councils of his subjects.

He who is expressive but incapable of putting his ideas into practice is an instrument for the state. And he who speaks kind words but does evil things is a curse to the state. Those who govern the state cherish the treasure, love the vessel, use the instrument, but get rid of the curse.

If you do not make people wealthy, you have nothing to nourish their dispositions. If you do not educate people, you cannot change their natural character. A household with five *mu* of homestead and a hundred *mu* of cropland will be made rich if its members are devoted to farming without being robbed of their time for work. Set up colleges and schools at which the Six Ceremonies[8] are instructed and the Seven Canons[9] are made clear, they will be properly guided. Just as it is sung in *The Book of Songs*:

"Give them food and drink,
    Teach them to do and think."[10]

Thus, the state affairs are done.

When King Wu entered Yin[11] for the first time, he erected at the residence of Rong Shang a board inscribed with his honest virtue, released Jizi from imprisonment, and wept at the tomb of Bigan, and all under Heaven returned to good.

Under Heaven, there are outstanding men of virtue in all states and generations. Men are lost because they do not ask the way, drowned because they do not make clear where to ford, and perish because they are fond of acting on their own. It is said in *The Book of Songs*:

"My words are about affairs true,
    Never think I am only joking.
    Just like an advice of old,
    Even a firewood gatherer has a clue."[12]

It advises people to inquire widely.

Where there are laws, abide by them; where no law is available, draw analogies. Judging by the root, you get to know the branches. Judging by the left side, you get to know the right side. All things proceed in their own ways but share the same principles.

When rewards and punishments are given according to the same rules and regulations, people will abide by them. Government enlightenment and popular custom will not work till they conform to each other.

In a family with an octogenarian, one son is excused from corvée labor; in a family with a nonagenarian, the whole family is excused from it. For the disabled or the

---

[8] The ancient six ceremonies in classics: capping, wedding, funeral, sacrifice, communal festival, presentation.

[9] Education on the relations of father and son, husband and wife, ruler and subject, young and old, brothers, friends and guests.

[10] Minor Court Hymns, *The Book of Songs*.

[11] The capital of Shang Dynasty.

[12] Major Court Hymns, *The Book of Songs*.

sick who take care of themselves, one family member is excused from the service. Those in mourning for a parent are excused for three years. Those engaging in other types of mourning like *zicui* and *dagong* are excused from it for three months. The immigrants from other feudal states and the newly-weds are excused from the service for one year.

Master Confucius spoke of Ju Zijia as unyielding but not as firm as Master Yan, of Master Yan as a practical minister but not as persistent as Chan Zi, of Chan Zi as a benefactor but not an equal of Zhong Guan, and of Zhong Guan as a man stressing efficiency and wisdom rather than morality and humanity, less cultivated and therefore not up to the minister of the Son of Heaven.

Mencius had an audience with King Xuan of Qi on quite a number of occasions but refused to discuss the state affairs. One of his disciples asked, "Why did you not talk about official matters with King of Qi when you saw him so many times?"

"I must make him dismiss his wicked ideas first," replied Mencius.

On his way to Yan, Zizhi Gongxing ran into Yuan Zeng. "How do you like His Majesty?" asked Gongxing.

"His aspiration is humble," replied Zeng. "Men with humble aspirations make light of their cause and therefore do not seek assistance. Without the help of worthy men, how can they be qualified for anything? Just like the Di and Qiang captives! They are not distressed by being tied and bound, but are worried that they would not be burned after death. They seek profit, even though it is as little as the fine down newly grown in fall and even if it is so harmful to the state as to destroy it. Could they be regarded as knowledgeable about how to plan state affairs?

Now let us suppose there is a man who has lost a needle. He searches a whole day but fails to find it. Later, however, he finds it. It is not that his eyes are brighter but that he has bent down to look more carefully for it. It is the same case with the reflection in mind.

Both the sense of righteousness and the desire for profit are things humans have. Even Yao and Shun were unable to get rid of the desire for profit in people; however, both emperors were able to make them love virtue more than they desire profit. Even Jie and Zhou were unable to get rid of the sense of righteousness in people; nevertheless, they were able to make them love virtue less but desire profit more. Thus, righteousness over profit marks good order; profit over righteousness indicates chaos. If a ruler stresses righteousness, profit will be conquered by righteousness; if he emphasizes profit, righteousness will be conquered by profit. For this reason, the Son of Heaven should not bother about quantity, a feudal lord should not comment on profit, a senior official should not talk about gain or loss, and a man of learning should not talk about management for wealth and property. The monarch of a state does not raise flocks and herds, a minister pledging allegiance to his monarch does not raise chickens or pigs, a senior minister does not secure personal gains, and a senior official does not plant fields or gardens. When the men of learning and above sneer at seeking personal profit, keep from competing with the people for business and are happy to grant favors but ashamed to accumulate wealth, the people in general will not be troubled by difficulty with money, and the impoverished will have something to do to support themselves.

King Wen conquered four states, King Wu destroyed two, and when Duke of Zhou completed the great cause, King Cheng and King Kang came to power and made no punitive campaign.

Emphasis on the accumulation of wealth, contempt for poverty, heavy load on the people, and punishment of those who fail to bear the burden give rise to evils and bring forth too numerous penalties.

If a ruler is fond of righteousness, the people will try to refine themselves in private. If he is fond of wealth, the people will run after profit at the risk of their lives. These two choices form a crossroads to order or chaos. A popular saying goes: "Do you want to be rich? Then tolerate disgrace, risk your life, break off the relations with your old friends, and run counter to righteousness." When a ruler loves to be rich, the people will follow his example. So how can chaos be avoided?

During a drought, Tang of Shang prayed to Heaven, saying: "Is my government not properly regulated? Are the people forced to overwork themselves? Why is there no rain for such a long time? Are my palaces and chambers gorgeous? Do my women intervene too often? Why has there been no rain for so long? Is it due to rampancy of bribery or flourishing of slanderers? Why has it been dry for such a long time?"

Heaven does not create the common people for the sake of a monarch; it establishes the monarch for the sake of the common people. For this reason, the division of land for different states since the ancient times is not to honor the feudal lords only; the disposition of offices and ranks and the establishment of titles and emoluments are not to honor the senior officials only.

The way of a ruler lies in the knowledge of how to use men and that of a minister in the knowledge of how to manage state affairs. For this reason, when Shun governed all under Heaven, he did not give orders to all things, yet everything was done. Farmers are skillful in growing crops but cannot make officials in charge of agriculture. So is the case with craftsmen and merchants.

It is propitious without consulting an oracle to replace the unworthy with the worthy. Victory is expectable without battle if the force of a well-ordered state is dispatched on a punitive expedition against a state in chaos.

The men of Qi wanted to attack Lu but feared Zhuangzi of Bian,[13] so they dared not pass by the town. The men of Jin wanted to attack Wei but were so afraid of Zilu that they dared not pass by the town of Pu.

He who is in want of knowledge may consult Yao and Shun, and he who is in poverty may go to the Treasury of Heaven for help. It is said that the way of the great Former Kings is that of Yao and Shun, and the broad learning of the Six Classics[14] is the wealth in the Treasury of Heaven."

A gentleman makes progresses in learning as fast as the molting of an insect: he learns when walking, standing, or sitting; he learns in facial expressions as well as in the manners of speaking. He neither leaves anything good undone nor puts off questions till tomorrow.

---

[13] AN official of Bian, a town in the Spring and Autumn Period, known for his courage.

[14] *The Book of Poetry, The Book of History, The Book of Changes, The Book of Rites, The Book of Music* and *The Spring and Autumn Annals.*

He who is good at learning exhausts the ways of things. He who is adept at putting things into practice examines all the difficulties involved.

A gentleman sets his aspirations as if he were in adversity. Even if the Son of Heaven or the Three Councilors of State inquire about government affairs, he says yes when it is right and no when it is wrong.

A gentleman does not lose his virtue when beset in difficulty, he is not careless when exhausted, and he does not forget the casual talks when facing troubles and difficulties.

You never really know the pine and cedar till winter comes. Similarly, you never realize till you run into difficulties that a gentleman never forgets even a single day to persist in doing what is right.

Even if it just drizzles, the water still sinks deep. What is great is so because it embraces what is small; what is obvious is so because it is the accumulation of what is subtle. A man of noble virtue looks gentle and kind; a man perfect in conduct is known far and wide. On the other hand, a petty man is dishonest in heart and seeks only what is superficial.

He who does not recount his teachers with admiration in his discourse means betrayal; he who does not recount his teachers with admiration in his teaching means deviation. An enlightened monarch does not accept such rebels and the gentry at court refuse to talk with them when they encounter them on the road.

He who is inadequate in action is excessive in speech; he who is untrustworthy pretends to be honest in talking. For this reason, *The Spring and Autumn Annals* approves of mutually repeated verbal agreement while *The Book of Songs* disapproves of repeated meetings for alliance, but their intention is one and the same. He who has a complete mastery of *The Book of Songs* does not offer interpretations, he who comprehends *The Book of Changes* completely does not practice divination, and he who is familiar with *The Book of Rites* does not serve as the master of ceremonies. They have the same frame of mind.

Master Zeng said: "It is good to listen to what a filial son says and look at what he does. If his words are heard, they will please people far away. If his actions are seen, they will please people nearby. When those nearby are pleased, they get closer. When those far away are pleased, they feel attached to him. To inspire love in those nearby and attachment in those far away is the way of a filial son."

When Master Zeng went on a journey, Master Yan followed him to the suburbs, saying, "I am told that a gentleman offers gift of advice while an ordinary person presents material things. As I have no money to spare, I'd like to present you with some words in the name of a gentleman. The wheels of a chariot or carriage are made of wood from Mount Tai. With pieces of wood placed in a shaper and left there for three or five months, the rims, spokes and hubs are made. But once the wheels are broken, they cannot return to their former shape. So, a gentleman cannot be too careful in building his own image. Be careful! Sweet herbs like angelica and *gaoben* steeped in sweet wine are for wearing only once before they are changed. An upright ruler steeped in sweet words are likely to be corrupted by slanders. So, a gentleman can never be overcautious in choosing his environment."

Culture and learning are to a man what carving and polishing are to jade, just like the description of learning in *The Book of Songs*:

"As knife and file make smooth the bone,
  So jade is wrought by chisel and stone."[15]

He's *bi*[16] was made of a stone found beside a well and did not become a treasure of the Son of Heaven[17] till it was cut by a jade worker. Zigong and Jilu were originally low in status. However, they were turned into outstanding men of learning after education in culture, learning, rite and morality.

Insatiable in learning and inquiry and tireless in adoring the men of learning—these qualities are access to the treasury of Heaven.

A gentleman does not talk about anything till his doubt is resolved; he does not tell anything before consulting others about it. His perseverance in so doing accelerates his daily progress.

A gentleman does not approve of much knowledge without being friendly to one's teachers, erudite learning without following certain standards, and being fond of many things but a master of none.

Those who neither read and recite when still young nor analyze and discuss in the prime of their lives will go nowhere even though they are with an aptitude for learning.

If a gentleman is whole-minded in teaching and his disciples are single-minded in learning, they will succeed soon.

In office, a gentleman is able to add to the reputation of his monarch and reduce the worries of the common people. Being in office but without abilities is a deceit. Enjoying a good salary without being able to do any good is usurpation. A man of learning does not necessarily serve in office; however, he who serves in office must learn.

Zigong told Confucius, "I am tired of learning and would like to stop to serve the monarch."

Confucius replied, "In *The Book of Songs* it says:

'Be kind and polite from morning to night,
  Be respectful and serious in the service.'[18]

It is hard to serve the monarch. So, how can you wait upon him and stop learning?"

"In that case," said Zigong, "I want to stop to wait upon my parents."

Confucius said, "*The Book of Songs* also says:

'For filial piety that is endless
  On you there'll be conferred bless.'[19]

---

[15] Ballads from the States, *The Book of Songs*.

[16] A priceless jem which is said to be found by He Bian, a native of Chu.

[17] Another version is "a treasure of the world."

[18] Eulogies, *The Book of Songs*.

[19] Major Court Hymns, *The Book of Songs*.

It is no easy to serve the parents. So, how can you attend to them and stop learning?"

"That being the case," replied Zigong, "then I would like to stop to take care of my wife and children."

Confucius again cited *The Book of Songs*:

"'He brings his lady in line with ritual
   And treats his brothers likewise
   Before proceeding to manage the state affairs.'[20]

It is no easy job taking care of one's wife and children. So, how can you take care of them and stop learning?"

"That being so," said Zigong, "I would like to stop to be with my friends."

Confucius cited *The Book of Songs* another time:

"'Friends should help one another,
   For mutual assistance adds to dignity.'[21]

It is not easy to be with friends. So, how can you stop learning to make friends?"

"If that is true," responded Zigong, "I would like to stop to crop the field."

Confucius cited *The Book of Songs* once more, saying:

"'Collect twitch-grass by day,
   And by night ropes are made.
   Hurry to repair your roof,
   Since sowing will start soon.'[22]

It is difficult to till the land. So, how can you work on the field and stop learning?"
"In that case, is there no chance for me to stop learning?" asked Zigong.
Confucius replied, "Look at the tomb in the distance. It is as high as a mound and it resembles a giant pot. That is where you can stop learning."
"How great death is!" exclaimed Zigong. "A gentleman stops there and a petty man ends there, too."
The passion of love in the Ballads from the States[23] is described as "satisfying the human desire without surpassing the boundary of ritual, whose genuineness may be compared to metal and stone and whose lyrics are accepted in ancestral temples." The composers of the Hymns Minor, failing to be used by the corrupted rulers, withdrew of their own accord and stayed humble. They complained against the contemporary

---

[20] Major Court Hymns, *The Book of Songs*.
[21] Major Court Hymns, *The Book of Songs*.
[22] Ballads from the States, *The Book of Songs*.
[23] One of the three sections of *The Book of Songs*, the other two being Hymns (Major and Minor) and Eulogies.

government and expressed their nostalgia for the past. The words are of rich and bright colors and the tone is of the sentiment of sorrow.

When a state is going to flourish, it attaches importance to teachers and masters. And when teachers and masters are honored, it means that laws and regulations are implemented. On the other hand, if a state is on the decline, it looks down on teachers and masters. And if teachers and masters are despised, people will become self-indulgent and, as a result, laws and regulations will be broken.

In ancient times, the ordinary men were not able to join government service till fifty. The princes of the Son of Heaven and feudal lords, however, underwent their capping ceremony at nineteen before attending to government affairs because their decent education was complete by then.

He who admires gentlemen is the right person to be educated. Failure to educate him is deemed to be inauspicious. In the contrary, he who admires those other than gentlemen is not the right person to be educated. To offer him education simply means to give robbers food or lend bandits weapons.

He who is unconscious of the inefficiency in his actions is most likely to indulge in exaggerated talk. However, the men of virtue in ancient times would not accept promotion against rite and morality even though they were humble and poor like the ordinary people and had only thin porridge for meals and broken coarse cloth for clothing. How could they be otherwise?

Zixia was from a poor family. His clothes were in tatters. Someone asked him, "Why don't you take an official position?"

"I refuse to serve those feudal lords who hold me in contempt," replied Zixia, "and I am not going to see those officials again since they look down on me. Hui Liuxia wore the same broken clothes as those guards at the back gate, but he was not despised. His noble conduct was not known for just one day. Besides, competing for profit as tiny as a nail may result in loss as big as your palm."

The ruler of men has to be cautious in choosing his ministers. Similarly, an ordinary person has to be careful in making friends. Friends must be friendly with and help each other. If they follow different roads, how can there be mutual assistance? When firewood is evenly spread out for burning, fire starts from the driest; when water is poured out on level ground, it flows toward the wet spot first. Since it is so clear that things of the same kind follow each other, how can there be any doubt when you judge a person by the friends he makes? Therefore, one must be careful to make friends with men of virtue. It is the foundation of morality. *The Book of Songs* says:

> "Do not push the ox-cart,
>   Or dust will rise and dart."[24]

It implies that one should never make friends with petty men.

He who is arrogant and deceptive thinks himself wise, but actually he is not. He who is weak and inconstant seems kind, but actually he is not. And he who is violent and aggressive looks courageous, but actually he is not.

---

[24] Minor Court Hymns, *The Book of Songs*.

Benevolence, righteousness, ritual and goodness are to men what wealth, property and food to a household. The more they have them the richer, the less the poorer, and those have none are poverty-stricken. Hence, those who are incapable of major responsibilities but reluctant to perform minor duties are going to destruction.

All things arise because of something else. Wherever they appear, they will go back there in the end.

Rumors and hearsays should be eliminated; merchandise and female charm should be kept at a distance. Troubles can be traced to imperceptible tiny sources and a gentleman should cut them off as soon as possible.

A credible person clarifies between what is definitely credible and what is probably credible. He refrains from telling what is doubtful or what he has not consulted about.

A wise man is clear about what things to do and fully comprehends their ways and therefore serve earnestly. For this reason, it is said, "It is difficult to please a gentleman, for if you attempt to make him happy with what is against reason, he is not pleased."

A saying goes like this: "As a rolling ball stops in a bowl or some other container, so rumors stop when they reach a wise man." This serves to explain why various schools and heterodox doctrines loathed the Confucians. If you cannot decide whether something is right or wrong, judge it with past experience, verify it with things nearby, and reflect on it with a fair mind. Then gossips stop and abusive words die there.

Master Zeng did not finish eating fish and said, "Keep the leftover in the rice water."

One of his disciples replied, "Better salt it, for it is harmful to you that way."

Master Zeng exclaimed with tears in his eyes, "I bore no ill will, did I?"

He was sad to have heard such different opinions so late in life.

Do not use your weakness to deal with the strengths of others. Hide and avoid your disadvantages and make best use of your advantages. Being extremely intelligent but disobedient to laws and regulations, being perceptive and eloquent but queer in conduct, being bold and resolute but lacking propriety—these are what a gentleman detests.

He is a sage who talks much and whose words are appropriate in category. He is a gentleman who speaks little but whose words are rightful. And he is a petty man who babbles much against rules and regulations. He may be skilled in debate but his words are drunken nonsense.

The laws of the state forbid picking up lost articles. The reason behind this is the hate for people who are accustomed to obtaining things against the system of rank and status. When each person observes his social status and fulfills his duties, there will be good order under Heaven. However, if no one does this, there will be chaos even if only a wife and a concubine are involved.

All men under Heaven have their own ideas; however, they have some positive opinions in common. For example, when speaking of the taste of food, they all recommend Ya Yi; when talking about music, they think highly of Maestro Kuang; when discussing good government, they turn to the kings of the Three Dynasties. Since the kings of the Three Dynasties had made the laws and regulations and established ritual and music, if anyone attempts to devise his own rather than adopt theirs, is it not the same as to change Ya Yi's cooking and Maestro Kuang's tones? Without observing the laws and regulations formulated by them, all under Heaven would die before long and all states would perish soon.

What drinks but does not eat is cicada. What neither drinks nor eats is mayfly.

Shun and Xiaoji loved their parents but were not loved by them. Bigan and Zixu Wu were loyal to their monarchs but did not win their trust. Zhongni[25] and Yuan Yan were wise but frustrated in their lives. Being compelled to live under a tyrant and unable to escape, one may hold what is good in esteem, advocate what is beautiful, talk about the strong points and not mention the shortcomings.

Being respectful all along but meeting a sticky end, this is because he slanders in private. Being knowledgeable but not employed, this is because he backbites. Being desirous to a fair reputation but becoming notorious, this is because he exaggerates.

A gentleman can make himself honorable, but he cannot ensure that others will honor him. He can make himself qualified for a certain job, but he cannot ensure that others will employ him.

Mandate and oath were beneath the Five Emperors.[26] Covenants and treaties were beneath the kings of the Three Dynasties. The practice of exchanging sons as hostages was beneath the Five Hegemons.

---

[25] The style name of Confucius.

[26] They are usually said to be the Yellow Emperor, Zhuanxu, Ku, Yao and Shun.

Chapter 28
The Vessel of Warning

Synopsis

This is an expression of Master Xun's thought through a collection of words and deeds of Confucius.

An analogy is made of the warning vessel usually placed on the right side of the royal seat, which tilts when empty, becomes upright when half full, and overturns when completely filled. Confucius intended to show that one should follow the way of retreat and modesty rather than indulge in self-exaltation and complacency.

A recount of the government affairs handled by Confucius when he was Executive Prime Minister and the Minister of Justice in the State of Lu showed that when a gentleman was in power, he should prevent against petty men who were good at confounding the public with their eloquence and forming parties for personal gains. The rulers were advised to implement the way of the Former Kings by employing the worthy to conduct education before administering punishment with caution.

By discussing the frustrations Confucius experienced in putting his learning into practice, gentlemen are encouraged to continue their diligent learning and self-cultivation before difficulties and prepare for opportunities to come.

Text

Confucius visited the ancestral temple of Duke Huan of Lu and spotted a lopsided vessel there.

"What is this?" Confucius asked the keeper.

"It is a warning vessel placed on the right of the royal seat," the latter replied.

"I have heard of such a thing," said Confucius. "If empty, it tilts; when half full, it is upright; and when full, it overturns." Turning to his disciples, he continued, "Add some water in it."

One of his disciples fetched some water and did so. When halfway full, the vessel became upright. When completely filled, it overturned. And when emptied, it again tilted.

Confucius drew a long breath and sighed, "Oh, how could there be any vessel that does not overturn when it is completely filled!"

Zilu asked, "May I ask if there is a way to maintain uprightness when completely full?"

"Yes," replied Confucius. "Intelligence and wisdom may be maintained by seeming stupidity, great merit under Heaven may be guarded by modesty, matchless courage and power may be kept by outward timidity, and great wealth within the four seas may be protected by humility. Such is the way of retreat and modesty."

When he served temporarily as prime minister of Lu, Confucius executed on the seventh day of his appointment the deputy censor named Mao.

"Mao is one of the celebrities in Lu," his disciples came and informed him. "But you killed him at the very beginning of your office. Was there not something mistaken?"

"Sit down," said Confucius, "and let me tell you why. Human wickedness is characterized by five qualities, robbing and stealing excluded. The first is being clear in mind but wicked. The second is being perverse in conduct and obstinate. The third is being hypocritical but powerful in argument. The fourth is being fond of memorizing foul things extensively. The fifth is being favorable to what is wrong and trying to rationalize it. Any individual with one of these bad qualities cannot avoid punishment by a gentleman. However, Mao possessed them all. Thus, wherever he dwelled, he could gather those who would follow him and form crowds, and whatever he would say could disguise evil ideas and confuse the public. He was so firm in his will that he could run against what was right and act on his free will. Such was the determined champion of petty men and therefore could not be left unpunished. For this same reason, Tang punished Yinxie, King Wen punished Panzhi, Duke of Zhou punished Guanshu, the Grand Duke punished Huashi, Zhong Guan punished Fuliyi, and Zichan punished Xi Deng and Fu Shi. These seven men lived in different ages but shared a common frame of mind, so they could not escape punishment. *The Book of Songs* sings,

> 'I feel deeply worried and uneasy
>   For I am hated by the petty and greedy.'[1]

When petty men form gangs, it is cause enough for worry."

When Confucius served as Minister of Justice in Lu, there was a legal dispute between father and son. Confucius put the son in prison and for three months did not resolve the matter. Then the father requested permission to drop the suit, and Confucius released the son. Jisun heard about the matter and was displeased, saying, "This old man has deceived me. He told me that filial piety must be stressed before a state can be well-governed. Now that he could kill one unfilial son to warn other men, but he released him instead."

---

[1] Ballads from the States, *The Book of Songs*.

Qiu Ran told Confucius of the complaint.

"Alas!" sighed Confucius deeply and said, "If the superiors have gone astray, will it do to kill their subordinates? To judge a case without conducting education in the first place is to kill the innocent. If the three armies were utterly defeated, it would not do to behead all of them; similarly, if a prison were not in good order, it would not do to punish all the criminals. In both cases, the real blame did not lie with the people. When an order is inefficiently implemented but punishment is severe, they result in cruel harm. Now when production is carried out in the right season but the collection of tax is without any restraint, they lead to ruthlessness. If merit is demanded without giving instructions in advance, it is tyranny. And penalties shall not be imposed till these three practices are checked. *The Book of History* says, 'Even if death penalty and other punishments are righteous, they should not be executed in haste. We can only say that we should have done our job with more considerations.' That is to say, education should be put in the first place."

Thus, the Former Kings proclaimed their way of government and they followed it themselves first. If the people failed to be transformed, they exalted the worthy to educate them. If they failed to be educated, they dismissed those who were not able in order to inspire fear in them. In three years' time, the common people would ordinarily become obedient. If some wicked men would disobey, punishments would be applied to them and then they would realize their guilt. This is praised in *The Book of Songs* when it sings,

> "A grand master is Yin, Oh!
> He is like the foundation of Zhou.
> He has the power of the nation in hand,
> Dependent on him is the whole land.
> The Son of Heaven he assists
> The people should not go astray, he insists."[2]

Things are different in the current world. So confusing are the teachings and so various are the punishments that the people are bewildered and led astray before they are caught in the net of justice and get punished. Thus, penalties are increasingly profuse but evil is still not defeated. An empty cart cannot climb up a short slope while a loaded one can overcome a high mountain. Why? Because the slope is less steep in the former case. A man cannot climb up a high wall but little kids can climb up a mountain to play. Why? Because the slope is gradual in the latter case. There has long been gentle slopes in the present world, can people be stopped from climbing them? *The Book of Songs* says,

> 'The road of Zhou was smooth like a whetstone,
> It was straight as an arrow shaft.
> It was where gentlemen walked along
> And petty men only cast a glance.
> Whenever I think of this,

---

[2] Minor Court Hymns, *The Book of Songs*.

Tears well up in my eyes.'³

Alas! Is it not sad indeed?"
The Book of Songs sings,

"When I gaze at the moon or the sun,
  It will remind me of my loved one.
  Between us is such a distance and divide,
  How can I expect him to come to my side?"⁴

Master Confucius remarked, "If they could bow deeply to each other, how could one not expect the other to come?"

Zigong once asked Confucius who was watching the east-flowing water, "Why is it that a gentleman will surely watch a great river whenever he sees it?"

Confucius replied, "Water nourishes all living things, yet there is no selfish intention in it. This resembles virtue. It takes a zigzag course and flows from high to low ground. This resembles righteousness. It goes forward with strength and vigor without a pause. This resembles Dao. If a channel is opened for it to flow, it rushes through as swiftly as an echo and does not fear a ravine a hundred fathoms deep. This resembles courage. Use it to check the ground and it tells whether its surface is flat. This resembles law. Fill up a container with it, and it becomes level without seeking help. This resembles justice. Delicate and fine, it extends anywhere and everywhere. This resembles penetration. Anything going in and coming out of it becomes fresh and clean. This resembles excellence in transformation through education. It naturally flows eastward in spite of twists and turns. This resembles will. For these reasons, a gentleman is sure to watch a great river whenever he sees it."

Confucius said, "I consider some things shameful, others despicable, and still others dangerous. I hold it to be a shame for anyone who does not work hard at learning when young and have nothing to teach others when old. I consider it something to be despised if anyone leaves his hometown to serve his monarch and become successful in life but fails to exchange reminiscences about the good old days when he runs into an old acquaintance. And I consider it dangerous to get along with petty men."

Confucius said, "I approve of learning that resembles the building of an anthill because it is continuous. But if it is like a mound that never grows, I dislike it."

Nowadays, some men are satisfied with what little trifles they have learned and desire to teach others.

When traveling southward to Chu, Confucius was besieged between the states of Chen and Cai. He and his disciples starved for seven days. Since they had only vegetable soup, the disciples looked very hungry.

Coming up to Confucius, Zilu said, "I have heard that those who do good are rewarded by Heaven with good fortune, while those who do evil are punished by Heaven with misfortune. Now you, Master, have long been putting into practice the

---

³ Minor Court Hymns, *The Book of Songs*.
⁴ Ballads from the States, *The Book of Songs*.

intensification of moral integrity, pursuit of righteousness, and cultivation of good virtues, but why are you reduced to such difficulty?"

Confucius replied, "Since you do not know, let me tell you why. Do you think that those who have wisdom are sure to be employed? Did you not see that Bigan had suffered evisceration? Do you expect that those who are loyal are certain to be used? Did you not see that Longfeng Guan had been executed? Do you imagine that those who remonstrate are sure to be trusted? Did you not see that Zixu Wu had ended with his corpse being displayed outside the east gate of Gusu? It is a question of opportunity whether anyone is to be used or not, it is a personal quality to be worthy or not, and many a gentleman with profound learning and great vision was born in wrong time! From this it can be seen that those who have not got the right opportunity are many! I am not the only one at all.

"Plants such as orchid and angelica grow deep in the forest. They do not depend on man to be fragrant. A gentleman does not learn for the purpose of being impressive; rather, he does for the purpose of being able to deal with troubles, to remain firm before hardship, and keep a clear mind about the relationship between life and death as well as fortune and misfortune. Being worthy or unworthy is a question of personal qualities. Doing or refusing to do is a question of attitude. Being promoted or frustrated is a question of opportunity. And life or death is a question of fate. Now suppose there is such a person who is worthy, is he able to get anywhere without the right opportunity? Or should he have the opportunity, what difficulties will there be for him? So, a gentleman broadens his learning, sharpens his vision, cultivates his virtue, corrects his conduct and waits for the right opportunities."

"Sit down, Zilu," continued Confucius, "and I will tell you. Prince Chong'er of Jin conceived in Cao his ambition to become a hegemon, King Goujian of Yue did the same at Kuaiji, so did Duke Huan of Qi when he was in Ju. Thus, one does not become far-sighted till he finds himself in difficulty, nor does he cherish great aspirations till he goes into exile. So, how can you conclude that I will not succeed in the future because of my present situation under the mulberry tree with its leaves falling!"

After visiting the north hall of the ancestral temple of Lu, Zigong came out and asked Confucius, "Just now I was looking around in the north hall of the Grand Temple without taking a break. But when I went back for another look at the north doors and found them pieced together. Is there anything particular about it? Or is it a fault in the carpenter's workmanship?"

Confucius replied, "Great attention is certainly paid to the building of the Grand Temple. The official in charge employs the best craftsmen who make designs according to the grain of wood so that it looks beautiful. It does not mean that there is a lack of good materials. It should be taken as being emphatic on patterns."

Chapter 29
On the Way of a Son

Synopsis

This is a collection of words and deeds of Confucius and his disciples demonstrating the moral pursuit of Confucianism in terms of conduct, will and speech. In personal conduct, Confucianism regarded filial piety as the foundation, which was made true by way of respect in behavior, humility in speech, and obedience in appearance and perfected by following Dao and moral principles rather than the wishes of one's monarch or parents. Personal will should be placed in the control of ritual even in private, as is shown in Confucius' refusal to answer Zilu's question of whether it was proper for the senior minister of Lu to lie on bed wearing a white cloak since Confucius considered it against ritual to criticize a senior official in his own city. As speech is the voice of the mind, a gentleman should admit his knowledge and confess his ignorance. In a word, the way of Confucianism is complete when will is controlled by ritual principles and speech is in agreement with ritual requirements.

Text

To be a good son at home and to be a good brother outside constitute the minor standards of human conduct. To be obedient to superiors and to be sincere to inferiors constitute the average standards of conduct. To obey Dao rather than the monarch and to follow moral principles rather than the wishes of one's father constitute the highest standards of conduct. When will is under the control of ritual principles and speech is in agreement with ritual requirements, the Confucian way is complete and even Shun could not have done better.

    A good son refuses to follow orders in three circumstances: When following an order endangers his parents and refusing it brings them security, his refusal means devotion. When following an order brings disgrace to his parents and refusing it win them glory, his refusal means righteousness. When following an order makes him savage as beasts and refusing it brings him in line with proprieties, his refusal means respect. Hence, it is unfilial to refuse an order when he should accept it; it is disloyal to accept an order when he should refuse it. If a son is clear why he should obey or disobey orders, why he can be respectful, loyal, sincere, and properly behaves himself in these respects, he may be called a man of great filial piety. This is reflected in an old book when it says, "Follow Dao rather than your monarch. Follow righteousness rather than your father." Hence, to maintain his respect when exhausted from hard labor, to carry on righteousness when suffering disasters and difficulties, and to retain love when being unluckily disliked because of certain dissatisfactions – none but a benevolent man can do it. And this is why such good virtue is thus praised in *The Book of Songs*: "A good son knows no end in filial piety."[1]

Duke Ai of Lu asked Confucius, "When a son obeys his father's order, is it an act of filial piety? And when a minister follows the command of his monarch, is it an act of loyalty?" The questions were repeated twice, but Confucius did not answer them.

Confucius came out in a hurry and told Zigong, "Just now His Majesty asked me, 'When a son obeys his father's order, is it an act of filial piety? And when a minister follows the command of his monarch, is it an act of loyalty?' He asked me three times but I made no response. What do you think of it?"

"It is filial for a man to obey his father's order and loyal to follow his monarch's command," replied Zigong, and then he asked, "could there be an alternative, Master?"

Confucius said, "What a petty man you are! You do not understand it. In the past, if a state of ten thousand chariots had four ministers who could present remonstrances, its borders would be well defended against invasion. If a state of a thousand chariots had three ministers who could present remonstrances, it would face no threat. If a state of a hundred chariots had two ministers who could present remonstrances, its ancestral temple would be protected against destruction. A father is unlikely to do anything against ritual if he has a remonstrant son. Similarly, a man of learning is unlikely to do anything against righteousness if he has remonstrant friends. So, if a son obeys his father's order, in what could he be regarded as filial? If a minister follows the order of his monarch, in what could he be said as loyal? Whether a man is filial and loyal or not, it depends on circumstances."

Zilu asked Confucius, "Here is a man who rises early and retires late, plowing and weeding, planting and gardening, till his hands and feet are callused, in order to wait on his parents, yet this man lacks a reputation for filial piety. Why?"

Confucius replied, "Perhaps he is not respectful in behavior? Or he is not modest in speech? Or he is not compliant in facial expression? An ancient saying goes, 'You may give us clothing and provide everything else for us, but we will not depend on you unless you are respectful.' Now this man rises early and retires late in order to wait on his parents, plowing and weeding, planting and gardening, till his hands and feet are callused. If he is respectful in behavior, modest in speech, and compliant in

---

[1] Major Court Hymns, *The Book of Songs*.

facial expression, why does he still fail to have the reputation of being filial? Is it perhaps because he keeps company with men who are inhumane?"

Confucius said, "Remember what I am going to say to you, Zilu. Even if a man has strength enough for a top warrior of state, he still cannot lift his own body. It is not because he is not powerful but because he is not in the proper situation to do so. For this reason, if he fails to behave properly when he comes home, it is his fault; if he does not become distinguished when he is away from home, it is the fault of his friends. Thus, if a gentleman behaves himself well at home and keeps company with worthy men outside, how could he not be known as a man of filial piety?".

Zilu asked Confucius, "The senior minister of Lu lies on bed wearing a white cloak.[2] Is this in accord with ritual?"

"Sorry," replied Confucius, "I do not know."

Zilu went out and told Zigong, "I thought our master knew everything. Actually, there are things he does not know."

"What did you ask him?" said Zigong.

Zilu replied, "I asked him if it was ritually proper for the senior official of Lu to lie on bed wearing a white cloak, and he said he did not know."

"Let me ask him on your behalf," Zigong suggested and went in. "Is it ritually proper to lie on bed with a white cloak on the back?" he asked Confucius.

"It is against ritual," answered Confucius.

Zigong came out and told Zilu, "You said there were things our Master did not know, didn't you? Actually, there is nothing he is ignorant of. The problem is that you asked a wrong question since it is ritually improper to criticize a senior official whose city you are now in."

Zilu came in full dress to see Confucius.

"Why are you so splendidly dressed?" Confucius asked. "In former days, the River[3] originated from the Min Mountains. At its starting point, the water can only float a winecup; but when it reaches the ferries, you cannot cross it without tying boats together or avoiding the strong wind. Is this not because of the abundant water in its lower course? Now you are so elaborately dressed and look so dignified, who under Heaven would be willing to offer you advice?"

Zilu hurried out to change his attire and returned good-naturedly. Confucius said, "Remember what I am going to say to you, Zilu. He who speaks prudently does not say anything as he pleases, he who acts prudently does not flaunts himself, and he who makes a display of wisdom and ability is a petty man. Thus, a gentleman admits his knowledge when he knows something and denies it if he does not. This is the essence of speech. He admits his ability when he can do something and denies it when he cannot. This is the perfection of conduct. It is wisdom if one keeps to the essence in speech; it is benevolence if one arrives at the perfection of conduct. And how could there be any question of inadequacy if one is both wise and benevolent?"

---

[2] During the 27-month mourning for one's deceased parent, a man should wear a white piece of cloth on the back and keep from sleeping on bed.

[3] The Yangtze River or Changjiang now.

When Zilu entered, the Master asked him, "What should the wise do? And what should the benevolent do?"

"The wise act in such a way that others come to know him," replied Zilu, "and the benevolent behave in such a manner that others come to love him."

The Master said, "You can be called a man of learning now."

When Zigong entered, the Master asked him, "What should the wise do? And what should the benevolent do?"

"The wise understand others," Zigong replied, "and the benevolent love others."

The Master said, "You can be called an educated gentleman."

When Yuan Yan entered, the Master asked, "What should the wise do? And what should the benevolent do?"

Yan Yuan replied: "The wise understand themselves first," said Yan, "and the benevolent love themselves first."

The Master said, "You deserve to be called an enlightened gentleman."

Zilu asked Confucius, "Does a gentleman have anxieties?"

"No," said Confucius, "a gentleman is happy about his aspirations before employment, and when employed he is happy about his accomplishments. For this reason, he is happy all his life without a single day of anxieties. On the other hand, a petty man is anxious to have a position before employment and is afraid of losing it when employed. For this reason, he is anxious all his life without a single day of happiness."

Chapter 30
On Self-Examination

Synopsis

This is another collection of the words of Confucius and his disciples emphasizing the importance of inner self-cultivation according to ritual principles which cannot be transcended even by sages. A comparison is made between gentlemen and jade with the implication of finding purity and perfection within rather than from outside. In dealing with people, whether it is for the purpose of taking or giving, one must make self-reflection and be forgiving when problems arise.

Text

As Ban Gongshu[1] cannot improve on the straightness of the marking line, a sage cannot transcend ritual, for ritual is something the common people observe without knowing why but the sages do on the basis of understanding.

Master Zeng said, "Do not estrange your relatives while drawing close to outsiders. Do not blame others because you yourself are not good. And do not cry out to Heaven when punishment falls on you. Is it not against reason if you estrange your relatives but draw close to outsiders? Is it not far off the mark if you blame others because you yourself are not good? Is it not too late if you call out to Heaven only when you have to suffer punishment? It sings in *The Book of Songs*,

> 'A trickling stream flows.
> Do not block it and it ever goes.
> When the hub breaks,
> You enlarge its spokes.
> When things have gone to ruin,

---

[1] Also known as Ban Lu, a famous carpenter in the state of Lu during the Warring States Period.

You sigh now and then groan.'[2]

Is it of any help to do so?"

Master Zeng was seriously ill. Yuan, his son, was holding his feet in the hands.

"Yuan," said Master Zeng, "remember what I am going to tell you. Fish, turtles, and crocodiles consider the pools too shallow; therefore, they dig holes underwater. Hawks, eagles, and kites consider the mountains too low; therefore, they build their nests atop the summits. Even so, they are still caught for the sake of bait. Thus, a gentleman will not suffer shame or disgrace if he does not gain profit at the cost of righteousness."

Zigong asked Confucius, "Why does a gentleman value jade but despise jake-like stone so much? Is it because jade is rare while jade-like stone is frequently found?"

Confucius said, "How can you say so, Zigong! Would a gentleman despise something because it is plentiful and value other things because of their rarity? A gentleman compares jade to good virtue. It is warm, smooth, and lustrous and is likened to benevolence. It is firm with patterns and is likened to wisdom. It is strong, tough and unyielding and is likened to righteousness. It is sharp but does not cause injury and is likened to moral conduct. It is breakable but unbendable and is likened to courage. It shows both flaw and virtue and is likened to honesty. Strike it and it sounds clear, sweet and audible in the distance and then stops all of a sudden, just like speech. Thus, a jadelike stone with beautiful carvings is no match to the brilliance of jade. It is just like what is sung in *The Book of Songs*:

"How I long for the gentleman
Who is warm and gentle like jade."[3]

Master Zeng said, "If I am not treated friendly by those who travel with me, it must be because I am not benevolent. If I am not respected by those who associate with me, it must be because I am not respectful. If I am not trusted in financial dealings, it must be because I am not trustworthy. If these are true, how could I blame others? He who blames others is at his wit's end; he who blames Heaven lacks knowledge. Is it not ridiculous to blame others when it is the fault of oneself?"

Huizi Nanguo asked Zigong, "Why is there always such a motley crew at your Master's gate?"

Zigong replied, "A gentleman is upright in attitude toward others. He does not refuse those who want to come, nor does he stop those who intend to leave. Since you may find many patients at the door of a good doctor and a lot of crooked wood beside a press frame, it is natural they are of a big variety."

Confucius said, "A gentleman has three principles of forgiveness. When a man fails to serve his monarch yet expects himself as a ruler to be served by his subjects, it is against the principle. When a man fails to requite the affection of his parents yet expects his son to be filial toward him, it is against the principle. When a man fails to be respectful to his elder brother yet expects himself to be respected by his

---

[2] Not available in the extant Chinese versions.

[3] Ballads from the States, *The Book of Songs*.

younger brother, it is against the principle. A man of learning who is clear about these principles can rectify his behaviors."

Confucius said, "A gentleman has three matters to consider carefully and they are things that must be pondered over. If he does not learn when he is young, he will not be able to do anything important. If he does not educate others when he is old, he will not be remembered. If he gets rich but fails to share his wealth, he will not be able to share with others when he himself is impoverished. For these reasons, a gentleman, when young, will learn if he considers carefully about what to do when grown up; he will engage in educating others in his old age when he expects himself to be remembered after death; and he will share his wealth with others when he is rich and considers carefully about the likelihood of being reduced to poverty someday."

Chapter 31
Conversations Between Duke Ai of Lu and Confucius

Synopsis

This is a collection of conversations between Duke Ai of Lu and Confucius and Duke Ding of Lu and Yuan Yan explaining the principles and methods the ruler of men should consider in using people if he intended to rule according to ritual. In judging and employing a man, instead of observing his outer behavior from the perspective of ritual, attention should be given to his virtue and ability. The ruler of men should be able to identify men on five levels, namely common men, scholars, gentlemen, worthy men, and sages.

In governing a country according to ritual, it is essential to know that self-cultivation is the foundation. While outer form like dress is necessary, inner strength is indispensable. It is meaningless to stress the form of etiquettes before being aware of worries, fears and difficulties in governing a country. And it is impossible to see the importance in emphasizing strategy and overlooking personal grudge before making good use of the people's talents without exhausting their strengths.

Text

Duke Ai of Lu asked Confucius, "I want to choose from among the most able in our state and share government affairs with them. Can you tell me how?"

Confucius responded, "Living in the present world yet not forgetful of the way of ancient times, and following the current customs yet wearing the ancient clothing—these are the ways in which some people behave themselves. Such men are rarely found to do evil, are they not?"

"Yes," answered Duke Ai, "but are those men worthy who wear a top hat, shoes with ornamented toe cap, and a girdle with an official tablet inserted in it?"

"Not necessarily," replied Confucius. "Those who wear ceremonial robes and hats and ride in a ceremonial carriage do not think of strong flavors, and those who wear mourning robes and straw sandals, lean on a ceremonial cane, and eat gruel do not think of wine and meat. There are cases in which one lives in the present world with the way of ancient times in mind and follows the current customs in ancient clothing but commits evils. But are they not rare?"

"Well-said!" exclaimed Duke Ai.

Confucius said, "Men may be divided into five grades: common men, men of learning, gentlemen, worthy men, and great sages."

"May I ask what sort of men may be called common men?" said Duke Ai.

Confucius said, "Those who are regarded as common men cannot use decent words when talking and do not feel depressed in the heart. They are ignorant of the necessity to choose from worthy men and good men of learning so that they are able to remove their worries. They lack a target in the actions they take and do not know how to behave when no action is to be taken. They pick and choose day after day but are not sure what is valuable. They follow the natural course of things as water does without a fixed destination. They are dominated by the five desires and are liable to corruption in mind. Such are properly called common men."

"Well said!" exclaimed Duke Ai. "May I ask what sort of men are called men of learning?"

Confucius replied, "The men of learning are those who follow certain principles although they may not have a mastery of the way of government and they know what to persevere in although they may not be perfect. For these reasons, they try to understand correctly what they learn rather than learn too many things, say what is proper rather than talk much, and make clear what they do is in accord with principles or standards rather than practice a great deal. Thus, when they succeed in understanding what they want to learn, expressing properly what they want to say, and fulfilling what they intend to do according principles or standards, they will be determined not to alter just as they will never force any change to their life or skin. Thus, to them wealth and eminent position do not mean much, nor does it make any difference to be lowly or humble. Such are properly called the men of learning."

"Excellent," commented Duke Ai. "May I ask what sort of men can be called gentlemen?"

Confucius responded, "Gentleman are those who tell the truth and, in their hearts, do not think themselves sufficiently virtuous, who cherish benevolence and righteousness but do not show off in their appearance, and who are clear-minded, considerate, and refrain from arguing with others so that they take all things easily and leisurely, as if they were not extraordinary. Such are properly called gentlemen."

"Superb!" Duke Ai cried out. "May I ask what sort of men can be said as worthy?"

Confucius answered, "They are those whose behaviors are in perfect accord with the rules without causing any harm to the fundamentals, whose ideas are sufficient to serve as models of all under Heaven without bringing any harm to themselves, and who are wealthy enough to possess the whole world without accumulating any for themselves. They distribute what they have to all people without being afraid of poverty themselves. Such are properly called worthy men."

"Wonderful!" exclaimed Duke Ai. "May I ask what sort of men can be called great sages?"

Confucius explained, "Great sages are those who have mastery of the great Dao in understanding, adapt themselves readily to boundless changes, and correctly distinguish among the dispositions and natures of myriad things. The great Dao is the fundamental principle on which formations and transformations are realized. Dispositions and natures are the basis on which judgements are formed on what is right or wrong and decisions are made on what to accept or reject. For these reasons, what they do is great as Heaven and Earth, and what they perceive is bright and clear as the sun and moon. They govern everything the way wind and rain nurture the living things, which is harmonious and pure. What they do is beyond imitation, as though they were carrying on what Heaven does. What they engage in is beyond comprehension, since the common people are so shallow that they do not even recognize things close at hand. Such are properly called great sages."

"Marvelous!" shouted Duke Ai.

Duke Ai asked Confucius about the ceremonial hat of Shun but got no response. Three times he asked, and three times Confucius did not reply.

Duke Ai said, "I asked you about Shun's hat, but why did you not answer my question?"

"In ancient times," replied Confucius, "the kings wore a simple crown of a helmet with a round-collar pendant. In their government, nourishing life was preferred and killing was hated. For this reason, phoenixes were found in the woods, unicorn kylins were seen in the wild of the suburbs, and the nests of crows and magpies were spotted everywhere. Your Majesty asked me about Shun's hat rather than those things, and that was why I did not react."

Duke Ai of Lu told Confucius, "As I was born deep in the palace and brought up in the hands of women, how is it that I have had no experience of sorrow, no experience of worry, no experience of toil, no experience of fear and no experience of danger?"

Confucius responded, "The questions raised by Your Majesty are questions of a sagely ruler. Since I am a petty man, their answers are beyond me."

Duke Ai insisted, "I can ask none other than you alone."

Confucius said, "When Your Majesty enters through the gate of his ancestral temple, ascends from the stairs on the right, and looks up, he will see the beams and rafters; when he looks down, he will see the altar. He will notice that the vessels are still there but their owners are gone. If he reflects on this, how could he not experience sorrow? At daybreak, Your Majesty rises, has his hair combed, and wearing his crown he goes to court at dawn for the audience, since a single matter not properly attended to might lead to disorder. If he reflects on this, how could he not experience anxiety? He goes to court at dawn and does not retire till evening. In his back court, held hostage or sent on exile are surely the sons and grandsons of other feudal lords. If he reflects on this, how could he not experience toil? When Your Majesty goes out through the four gates of Lu to the suburban regions, he will see many huts left among the ruins of perished states. If he reflects on this, how could he not experience fear? And I have heard that the monarch is a boat and his subjects the water. Water can support a boat; it can capsize it, too. If he reflects on this, how could he not experience danger?"

Duke Ai of Lu asked Confucius, "Does wearing the girdle and ceremonial hats contribute to benevolence?"

"Why does Your Majesty ask such a question?" Confucius responded respectfully. "If someone refuses to listen to music in mourning apparel and with a ceremonial staff, it is not because his ears fail him but because he is wearing the funeral costume. If he abstains from strong flavors when wearing sacrificial robes with embroidered designs and patterns, it is not because he lacks the sense of taste but because he is in such ritual clothing. Besides, I have heard that those who are good at trading try to prevent loss of their stores and those who are respectable do not engage in business transactions. If Your Majesty examines what is of benefit and what is not, he will surely know the answer."

Duke Ai of Lu asked Confucius, "I'd like to know how to choose the people of talents."

Confucius gave the following suggestions: "Do not choose those who seek to prevail over others. Do not choose those who seek to overwhelm others by their power. And do not choose those who have a silver tongue. Those who seek to prevail over others are greedy. Those who seek to overwhelm others by their power are rebellious. And those who have a silver tongue are unreliable. Only when a bow is well-adjusted does one get its strength, only when a horse is fairly tamed does it give its full play, and only when a man of learning is trustworthy and sincere does one make use of his intelligence and abilities. A man of learning who is multi-talented but not trustworthy may be likened to a wolf and therefore should not be approached. It is said that Duke Huan employed a traitor[1] and Duke Wen used a robber.[2] Thus, an enlightened ruler emphasizes strategy and overlooks his grudge while a benighted ruler does just the opposite. And he who places his strategy over grudge will become strong, while he who places grudge over strategy will perish."

Duke Ding of Lu asked Yuan Yan, "Is Bizhi Dongye an expert at chariot driving?"

"Yes," said Yuan Yan, "but if he goes on driving his way, his horses will flee."

Duke Ding was not pleased at these words. Coming inside, he said to those who were around him, "Even a gentleman backbites!"

Three days later, a stable keeper came with a report: "Bizhi Dongye's horses ran away. Both outside horses broke their reins, and the two inner horses are back to the stable."

Duke Ding jumped up and stepped across his mat, saying, "Send a chariot for Yan and hurry!"

When Yan arrived, Duke Ding said, "The other day when I asked you about Bizhi Dongye, you told me that he was a good driver but his horses would run away. How did you know it would happen?"

Yan answered, "I predicted it from the general rules. In the past, Shun was skillful at employing the people and Fu Zao was adept at handling horses: Shun did not press

---

[1] Referring to Zhong Guan.
[2] Referring to Di Bo or Fuxu Li.

his people to their limits and Fu Zao did not wear out his horses. For this reason, no one fled under Shun's rule and no horse ran away from Fu Zao. Now when he drives, Dongye takes hold of the reins when he mounts on the chariot and gets the horses and their bits in place. In making the animals trot, canter, gallop, and race, he fully observes the rites. In overcoming obstacles to reach distant places, he exhausts their strength. In spite of that, he still urges them on without a pause. From this I expected what would happen."

"Good," exclaimed Duke Ding, "Can you explain a little further about it?"

Yuan Yan said, "I have heard that a bird will peck, a beast will bite, and a man will cheat when they are driven desperate. From ancient times to the present, there has never been a case in which a monarch is free of danger when the common people are reduced to dire straits."

Chapter 32
Sidelights

Synopsis

This is a collection of stories extracted from historical data, roughly arranged according to the characters from high to low in position. Since modesty is usually praised and self-complacency arouses resentment, these stories are used to show the necessity to be loyal, honest, modest and respectful before making genuine progress in virtue and great accomplishments and remaining free from trouble. It is concluded by a high commendation of Master Xun's virtue, talent and learning by his disciples and a deep sympathy expressed for his bad luck in those turbulent years.

Text

Yao asked Shun, "If I want all under Heaven to come to me, what should I do then?"

Shun replied, "Be concentrated on government affairs without any slip, attend to tiny matters diligently, keep your faith and promise without becoming tired, and all under Heaven will come to you. Concentrate on the affairs of government as long as Heaven and Earth, give attention to tiny matters as the sun and moon do, keep loyalty and sincerity within, make them apparent without, and expose them to all within the four seas, and all under Heaven will be found as though it were in a corner of your room. What necessity is there then for you to try to win it?"

Marquis Wu of Wei was so capable of proper schemes that none of his ministers could surpass him. For this reason, he had a happy look on his face when court was concluded.

"Have you ever heard from anyone around you about what King Zhuang of Chu said?" Qi Wu came up and asked.

Marquis Wu replied, "What did he say?"

Qi Wu said, "King Zhuang of Chu was so capable of proper schemes that none of his ministers could surpass him; however, he withdrew from court with a worried look on his face. Wuchen, the Duke of Shen, came up and asked, 'Why does Your Majesty look worried after the audience?' King Zhuang explained, 'I am worried because none of my ministers could improve on the plans I have made. As was pointed out by Hui Zhong, "A feudal lord makes a true king if he can get instructions from a master, he can become a hegemon if he is assisted by friends, he can keep his state secure if he can have his doubts resolved, and he is doomed if he makes plans himself and none is able to surpass him." Now that I am so unworthy and none of my ministers can improve on my plan, my country is facing imminent destruction! That is why I am worried.' King Zhuang of Chu was worried about this, but Your Majesty is happy about it!"

Marquis Wu of Wei took a step backward and bowed twice, saying, "Heaven has sent you to remedy my faults."

When Boqin[1] was about to return to Lu, Duke of Zhou addressed his son's tutor, "Since you are leaving now, why do you not report on my son's good virtues?"

The tutor replied, "He is magnanimous toward others, independent in handling affairs, and cautious. These three qualities constitute his good virtues."

"Alas!" exclaimed Duke of Zhou. "How can you regard as good virtues what others despise? A gentleman is fond of following moral principles in doing things, so the people return to the right road. He is magnanimous because of his failure to discriminate between good and bad, yet you praise him for it! He is fond of doing things by himself because of narrow-mindedness. Even though a gentleman has the strength of an ox, he does not seek to prevail over the animal in matters of strength. Even if he can run as fast as a horse, he does not desire to excel over the animal in a race. He could be as wise as a man of learning, but he does not seek to do others down in matters of knowledge. Contention involves disputes among peers caused by personal feelings, yet you praise him for it! His being cautious can be accounted for by his shallowness and ignorance. I have heard that one should never refuse to see a man of learning because he is afraid of lowering himself in doing so. Instead, when he gives audience to a man of learning, he should ask himself, 'Am I not clear-minded somewhere somehow?' If he is not fond of making an inquiry of anyone, he will learn less. As a consequence, he will be shallow or ignorant. Being shallow and ignorant is the way of despicable men, yet you praise him for it!

"Let me tell you: I am a son of King Wen, a younger brother of King Wu, and an uncle of King Cheng. I am no humble man under Heaven. However, I have visited a number of ten men with greeting gifts for them and a number of other thirty men reciprocating their greeting gifts, given a polite interview to over a hundred men, and granted permission to more than a thousand men for them to complete their account of affairs. From among these men, I have won only three worthy men who can correct my behaviors and help settle all affairs under Heaven. I chose the three men from among hundreds or thousands rather than from the ten or the thirty. I treated the men of learning from higher positions less courteously than those from lower

---

[1] Duke of Zhou's son who was enfeoffed Marquis of Lu.

positions. All men believe that I am fond of the men of learning and condescend to meet them, so they come to me. Their arrival makes it possible for me to perceive the true state of things and as a matter of course become aware of what is right and what is wrong. Be careful about this! If you treat others with arrogance because you think you govern the state of Lu, you are in danger! You may be arrogant to those who depend on their emolument for a living, but you can never be so to those who behave properly and make others do the same. These men forget their noble status and choose to be humble, forsake their wealth and stay poor willingly, abandon their ease and comfort and turn to hard work, and refuse to change their mind even though they are sunburned. For this reason, the guiding principles for all under Heaven have been handed down and the ancient laws and regulations have been preserved."

When the border warden of Zengqiu[2] met Ao Sunshu the prime minister of Chu, so the story goes, he said, "I have heard that he who occupies a position for a long time incurs the jealousy of the men of learning, he who has a generous official salary excites resentment among the common people, and he who enjoys a noble status evokes hatred in his monarch. Now you, as prime minister, fulfill the three conditions but how is it that you have offended neither the men of learning nor the commoners of Chu?"

Sunshu replied, "I have been prime minister of Chu three times, but each time in office I feel humbler in mind, each time my salary got increased I would share more widely, and each time my status was exalted I grew more respectful. For these reasons, I have avoided causing any offence to the men of learning and the common people."

Zigong told Confucius, "I would like to be humble to others but I do not know how."

"If you really want to be humble to others," said Confucius, "follow the example of the earth: dig deep into the ground and you get sweet spring waters there; cultivate the land and there is an abundant harvest of the five grains. Grasses and trees as well as birds and beasts multiply on it. While alive, creatures move on it; after death, they are buried in it. Multitudinous are its merits, yet it claims none. If you want to be humble, do as the earth does."

Formerly in Yu, no heed was given to the remonstrance of Zhiqi Gong[3] and the state was annexed by Jin. In Lai,[4] Zima was not used and the state was annexed by Qi. Zhou of Yin had Prince Bigan disemboweled and he was replaced by King Wu. Thus, those who failed to draw near to the worthy and employ the wise suffered tragic death and lost their countries.

Those who promote their doctrines commented, "Qing Sun was not as good as Confucius." It was not true actually. Qing Sun had to live in an age of chaos under the intimidating threat of stern punishments. There was not a worthy ruler then. What

---

[2] A place formerly belonging to Zeng, a state of the Spring and Autumn Period, located in the current Yuanfeng County, Shandong, which was annexed by the State of Ju in 566 BC.

[3] A senior official of the State of Yu.

[4] A state in the Spring and Autumn Period, located in the current southeast of Huang County, Shandong, which was annexed by the State of Qi in 567 BC.

was worse, there were the brutal aggressions of Qin. Under such circumstances, none of the ritual and moral principles was observed and transformation through education was impossible, so that those who were benevolent were dismissed or frustrated, all the world was locked in darkness, those who possessed more integrity were ridiculed, and the feudal lords schemed against one another. Living in such an age, the wise had no opportunity to think for the benefit of their countries, the able had no opportunity to participate in governing their states, and the worthy had no opportunity to play their part in their state affairs. As a result, the rulers were kept in the dark and were ignorant of what was happening, and the worthy were rejected rather than accepted. Nonetheless, Qing Sun cherished in his heart the lofty aspiration to become a sage, concealed under the pretense of madness and presented to the world as stupid. Such quality is praised in *The Book of Songs* when it says,

> "Being wise and discreet,
>   He remains whole and complete."[5]

This is why he was not so widely known, not followed by so many disciples, and not so brilliant. However, scholars nowadays learn from the words and teachings he left behind, which sufficiently serve as standards and examples for all under Heaven. Where his doctrines are put into practice, they work wonders. Where his teachings are accepted, transformations are achieved. Observe his good conduct and you find he was not surpassed by Confucius. But the world did not regard him as a sage, for it failed to make a careful examination on what he said and did. What can be done about it? The world was not in good order and Qing Sun was living in a wrong time. He was virtuous as Yao and Yu, but his virtue was rarely recognized. His plans and strategies were viewed with suspicion rather than adopted. His wisdom was divine and his conduct was upright and accorded with Dao. Both could be taken as the rules of conduct. Alas for such a worthy person! He was fit to be a monarch. What a pity it was that the world was unwise, for despots like Jie and Zhou were treated kindly while the worthy and good got killed, for instance, Bigan was disemboweled, Confucius once got trapped in Kuang, Jieyu fled the world, Jizi feigned madness, Chang Tian rebelled, and Helü abused his power. Those who did evil obtained good fortune, while those who were benevolent suffered misfortunes. Those who promote their doctrines today fail to make investigations and they make judgements by fame and reputation. Now that the times were different, how could he have gained such a fame or reputation? Since he was not employed in a government position, how could he have made accomplishments? Yet, since he cherished fine aspirations and highly developed his moral worth, who can say he was not worthy?

---

[5] Major Court Hymns, *The Book of Songs*.

Printed in the USA
CPSIA information can be obtained
at www.ICGtesting.com
CBHW051620301024
16481CB00014B/31